W9-BXM-381

TRAGEDY: MODERN ESSAYS IN CRITICISM

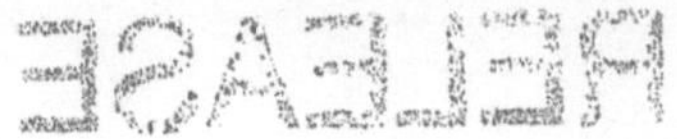

PRENTICE-HALL ENGLISH LITERATURE SERIES
Maynard Mack, *Editor*

PRENTICE-HALL INTERNATIONAL, INC., *London*
PRENTICE-HALL OF AUSTRALIA, PTY., LTD., *Sydney*
PRENTICE-HALL OF CANADA, LTD., *Toronto*
PRENTICE-HALL FRANCE, S.A.R.L., *Paris*
PRENTICE-HALL OF JAPAN, INC., *Tokyo*
PRENTICE-HALL DE MEXICO, S.A., *Mexico City*

TRAGEDY: MODERN ESSAYS IN CRITICISM

EDITED BY

Laurence Michel
State University of New York at Buffalo

Richard B. Sewall
Yale University

Prentice-Hall, Inc., Englewood Cliffs, N.J.

LIBRARY OF CONGRESS CATALOG NO.: 63-14305

PRINTED IN THE UNITED STATES OF AMERICA C

Preface

The study of tragedy has broadened and deepened ever since Nietzsche. For the last twenty-five or thirty years, it has attempted not only revaluations of the tragic drama and theatre, but also probings into and prescriptions for the underlying ethos and "classic form" of the thing itself.

Secondly, presumptions about tragedy, and the word "tragic," keep cropping up in contexts which, a generation or two ago, would not have been thought particularly receptive to these terms. Aristotle had said the last word on the Greeks, Bradley on Shakespeare, and that was that. Now, however, the terms and insights have renewed their franchise and have been found useful and stimulating in the most unexpected realms of discussion. This phenomenon is reflected in writing about the arts and sciences, politics, sociology, anthropology, and psychology: religion, theology, and philosophy: *Zeitgeist* and *Weltanschauung*. In the colleges, courses in tragedy have become the cores whence other courses radiate, drawing upon what is variously recognized as "the tragic form," "the tragic sense of life," "the spirit of tragedy," "the tragic vision."

This volume is designed to make available a representative body of modern thought on tragedy and to display the new terminology at work. The editors have chosen (with the frustrations usual to anthologizing) those essays which seem to be most serviceable or exciting, most valuable, most challenging; those not readily available elsewhere; and those which "say a new word."

The list could easily be tripled, even now. Many pieces were chosen over others quite as illuminating (and making much the same points) because they are particularly wealthy and pertinent in reference or allusion to the surrounding criticism, or because they helpfully summarize a body of thought before modifying or building on it. Some of the pressures are relieved by the existence of such collections as Nathan A. Scott's *The Tragic Vision and the Christian Faith* (New York, Association Press, 1957) and Cleanth Brooks' *Tragic Themes in West-*

ern Literature (Yale, 1955). Morris Weitz has conveniently grouped Aristotle, Hume, Nietzsche, Hegel-Bradley, and J. W. Krutch in his *Problems in Aesthetics* (New York, Macmillan, 1959). Francis Fergusson's seminal study *The Idea of a Theatre* (1949) has been given wide currency in a paperback edition; G. Wilson Knight's *oeuvre* has attained the status of its own index-volume. Some essays which would be appropriate here are to be found already in other specialized gatherings. Of particular note are Arthur Sewell's "Tragedy and the Kingdom of Ends" in the Oxford Galaxy *Shakespeare,* and Stephen Whicher's "Emerson's Tragic Sense" and Frederick Hoffman's "No Beginning and No End: Hemingway and Death" in the Galaxy *Interpretations of American Literature.* It is hoped that this selection will map further roads into that country of the mind which is the realm of tragedy.

A word about the structure of this anthology. The first group of essays (Unamuno through Weisinger) places the discussion of tragedy in its largest context and at the center of the human concern. Beginning with Unamuno's "man of flesh and bone," it ends by putting tragedy in the perspective of some great archetypal experiences of the race. The next two essays (Sewall and Krieger) develop further the specific literary problem—how, and to what degree, this central concern, and what has issued from it, are brought into some sort of formal control by the writers of tragedies. A third group (Kitto through Rossiter) shows the importance of historical perspective in the study of particular tragedies—what "tragedy" meant *there* and *then* (e.g., to the Greeks and the Elizabethans). The essays by Barnet, Michel, Auden, and Drucker explore a matter of increasing contemporary interest—the relation of Christianity to tragedy. The problem of catharsis, which has by turns illuminated and beclouded the discussion of tragedy since Aristotle, is forthrightly attacked in the selections from Else and Morrell and in the lively Hill-Bateson exchange. Another group presents some striking individual perspectives: Henn's image of the "net," Leavis' objections to Santayana, Hayes' review of Giraudoux' play. And, finally, Fiedler and Bredvold address a question which has recurred persistently from Joseph Wood Krutch's famous essay of 1930, "The Tragic Fallacy," to George Steiner's *The Death of Tragedy* in 1961: is tragedy possible in our time?

Tragedy is not dead, of course, nor is its continued vitality merely a conspiracy of the school teachers. This volume is not an effort at resuscitation; rather, it is a testimony to the potency of an idea, "a complex of thought and feeling," of urgent and even terrifying relevance to our time. For if tragedy were really dead, if the values which it presupposes and affirms were suddenly negated (or, by no means an unlikely threat, gradually worn away by the corrosive elements in our culture), then we would be in a sorry way indeed. In George Orwell's *1984,* the hero, Winston Smith, has a startling insight; from the faceless, monolithic world of statism, he looks back to his youth, when the individual was a reality and suffering had dignity:

> The thing that now suddenly struck Winston was that his mother's death, nearly thirty years ago, had been tragic and sorrowful in a way that was no longer possible. Tragedy, he perceived, belonged to the ancient time, to a time when there were still privacy, love, and friendship, and when the members of a family stood by one another without needing to know the reason. . . .

The angle is oblique, but Winston's insight shows how close we are, in our concern for tragedy, to the center of things. The logic of all this, the steps in the reasoning and the evidence for these conclusions, are made plain in the essays that follow.

Contents

Tragedy: Modern Essays in Criticism

The Man of Flesh and Bone

MIGUEL DE UNAMUNO

Homo sum; nihil humani a me alienum puto, said the Latin playwright. And I would rather say, *Nullum hominem a me alienum puto:* I am a man; no other man do I deem a stranger. For to me the adjective *humanus* is no less suspect than its abstract substantive *humanitas,* humanity. Neither "the human" nor "humanity," neither the simple adjective nor the substantivized adjective, but the concrete substantive —man. The man of flesh and bone; the man who is born, suffers, and dies—above all, who dies; the man who eats and drinks and plays and sleeps and thinks and wills; the man who is seen and heard; the brother, the real brother.

For there is another thing which is also called man, and he is the subject of not a few lucubrations, more or less scientific. He is the legendary featherless biped, the ζῷον πολιτικόν of Aristotle, the social contractor of Rousseau, the *homo economicus* of the Manchester school, the *homo sapiens* of Linnæus, or, if you like, the vertical mammal. A man neither of here nor there, neither of this age nor of another, who has neither sex nor country, who is, in brief, merely an idea. That is to say, a no-man.

The man we have to do with is the man of flesh and bone—I, you, reader of mine, the other man yonder, all of us who walk solidly on the earth.

And this concrete man, this man of flesh and bone, is at once the subject and the supreme object of all philosophy, whether certain self-styled philosophers like it or not.

In most of the histories of philosophy that I know, philosophic systems are presented to us as if growing out of one another spontaneously, and their authors, the philosophers, appear only as mere pretexts. The inner biography of the philosophers, of the men who

From *The Tragic Sense of Life in Men and Peoples,* trans. J. E. Crawford Flitch, London, 1921, pp. 1-3, 15-18. Reprinted by permission of Macmillan & Co. Ltd.

philosophized, occupies a secondary place. And yet it is precisely this inner biography that explains for us most things.

It behoves us to say, before all, that philosophy lies closer to poetry than to science. All philosophic systems which have been constructed as a supreme concord of the final results of the individual sciences have in every age possessed much less consistency and life than those which expressed the integral spiritual yearning of their authors.

And, though they concern us so greatly, and are, indeed, indispensable for our life and thought, the sciences are in a certain sense more foreign to us than philosophy. They fulfil a more objective end—that is to say, an end more external to ourselves. They are fundamentally a matter of economics. A new scientific discovery, of the kind called theoretical, is, like a mechanical discovery—that of the steam-engine, the telephone, the phonograph, or the aeroplane—a thing which is useful for something else. Thus the telephone may be useful to us in enabling us to communicate at a distance with the woman we love. But she, wherefore is she useful to us? A man takes an electric tram to go to hear an opera, and asks himself, Which, in this case, is the more useful, the tram or the opera?

Philosophy answers to our need of forming a complete and unitary conception of the world and of life, and as a result of this conception, a feeling which gives birth to an inward attitude and even to outward action. But the fact is that this feeling, instead of being a consequence of this conception, is the cause of it. Our philosophy—that is, our mode of understanding or not understanding the world and life—springs from our feeling towards life itself. And life, like everything affective, has roots in subconsciousness, perhaps in unconsciousness.

It is not usually our ideas that make us optimists or pessimists, but it is our optimism or our pessimism, of physiological or perhaps pathological origin, as much the one as the other, that makes our ideas.

Man is said to be a reasoning animal. I do not know why he has not been defined as an affective or feeling animal. Perhaps that which differentiates him from other animals is feeling rather than reason. More often I have seen a cat reason than laugh or weep. Perhaps it weeps or laughs inwardly—but then perhaps, also inwardly, the crab resolves equations of the second degree.

And thus, in a philosopher, what must needs most concern us is the man.

Take Kant, the man Immanuel Kant, who was born and lived at Königsberg, in the latter part of the eighteenth century and the beginning of the nineteenth. In the philosophy of this man Kant, a man of heart and head—that is to say, a man—there is a significant somersault, as Kierkegaard, another man—and what a man!—would have said, the somersault from the *Critique of Pure Reason* to the *Critique of Practical Reason*. He reconstructs in the latter what he destroyed in the former, in spite of what those may say who do not see the man himself. After having examined and pulverized with his analysis the traditional proofs of the existence of God, of the Aristotelian God, who is the God corresponding to the ζῷον πολιτικόν, the abstract God, the unmoved prime Mover, he reconstructs God anew; but the God of the conscience, the Author of the moral order—the Lutheran God, in short. This transition of Kant exists already in embryo in the Lutheran notion of faith.

* * * *

If a philosopher is not a man, he is anything but a philosopher; he is above all a pedant, and a pedant is a caricature of a man. The cultivation of any branch of science—of chemistry, of physics, of geometry, of philology—may be a work of differentiated specialization, and even so only within very narrow limits and restrictions; but philosophy, like poetry, is a work of integration and synthesis, or else it is merely pseudo-philosophical erudition.

All knowledge has an ultimate object. Knowledge for the sake of knowledge is, say what you will, nothing but a dismal begging of the question. We learn something either for an immediate practical end, or in order to complete the rest of our knowledge. Even the knowledge that appears to us to be most theoretical—that is to say, of least immediate application to the non-intellectual necessities of life—answers to a necessity which is no less real because it is intellectual, to a reason of economy in thinking, to a principle of unity and continuity of consciousness. But just as a scientific fact has its finality in the rest of knowledge, so the philosophy that we would make our own has also its extrinsic object—it refers to our whole destiny, to our attitude in face of life and the universe. And the most tragic problem of philosophy is to reconcile intellectual necessities with the necessities of the heart and the will. For it is on this rock that every philosophy that pretends to resolve the eternal and tragic contradiction, the basis of our existence, breaks to pieces. But do all men face this contradiction squarely?

Little can be hoped from a ruler, for example, who has not at some time or other been preoccupied, even if only confusedly, with the first beginning and the ultimate end of all things, and above all of man, with the "why" of his origin and the "wherefore" of his destiny.

And this supreme preoccupation cannot be purely rational, it must involve the heart. It is not enough to think about our destiny: it must be felt. And the would-be leader of men who affirms and proclaims that he pays no heed to the things of the spirit, is not worthy to lead them. By which I do not mean, of course, that any ready-made solution is to be required of him. Solution? Is there indeed any?

So far as I am concerned, I will never willingly yield myself, nor entrust my confidence, to any popular leader who is not penetrated with the feeling that he who orders a people orders men, men of flesh and bone, men who are born, suffer, and, although they do not wish to die, die; men who are ends in themselves, not merely means; men who must be themselves and not others; men, in fine, who seek that which we call happiness. It is inhuman, for example, to sacrifice one generation of men to the generation which follows, without having any feeling for the destiny of those who are sacrificed, without having any regard, not for their memory, not for their names, but for them themselves.

All this talk of a man surviving in his children, or in his works, or in the universal consciousness, is but vague verbiage which satisfies only those who suffer from affective stupidity, and who, for the rest, may be persons of a certain cerebral distinction. For it is possible to possess great talent, or what we call great talent, and yet to be stupid as regards the feelings and even morally imbecile. There have been instances.

These clever-witted, affectively stupid persons are wont to say that it is useless to seek to delve in the unknowable or to kick against the pricks. It is as if one should say to a man whose leg has had to be amputated that it does not help him at all to think about it. And we all lack something; only some of us feel the lack and others do not. Or they pretend not to feel the lack, and then they are hypocrites.

A pedant who beheld Solon weeping for the death of a son said to him, "Why do you weep thus, if weeping avails nothing?" And the sage answered him, "Precisely for that reason—because it does not avail." It is manifest that weeping avails something, even if only the alleviation of distress; but the deep sense of Solon's reply to the impertinent questioner is plainly seen. And I am convinced that we should solve many things if we all went out into the streets and uncovered our griefs, which perhaps would prove to be but one sole common grief, and joined together in beweeping them and crying aloud to the heavens and calling upon God. And this, even though God should hear us not; but He would hear us. The chiefest sanctity of a temple is that it is a place to which men go to weep in common. A *miserere* sung in common by a multitude tormented by destiny has as much value as a philosophy. It is not enough to cure the plague: we must learn to weep for it. Yes, we must learn to weep! Perhaps that is the supreme wisdom. Why? Ask Solon.

There is something which, for lack of a better name, we will call the tragic sense of life, which carries with it a whole conception of life itself and of the universe, a whole philosophy more or less formulated, more or less conscious. And this sense may be possessed, and is possessed, not only by individual men but by whole peoples. And this sense does not so much flow from ideas as determine them, even though afterwards, as is manifest, these ideas react upon it and confirm it. Sometimes it may originate in a chance illness—dyspepsia, for example; but at other times it is constitutional. And it is useless to speak, as we shall see, of men who are healthy and men who are not healthy. Apart from the fact there is no normal standard of health, nobody has proved that man is necessarily cheerful by nature. And further, man, by the very fact of being man, of possessing consciousness, is, in comparison with the ass or the crab, a diseased animal. Consciousness is a disease.

Among men of flesh and bone there have been typical examples of those who possess this tragic sense of life. I recall now Marcus Aurelius, St. Augustine, Pascal, Rousseau, *René, Obermann,* Thomson,[1] Leopardi, Vigny, Lenau, Kleist, Amiel, Quental, Kierkegaard—men burdened with wisdom rather than with knowledge.

And there are, I believe, peoples who possess this tragic sense of life also.

It is to this that we must now turn our attention, beginning with this matter of health and disease.

[1] James Thomson, author of *The City of Dreadful Night.*

The Tragic: Awareness; Basic Characteristics; Fundamental Interpretations

KARL JASPERS

Awareness of the Tragic

Knowledge of the Tragic: The Insight Gained from Tragedy. At first, as we have seen, religion, art, and poetry were one. What was formulated in their original visions is nothing less than the total content of our consciousness. Consider a single instance from this vast area: tragic fate and deliverance. All the many varieties of tragedy have something in common. Tragedy views in tremendous perspectives all that actually exists and occurs; and in its climax of silence, tragedy suggests and brings to realization the highest possibilities of man.

These tragic visions and perspectives contain a hidden philosophy, for they lend meaning to an otherwise meaningless doom. Although we cannot translate this hidden philosophy into intellectual terms, we can by philosophic interpretation throw it into bolder relief. We acquire this hidden philosophy by re-experiencing its original visions. There can be no substitute for this world of visions. As an organon of philosophy, it is an essential part of philosophic thought. But in finding its own fulfillment, this world of visions goes beyond philosophy, which must reach it once again as something distinct from philosophy itself.

All great expressions of tragic knowledge are cast in the mold of history. In style, theme, and intention, they unmistakably bear the signature of their time. But in its concrete historical form no knowledge can be timeless and universal. In every case, man must acquire it anew to bring its truth to life for himself. The differences in the expressions of tragic knowledge are for us historical facts.

Such differences and contrasts among the historical expressions of the tragic pattern cast light upon one another. What is more, they provide the basis for any knowledge of ourselves.

It is through these differences and contrasts that we apprehend the

From *Tragedy Is Not Enough,* trans. K. W. Deutsch, 1952, pp. 27-40; 41-56; 97-100. Reprinted by permission of Victor Gollancz, Ltd. and The Beacon Press.

various degrees of tragic consciousness, the various possibilities of interpreting existence by means of the tragic, and the mainsprings of final deliverance in tragedy. The historical expressions of tragic knowledge provide for us a system of possible approaches to understanding.

Historical Survey. Let us recall the great instances of tragic knowledge as they were expressed in vision and artistic form:

1. Homer; the Edda and Icelandic sagas; heroic legends of all peoples, from Europe to China.
2. Greek tragedy: Aeschylus, Sophocles, Euripides. Only here tragedy arose as independent poetic genre, all later tragedy being either dependent on or—through Seneca inspired by it.
3. Modern tragedy represented by three national figures: Shakespeare, Calderón, Racine.
4. Lessing; tragedy representing the ideals of German culture: Schiller and, subsequently, the nineteenth century.
5. Other poetry of awe and terror asking their own questions of the problem of existence: the Book of Job; several Indic dramas (none of which, however, is entirely tragic).
6. Tragic knowledge in Kierkegaard, Dostoevsky, Nietzsche.

Heroic sagas display the tragic world view as self-evident. This embodies as yet no intellectual struggle with a problem, and as yet no yearning for deliverance. Stark disaster, death and doom, unflinchingness and glory: these are what matter.

Great tragedy, Greek as well as modern, arises in eras of transition: it comes up like a flame from the fires that consume an epoch. It declines in the end to mere decoration.

Greek tragedy is a semi-ritual acting out of man's desperate struggle for knowledge of the gods, the meaning of existence, and the nature of justice. At first it is part of the belief in order and deity, in basic and valid institutions, and in the city-state. In the end it may cast doubt upon all these products of history, but it never questions the Idea of Justice or the reality of Good and Evil (Euripides).

Shakespeare, on the contrary, moves across a purely secular stage; in his dramatic personages a proud society recognizes its own heightened image. Human life understands itself in terms of its potentialities and perils, its greatness and nothingness, its human and diabolical strains, its nobleness and meanness, its sheer joy of being alive and its bewildered terror at failure and destruction, its love, dedication, and openness of heart, and then again its hatred, narrowness, and blindness.

All in all, humanity sees itself confronted by an unanswerable problem, by the ultimate collapse of every effort to realize its promise—all this against the background of unshaken order and a strongly felt contrast between Good and Evil.

Calderón and Racine are high points of Christian tragedy. In them tragedy is charged with a new kind of tension. In them, instead of destiny and demons, we have Providence and Grace, even damnation. Instead of the question asked only that it might be answered by ultimate silence, all is now sustained by the certainty of the Beyond and an all-merciful God. Instead of the unceasing struggle for truth, which the poet carries through from one composition to the next, and instead of the play with symbolic ciphers, we now see truth actually present in the knowledge that both the sinful world and God Himself are indeed realities. But within the tensions of this new polarity, the genuinely tragic has become extinguished by Christian Truth. The tragedies of Calderón and Racine, because they are of Christian faith, look to more distant horizons; but compared with Shakespeare they are quite narrow in problem and approach, in poignancy and richness of character, in scope and in freedom of outlook.

Absolute and radical tragedy means that there is no way out whatsoever. Although it might possibly be found in some of Euripides' plays, it does not become really evident until it appears in nineteenth-century drama. Here, however, the collapse of all but merely æsthetic standards at last takes tragedy into a bottomless pit.

Tragic Knowledge of Existence and Untragic Security. The greatest chasm separates those civilizations that never achieve tragic knowledge —and consequently its vehicles, tragedy, epic, and novel—from those whose way of life is determined by poignant awareness of the intrinsic part tragedy plays in man's existence.

Looking back, we can see how history was rent asunder by the birth of Tragic Man. His tragic insight need not be the product of a flowering civilization, but may be quite primitive. But, primitive or not, man seems truly awake only when he has such knowledge. For now he will face each realization of his ultimate limits with a new restlessness that drives him beyond them. Nothing that is stable will endure, for nothing that is stable will satisfy him. Tragic knowledge is the first phase of that historical movement which takes place not only in external events but in the depths of man himself.

Pre-tragic knowledge is rounded out, complete, and self-contained.

It sees man's suffering, doom, and death. There is deep sorrow in such knowledge, and deep joy. Sorrow becomes accepted as part of the eternal cycle of living and dying, death and resurrection, and everlasting change. A God dying and returning, the seasons of the year celebrated as the occasions of this death and rebirth, these are the basic realities. Nearly everywhere on earth we find mythical conceptions of a mother-goddess as the bringer of life or death; she bears and nurses all, loves and lets ripen—but also takes everything back into her womb, kills without mercy, and destroys in tremendous disasters. But such images of fate are not yet tragic knowledge. They represent no more than man's reassuring knowledge of a mortality in which he feels at home. Essentially this knowledge is unaware of history. Here, everything at all times has the same degree of reality. Nothing strikes man as outstandingly important; everything is equally important. Whatever is present is fully and exhaustively present as that which it is.

Tragic knowledge, on the contrary, contains an element of history. Cyclical patterns are merely its background. The crucial events are unique and are always moving on. They are shaped by irrevocable decisions, and they never recur.

But pre-tragic knowledge is not always superseded by tragic knowledge. It may be possible for pre-tragic knowledge to preserve its own truth intact alongside the tragic outlook of other civilizations. No such tragic outlook develops wherever man succeeds both in achieving a harmonious interpretation of the universe and in actually living in accord with it. That is to a great extent what happened in ancient, especially in pre-Buddhist, China. In such a civilization, all misery, unhappiness, and evil are merely temporary disturbances which never need occur. There is no horror, rejection, or justification of the ways of this world—no indictment, only lament. Man is not torn in desperation: he suffers and even dies with composure. There are no hopeless entanglements, no dark frustrations; all is basically clear, beautiful, and true. To be sure, terror and horror are part of experience and are as familiar to this civilization as to those civilizations awakened to an awareness of the tragic. Yet serenity remains the dominant mood of life; there is no struggle, no defiance. A deep awareness of the past connects man with the ancient foundation of all things. What man seeks here is not any kind of historical movement, but rather the ever-new re-establishment of an eternal reality that is both orderly and good. Wherever the tragic sense appears, something extraordinary is lost: the feeling of security without the shadow of tragedy, a natural and sublime humanity, a sense of being at home in this world, and a wealth of concrete insights—all of which were real for the Chinese at one time. The relaxed and serene face of the Chinese still contrasts with the tense and self-conscious expression of Western man.

Tragic Knowledge in Epic and Drama. The mythical mind sees the world's basic disharmony reflected in the multiplicity of gods. No man can do justice to all of them; somewhere the cult of one god is bound to offend against that of another; the gods are at war among themselves, and they use men's destinies as stakes in their battles. But even the gods are not all-powerful; above both gods and man, dark Moira holds her sway. The questions "Why?" and "Wherefore?" call forth many answers, depending upon the situation, but provide no single answer. Man may encompass the whole wealth of his environment, the whole range of his potentialities. He experiences the extremes. But he does not strain his every fiber in the search for an inclusive unity, and thus he is not yet committed to seek at any price the answer to his question.

Tragic insight of this early type is found in Homer: in the sheer joy of seeing, in the worship of the gods, and in unquestioned steadfastness and endurance.[1]

This same endurance, this same calm defiance in the face of destiny, becomes deliberate in the *Edda* and sagas, and although it is not so richly drawn as in Homer, it is there more impassioned and boundless.

All these views are like tragic knowledge that is only half-grown. They do not distinguish the various kinds of catastrophe,[2] nor the last unfathomed depths of tragic failure. The man of the heroic age does not yet crave for liberation of the soul: his soul is content if it can find strength to endure. Somehow his questions stop too soon. He accepts life and death too easily as unproblematic and self-evident. His epic point of view differs from the pre-tragic (as in old China) only in this

[1] Yet, if spirituality and inwardness are taken (with John H. Finley, Jr.) as the *Iliad's* tragic qualities, then surely the *Odyssey* with its intellectuality and social ethos is far closer to high comedy.

[2] *Weisen des Scheitern:* lit., "ways of stranding or of suffering shipwreck." This is Jaspers' term for failure. Though a language of seafarers, English does not use "shipwreck" in this sense. Much could be made of the apparent paucity in modern English and American of a vocabulary for failure as opposed to one for success; failure tends to be seen solely as an unfortunate interlude, briefly acknowledged but passed over as without positive significance. By contrast, German thought, quite apart from the Existentialist movement, is "conditioned" by its very language and literary tradition to dwell on failure as a general process with a discernible structure. . . .

—that it does not shroud the world's discrepancies in a veil of harmony.

Greek tragedy takes its raw material from this world of myth and epic. But there is a difference. Men no longer bear their tragic knowledge calmly, but pursue their questions ceaselessly. Men ask questions and find answers when they transform the myths themselves. Only now the myths attain their full maturity and depth, but no version of them can henceforth remain stable. Each great tragic poet will recast the myths to suit his purposes. Finally those myths are wholly consumed in man's passionate struggle for truth—in the poet's dialogue with the divine—until nothing remains but their ashes: poetic images that still charm but no longer compel.

The questions of tragedy are already philosophical in substance, but they are still formulated in visual, dramatic terms. They have not yet reached the rational method of philosophy. These are the questions directed to the gods: Why are things the way they are? What is man? What leads him on? What is guilt? What is fate? What are the ordinations valid among men, and where do they come from? What are the gods?

These questions search for a road to gods who are just and good, to the one God. But as man travels along this road, tradition slowly disintegrates. It cannot measure up to the new standards of right, goodness, and omnipotence as they become increasingly rational. Skepticism is the end of this high-minded search that is sustained by the contents of tradition brought to their utmost purity and beauty.

In this dramatic re-examination of tradition—acted out at the sacred festivals in honor of Dionysus—the poet wills and achieves something more than man's earlier delight in the untiring representation of nature, men, and gods. Of that delight Hesiod had sung, praising the Muses:

> Aye, though fresh troubles have crazed a man till he knows
> nothing but dread and despair, should a singer praise,
> as the Muses' servant, the glory of ancient days,
> the heroes and blessed gods of Olympus-crest,
> the man will forget that he ever was darkly distressed,
> such powers of healing to gifts of the Muses belong.[3]

Tragedy wants more: the catharsis of the soul. Admittedly, even Aristotle does not make clear to us just what this catharsis is. This

[3] *Theogony,* lines 98-103. Jack Lindsay translation in *The Oxford Book of Greek Verse in Translation* (New York: Oxford University Press, 1938), p. 149. Reprinted by permission of the Clarendon Press, Oxford.

much is certain: it is an experience that touches the innermost being of each man.[4] It makes him more deeply receptive to reality, not merely as a spectator, but as a man who is personally involved. It makes truth a part of us by cleansing us of all that in our everyday experience is petty, bewildering, and trivial—all that narrows us and makes us blind.

Tragedy Transcended in the Philosophic Interpretation of the World and in Revealed Religion. Tragic knowledge uses myth in these two forms: in the epic, as knowledge that without question accepts as real a world of visual images; in tragedy, as knowledge that asks searching questions about deity. Each of these tragic forms in turn provides a way for man to overcome the tragic itself: the epic is the root of every Enlightenment, with its philosophic interpretation of the world; tragedy is the root of revealed religion. Ultimately, both forms are inadequate.

Neither the pre-Socratics nor Plato, with their speculative testing of reality[5]—a testing which is both the opposite and the complement of tragedy—draws the consequences from man's ultimate awareness of his ignorance,[6] at which the tragic poets gradually arrived. It is left to the sober encyclopedic philosophy of the post-Aristotelian era to draw such consequences and to dissolve the faulty conceptions of God endorsed by tradition.[7] This late philosophy then conceives of the universe as a harmony, whose every dissonance is merely relative.

It relativizes the importance of individual destinies, accepting each man's personality[8] as something unshakable, something which merely acts out its destiny in the world like a part in a play, doing so without identifying itself with the part. Here tragic knowledge has lost its weight; its final attitude to existence is no longer the stubbornness of the unyielding hero or the catharsis of the soul entangled in this world. Rather, tragic knowledge in this last stage becomes Apathy, the indestructible serenity of indifference to suffering.

[4] *Das Selbstsein des Menschen:* lit., "selfhood." By "selfhood" Jaspers means individual consciousness and conscious inner activity—the process as its own product. Man is aware of his own inner tensions and his inner activity in shaping them and making them conscious. See *Von der Wahrheit,* pp. 540ff.

[5] *Seinsvergewisserung.* This involves verifying one's own inner condition and relationship with one's environment.

[6] *Nichtwissen.* This is not so much "ignorance" as "inability to know more"; the negation refers to the future rather than to the present.

[7] This, of course, merely completes a process begun as early as Hesiod and Xenophanes. See Werner Jaeger, *The Theology of the Early Greek Philosophers* (New York: Oxford University Press, 1948); and F. Solmsen, *Hesiod and Aeschylus* (Ithaca: Cornell University Press, 1949).

[8] *Selbstsein.*

When brought face to face with tragic knowledge, philosophic Apathy fails to carry liberation far enough. In the first place, Apathy is mere endurance. It may claim for precedent the heroic defiance of mythical times, but it lacks the passion of that defiance; almost empty of content, it shrinks to a mere pinpoint of meaningless self-assertion. In the second place, Apathy remains a theory, however impressive, which can hardly be carried through in practice by the majority of people. It is for these reasons that man, out of his tragic knowledge and philosophic emptiness, yearns for a deeper liberation. This liberation is the promise of revealed religion.

Man wants to be saved, and he is saved. But not entirely of his own doing. He is relieved of the burden of this impossible task. Christ's sacrificial death and Buddha's revelation not merely offer help to man, but actually create for him that power with which he has only to cooperate in order to be free.

The revealed religion of Judaism and Christianity views the discrepancies of life, of man, of all that finds tragic expression, as imbedded in the origin of man: original sin is rooted in Adam's Fall. Redemption springs from Christ's death on the cross. All the things of this world are, as such, corrupt: man is steeped in inescapable guilt before he ever incurs guilt as an individual. He has become involved in the one all-pervading process of incurring guilt and finding salvation. He partakes of both through himself, though not through himself alone. He is guilty already through Original Sin, and he is to be saved through grace. Now, however, he takes his cross upon himself. He no longer merely endures the sorrows of existence, its discrepancies and tearing conflicts[9]—he deliberately chooses them. This is tragedy no longer. The darkness of terror is pierced by the radiance of blessedness and grace.

Seen from this point of view, Christian salvation opposes tragic knowledge. The chance of being saved destroys the tragic sense of being trapped without chance of escape. Therefore no genuinely Christian tragedy can exist. For in Christian plays, the mystery of redemption is the basis and framework of the plot, and the tension of tragic knowledge has been released from the outset with the experience of man's perfection and salvation through grace.

At this point, tragedy loses its compelling character: man is aroused

[9] *Das Zerrissene.* Kuhn, *Encounter*, pp. 124ff., shows how this term was first used in the early Hegel's theological writing to denote—in Kantian terms—the critical mental "cleavage" suffered by the Jews previous to the coming of Christ.

by it, not touched in his innermost being. What is essential to the Christian cannot even emerge in tragedy. What is religious in the specific Christian sense forever escapes poetry, for it can only be realized existentially (through and in living), and it cannot be contemplated as an aesthetic phenomenon. In this sense a Christian is bound to misunderstand, say, Shakespeare: Shakespeare succeeds in making everything the subject of his drama, for under every possible aspect he shows man as he really is. But the specifically religious—and only this—escapes him. When confronted with Shakespeare's dramatic works, the Christian knows, as a matter of deep personal experience, that they do not reveal to him, or even touch upon, the boon that is his through faith. It is only indirectly that Shakespeare seems to the Christian eye to lead up to the experience of faith—in the open, jagged [10] fractures of his work, in what it leaves unresolved, in the tenseness of his characters, and in their straining, unspoken and unconscious, toward the chance of being saved.

The substance of this tragic knowledge must escape the Christian. Nevertheless, this tragic knowledge, if it remains philosophic and develops along purely philosophic lines, is also a way for man to transcend his limitations. It offers a unique form of deliverance, but it is not understood from the Christian point of view, and it loses its content whenever it ends in philosophic Apathy.

Every one of man's basic experiences ceases to be tragic in a Christian context. Guilt becomes *felix culpa,* the "happy fault"—the guilt without which no salvation is possible. Judas' betrayal was necessary for Christ's sacrifice and death, the source of salvation for all believers. Christ is the deepest symbol of failure in this world, yet he is in no sense tragic. In his very failure he knows, fulfills, and consummates.

Basic Characteristics of the Tragic

The tragic looms before us as an event that shows the terrifying aspects of existence,[11] but an existence that is still human. It reveals its entanglement with the uncharted background of man's humanity.[12] Paradoxically, however, when man faces the tragic, he liberates him-

[10] *Durch die offene Bruchfläche.*

[11] *Dasein* is man's empirical, worldly existence. It is sharply distinguished from the authentic existence that is the Uncharted Background. But for the sake of readability, *Dasein* has often been rendered simply as "existence." Where Jaspers' context has left some doubt as to which is meant (as in Note 19), the German has been given in the note.

[12] *Menschsein.*

self from it. This is one way of obtaining purification and redemption.

Breakdown and failure reveal the true nature of things. In failure, life's reality is not lost; on the contrary, here it makes itself wholly and decisively felt. *There is no tragedy without transcendence.* Even defiance unto death in a hopeless battle against gods and fate is an act of transcending: it is a movement toward man's proper essence, which he comes to know as his own in the presence of his doom.

Where awareness of the tragic has become fundamental to man's awareness of reality, we speak of tragic readiness.[13] But we must distinguish between awareness of the transitoriness of things and genuine awareness of the tragic.

When he thinks of transitoriness, man views the actual events leading up to death, as well as the ephemeral character of all life, as parts of the natural cycle of growth, decay, and renewed growth. He recognizes himself as within nature and identifies himself with it. Here man comes upon a secret that makes him tremble. What is the soul which, independent of the flux of time, knows itself to be immortal, although aware of the finiteness of its worldly existence, aware that it is doomed to pass away in death? Yet, neither this fact of mortality nor this secret of the soul can rightly be termed tragic.

Genuine awareness of the tragic, on the contrary, is more than mere contemplation of suffering and death, flux and extinction. If these things are to become tragic, man must act. It is only then, through his own actions, that man enters into the tragic involvement that inevitably must destroy him. What will be ruined here is not merely man's life as concrete existence, but every concrete embodiment of whatever perfection he sought. Man's mind fails and breaks down in the very wealth of its potentialities. Every one of these potentialities, as it becomes fulfilled, provokes and reaps disaster.

A yearning for deliverance has always gone hand in hand with the knowledge of the tragic. When man encounters the hard fact of tragedy, he faces an inexorable limit. At this limit, he finds no guarantee of general salvation. Rather, it is in acting out his own personality, in realizing his selfhood [14] even unto death, that he finds redemption and deliverance.

He may find this deliverance through his sheer strength to bear the unknown without question, and to endure it with unshakable defiance.

[13] *Tragische Haltung.* This is the inner attitude of composure in the face of tragedy; it resembles Hamlet's "the readiness is all."

[14] *Im Akt seines Selbstseins.* The inner movement implied in Note 4 is here explicitly stated: selfhood is the product and the activity of consciousness.

This, however, is the mere seed of deliverance, its barest possible form. Or he may find deliverance by opening his eyes to the nature of the tragic process which, brought to light, can purify the mind. Finally, deliverance may already have preceded contemplation of the tragic process in the case where some faith has, from the outset, led life onto the road to salvation. Then, tragedy appears as overcome from the beginning as man transcends to the unseen, to God, the background of all backgrounds.

Ways of Interpreting Tragic Knowledge. The meaning of those tragedies that lie before us as the work of poets cannot possibly be reduced to a single formula. These works represent man's labor dealing with his knowledge of the tragic. Situations, events, social forces, religious beliefs, and types of character are the means through which man expresses the tragic.

Every one of the great poems has a meaning which cannot be exhausted by interpretation. They offer no more than directions for interpretation to pursue. Where complete rational interpretation is possible, poetry becomes superfluous—indeed, there has never been truly poetic creation from the very beginning. Where interpretation can make some elements stand out clearly, it heightens their accessibility precisely by virtue of a profound vision that is uncharted, that is not exhaustible by any analysis or interpretation.

In all poems the intellectual construction of the poet asserts itself. In proportion, however, as the thought emerges as such without being made incarnate in dramatic figures, poetry grows weaker. To that degree, then, the work is generated not by the power of tragic vision but by philosophical preference. This is not to say that thoughts in tragic poetry may not have crucial philosophical significance.

Now that we have reviewed tragic knowledge as a whole, our interpretation must give more searching answers to three problems:

1. What do the objective aspects of the tragic look like? What is the pattern of tragic existence and of a tragic course of events? How is it conceived in thought? Our interpretation of tragic subjects in poetry will yield the answer.

2. How do the subjective aspects of the tragic work themselves out? How does the tragic enter into consciousness? How is tragic knowledge achieved and, through it, deliverance and redemption?

3. What is the meaning of any fundamental interpretation of the tragic?

The Tragic as Subject of Poetry. Without trying to define the tragic, we visualize the stark immediacy of tragic events as they have achieved form and expression in poetry.

Our interpretation must hold fast to the content of the poet's original vision, to what already has been expressed and interpreted in his work. Interpretation adds to this vision the meaning which is or might be implied in it, whether or not the poet had explicitly thought of it.

In poetry, tragic consciousness gives body to its own thought: it is only through the tragic mood that we can sense tension and disaster in events affecting us directly or in the world as a whole.[15] Tragedy shows up in battle, in victory and in defeat, in guilt. It is the measure of man's greatness in breakdown and failure. Tragedy reveals itself in man's unconditional will to truth. There it stands revealed as the ultimate disharmony of existence.

The Tragic Atmosphere. Life and death, the cycle of blossoming and withering away, the fact of transitoriness, do not yet establish in themselves any tragic atmosphere. The onlooker can calmly contemplate this process in which he is himself included and by which he is sheltered. The tragic atmosphere arises as the strange and sinister fate to which we have been abandoned. There is something alien that threatens us, something we cannot escape. Wherever we go, whatever we see, whatever we hear, there is something in the air which will destroy us, no matter what we do or wish.

This mood occurs in Indic drama as the vision of a world which is the setting of our life, a setting in which we have been abandoned without any protection. Thus, in *Kausika's Wrath:*

> The whole world seems a carrion-ground,
> A plain of corpses slain by Siva's servant, Time.
> The firmament at dusk seems red
> With blood of victims executed.
> Like embers of a pyre
> The feeble sun-disk glows; stars above
> Seem but a boneyard in the sky;
> And, like a skull bleached white,
> Glares the pale moon . . .[16]

[15] *Weltsein.* As the sum of all knowable objects in our experience, this includes ourselves as part of this world. See *Von der Wahrheit,* pp. 88ff.

[16] Editor's version of Jaspers' excerpt from Kshemisvara, *Kausikas Zorn,* as edited and translated into German by L. Fritze (Leipzig: Reclam, 1882), p. 64. Innocent King Haristshandra is cruelly destroyed by the magician Kausika. For a

Moods of horror dominate some works of Brueghel and Hieronymus Bosch, as well as Dante's *Inferno.* But this mood is nothing more than foreground. We must look for something deeper, but we cannot find it without first passing through these terrors.

The tragic atmosphere in Greek drama is not the mood of all nature.[17] Rather it is related to particular events, particular human figures, perhaps as the tension that grips everything even prior to any specific deed or occurrence, the tension that warns of doom, though no one yet knows what form the doom will take. Aeschylus' *Agamemnon* gives us an example, and one of singular magnificence.

The tragic mood assumes the many shapes of so-called pessimism and its various pictures of this world, whether in Buddhism or in Christianity, in Schopenhauer or in Nietzsche, in the *Edda* or in the *Nibelungenlied.*

Battle and Collision. Truth and reality split apart. In consequence of this split, men must support each other in community, and they must battle in collision. Tragic knowledge sees those battles which are unavoidable. The question for the tragic poet is precisely this: Who is battling whom, and what is really colliding with what?

Immediately, the battle which has found poetic expression is the battle of men against men, or of man against himself. Incompatible needs, duties, motives, and qualities of character are locked in combat. Psychological and sociological analysis seems to make these battles understandable in terms of fact. But the poet sees farther and deeper. It is his task to render tragic knowledge visible, and all these limited realities serve him merely as raw material. Through this raw material he points out what is truly at issue in this conflict. The conflict is now understood according to the interpretations of the antagonists, or of the poet and, through him, the spectator. These interpretations of the battle are themselves realities. For significance so uncovered has always generated the strongest motive power. This significance emerges in the plot of the tragedy.

Such interpretations, when embodied in the work of art itself, are either immanent or transcendent. Tragedy may be immanent, as in a battle between the individual and the universal, or as in a battle of different ways of life that succeed each other in history; or it may be

---

detailed discussion of the sense in which this, and Indic drama generally is "tragic," see Weber, *Das Tragische,* pp. 125-78.

[17] *Weltstimmung.*

transcendent, as in a battle between men and gods, or as in a battle between the gods themselves.

The Individual and the Universal. The individual is opposed to universal laws, norms, necessities: untragically, he represents mere willfulness opposing the law; tragically, he represents the genuine exception which, though opposing the law, yet has truth on his side.

General principles are concentrated in the forces of society, in social stratification, rules, and offices. Hence society may give rise to tragedy. On the other hand, general principles may be concentrated in human character as an imperative of eternal laws which run counter to the drives and the personality of the individual. Hence there are also tragedies that arise from character.

Commonly, tragic works based on such interpretations are poetically weak. Human drives which are entirely concrete, and general rules which are entirely abstract, can meet in conflicts that may be rationally developed. But they do not take visible shape as compelling visions of the depths of existence. The very transparency of these alternatives exhausts the problem. Where there is no sense of the infinite vastness of what is beyond our grasp, all we finally succeed in conveying is misery—not tragedy. This is the peculiar predicament of modern tragedy since the Enlightenment.

The Clash of Ways of Life. A comprehensive philosophy of history should interpret the changes in man's condition as a meaningful succession of historical ways of life; in every epoch these ways of life account for the general situation and the prevailing patterns of action and thought. They do not replace each other suddenly. The old is still alive while the new unfolds itself. The mighty breakthrough of the new is bound at first to fail against the staying power and coherence of the old way of life not yet exhausted. Transition is the zone of tragedy.

According to Hegel, the great heroes of history are tragic figures in this sense. They embody the new idea, purely and uncompromisingly. They arise in sunlike splendor. Their real significance goes unnoticed at first, until the old way of life senses its danger and gathers all its forces to destroy the new in the form of its outstanding representative. Whether Socrates or Julius Caesar, the first victorious protagonist of the new principle becomes, at the same time, the victim at the border of two eras. The old is justified in asserting itself, for it still functions; it is still alive and proves itself through its rich and elaborate traditional patterns of life, even though the seed of decay has already begun its fatal germination. The new is justified also, but it is not yet protected by an established social order and culture. For the time being it is still functioning in a vacuum. But it is only the hero, the first great figure of the new way of life, whom the old, in a last frantic rally of all its forces, can destroy. Subsequent breakthroughs, now untragic, will succeed. Plato and Augustus Caesar are brilliantly triumphant; they realize the vision; they mold men through their works; they shape the future. But they live with their gaze fixed upon the first hero who was the victim.

This interpretation represents a particular philosophy of history. It sets out to speculate only about what is immanent in this world, but proceeds to assign substance and personality to historic units which actually cannot be verified. It ends by endowing historical patterns with quasi-demonic self-direction.

Men Against Gods. The battle takes place between the single individual and the "powers," between man and demons, between man and the gods. These powers are elusive. They escape man if he would grasp or just understand them. They are both there and not there. The same god is helpful and vicious.

Man does not know. Unknowingly and unconsciously he falls prey to the very powers that he wanted to escape.

Man rebels against the gods, as Hippolytus, the chaste youth in the service of Artemis, revolted against Aphrodite. He is overcome in battle with the unconquerable one.

Gods Against One Another. The battle is a collision of the powers, of the gods themselves: man is only a pawn in these terrible games, or their scene, or their medium; but man's greatness consists precisely in his act of becoming such a medium. By this act, he becomes imbued with a soul and identical with the powers.

In the *Antigone* of Sophocles, the hidden gods of chthonic or political origin are basically such powers locked in mutual combat. But in Aeschylus' *Eumenides* the battles of the gods are quite manifest and in the foreground, determining the needs of men. In the *Prometheus* such battles are represented even without man's entering upon the scene.

Tragic world views always contain evidence of struggles. But is struggle tragic in and for itself? Or if not, what makes it tragic? To decide this question, we must explore further aspects of the tragic world view.

Victory and Defeat. Who or what conquers in tragedy? Men and the powers are colliding. The outcome suggests decision in favor of the conqueror: the losers are wrong. But this is not true. Rather, we discover the following aspects of the tragic:

1. Victory is not his who triumphs but his who fails in defeat. In suffering failure, the loser conquers. The apparent victor is in truth inferior; his victory is fleeting and hollow.
2. *What conquers is the universal,* the world order, the moral order, the universal laws of life, the timeless—but the very recognition of such universality implies its rejection: the nature of the universal is such that it must crush this human greatness which opposes it.
3. *In reality nothing conquers.* Instead, everything becomes questionable, the hero as well as the universal. Compared with the *transcendent,* all is finite and relative, and therefore deserves to be destroyed, the particular as well as the universal, the exception as well as the rule. Both the exceptional man and the sublime order have their own limits, beyond which they break down. What conquers in tragedy is the transcendent—or rather even this does not conquer, for it makes itself felt only through the whole situation. It neither dominates nor submits; it simply exists.
4. In victory and in defeat, in the very process of achieving a solution, a new historical order is born, transitory in its turn. Its significance applies first to the particular knowledge of the tragic from which it arose. The rank of a tragic poet is then determined by the content which he draws from victory and defeat, and from their resolution.

Guilt. Tragedy becomes self-conscious by understanding the fate of its characters as the consequence of guilt, and as the inner working out of guilt itself. Destruction is the atonement of guilt.

To be sure, the world is full of guiltless destruction. Hidden evil destroys without being seen; it acts without being heard; no worldly authority so much as hears about it, any more than when someone was being tortured to death in the dungeon of a castle. Men die as martyrs without being martyrs, in so far as no one is present to bear witness or to learn of their martyrdom. Every day some defenseless creatures are being tortured and destroyed on this earth. Ivan Karamazov flies into a mad rage at the thought of the children killed for mere pleasure by the warring Turks. But this whole heart-rending, gruesome reality is not tragic, in so far as disaster is not the atonement of a guilt and is unconnected with the meaning of this life.

The question of guilt, however, is not limited to the actions and lives of individual men. Rather, it refers to humanity as a whole, of which every one of us is a part. Where are we to look for the guilt that is responsible for all this undeserved disaster? Where is the power that makes the innocent miserable?

Wherever men saw this question clearly, they conceived of the idea of complicity in guilt. All men are jointly committed and jointly liable. Their common origin and their common goal account for this. A token of this, though not an explanation, is that we feel shaken and perplexed [18] at the following thought, which seems absurd to our limited understanding: I am responsible for all the evil that is perpetrated in the world, unless I have done what I could to prevent it, even to the extent of sacrificing my life. I am guilty because I am alive and can continue to live while this is happening. Thus criminal complicity takes hold of everyone for everything that happens.

We must therefore speak of guilt in the wider sense of a guilt of human existence as such,[19] and of guilt in the narrower sense of responsibility for any particular action. Where our own guilt is not limited to certain specific wrongdoings but, in a deeper sense, is found in the very nature of human existence, there the idea of guilt becomes truly inclusive. Tragic knowledge, therefore, distinguishes these two kinds of guilt:

First: Existence is guilt. Guilt in the larger sense is identical with existence as such. The idea, already found in Anaximander, recurs in Calderón, although in a different sense—that man's greatest guilt is to have been born.

This is revealed also in the fact that my very existence causes misery. Indian thought has an image for this: with every step, with every breath, I destroy living beings. Whether I act or not, merely by existing I infringe upon the existence of others. Passive or active, I incur the guilt of existence.

A particular life is guilty through its origin. True, I did not desire this world nor my particular existence in it. But I am guilty against my will, simply because it is I myself who have this origin. My descent from guilty ancestors causes my own guilt.

Antigone is born contrary to the law as the daughter of Oedipus and

[18] *Betroffenheit.* In English, to be "perplexed" is to be baffled by circumstance. In German, however, one is *betroffen* when one is not only baffled but touched to one's core.

[19] *Schuld des Daseins schlechthin:* lit., "the guilt of human existence as such."

his own mother. The curse of her descent is active within her. But her very exclusion from the norm of legitimate descent accounts for her singular depth and human feeling: she possesses the surest and most unshakable knowledge of the divine law. She dies because she is greater than the others, because her exceptional case embodies truth. And she dies gladly. Death to her means release; all along her road of action she is at one with herself.

A particular character is guilty because of what he is.[20] Character is itself a form of destiny—in so far as I detach myself from my own character and turn to look upon it.

What baseness there is in me, what desires to do evil, what unregenerate pride there is in my perversity—all this I myself have neither wanted nor created. Yet I am guilty of all this. And my guilt begets my destiny, whether I die unwillingly and unredeemed, or whether I am destroyed in trying to transcend my base nature by summoning up a deeper resource of my being—a resource which enables me to reject what I was, even though I cannot become what I long to be.

Second: Action is guilt. Guilt in the narrower sense is found in any distinct action I carry out freely in the sense that it need not occur and could also occur differently.

Guilty action may consist in flouting the law; it is personal arbitrariness consciously opposing the universal for no other reason than its own arbitrariness. It is the consequence of culpable ignorance, of half-conscious transpositions and concealments of motives. Nothing else is involved in such willfulness beyond the misery of meanness and evil.

The situation is different when tragic knowledge recognizes the guilt of an action. Truthful and morally necessary action, although springing from the foundation of freedom, may entail failure. Man cannot escape his guilt through right and truthful conduct: guilt itself seems incurred guiltlessly. Man takes this guilt upon himself. He does not try to evade it. He stands by his guilt, not out of personal stubbornness, but for the sake of the very truth, which is destined for failure in his necessary sacrifice.[21]

Man's Greatness in Failure. Tragic knowledge cannot be extended and deepened without seeing in man the quality of greatness over and above his atonement of guilt.

[20] This was the "Orphic" view of Rohde and Nietzsche, now generally abandoned on the basis of new manuscript evidence brought forward by Diels. See, e.g., Jaeger, *Theology*, pp. 34ff.

[21] *Schuld des Soseins.* This is guilt, not of existence, origin, or action, but arising from the stubbornness and meanness in one's character.

That man is not God is the cause of his smallness and undoing. But that he can carry his human possibilities to their extreme and can be undone by them with his eyes open—that is his greatness.

What we essentially learn from tragic knowledge, therefore, is what makes man suffer and what makes him fail, what he takes upon himself in the face of which realities, and in what manner or form he sacrifices his existence.

The tragic hero—man heightened and intensified—is man himself in good and evil, fulfilling himself in goodness and canceling out his own identity in evil.[22] In each case his existence is shipwrecked by the consistency with which he meets some unconditional demand, real or supposed.

His resistance, stubbornness, and pride drive him into the "greatness" of evil. His endurance, his dauntlessness, his love, raise him up into the good. Always he grows in stature through the experience of life at its limits. The poet sees in him the bearer of something that reaches beyond individual existence, the bearer of a power, a principle, a character, a demon.

Tragedy depicts a man in his greatness beyond good and evil. The poet's view resembles that of Plato: "Or do you suppose that great crimes and unmixed wickedness spring from a slight nature and not from a vigorous one . . . while a weak nature will never be the cause of anything great, either for good or for evil?" It is from the most gifted type of man that "these spring who do the greatest harm to communities and individuals, and the greatest good . . . but a small nature never does anything great for a man or a city." [23]

* * * *

Fundamental Interpretations of the Tragic

The Distortion of Tragic Knowledge into a Tragic World View. Every effort to deduce tragedy alone as the dominant law of reality is philosophically unsound. We object to it, as to every metaphysics that would

[22] *Im Bösen sich vernichtigend.* This implies both physical and spiritual self-destruction.

[23] Plato, *Republic,* VI, 491 e, 495 b. Shorey translation (Loeb Classical Library).

approach Being and Reality deductively and that would make descriptive statements about the nature of Being or God—we object to it because it seeks to make them both absolute and finite. Even those profound dualisms which are postulated as existing at the very base of reality and assumed to account for the origin of tragedy (for instance, that aspect of God which is not Himself) are only code symbols of relative validity within philosophic thought, and no deductive knowledge can be derived from them. Tragic knowledge is open knowledge, well aware of its own ignorance. To freeze it into a pan-tragism of whatever kind is to distort it.

How a tragic philosophy becomes narrow and perverted may be studied in the case of the poet Hebbel. His systematic interpretation becomes absurd, monstrous, and fanatical. The result is poetry contrived by speculation, the loss of all true spiritual depth—poetry reduced on the one hand to nothing but psychology, and on the other to speculatively heightened grandeur. At the same time, as in flashes of lightning, Hebbel achieves some striking insights and perspectives. But his consciousness of tragedy is no more than consciousness of misery decked out in philosophic trimmings.

As a concept of aesthetics, too, the tragic has acquired a coloring which corresponds to this misleading type of tragic philosophy, as when Bahnsen speaks of tragedy as the universal law, or Unamuno of the tragic sense of life.

The most sublime aberration of a tragic world view occurs when the truly tragic is turned into an absolute and made to appear as if it constituted the essence and value of man.

Tragedy is distinct from misfortune, suffering, and destruction, from sickness or death, and from evil. It is so distinct by virtue of the nature of its knowledge; this knowledge is general, not special; it is question, not acceptance—accusation, not lament. Tragic knowledge is further distinct by virtue of the close connection between truth and catastrophe: tragedy grows more intense as the clashing forces increase in scale and as the necessity of their conflict deepens. All misfortune becomes tragic only through the context in which it occurs, or to which we relate it; through the consciousness and knowledge of those who suffer and those who love; through the interpretation, by tragic knowledge, of misfortune as meaningful. But in and for itself, misfortune is not tragic; it is simply the burden that all must bear. Tragic knowledge invades and breaks through, but does not master, reality—there is too much it leaves untouched, forgotten, or unexplained. It lures us into an exalting realm of grandeur; and thus, despite all clear-eyed honesty, it obscures the truth.

Tragedy becomes the privilege of the exalted few—all others must be content to be wiped out indifferently in disaster. Tragedy then becomes a characteristic not of man, but of a human aristocracy. As the code of privilege, this philosophy becomes arrogant and unloving; it gives us comfort by pandering to our self-esteem.

Tragic knowledge thus has its limits: it achieves no comprehensive interpretation of the world. It fails to master universal suffering; it fails to grasp the whole terror and insolubility in men's existence. This is clearly shown by the fact that although everyday realities—such as sickness, death, chance, misery, and malice—may well become the media through which tragedy makes its appearance, they are not so considered from the outset simply because they are not in themselves tragic. A tragic philosophy lives in an aura of grandeur; it offers us personal fulfillment, as the fortunate result of an appropriately successful disaster, and thus lifts us high above reality. But in so doing, this philosophy narrows down our awareness. For in so far as men find release in an experience of this kind, they find it only at the price of concealing from themselves the terrifying abysses of reality. Misery—hopeless, meaningless, heart-rending, destitute, and helpless misery—cries out for help. But the reality of all this misery without greatness is pushed aside as unworthy of notice by minds that are blind with exaltation. And all the while, man presses for redemption from his terrible realities, which lack the glamor of tragedy.

Together with this unloving blindness, we find a watered-down aesthetic jargon in current phrases about tragedy, a jargon that conveys the essence of tragedy but at the same time distorts its meaning. This jargon untruthfully makes reality appear remote, and all too easily relieves us from having to see the misery of the world as it really is. Thus it is glibly remarked that tragedy reveals the worthlessness of life itself, of all individual finite human life; that the doom of greatness is precisely one of its characteristics; that the world is set up to break and destroy the unusual individual. By such diffuse generalities, so plausible in their vagueness, we cover up the actual ills of reality with a tissue of lies.

On the Tragic

MAX SCHELER

In the following we will speak of no particular art in which the tragic is portrayed. It is impossible to arrive at the phenomenon of the tragic through the art product alone, although the results of examining its extant forms might be most fruitful in discovering what it really is. The tragic is rather an essential element of the universe itself. The material made use of by the art product and the tragedian must contain beforehand the dark strain of this element. To determine what makes a tragedy genuine we must first have as precise a notion as possible of the phenomenon.

It is doubtful whether the tragic is essentially an esthetic phenomenon. We are speaking of life and history in general without placing ourselves in any particular esthetic circumstance, no matter how unusually full of tragic events and circumstances. The question of how the tragic works on our emotions or of how we come to "enjoy" the tragic in some art form we are purposely avoiding. These things can not tell us what the tragic is. The usual "psychological" method of observation, proceeding from the investigation of the experiences of one observing a tragic incident to its "objective understanding," tries to discover and describe the evocations of these experiences. Such a method avoids the issue rather than clarifies it.[1] It tells us only what the tragic does, not what it is. The tragic is above all a property which we observe in events, fortunes, characters, and the like, and which actually exists in them. We might say that it is given off by them like a heavy breath, or seems like an obscure glimmering that surrounds them. In it a specific feature of the world's makeup appears before us, and not a condition of our own ego, nor its emotions, nor its experience of compassion and fear. What goes on in the observer of the tragic as he feels this heavy breath and sees this shimmering darkness that encircles

From *Cross Currents,* Vol. IV (1954), pp. 178-91, trans. Bernard Stambler; published originally under the title *Zum Phänomen des Tragischen,* Francke Verlag, Bern, Switzerland. Reprinted by permission.

[1] Even the famous definition of Aristotle: The tragic is that which arouses pity and fear.

the head of the "tragic hero" is not related to his ability to understand this phenomenon by using his own symbolical way of looking at this feature in the world's makeup. There are people who are blind, or half blind, to the tragic—like Raphael, Goethe, and Maeterlinck.[2] One must know what the tragic is to depict this experience. Moreover, the experience is historically far more variable than the tragic itself. A tragedy of Aeschylus arouses entirely different emotions today than in his time, although the tragic is just as perceptible to both ages.

The mental processes of understanding the tragic, the inner perception of how it is brought to us, are to be distinguished from what one experiences in observing the tragic. This is not the same as the "experience" theory of the tragic. It has nothing to do with depicting the way it works on us psychologically. However, the former places the problem close to the essence of the tragic and its essential manifestations. Consequently, it should not be disregarded.

How then should we proceed? Should we indiscriminately gather together examples of the tragic, selecting those events that impress men as being such, and then ask what they possess in common? This would be a method of induction that would lend itself well to experimental support. Yet this would bring us only to the observation of our own ego when the tragic works upon us. What right have we to trust men when they call something tragic? A plurality of opinion does not help here. Without knowledge of what the tragic is, must we be forced to decide between the opinions that have weight and those which do not? But even taking this for granted, we would still have to justify ourselves. We would have a confused mass that we would call tragic. What would the common element be that would justify this judgment of ours? Nothing more than the fact that they are all called tragic.

All induction would presuppose that one knows beforehand what the essence of the tragic is, and not just what events are tragic. Our method of procedure will be different. The few examples and statements of others that may be given are not to serve as the basis for abstracting by induction a concept of the tragic. They will rather give us some rough draft in which to see the basic use of the word and the phenomenon expressed therein, without taking into account who uses the word and to what intent. They will provide the basis for seeing in what experience this phenomenon comes to its given state. We do not assume that the examples are facts in which the tragic adheres as a property. They are only something which will contain the basic mani-

[2] Cf. Maeterlinck's *La Sagesse et la Destinée.*

festations of the tragic. They will provide us with the opportunity of searching out these manifestations and finally of arriving at the tragic itself. It is not a question here of proofs but of indications or signs.

One should also guard against treating the tragic as a phenomenon with its own metaphysical, religious, and otherwise speculative interpretations. The tragic is not the result of an interpretation of the world and the important events of the world. It is a fixed and powerful impression that certain things make and one which can itself be subjected to many different interpretations. Theories like that which Maeterlinck proposes, basically the theory of every Rationalism and Pantheism, are totally wrong. According to these theories the tragic is the result of a false and unstable interpretation of the world. The tragic is attributed to the ways of thinking in uncivilized times with uncontrolled emotions. Or it is a sort of sudden bewilderment in the face of the defects of the world against which one knows of no help, or—what is the simple consequence of this as stated by Maeterlinck—no helper is at hand, no helper to put the matter in order. They obscure rather than clarify the essence of the tragic; their own outlook and times prevent them from seeing it. We, however, reason that these interpretations of the world are wrong because they have no place for the undeniable fact of the tragic and that any age which does not perceive it is insignificant.

Metaphysical interpretations of the tragic are most interesting. But the phenomenon itself is taken for granted by them. Certain metaphysicians like Eduard von Hartmann make God Himself the tragic hero. Others think the tragic lies only on the surface of things and that underneath all tragedies lies an imperceptible harmony, into which they are finally resolved. But to know where the tragic has its source, whether in the basic structure of existence or in human passions and unrest, is to know already what the tragic is.

Every interpretation fails before the inflexibility of reality which reduces it to silence.

This question of the tragic is only one example of the importance of contrasting the changing whims of the times with the facts of reality.

The Tragic and Values

All that can be called tragic is contained within the realm of values and their relationships.

In a universe free of values, such as that constructed by mechanical physics, there are no tragedies.

Only where there is high and low, nobleman and peasant, is there anything like a tragic event.

The tragic is not a value like beautiful, ugly, good, or bad. The tragic appears in objects only through the interplay of their inherent values.

It is always founded on values or connected with values. To repeat, it is found only in that realm where there are objects of value and where these work in one way or another on each other.

Serenity, sadness, grandeur, and earnestness can be classified among the more tranquil values. The tragic is absent here. It appears in the realm of changing values and circumstances. Something must happen for it to appear. There must be a period of time in which something is lost or destroyed.

In empty space—Schiller notwithstanding—dwells much sublimity, but not the tragic. In a spaceless world the tragic might be possible, but never in a timeless world. In its basic connotations the tragic always implies a determined effectiveness in doing and in suffering. The tragic "character" remains such only as long as he has the necessary dispositions for tragic acting and suffering. Even a situation calling for opposition of forces or their reconciliation is only tragic as long as it contains this effectiveness. If the tragic is to appear, however, this effectiveness must take on a definite direction, a direction toward the annihilation of a positive value in a determined hierarchy. The strength which annihilates it must possess this value itself.

To belong to the category of the tragic some value must be destroyed. With regard to man it does not have to be his existence or his life. But at least something of his must be destroyed—a plan, a desire, a power, a possession, a faith. The destruction as such is not tragic. It is rather the course that an object of lower or equal positive values, never of higher values, is able to force upon it. We can hardly call it tragic for a good man to defeat and bring about the downfall of an evil man, nor for a nobleman to do the same to a peasant. Moral approval precludes a tragic impression here. This much is certain. It is also certain that it must be an object of high positive value that destroys a value. (Values such as the honest with respect to the wicked, the good with regard to the bad, and the beautiful compared to the ugly, are here called positive. All values have this opposition and duality, even excluding their degree of "higher" and "lower.") The tragic is apparent only where the strength to destroy a higher positive value proceeds from an object possessing this positive value. The manifestation is, moreover, purest and clearest where objects of equally high value appear to undermine and ruin each other. Those tragedies most effectively portray the tragic phenomenon in which, not only is every one in the right, but where each person and power in the struggle presents an equally superior right, or appears to fulfill an equally superior duty. If an object of higher positive value, let us take for example a good, just man, is overpowered by some insignificant evil object, the tragic is at once senseless and irrational. In place of arousing tragic pity, it arouses painful indignation. Tragic pity can never fall completely into the depths of pain and disgust, but must maintain some semblance of coolness and calmness.

The tragic is first of all a struggle that is occasioned in an object of high positive value, i.e., of a high moral nature, generally treating of the family, marriage, or the state. The tragic is a "conflict" which takes place between the positive value and the very object which possesses it. The great art of the tragedian is to set each value of the conflicting elements in its fullest light, to develop completely the intrinsic rights of each party.

On the Tragic and Grief

It is true that in some way all tragic events are sad, but in a very definite sense. This is precisely what fate is, an event surrounded by this quality of sadness.[3] On the other hand it arouses sorrow in the feelings of men. It makes the soul sad.

Not all sad persons are tragic characters, however. Every death is sad and makes those left behind sad as well, but assuredly not every death is tragic. Let us disregard for a moment that type of grief that is produced in us independently of any perception of values, almost as if caused by a "neutral" feeling. We would rather consider the "grieved over something." The nature of a certain event arouses our sentiments and produces this feeling in us. It should not appear to be caused by our individual wishes or aims, but only by the worth of the object. The tragic grief has a double characteristic, one rooted in itself, the other in its subject.

This kind of grief is free from all indignation, anger, reproach, and that accompanying the desire "if it had only been otherwise." It is a

[3] That the quality of the sad is definitely not a "feeling," nor a so-called "empathic feeling," cf. the essay, "Idole der Selbsterkenntnis."

calm, quiet fullness; a special kind of peace and composure is characteristic of it.

The atmosphere of tragic grief will be absent if we are aroused to do something about it. Once the event has been completed and brought to its climax, any indication of a compromise or of some chance to avert the catastrophe makes tragic grief impossible.

Tragic grief contains a definite composure. It is thus distinguished from all specifically personal griefs, those which come from a personal experience of being "sad about something." It comes to us from the outside through the soul; it is occasioned by events that are "tragic." The tragedies of Aeschylus show especially well how to awaken this atmosphere of grief in its utmost purity.

We will not point out the twofold characteristic feature of the tragic which causes this atmosphere. One is the very nature of the world's makeup; every individual sad event is thus determined. The other is based on the appearance of an uncompromising inevitability of the destruction of a value, a species of destruction which every tragedy must contain.

In every genuine tragedy we see more than just the tragic event. We see over and above it the permanent factors, associations, and powers which are in the very makeup of the world. It is these which make such a thing possible.[4] In every tragic event we are directly confronted with a definite condition of the world's makeup without deliberation or any sort of "interpretation." This confronts us in the event itself; it does not result from what it does to the things which brought it about. It is only momentarily connected with the event and is independent of the elements that make it up. It is present in the form of a slight presentiment.

Every objective grief like that of a tragic event has its own depth. (I take the word here in a transferred meaning like the "depth" of a room.) It has its own immensity, too, which distinguishes it from a very limited, determined event. The depth is brought about by the fact that its subject is twofold. One is the element of the event that has been seen by us. The other is that point in the world's makeup that is exemplified by the event and of which the event is but an example. Grief seems to pour out from the event into unlimited space. It is not a universal, abstract world-makeup that would be the same in all tragic events. It is rather a definite, individual element of the world's construction. The remote subject of the tragic is always the world itself, the world taken as a whole which makes such a thing possible. This

[4] We mean "such a thing" in the sense of "a so-constituted value."

"world" itself seems to be the object immersed in sorrow. In the foreground of this darkness of sorrow we see the specific event and fate standing out all the more clearly.

The element in the world's makeup which produces these situations seems to do so without any warning. In producing them it ignores the peculiarities of the causes of the event and even its normal effects. It is this which causes the second essential element of the tragic, its inevitability.

We will clarify this later. Right now we are interested in the peculiar atmosphere which it lends to the tragedy.

There is a whole category of feelings and affections that can be connected with the destroying of a value. Their essence is in being "preventable," even if in a particular case they may or may not have been prevented. It doesn't matter what these feelings might be—dread, fear, anger, horror, or the like; they all have in general the characteristic of "excitement." Thinking about the possibility of its turning out otherwise, or even better, causes this excitement. In men it is more frequently caused by the thought, "If so and so had only acted differently." This excitement is able to take hold of a man only because he is a practical being and, as it were, the potential actor in any event.

It softens when the inevitability is seen as an impossibility. The grief does not cease to be what it is, but it assumes the character of the feelings of dissatisfaction, excitement, and pain. These are taken in the same narrow sense as the physical feelings of fear, horror, and the like.

Tragic grief is pure, without physical arousement. In a certain sense even a feeling of "contentment" is joined with it.

There is no desire to do away with the event which led to the destruction of some value. This is abolished by seeing its inevitability.

We see that the tragic seems to have its ultimate roots in the essential makeup of the world itself. It is this which clears away all sense of culpability or responsibility. When we see this in the nature of the event a certain reconciliation takes place. It is a species of reconciliation which fills us with peace and rest and with resignation. This resignation banishes the weakness and pain that would come from contemplating a better-made world.

Thus the specific sadness of the tragic is really an objective character of the event itself. It is independent of the individual circumstances of the beholder. It is free from the feelings provoked by excitement, indignation, blame, and the like. It has a depth and immensity. It is not accompanied by physical feelings or by what can be called real pain. It has a definite resignation, contentment, and a species of reconciliation with the existence which it chances to have.

The Tragic Knot

We asserted previously that in the tragic a struggle takes place between two objects possessing high positive value and that one of them must be overcome. There is one case where this is fulfilled to the highest degree. It happens when the objects are not different events, persons, or things, but coincide in one event, person, or thing; even better, in one and the same quality, power, or ability.

It would be most tragic if the same power which has brought either itself or another object to a very high positive value becomes its destroyer—especially if this takes place in the very act of its achievement.

If we are observing a certain action which is realizing a high value, and then see in that same action that it is working towards the undermining of the very existence of the being it is helping, we receive the most complete and the clearest of tragic impressions.

The same tragic impression occurs when a special courage or boldness which permits a man to accomplish an heroic deed undermines him because it exposes him to a danger that a moderately prudent man would avoid—"If only I were prudent enough I would not be called Tell." Another example is the man with high ideals toward a spiritual goal who permits them to become shipwrecked on the little things of life. Everyone according to Madame de Staël's dictum has the mistakes of his virtue: the same traits of character which permitted a man to do his best have brought him to catastrophe.

We don't have to talk only of human beings here. An art gallery can be destroyed by the very fire that was kindled to preserve the picture. The event has a sharp tragic character. The flight of Icarus is tragic. The very wax which glued his wings to him melts in the same degree as he flies toward the sun.

The use of the phrase, "the tragic knot," is a pertinent metaphor. It illustrates the inner entanglement between the creation of a value and the destruction of a value as they take place in the unity of the tragic action and the tragic event.

Something else can be deduced from the aforesaid. It is not the relationship between values that constitutes the "stage" for the tragic event, nor is it the connection of causal events which it contains. It is rather a special reference of the value relationships to the causal relationships. It is an essential characteristic of our world—and thus of every world—that the course of the causal events disregards completely the value of things. The exigencies of values as they develop toward a unity or as they unfold themselves toward their ideal fulfillment is not taken into account by the causal series. The simple fact that the sun shines on the good and bad alike makes tragedy possible. At times it may happen that the causal relationships simultaneously coincide with an increase of the values. This is accepted as only accidental. It is not occasioned by intrinsic determination. Nor is it occasioned by a consideration of what the values need to reach their fulfillment or that the causality is at hand to produce them.

Without this basic condition there can be no tragedy.

There would be no tragedy in a world which operated on an established system of laws whereby each thing had the powers and capabilities commensurate with its values, and whereby its activity was directed only towards the exigencies of developing or unifying these values. Tragedy would likewise be impossible in a world operating on a system of laws whereby the powers would be directed against the exigencies of these values, purposely opposing them. The tragic would thrive in a satanic world as well as in a divine—a fact that Schopenhauer forgot in his discussion of the tragic.

We see the tragic only when in one glance we embrace both the causality of things and the exigencies of their immanent values. In this unified glance the mind tries to synthetize the conditions in which it finds these values so as to arrive at the unity it is trying to achieve. Then it follows the course of events in their causal sequence. The result is a clear insight into the independence of these two things. It is here that we may see the formal "background" of all tragedies.

Obviously, it is not in the mere knowledge of this circumstance that the tragic exists. The tragic comes into sight only when this independence of the two elements becomes embodied in a concrete event.

What has just been said casts new light on our definition. For never is our insight so clear and so concentrated as when we see that the same action may in some places produce a high value and in others—quite indifferently—destroy this value.

Here then—where we are able to see the unity of an action at a single glance and not by discursive connection, limb by limb—here is a circumstance known previously only by concept which has now come tangibly within our grasp.

What do we mean when we say that in the tragic the destruction of value is "necessary"? Surely not the destruction of causality in general!

Is the question then one of "causal" necessity or is it likely to be one of quite another kind of necessity? Here one might begin to discriminate and say that it is indeed causal necessity but of a particular kind, that is, "inner necessity," and consequently a necessity which depends not on influences breaking in from the outer world but rather on the eternal nature of things and men. Only as such can things and men undergo the tragic fate. Actually, this concept of the tragic—widely held though it may be—is not borne out by the facts.

When a man who seems destined for a certain fate, either by congenital disease or by any sort of natural predisposition, is brought low the first time that external circumstance has a chance to work upon him—such an event does not seem tragic to us even if the highest values inhered in him, values independent of this natural predisposition. Thus Ibsen, with all his artistic genius, has not succeeded in making of Oswald, in *Ghosts,* a tragic figure, since the worm of destruction gnawing at Oswald is the result of a disease he has inherited from his father. We miss here something that belongs to the essence of the tragic hero: that the evil which drives the hero to his downfall pertain to those against whom the struggle is being waged, and also that such a struggle be actually waged.

Both these requirements are missing in *Ghosts*. Nor is the tragic hero to be found in him who immediately surrenders to the inimical, and who at the first dismissive word, immediately abnegates and resigns himself. The "necessity" of which we are now speaking must rather be of such a kind as to take its course even after the performance of all the "free" actions that may be tried in an attempt at flight. When we see the catastrophe opposed by all free efforts of will and means, and can still trace its irruption as "necessary"; when we can even trace, through the turmoil and anguish of this struggle to avert the catastrophe, a species of transcendent necessity: then and then only do we have an example before us of tragic "necessity."

Tragic necessity is not the necessity of the course of nature, a necessity which lies beneath freedom and the power of the will and which may be conceived as the free essence which permits the best linking of events in nature. Rather is tragic necessity of such a kind that it lies *above* freedom: it is to be found only in the conclusion of free acts or of "free causes" in the total sphere of causality, in which may be found even "unfree causes," that is, those which are the results of prior causes.

Wherever men are presented as "milieu-defined," as completely determined by "relationships," as in the naturalist "drama," we have a much less likely source of the tragic than in the drama which gives us the impression that consciously free choices are clearly and conclusively driving the events of the play to its catastrophe. Consequently neither naturalism and determinism on the one hand nor the rationalistic thesis of a "freedom of the human will" limited only by the chances of nature can provide a comprehension of the tragic, or anything more than the beginning of such comprehension. Both these views of the world have no place for the tragic since they make no provision for essential necessity reaching out above the qualities of nature and free choice.

There is still another reason why it is inadequate to define as "inner" that species of necessity we are here discussing. Immanent cause is that which in a thing or in a person exists as latent predisposition, or capacity, or skill, which functions at the inception of true relationships to other things or situations or persons. Wherever we encounter a strictly defined predisposition to the decline of value we must recognize an absence of the true development, of the veridical renewal, of the inner historicity which is needed for the tragic event: in such a situation the catastrophe itself would be predictable if we had a firm and exact picture of the character. The tragic however contains this paradox that when we behold the destruction of value it seems completely "necessary" and at the same time completely "unpredictable." Though the catastrophe may come closer and closer, driven by all the contributory factors (whether free or not), and each new event is visibly pregnant with danger, yet there must still remain one moment when everything —even by ideal calculation—could still turn out quite differently: whereupon from all this complexity is brought forth a deed which resolves these lurking factors into the unity of one species of reality by a means not rationally predictable.

The seemingly "propitious turn of events" just before the catastrophe, which so many tragic poets have been fond of, is a special means to exclude from the audience even the slightest appearance of "predictability." Even the increase of tension, which every tragedy must arouse, would not be possible if the catastrophe did not seem to us to be well founded from the beginning in the latent inner qualities of the characters and their relationships. It is *concrete* causality, which has nothing to do with "natural law," which governs tragic events as it also governs the irreversible motions of the constellations in their consummation of causality—that species of causality which is rightly called the truly "historical." For this we must return to the assertion of Schopenhauer that tragedy never exhibits true "character development" but only "character revelation," revelation of what was previously latent as disposition and character.

Even the tragic transformation of a character, the alteration of disposition and mentality, the essential and latent diversion from the previous course of life—even this transformation is seldom either the catastrophe itself or even an important part of it. A specifically tragic phenomenon is to be seen in the interruption—even in the midst of external victories—of a course of life directed towards certain values as goals. Tragic necessity is to be seen above all in the essence and essential relations of the inevitability and inescapability of things founded in society.

Even these negative definitions indicate that the species of "necessity" we have been talking about becomes apparent only when every conceivable kind of skill seems to be brought into play to halt the destruction of value and to preserve the value in question. Consequently two species of value-destruction are essentially untragic: first, those instances which are tinged with guilt because someone has failed in a duty definitely assigned to him; second, those instances which might have been avoided by the use of available techniques and means. In general, then, the quality of the tragic is lacking when the question "Who is guilty?" has a clear and definite answer.

Only where no such answer can be given does the stuff of tragedy begin to appear. We may use the term "tragic" only when we feel that everyone concerned in the story has hearkened to the demands of his duty with the utmost of his capabilities, and yet the disaster has had to occur. The tragic consists—at least in human tragedies—not simply in the absence of "guilt" but rather in the fact that the guiltiness can not be localized. Wherever we can substitute, in place of a man who plays a role in the unfolding of a catastrophe, another man who is like the first but morally better—that is, one who has a finer sympathy for moral opportunities as well as a greater energy of the moral will—to the extent that we can perform such substitution the growth of a feeling of tragedy is stunted by the amount of blame we can pin on the responsible person.

In such an instance "necessity" is missing as a quality of the tragic phenomena. Consider, for example, the death of Christ; suppose we were able to have the idea that his death, instead of being an essential relationship between His divine purity and the profaneness and opposition of an obdurate "world," had been brought about by the particular moral laxity of Pontius Pilate, or by the wickedness of an individual named Judas, or by the inimical deeds of the Jews. If we were then able to imagine Jesus of Nazareth surrounded not by these men but by a group morally "better," or if we could place him in a different historical context where he would come to higher recognition and repute—if we could do these things the impression of the tragic would vanish.

The death of Jesus is tragic only when it is presented—everywhere and forever—as the consistent adherence to the higher duty of all the parties concerned. An execution, for example, can never have a tragic culmination. The tragic appears when the idea itself of "justice" appears as leading to the destruction of higher value. An execution, if it is unavoidable, awakens deep sympathy; if it were avoidable it might arouse deep anger or irritation, but never tragic sympathy.[5]

If it is true that a disaster becomes tragic only when everyone has done his duty and, in the usual sense of the word, no one has incurred "guilt," it becomes part of the essence of tragic conflict that this conflict be guiltless and unavoidable even before judges who approach the ideal in wisdom and virtue. The tragic misdeed is even definable as that which silences all possible moral and legal powers of judgment; and, on the other hand, every conflict is essentially untragic when by moral and legal lights it is seen to be obvious and simple. Every essential confusion of the bounds of right and wrong, of good and evil, in the unity of action; every maze of threads, of motives, of views, of duties, so presented as to seem to lead equally well to a judgment of "right" or "wrong"; every complication which is not based on necessary moral and legal wisdom but which instead produces from the circumstances alone an absolute confusion of our moral and legal powers of judgment—every such complication pertains to the subjective side of tragic feeling and thereby transposes us completely from the realm of possible "right" and "wrong," from possible "accusation" and "indignation." "Tragic guilt" is of a kind for which no one can be blamed and for which no conceivable "judge" can be found.

Out of this error of our moral judgments, out of this pardonable search for a subject upon whom to pin this "guilt," a guilt which appears to us as such with crystal clarity—only out of this appears that specific tragic grief and tragic sympathy of which we have been speak-

[5] It is for this reason that Aeschylus, in his *Eumenides,* furnishes the judges of the Areopagus with both black and white marbles to indicate the guilt or innocence of Orestes.

ing, along with its unique peace and reconciliation of the emotions. Now too the shifting of that which is to be feared to the cosmos itself appears as the essence of the reconciliation of the individual men and wills with the culminating deeds and events in which they have been taking part.

In this way, tragic guilt becomes something other than definable "right" and "wrong," or than "obeying obligation" or "defying obligation."

But individual men have quite different microcosms of values, dependent on the extent of their actual moral awareness and even on the extent of their possible moral awareness. Only on these bases can be measured their possible "duties" and areas of duty—quite independently of all the peculiarities of their empirical real situations. If every individual does his "duty," to the extent that he does this he behaves *morally;* not otherwise can he do something of equal *value* or *be* in any way of equal value. How deep his gaze thereby penetrates into the macrocosm of moral value, which contains the entire extent of the realm of possible good and evil, and how deep a hold he takes within this macrocosm, are in no way to be decided by the extent to which each individual dutifully produces the "best" of the realm of values with which he has been endowed. It is not duty and the performance of it that "ennoble"—as the Kantian, short-sighted ethic puts it—but rather "noblesse oblige": this is the original nobility of man, which establishes for him quite varied arrays of possible duties—duties which stand in varied relationships to the moral world and are variously "significant" for it.

It makes a difference whether the man doing his duty is a grocer or a noble king; the first one in a vague way obeys a few moral value-distinctions, doing his "duty" with a couple of poor concepts of choice, while the other, living in the fullness of manifold human and other moral relationships, with a finely articulated and higher realm of moral value-distinctions before his eyes, does his "duty" while he demonstrates the highest value given to him, and in will and deed realizes this value. The latter man in this action must conduct himself as occasionally opposed to duty, while the man blind to value blandly performs *his* "duty." If we were now to say that in a true tragic presentation everyone must do his "duty," or at least that it would be prudent so to do, and that—even if everyone has done his duty—the destruction of value and the consequent lessening of the total moral value of the world must nevertheless take place, we would thereby still not know how to exclude this quite different dimension of the moral value-distinction of the individual and of his being taking part in the tragedy. It is rather a quite different species of the tragic which, in this dimension of being, bruises "noble" individuals against the strongly articulated "duties" of the mob. And it appears to be a particular melancholy-ironic glory of this kind of tragedy that the noble individual should accept a moral guilt that his companions do not accept. To the extent that the noble person can more easily become "guilty" than the ignoble—in accord with his richer and higher realm of duties—he is susceptible to a moral "risk" which ever bears with it something potentially tragic, as this risk simultaneously praises and blames his noble nature. The Prometheus of technic, who stole fire from Zeus, is a tragic figure; but even more tragic are the moral Prometheuses in whose eyes a moral world comes with the brilliance of lightning, a moral world that never previously existed. . . . While they are realizing values and acquiring duties which the vulgar do not yet know how to see as value or to feel as duty, the vulgar are themselves only doing their "duty" while the noble see as "evil" what may still be "good" for the vulgar. Here is one instance of the tragic "fall" for the "noble," in that his every eventual moral disapproval of the vulgar must necessarily remain silent—to the extent that only through "good consciences" can his sacred "duty" be accomplished.

We can now penetrate more deeply into "tragic guilt" if we are careful to remain clear on the matter of what, in such a case, is the completion of the duty of the noble. Let it be a proposition here—with no attempt at proof—that moral "good" is the relation by which we realize or tend to realize in a given action that a preference indicates a more highly conceived value.[6] To prefer the higher vlaue is always equivalent to depreciating the lower value, that is, to discontinue the realization of this lower value. However, all "moral norms," i.e., all imperative rules of a general type, are only exercises in what to will and what to do, as suggested by the average levelling of values in any given epoch resulting from the "situations" which are typical of and regularly recurring in this epoch; still, even this levelling of values provides "higher" values which must be realized. Every material rule of morality contains the presuppositions of the particular positive world of good appropriate to its level of civilization. What happens then when the "noble" man perceives a value which is higher than the average, a value which is generally trodden under in the levelling of values, and

[6] Cf. my book, *Der Formalismus in der Ethik und die materiale Wertethik,* vol. I, Niemeyer, Halle, 1914.

accomplishes his advance in the moral cosmos of value, an advance that the vulgar are not yet ready to grasp? In such a case it must be obvious to him that what appears "good" and "dutiful" according to the ruling morality now becomes wicked and evil—and by the same token becomes for him "opposed to duty." And this realization is not avoidable but rather—to use a term of Kant's—a "necessary perception" ("*notwendiger Schein*"). And since everything that can be generally a "moral law"—even to the most complete codification and strongly logical presentation of these laws—inevitably exhibits the positive material world of values of the "time," the "time" itself being determined by the prevailing system of value-levelling—such a man must violate the prevailing moral precept and also violate everything in the moral world that comes into the orbit of such precepts. He must necessarily appear "guilty" even before the fairest judge, when he is in fact guiltless and is so seen by God alone. That this is so is not an irregularity but rather part of the essence of all moral development. Here I mean to point out the root of that necessary and "guiltless guilt," which has hitherto been expressed in this paradoxical form only with a feeling for the justice of it. What is essential here is the necessity of the deception into which the most just moralist must blunder when confronted with the "tragic hero." Although the tragic hero with moral awareness[7] is obviously essentially the opposite of a sinner, he can not be distinguished from a sinner by the age in which he lives. Only to the extent that his newly experienced value becomes established and becomes the prevailing "morality" can he be seen and known—and then only in historical retrospect—as a moral hero. And so there are no present tragedies—there are only tragedies of the past. The tragic man necessarily goes his way in his "present" quiet and speechless. He strides unrecognized through the mob; he may even be there considered a sinner. The error of an instance which separates genius from sinner is here not an accidental but a necessary error. Here, in this tragic fate of the moral genius we can perhaps grasp, in a single species and fashion, the nerve of fate, the complete unpredictability of moral development in man. And even in the absolutely inevitable "fate" and the related absolute loneliness of the moral genius we can see a moment of the type of the tragic, as it may have happened to Jesus in Gethsemane. Here likewise appears the total fate of the world as it appears compressed into the experience of one man, as though in this moment he were standing alone and yet in the "middle," in the center of all the

[7] We are speaking here only of this kind and not of the tragic hero in general.

forces that animate the universe. His experience is as though whole epochs of history occurred in him, yet with no one else being aware of his experience—as though everything lay unified in his hand. And perhaps through this something more may become clear: the tragic hero of this kind is not guilty of his guilt, but rather it "happens" to him: this justifiable circumlocution repeats a very characteristic moment of "tragic guilt." That is: that the "guilt" comes to him and not he to the guilt! . . . *"Ihr fuhrt ins Leben ihn hinein. . . ."*

Nevertheless this "fall" into guilt does not mean that the tragic hero, either through immoderate passion or through stress and a drive in one direction, is so moved that this drive becomes the central point of his ego and his will consequently is impelled in this same direction. This is also the case in the usual moral guiltiness—at least in great measure; and quantities cannot here serve as a basis for differentiation. Even in the midst of the most powerful stresses the will which "follows" such a direction remains a new action, an action not entirely determined by this stress! The tragic guilt into which the hero "falls" is much more accurately characterized by calling it a "guilty" doing or renunciation of doing which darkens the areas of his possible choices and so makes a certain kind of guilt unavoidable, since the choice of the "best" meaning is necessarily in error.

Moral or "guilty guilt" is based on the act of choice; tragic or unguilty guilt is rather based on the sphere of choice! The act of choice is consequently for the tragic hero free of guilt—just the reverse of what obtains in moral guilt, in which the sphere of choice also entails objectively guiltless possibilities, and only the guilt of the act is important. And so the tragic hero "becomes guilty" while doing a guiltless thing.

The consequence of what has been said is the absurdity of the schoolmasters' theory that a moral guiltiness is to be sought in tragedies, and that the tragic poet instead of being a respectable performer of a tragic phenomenon is made into a moral judge over his heroes, whom he punishes for their deeds while at the same time he animates them to perform those deeds. Only total blindness for the phenomenon of tragedy could hatch out this silliest of all theories.

But we should also fall into error if we should try to make the correct concept of tragic guilt serve as the complete definition of the tragic phenomenon. However, since from its earliest presentations the tragic has been a universal phenomenon, not one specifically human or limited to static will, such a definition is self-destructive. However, note this: where a "tragic guilt" is actually portrayed—and it is not the deed of the hero which brings the guilt upon him or is involved in the "catastrophe," nor is his downfall the bearer of the tragic phenomenon, but rather the "guilt of error" itself, and consequently the fact that purity of will falls into guilt—here is the very bearer and root of the tragic.

In this way it is tragic that Othello falls into the guilt of having to kill his beloved, and that guiltless Desdemona should be killed by her beloved who loves her. In his own words, "For, in my sense, 'tis happiness to die," the death of Othello is not punishment for his deed, which as "punishment" must terminate a conscious evil; rather is it deliverance. Tragic guilt is therefore not a condition of the tragic phenomenon —which would indeed be a *circulus in demonstrando,* if the guilt had to be not any sort of "guilt" but only "tragic" guilt—but it is a species of the tragic itself, and to the extent that we are here dealing with moral value, it is therefore a species of absolute value—so to speak, the culminating point of the tragic. Neither death nor any other mischance but only his "fall into guilt" constitutes the tragic fate of the hero.

The Tragic Attitude Toward Value

HENRY A. MYERS

I

What is the tragic attitude toward value, and what is the source of our pleasure in tragedy? The answers to these questions, which seek to get at the nature of a representation and the effect of that representation upon a spectator, must be related as intimately as two points of view of one and the same thing are related, for both lead us to the essence of tragedy, to that element constant in all tragedies which distinguishes the form from other kinds of representation and expression. This distinct character of tragedy as a form is an empirical fact to be explained by theory rather than a fact established by theory. We feel this attitude and appreciate it without necessarily being able to describe it intellectually. Without knowing the precise chemistry which distinguishes wine from water, we are nevertheless able to distinguish one from the other; and in the same way, without knowing the exact logic which constitutes the tragic attitude toward good and evil, we are yet able to distinguish tragedy from optimism and pessimism. The tragic attitude is not optimism, for it does not represent the little that is evil in the world as rapidly diminishing, and it is not pessimism, for it does not represent that inevitable obliteration of good which leads one away from the unyielding persistence of the tragic hero and toward the resignation and acceptance of forgetfulness. In like manner tragedy affords its own kind of pleasure to the spectator. We know by experience rather than by hypothesis that St. Augustine is wrong in thinking that the same curiosity, "the lust of the eyes," leads us to the theatre and to the scene of sensational or shocking events. We have seen shocking events, and we have seen tragedies. They are not the same.

But it is easier to know this than it is to tell how we know it, for tragedies are, at least when partially considered, spectacles of evil. And it is this partial consideration which brings about the superficial para-

From *Tragedy: A View of Life,* 1956, pp. 4-16, 21-27, 155-58. Reprinted by permission of Cornell University Press.

dox of tragedy. Tragedy is a spectacle of evil. Evil is precisely that which we do not enjoy. Yet we do enjoy tragedy.

To escape from this superficial paradox it is necessary only to maintain that tragedy is something more than a spectacle of evil, but then it is necessary to explain what the further element is and how it brings us pleasure. Since that further element must be good, it must be one of the three goods here possible. It must be the triumph of good over evil in the action itself; or it must be the triumph of the play as a whole, considered in respect to its diction, melody, and artistic proportion, over the evil in the action proper; or it must be the relation of constant implication between good and evil in the action, a relation which could please us by its suggestion of order and law and by its insistence upon the harmony of events.

Several considerations lead us to doubt whether the source of our pleasure in tragedy lies in the triumph of good over evil in the action itself. There is, to be sure, a class of tragedies in which, at the climax, the emphasis is upon a note of triumph and victory. *Faust, Romeo and Juliet,* and *The Dybbuk* are such tragedies of victory. The evil represented in the action is the separation of the lovers, and in each the climax is reached with the union of the lovers. If we were able to confine our attention to this union alone we might find in the ultimate triumph of good over evil the source of our pleasure in tragedy. But the union of the lovers is more than a mere union; it is a union in death, a union that is also a separation, a good that is also an evil. At the end of these tragedies we do not look forward to the happy future of Faust and Margaret, Romeo and Juliet, Channon and Leah, united in heaven; indeed, we do not look into the future at all; we look backward over the action and feel that it brought out the good complementary to the evil represented. We accept the element of finality in the end of these characters; their destinies are completed; and we look upon the last scene as symbolic of their past rather than as prophetic of their future, finding in it the suggestion of an order that will not allow good or evil to stand alone.

There is another reason for rejecting the theory that our aesthetic pleasure arises from a happy ending, from the triumph in the action of good over evil. If this were true of the tragedies of victory, how could we account for the tragedies of defeat? Marlowe's tragedies, Shakespeare's *Macbeth,* and Ibsen's *Master Builder* proceed in a manner diametrically opposed to that of the three plays we have considered. The good for the central characters in these plays is the achievement of power, and evil for them is the loss of this power in defeat. The action of the tragedies proceeds through the development of this power to the inevitable realization of its loss; defeat furnishes the climax of each of the plays. If we follow the happy-ending theory in respect to the tragedies of victory, saying that it is the triumph of good over evil in the action which furnishes us aesthetic pleasure, we must further say that in the tragedies of defeat an exactly opposite event, the triumph of evil over good, is the source of our pleasure. Thus we should have no common theory applicable to all tragedies.

Nor can the issue be avoided by maintaining that all the spectators of the tragedies of defeat are pharisaical enough to derive their aesthetic pleasure from gloating over the downfall of a man who yielded to temptation. This theory is even less flattering to the spectators of tragedy than the theory that the source of our pleasure lies in the beauty of the diction and the artistic proportions of the tragedy, a theory which implies that the spectator can bear up nobly under the sorrows of others if they are accompanied by soft music and fitting words.

If the source of our pleasure lies neither in the triumph of the artistic beauty of the tragedy over the evil in the action represented nor in the ultimate triumph of good over evil in the action itself, the justification of tragedy as a representation and as a source of aesthetic pleasure can be found only in the realization that tragedy deals with the ultimates of value, good and evil, and that approaching its task either from the side of good, as in the tragedies of defeat, or from the side of evil, as in the tragedies of victory, the action must work out and realize the complementary opposite, good or evil as the case may be, presenting it as a necessary and inevitable concomitant. Tragedy, therefore, is not a spectacle of evil; it is a spectacle of a constant and inevitable relation between good and evil, a dramatic representation of a law of values. Such is the true significance of the *metabasis*, the change of fortune. It is two-sided always, and since the climax of tragedy is always retrospective, not prophetic, our minds are fastened always on the two necessary sides of value.

The representation of this relation between good and evil is the tragic attitude toward value; and the perception of this relation, and not the good of the action itself, is the source of the spectator's pleasure; and the relation itself, which has various significances in different contexts—metaphysical, aesthetic, dramatic, and ethical—is the essential element in tragedy. It is a relation which makes itself known to feeling long before it can be expressed in a formula. The artist in tragedy does not have it in mind as a conscious goal. He experiments until he feels that he has achieved the tragic attitude; nothing else will satisfy him. Although utterly free from theory, even although guided by a false theory, he may be infallible in taste and feeling. This priority of feeling over pure knowledge holds also for the spectator and for the philosopher. The spectator must feel the effect before he can wonder at the cause, and the philosopher must recognize the tragic attitude by feeling before he can write his dissertation on the elements, intellectual content, and essence of tragedy.

It is not the function of any single tragedy to represent this relation abstractly. Tragedy is not allegorical; each tragedy deals with a specific evil and its relation to the concomitant good. It is the philosopher in thought and the spectator in feeling who transcend the particular tragedy, who generalize about the form. Feeling that this is a specific case of the universal relation between good and evil, the spectator surrenders himself to the standards and values of the tragic hero. Perhaps in his own life he could not value love as intensely as Romeo did, nor gratitude as intensely as Lear did, nor success as intensely as Macbeth did, but for the duration of the tragedies he must be a Romeo, or a Lear, or a Macbeth. Only thus can he truly witness tragedy. He must put himself into the frame of mind of the tragic hero if the tragedy is individualistic, as most of Shakespeare's are, or into the climate of opinion of an age if the tragedy represents the values of a society, as is largely true of Greek tragedy.

The most popular climate of opinion in modern tragedy is that of romantic love, in which the good of the action is the union of the lovers, and the evil, consequently, their separation. Such essentially are Shakespeare's *Romeo and Juliet* and *Antony and Cleopatra,* the various versions of the Tristan and Isolde story, Ansky's *Dybbuk,* Hugo's *Hernani,* and O'Neill's *Desire Under the Elms.* Next in popularity has been the tragedy of ambition, in which good and evil are represented by power and the loss of power, as in Marlowe's tragedies, Shakespeare's *Macbeth,* and Ibsen's *Master Builder.* But the modern temper, which stresses individuality of values as opposed to the classical unity of value, gives rise to a great variety of tragic themes. Shakespeare has produced in *Hamlet,* in which the good is death and the evil is life, a tragedy which in the hands of a lesser writer would have degenerated into pessimism; in *Julius Caesar* a tragedy in which patriotism is the foreground value (of Brutus); in *Coriolanus* a tragedy of heroic pride; in *King Lear* a tragedy of gratitude and ingratitude. Virtue (in its true sense) is the foreground value in Milton's *Samson*. Goethe's *Faust* unites three climates of opinion in one tragedy; it is a tragedy of romantic love in respect to the Faust-Margaret story, a Christian tragedy in respect to the Faust-Mephistopheles story, and a third kind of tragedy, rising out of the other two, peculiarly modern in its emphasis upon the opposition between idle speculation and self-sacrificing labor.

The marked differences in themes in the history of tragedy serve, as nothing else could, to point out the element of identity in tragedy, its representation of a unique relation between good and evil. Further investigation of this relation should result in discovering the meaning of the tragic attitude toward value and the source of our pleasure in tragedy.

II

What is the metaphysics implicit in tragedy? Viewed in this context, tragedy is significant for the relation which it suggests between good and evil abstractly considered. We may set forth several postulates clearly indicated in tragedy.

1. *Tragedy represents supplementary elements of relativity and absoluteness in values.* Tragedy affirms a relativity of values in that it replaces the dream of a universal *summum bonum* with the recognition that goods are relative to persons and to times. The classical unity of value which held sway at the time the dream of a *summum bonum* first gained expression is a historical phenomenon which gave way to the personal values represented in Shakespeare. Yet through this very element of relativity tragedy best expresses its conception of the orderly and absolute nature of values. Every good is shown to imply its concomitant evil, and vice versa, and a constant relation is shown to exist between any and all pairs of the opposites. This absolute aspect of the problem of values is easily reached by the philosopher, who finds the tragic attitude the same in all climates of opinion. In addition, tragic artists have occasionally, by resorting to symbolism, explicitly stressed the universal applicability of their work. Ansky's *Dybbuk,* for example, which follows the tradition of the tragedy of romantic love in leaving the lovers at once united and separated at the end, is introduced and concluded by verses which apply the attitude of the tragedy to all values.

Why, from the highest height
To deepest depth below
Has the soul fallen?
Within itself, the Fall
Contains the Resurrection.[1]

Tragedy is never one-sided, never falls into the error common to optimism and pessimism, never fails to see the Resurrection implied in the Fall and the Fall implied in the Resurrection. By chance or design Ansky hit upon the very symbolism used by Goethe as the final significance of *Faust*. Out of the theme of the Faust-Mephistopheles story, and out of the accompanying theme of the Faust-Margaret story, Goethe drew a meaning universally applicable to values. The two most famous quotations from the tragedy, the first from the Prologue in Heaven, the second from the last scene of Part II, make clear this application.

While Man's desires and aspirations stir,
He cannot choose but err.

Whoe'er aspires unweariedly
Is not beyond redeeming.

Often quoted, these famous statements are seldom quoted together, yet the whole attitude of the tragedy is bound up with the recognition of the relation between both. Taken alone, the first is perfectly representative of pessimism, the second, of optimism. Taken together, they represent the tragic attitude toward value. The first is not obliterated by the second; Faust may be saved, but he has erred none the less; Mephistopheles has worked good, but he has willed evil. Through symbolic stories Goethe achieved a statement of the tragic axiom.

Students of literary criticism will see in this analysis of *Faust* a solution to the controversy concerning the relation of Part I to Part II. *Faust* is a tragedy of victory with a tripartite theme. As a tragedy of victory the evils are realized first, the goods last. At the end of Part I the evils are fully realized. Through idleness and speculation Faust has erred by seeking his own selfish good; he has placed his soul within the grasp of Mephistopheles; and he has been separated from Margaret. To fulfill the need of a true tragedy the concomitant goods must be realized in Part II, and this is precisely what Goethe has brought about. Through his error Faust is brought finally to the good of self-sacrifice;

[1] From *The Dybbuk* by S. Ansky, trans. Henry G. Alsberg, by permission of Liveright Publishers, New York (copyright R 1953 Henry G. Alsberg and Winifred Katzin).

this self-sacrifice makes possible his salvation from Mephistopheles; and as a final touch, he is united with Margaret in heaven. Anyone who maintains that Part I is complete as a tragedy obviously neither feels nor understands the tragic attitude.

2. *The choice of a good by the tragic hero or the dictation of a good by the classical unity of value or another climate of opinion determines the nature of the evil in the play.* The evil will be of the same order and the exact opposite of the good. That is to say, if life is the good for the Greeks, death will be the supreme evil; if gratitude is the good for Lear, ingratitude will be the supreme evil; if power is the supreme good for Macbeth, loss of power will be the supreme evil. Simple as this may seem, it clarifies some points which have confused critics. Obviously, for example, a tragedy cannot be compounded out of the good of one climate of opinion and the evil of another. The man of successful ambition who is the victim of ingratitude is not a tragic figure. The romantic lover who gives up the wealth and power of the world is not a tragic figure. Nor would it be compensation to Lear to restore him to his kingdom; it is ingratitude that rankles in his soul, and only the devotion of Cordelia can set that right. That is why the many deaths in Shakespeare's tragedies are incidental to the plot, often mere parts of the mechanics of the plays. Tybalt and Paris die in the interests of the plot; the spectator is so absorbed in the efforts of the lovers to be united that he is scarcely affected. The deaths are incidental and free from the shocking and sensational character of similar incidents in older drama precisely because life is never the good in Shakespeare's great tragedies. In *Hamlet,* indeed, death itself gradually looms up as the good of the play. There are three stages in Hamlet's acceptance of death as the greatest good; the first has the force of an emotional reaction ("O, that this too, too solid flesh would melt"); the second is in the form of an intellectual query ("To be or not to be: that is the question"); and the third, summarized in his plea to Horatio not to join him in death, contains the force and audacity of absolute conviction ("If thou didst ever hold me in thy heart, Absent thee from felicity awhile"). Although an extreme case, this is probably the best study of the psychology of value yet made.

3. *According to the tragic attitude, good and evil necessarily imply one another.* It is impossible, according to the tragic attitude, for one to find only good or only evil in life. Thus, those who see only the good or the evil of a climax of a tragedy are not truly witnessing tragedy. The culminating scenes are retrospective, not prophetic. In

the tragedies of defeat these scenes are not wholly suggestive of evil. Oedipus and Macbeth are fallen, but they are fallen kings. We are not allowed to forget that. Were it otherwise, we should have pathetic rather than tragic figures. In the same manner, Orestes is acquitted, but he has suffered and his sufferings are not obliterated. A most effective representation of the necessary copresence of good and evil is to be found in *The Master Builder,* where Solness, whose greatest fear is that Fortune may turn her unkindly face upon him, does not realize that by virtue of that very fear Fortune has always shown him both of her masks. And *Macbeth,* of course, is the masterly study of a fear that grows in exact proportion to the hero's triumphs.

4. *The more intensely the tragic hero appreciates the good, the more intensely will he suffer from the evil.* This postulate meets the objection of those who feel that an Iago or an Edmund suffer no more for their villainy than do the innocent Cordelia or the honorable Othello. It is not the object of tragedy to balance the sufferings of the victims of infamy against the punishment of the infamous. The deep feelings of Othello cannot be equated with the punishment of the cold Iago, nor can the sufferings of mighty Lear be balanced by the end of the scheming and emotionally undeveloped Edmund. Only a Lear can equal a Lear; only an Othello can equal an Othello. The devotion of Cordelia rather than the deaths of Edmund and the wicked daughters compensates Lear with a feeling that is as pure and intense as was his rage at ingratitude.

The essence of tragedy, the relation it represents between good and evil, which yields these postulates when viewed metaphysically, has further significance from the point of view of aesthetics. In it we can at last be certain of the source of our pleasure in tragedy, for it removes the paradox contained in the partial analysis of tragedy as a spectacle of evil. If the essence of tragedy is that it presents evil only in order to establish an inevitable order between evil and good, then certainly this order itself, and not the evil alone, comprises the organic unity of a tragedy and the basis of aesthetic delight. But since different contexts alter the meaning of concepts, the relation between good and evil, which was simply one of necessary implication in terms of metaphysics, becomes a harmony in terms of aesthetics.

The harmony of the opposites, good and evil, which constitutes the beauty of tragedy is only one kind of that general harmony which is apparently inseparable from beauty. The harmony of music is another kind, the harmony of painting another, of poetry, another. The old definition of beauty objectively considered as unity in variety may well be condensed to its meaning of order, for harmony in its oldest philosophical sense is equivalent to fitness or order. Evils and goods, according to the tragic attitude, are not matters of chance or caprice; they are in an inevitable relation to one another; and it is this relation, this order, which delights us in tragedy, just as its equivalents delight us in the other arts. But our delight in tragedy is justifiably the most intense, for tragedies order good and evil, the values most vital to us.

* * * *

Indeed, looking through the outward form of tragedy to its inner axioms, we come to look upon the heroic element as an adjunct to dramatic representation. The law of values represented in tragedy is for plain people as well as for heroes, and tragedy, a representation of life, reflects upon the process of living itself. The tragic essence, which yields the metaphysical axioms of value, the secret of our aesthetic pleasure, and the meaning of the dramatic modes, has a further significance in terms of the conduct of life. The metaphysical implication between good and evil, which in aesthetic terms is a harmony constituting the beauty of tragedy, becomes in ethical terms a justice constituting the truth of everyday experience and the meaning of life in terms of good and evil.

If this be so, how does tragedy function as material for a philosophy of values? First, it is evident that the essence of tragedy, representing as it does an inevitable relation between good and evil, satisfies the principle of such a philosophy that values must be subjected to law, and not to chance, caprice, or fortune. Second, tragedy meets the further principle of a philosophy of values in that the order which it represents is something more than the blank necessity which characterizes impersonal disciplines. The general order of the world, tragedy indicates, has a specific and personal meaning in terms of good and evil. It is not enough to say, confining ourselves to metaphysical terms, that a necessary implication exists between good and evil. In the light of aesthetic problems that necessary implication is a harmony which is the source of our pleasure; and in the light of problems of conduct that necessary implication is a justice which gives warmth and value to eternal law itself.

Some indication of the manner in which true tragedy affirms the two necessary principles of a philosophy of values may be found in a comparison of the *Oresteia* of Aeschylus with the modern imitation by

O'Neill, *Mourning Becomes Electra.* In the Aeschylean trilogy an inevitable order of values is indicated by the sequence of tragic events, a sequence rooted in the very beginnings of the foredoomed halls of the house of Atreus. Aegisthus avenges his father, and Clytemnestra, her daughter, Iphigenia, in the death of Agamemnon. Orestes, in turn, avenges the death of Agamemnon in the deaths of Clytemnestra and Aegisthus, and in turn the Furies of Clytemnestra pursue Orestes. O'Neill has displayed an almost point-by-point fidelity to the original in building a modern parallel. With necessary differences in motivation, Orin and Lavinia replace Orestes and Electra, Christine and Brant replace Clytemnestra and Aegisthus, and Mannon replaces Agamemnon. The same inevitability is suggested in an analogous sequence of events. Up to this point *Mourning Becomes Electra* is a successful imitation, but O'Neill is unable to follow Aeschylus in establishing the second principle of a philosophy of values. Aeschylus is not content with the mere orderly sequence of values; his culminating task is to represent the nature of the order of values. This he accomplishes through what is for us symbolism. The sequence of events is broken by the trial of Orestes, at which justice obtains in the acquittal of Orestes and the appeasement of the Furies. The inevitable order of human values makes manifest a justice ordained by the gods. Into this symbolic realm O'Neill cannot safely follow, and as his tragedy ends, we know nothing more than that the orderly sequence will be carried out to the bitter end, that, as Lavinia turns back into the house, we have come to the last link in the chain of necessary events. The chain remains a chain, and O'Neill's tragedy, because it can furnish nothing to replace the symbolism of the older trilogy, remains in a pre-Aeschylean attitude toward values; values are ruled by stern necessity, but that necessity is not seen in its true light as justice.

By its interpretation of the eternal law of values as justice tragedy places itself under the unity of Western culture. Whether it be as a representation of life or as artistic addition, only in the category of justice have the poet, the philosopher, and the religious teacher rested content with the meaning of life. Thus it had been with Homer, Heraclitus, and Aeschylus; and after Plato turned from the life of the individual to the activities of the state in search of justice, Christianity swept over him and over Greek philosophy, subordinating them to its vision. For beneath the softer surface of Christianity, Augustine and Thomas found that durable skeleton of eternal justice which has been represented in art by Dante and Milton; and this central thread of Greek and medieval culture still runs through the modern *Weltanschauung,* as we discover in Leibniz's theodicy, Hegel's philosophy of history, Emerson's theory of compensation, and Whitman's *Leaves of Grass.*

But the very concept of justice is in its development the product of creative imagination, and poets and tragic artists have been the largest contributors to its elaboration and perfection. The common conception of justice as a balance or equilibrium derives from the conception behind the picture of the golden scales of Zeus in the *Iliad.* From this conception all theories of justice start and diverge according to the notions of how the equilibrium is achieved. Tragedy is rich in such diverging conceptions, ranging from the poetic justice which we have found to be a minor dramatic device through the symbolism of Greek tragedy to its most important contribution to a philosophy of value, the unique conception of justice latent in the dianoetic background of tragic art.

In its search for the meaning of justice tragedy concerns itself with the individual rather than with the political animal of Aristotle, a point which clearly differentiates tragedy from the social-problem play. No matter how much the action of the plot may be related to social conditions or political or economic events, the attitude of tragedy clearly is that the citizen is merely a limited aspect of the man. The tragic hero may or may not follow the bent of his society; some yield to Caesar, and others, like Antigone, are guided by another law.

The tragic attitude toward material things is identical with its attitude toward the state. The individual works out his destiny through social institutions and through material things, but it is he, and not these things, who is the center of gravity in the problem of values. Societies and things have value only insofar as they are valued, only insofar as they enter into the lives of individuals. This is indicated by the climates of opinion in tragedy and established by the axioms of relativity (Axioms 1, 2). The inevitable order in things valued exists only by virtue of the inevitable order in the individual's capacity to value (Axioms 3, 4).

It is this preoccupation with the values of the individual that makes tragedy necessary material for a philosophy of value. The methodology of philosophy is invaluable in solving certain problems in the realm of values, but methodology, on account of its impersonal nature, must be applied to the arts of personal feeling before the true nature of values can be fully grasped. There is contained in the dramatic modes of representation in tragedy something indigenous to the form—a unique conception of eternal justice in terms of individuals—which cannot be discovered elsewhere.

This conception of justice is not consonant with the notion of justice at the level of the *lex talionis,* the law of the claw, for, as we have seen, tragedy recognizes the impossibility of exacting an eye for an eye, of bringing upon the emotionally undeveloped Edmund and Iago sorrows as great as those of Othello and Lear. Indeed, its conception is not in agreement with any of the traditional notions of either distributive or retributive justice. Because it is artistically self-sufficient, never carrying the spectator beyond the action, and because its climax is always retrospective, it cannot admit the eternal justice of rewards and punishments represented in Dante. There is in it no question of the distribution of material goods for the achievement of justice, for such goods are meaningless to an Oedipus, a Lear, an Antigone.

Tragedy has been led by the inequality of men to reject the concepts of justice at these levels. The feelings of one individual can seldom, perhaps never, be duplicated; hence the exaction of an eye for an eye is impossible; hence the equal distribution of goods is not a just government of values. A just government of values could only obtain by so regulating the individual's capacity for feeling that it would carry with it his fate and the justice of his life. Tragedy proclaims a law effecting this just government of values. Although, in the realm of values, no two men are equal in respect either to capacity for feeling or to choice of values, each individual is exactly equal to himself, and the eternal justice which cannot be found in attempting to equate Othello with Iago or Lear with Goneril and Regan can be found in the observation that an Othello is exactly equal to himself and a Lear exactly equal to himself. Operating through the two-sided nature of value (Axiom 3), eternal justice is manifest in the perfect measure governing the life of the individual (Axiom 4). Romeo, Solness, Orestes, Hedda, Iago, Faust, and Channon are all unequal in capacity for feeling and choice of values, but one and the same law of values orders inevitably the good and the evil in the life of each.

This conception of justice, which is the essential contribution of tragedy to the philosophy of values, rejects the moral law at the levels of the *lex talionis* and the theories of distribution and retribution, but it affirms the moral law on the plane where virtue is taken to be its own reward. The nicety of the tragic law is such that the piety and love of virtue of Antigone are sufficient psychologically to motivate her tragic action, just as Samson's need to exercise his virtue overcomes the psychological obstacle contained in the tragic fact that in exercising it he will bring it to an end in death.

Following the tradition which conceives of the notions of equilibrium, balance, and equality as lying at the center of the idea of justice, tragedy denies that this equality can be found in the relation of the citizen to the state (as in Plato's *Republic*), or in the relation between individual and individual (as in the *lex talionis*), but affirms that it can be found in the relation of the individual to himself, in his perfect self-equality. The equality of good and evil which constitutes justice can be found only in the individual, whose capacity for experiencing good is exactly equal to his capacity for experiencing evil.

It is perhaps well to note that an intellectual grasp of this tragic attitude is an invaluable supplement to tragedy rather than a substitute for it, for tragedy, as an experience, constantly reminds us that the law of values, abstracted and formulated by philosophy, is only an intellectual reflection of the lives and actions of individuals.

* * * *

Since it is positive and affirmative, great tragic poetry satisfies our deepest rational and moral inclinations. As rational beings, we are always looking for patterns, for order, for meaning, in experience; as moral beings, we can be satisfied only by discovering in the realm of good and evil the special kind of pattern or order which we call justice. Tragedy reconciles us to evil by showing us that it is not a single, separate phenomenon but one side of change of fortune, and makes us feel that the change of fortune of a representative man is just.

Melodrama, it must be admitted, also satisfies our rational and moral nature: it too presents an order which is just. The inadequacy of melodrama arises from the fact that the just order which it represents will not stand the test of critical judgment. The first premise of melodrama distorts the facts of life. Men, we know, are neither angels nor devils. When we know only the good side of someone and know nothing of his weaknesses, we rightly think of him as being a bit too good for this world. And when, forgetting our better understanding of human nature, we think that someone has for his object in life a goal which he knows to be evil and evil only—as Mephistopheles has for his goal the downfall of Faust—we correctly think of him as diabolical. If such a person did live on earth, he would be a devil, not a man.

The conclusion of melodrama, which follows inescapably from its first premise, is also false to the facts as we know them. Poetic justice is more often the exception than the rule; indeed we call it "poetic" justice because we have found it oftener in literature than in life. Sometimes, it is true, the innocent are rewarded and the guilty punished; more often the innocent and the guilty escape together or are punished together, as in war; sometimes the innocent suffer while the guilty go free.

No one has ever questioned the superiority of tragedy over melodrama. All who have known and enjoyed both testify that tragedy is greater and more effective because it presents a more convincing picture of man and of the relation between his grief and his gladness.

Tragic insight offers us a mean between all melodramatic extremes —between the extremes of optimism and pessimism, between the extremes of fatalism and utopianism, and between the view that man is naturally good and the view that he is inherently depraved.

The tragic artist is neither optimist nor pessimist: he represents good and evil as eternally necessary aspects of experience, and the relation between them as just. Change of fortune is the condition of man's destiny on earth; no man can hope to be happy and happy only; no man need fear that he may sink into endless misery. To the tragic poet man is like the sunflower. It is the nature of the sunflower to turn toward the sun, but it is its destiny to live half in sunshine, half in shadow. Similarly, it is the nature of man to seek happiness, but it is his destiny to suffer as well as to enjoy.

Tragedy reminds the utopian that suffering and all forms of evil are always with us—that change of fortune is the fundamental and inevitable condition of our experience. Whoever seeks to evade this inevitable condition merely hastens its fulfillment. Perhaps that is why, in an age dedicated to the task of bringing to all freedom from fear and insecurity, we are all so fearful and insecure. Certainly, by tragic irony, the utopian hopes of man are today closer to reversal than to realization.

On the other hand, tragedy reminds the fatalist that man can get what he wants—if he is willing to pay the price. Although he pays a heavy price for success, the tragic hero does reach his goal. Oedipus finds the unknown murderer; Orestes and Hamlet punish the murderers of their fathers; Medea crushes Jason; Tamburlaine conquers kingdoms and empires; Doctor Faustus has his four and twenty years, and Faust his fair moment; Romeo is united with Juliet in life and in death; Lear has ample proof of Cordelia's love, as does Othello of Desdemona's; Everyman is saved; Samson destroys the Philistines; Solness climbs the tower; Ahab hurls the harpoon at Moby Dick. Tragedy is not a spectacle of futility and frustration; it is a demonstration of the universal moral law: man gets what he pays for, and pays for what he gets.

The tragic view of man's moral capacities is again a mean between two extreme views. The tragic hero—the representative man—is neither eminently virtuous nor totally depraved. He has equal capacities for good and for evil; he is free to choose between a good deed and wrong-doing, and is responsible for his choice.

These are the main features of the tragic spirit. It lifts us above self-pity and reconciles us to suffering by showing that evil is a necessary part of the intelligible and just order of our experience. It lifts us above the divisive spirit of melodrama by showing that men are neither naturally good nor inherently evil. It saves us from the pitfalls of utopianism and fatalism. It teaches moderation by showing that the way of the extremist is short, but at the same time it shows the man of principle that an uncompromising stand is not without its just compensations. And most important, it teaches us that all men are united in the kinship of a common fate, that all are destined to suffer and enjoy, each according to his capacity.

Tragic Reality

OSCAR MANDEL

The tragic idea on which so many works of art rest is one of the great platitudes which stagger only when we look at them as though we had never noticed them before. It is well, on the whole, that the most frightening ideas are so evident and so commonplace that they only occasionally alarm us, in the night perhaps, when we are alone, at times of great sorrow, or in cetain unusual moods or situations. Yet such ideas—and their joyous counterparts too—continue to provide the raw materials for all the arts. In each generation, the artist is called upon to reword them in the idiom of the day. When he tires of them, his art becomes esoteric, mannered, decadent. The search for the altogether new, the determination to express an emotion never felt before, issues in exquisite art for the coterie. But the *outré* does not in its turn become the norm; rather it provokes another reaction, and a robust return to the undying platitudes. If it did become the norm, art would really progress, whereas of course it does no such thing. Like the clouds, whose shapes and colors are never twice the same, yet which always rise from the same natural cycle and catch the same sun, art moves from age to age through unrepeated shapes, but is always itself in essence.

The human situation which lies at the root of tragic art is thus simple, perpetual, and (when it makes itself felt) awesome. The situation is not simply that human effort fails, but that failure lies implicit in the effort. Some men—and, indeed, some cultures—are so preoccupied with their realization of this radical shortcoming of human existence that they withdraw from all activity and condemn the will. Others are content with the limited successes which life offers between the two eternities on either side of it, and, leaving death out of the problem by a kind of daily prestidigitation, assent to a conditional optimism. Most men are granted even better: death does not preoccupy them at all, "they are not philosophers," and they live as buoyantly as if they

From *A Definition of Tragedy* by Oscar Mandel, 1961, pp. 162-68. Reprinted by permission of New York University Press.

were immortal. We could call this stupidity; but it seems more like a last kindness of Nature, when she inflicted on man the foreknowledge of his own death.

Death with its inevitable victory over effort is then the first tragic fact. The second tragic fact is a socio-psychological one: the very act of living in the society of others brings with it—unavoidably, "naturally" —friction, hate, misery. The tragic purpose is the desire, or rather the need, to live among one's kind. If the radical flaw in this desire is interpreted as the perpetuation of an offense committed against God, we can speak of original sin. Sin as the misalliance between man and man (Cain murdering Abel) is indeed original, that is to say, essential, built into the very fact of sociable life. Thus the act of birth is tragic not only because it is simultaneously the condemnation to death (so that, as we watch our newborn child, we may fancy that we have brought another death into the world), but also because it fastens on the child the inevitability of suffering among his own species.

Pues el delito mayor
Del hombre es haber nacido

says the prince Segismundo in *La Vida Es Sueño*: the greatest crime of man is to be born. In the universal ritual of the seasons, the interlock of birth and death, spring and winter, fertility and sterility, is acutely realized. Once more, the distance between catastrophe and inevitable catastrophe is decisive. A man's crop may be blighted by the magic spells of an enemy: that is one thing. Quite another is the necessary blight brought by the winter, for that one is built into the hopeful act of sowing itself. One could not confuse the two species of event.

We meet with tragic fact at every level. We hear of the folly of being wise, which is undoubtedly a tragic notion, and of evil as the *sine qua non* of good. Some cultures, it appears, grew into their glory by means of oppression and slavery. In our own time, we look on troubled while at every leap of the day our wealth, our comfort, our control of the world increase, and a dreadful spiritual desiccation keeps pace, the shadow growing with the body. The sense of doom, which is so characteristic of contemporary art and philosophy, and penetrates even into the speeches of some public men, does not *happen* to co-exist with the material and social achievements of our times; it rose out of the very heart of success. At the point of the perfect "organization of human resources" comes the death of the soul. Eventually we ask whether the flaw does not lie at the root of every reform. How many advances, liberations, revolutions, hailed as new epochs in human affairs, are really progressions from Scylla into Charybdis? Here peons are given land, only to starve on it. There, a colonial people is set free, only to bleed in civil wars. Elsewhere patriots overthrow a tyrant to become tyrants themselves. And where is success? Is not the Stoic right when he preaches a return to the soul itself? Is not the grasping for wealth, liberty, security, and perhaps even love, self-defeating—rotten in the act itself?

These are mere suggestions, obvious enough. One does not have to subscribe to them *in toto* to feel how tragic art naturally emerges out of life's own conditions. Historical tragedies, in which the protagonist is a nation or an entire civilization, strike us with especial force. Nothing is so melancholy as a study of Europe since the Industrial Revolution. We read here powerful tragedies of guilt and good intentions, classic in all their lines. Logically, but only logically, the new capitalists of the nineteenth century had two ways open to them. They could disregard the notions of justice entertained in theory by most Europeans, and ride roughshod over the masses of people who were now in their hands; or they could create a system of distribution by which they would restrict their own wealth but satisfy the proletariat and the natives in the colonies, and at the same time glut the world with riches. Needless to say, the capitalists, in the image of the feudal landlords who preceded them, took the luxurious alternative of driving their slaves to the uttermost. This continuous act of guilt (we are dealing with a continuous tragedy enacted in reality) bore as its necessary consequences the class wars and the colonial revolutions of our own day. That the downtrodden should get the better of it was by no means certified in the original configuration; but the tragedy was consummated, regardless of its outcome, in the terrors, miseries and massacres of the last generations.

No less tragic has been the social upheaval in itself. Here too we recognize without difficulty a tragic purpose: call it the longing for social justice, though a better name for it is the natural greed of the dispossessed. In Shelley's times a gentleman might foresee a noble unchaining of the Outraged People, whether Greeks against Turks or British mill workers against Gradgrinds. We know better (as the Romans who had survived Marius knew better) what a rising of the people, however just in itself, brings to the world in new miseries, dictatorship by demagogues, civil and international wars, fresh spoliations and unforeseen oppressions, and, as always, the butchery of the innocent. Such are not adventitious but altogether inevitable consequences of these upheavals; there are no clean revolutions. Tough theory-makers proclaim that the end justifies the means—a tragic concept: blood *must* be shed as we march to the City of God.[1]

Historical tragedy has its counterpart in the tragedy of historical figures—of leaders whose leadership necessarily miscarried and drove men in directions other than they had imagined. Christ did not live to see the havoc wrought by, and the perversions imposed on, his doctrines; but Ghandi witnessed the slaughter which was released by the very act of independence in India, and Chamberlain lived long enough to see the unavoidable bankruptcy of his well-meant policies. We may count it an axiom, which leaders of mankind unfortunately ignore, that in every great movement—religious or social—success means failure, popularity is corruption, the triumph of purity is the end of purity.

While great men make impressive tragic figures, we meet with tragic situations at every turn among the mass of mankind. We are all acquainted with cases of sacrifice for the "greater good"—say the relinquishment of pleasure for the sake of religion, of love for the sake of a parental tie, of life for the sake of the fatherland. We may observe, with regard to the last instance, that propagandists do not usually present the patriot's conscious self-sacrifice with a tragic emphasis; they neglect the pain for the exaltation of death, the danger for them, in the tragic view, being that it is a wonderful moderator of fanaticism and enthusiasm. Such is the picture we have of those Japanese warriors who, we are told, crashed with their planes on a target out of single-minded patriotism. And it is incontestably true that fanatics do not make tragic figures.

Some who have reflected on the source of art have been distressed by a strange parasitism: all the arts seem to depend in large measure upon human suffering. The tragic pattern repeats itself: if we strive for great art, we must exploit and welcome the inhumanity of man to man. And it is more than a romantic legend to represent many artists as relying on their own suffering for the creative act. The unhappy Tennyson was a great poet; satisfied and at peace, he became, in Fitzgerald's phrase, a poetic machine. But not only artists: men in any profession may have to pay for success with a terrible hurt to another

[1] In a remarkable scene of *Point Counterpoint,* Aldous Huxley denounces any millennium which depends on the murder of even one vile person. The same problem occurs, of course, in Dostoievsky.

part of themselves. Tragic situations are so much taken for granted in our thinking—who does not know that men blindly persevere in professions for which they have no talent, or that they love on where they cannot be loved in return?—that to speak of them aloud is to belabor the commonplace. But then, as we have seen, to make the commonplace come alive—"to give," in Coleridge's words, "the charm of novelty to things of every day"—is one of the abiding goals of art.

We can go further. Aldous Huxley, in *Brave New World,* discovered that happiness itself is a blight, and that all the emotions that we really cherish derive from our misery. Not only the aesthetic experience, but love and pity and courage and admiration imply the existence of evil. We reach therefore the paradoxical condition of welcoming pain; and the hero of the novel turns into a flagellant! Anatole France arrives at the same conclusion regarding pain: "We owe to it all that is good in us, all that gives value to life," he writes in *Le Jardin d'Epicure.* There is then scarcely a virtue in our lives which does not require us to demand, if not to love, the presence of evil. This condition can actually be stated in two manners. If we begin with the desire for good—say a wish to write immortal poetry, or to love like Antony—then we face the tragic requisite of evil somehow and somewhere, for a blithe person in a blithe world will not write immortal poetry or love like Antony. Fortunately we can reverse the statement, and beginning with an evil we can say that it may often involve an inevitable good fortune. *"La fin du bien est un mal,"* goes one of La Rochefoucauld's posthumous maxims, *"et la fin du mal est un bien"*—"the end of a good is an evil, and the end of an evil is a good." [2] Perhaps this is not necessarily a cheering thought, but it cannot be denied that a villain may attempt a villainous deed, and by the nature of the drive and the context emerge unavoidably with a good. Political life is particularly susceptible to this species of tragedy-in-reverse: witness the good which, all historians agree, came of the Crusades.

In Anatole France's little book there is an entertaining story concerning the shade of Cadmus, come to visit the author in his library. The Phoenician is a rough and unprincipled captain, whose sole occupation while he lived was self-enrichment. He did not scruple to loot old treasures and massacre the innocents; but in his avidity for

[2] In contrast with Cardinal Newman: "Good is not only good, but reproductive of good; this is one of its attributes; nothing is excellent, beautiful, perfect, desirable for its own sake, but it overflows, and spreads the likeness of itself around it." (*The Idea of a University,* VII, 5.)

more wealth, he also found it useful to improve on the cumbersome method of writing (hence of keeping accounts) which was then current. In a word, in order to satisfy his rapacity, he invented the alphabet. The moral is that somewhere in the chain of events that leads to any object there is good and there is evil, take the words in almost any sense. And whether we have tragedy or tragedy-in-reverse often depends only on the point at which we break the chain.

This leads us to the final point that tragedy does not exhaust life, even though it is a condition of life. Life itself is stalked by death, but life is made up of many lives, as it were: it is constituted by a series of experiences. Sartre has made an attempt to prove that every act in this series is an expression of its own futility. Common experience refutes him. Futility is a judgment, and we know that many people do not judge their action as futile, whatever the philosopher may say. Sartre then accuses these people of being *salauds,* which is usually translated as "stinkers," but is rendered better by the vulgar "bastards." With this, however, the argument comes to an end, and each side withdraws to its fortifications, the bastards simply refusing to experience the suffering which the philosopher assures them they ought to feel.

Tragedy involves suffering. What men feel to be successful actions cannot be argued away as such on ontological grounds; success, indeed, is the feeling of success. The real tragedies we have touched on in this section involve felt, not theoretical, failure. Death itself is not necessarily an evil. Only those who hate and fear it can say that it is the fundamental blight of life; only for them is life tragic at the root. The great paradox is that the less tragic a man's life has been, the more tragic is the fact of death. Death is bitter only because life was good. But if that is so, the tragic view of life can be, as we maintained before, only one of the aspects under which life is considered. Were every act doomed to tragic failure, life as such would no longer be tragic, for we should be forced into the odd position that its inevitable consequence, death, was the basic victory of man.

The Mythos of Autumn: Tragedy

NORTHROP FRYE

Thanks as usual to Aristotle, the theory of tragedy is in considerably better shape than the other three *mythoi,* and we can deal with it more briefly, as the ground is more familiar. Without tragedy, all literary fictions might be plausibly explained as expressions of emotional attachments, whether of wish-fulfilment or of repugnance: the tragic fiction guarantees, so to speak, a disinterested quality in literary experience. It is largely through the tragedies of Greek culture that the sense of the authentic natural basis of human character comes into literature. In romance the characters are still largely dream-characters; in satire they tend to be caricatures; in comedy their actions are twisted to fit the demands of a happy ending. In full tragedy the main characters are emancipated from dream, an emancipation which is at the same time a restriction, because the order of nature is present. However thickly strewn a tragedy may be with ghosts, portents, witches, or oracles, we know that the tragic hero cannot simply rub a lamp and summon a genie to get him out of his trouble.

Like comedy, tragedy is best and most easily studied in drama, but it is not confined to drama, nor to actions that end in disaster. Plays that are usually called or classified with tragedies end in serenity, like *Cymbeline,* or even joy, like *Alcestis* or Racine's *Esther,* or in an ambiguous mood that is hard to define, like *Philoctetes.* On the other hand, while a predominantly sombre mood forms part of the unity of the tragic structure, concentrating on mood does not intensify the tragic effect: if it did, *Titus Andronicus* might well be the most powerful of Shakespeare's tragedies. The source of tragic effect must be sought, as Aristotle pointed out, in the tragic *mythos* or plot-structure.

It is a commonplace of criticism that comedy tends to deal with characters in a social group, whereas tragedy is more concentrated on a single individual. We have . . . reasons . . . for thinking that the typical tragic hero is somewhere between the divine and the "all too human." This must be true even of dying gods: Prometheus, being a god, cannot die, but he suffers for his sympathy with the "dying ones" (*brotoi*) or "mortal" men, and even suffering has something subdivine about it. The tragic hero is very great as compared with us, but there is something else, something on the side of him opposite the audience, compared to which he is small. This something else may be called God, gods, fate, accident, fortune, necessity, circumstance, or any combination of these, but whatever it is the tragic hero is our mediator with it.

The tragic hero is typically on top of the wheel of fortune, halfway between human society on the ground and the something greater in the sky. Prometheus, Adam, and Christ hang between heaven and earth, between a world of paradisal freedom and a world of bondage. Tragic heroes are so much the highest points in their human landscape that they seem the inevitable conductors of the power about them, great trees more likely to be struck by lightning than a clump of grass. Conductors may of course be instruments as well as victims of the divine lightning: Milton's Samson destroys the Philistine temple with himself, and Hamlet nearly exterminates the Danish court in his own fall. Something of Nietzsche's mountain-top air of transvaluation clings to the tragic hero: his thoughts are not ours any more than his deeds, even if, like Faustus, he is dragged off to hell for having them. Whatever eloquence or affability he may have, an inscrutable reserve lies behind it. Even sinister heroes—Tamburlaine, Macbeth, Creon—retain this reserve, and we are reminded that men will die loyally for a wicked or cruel man, but not for an amiable backslapper. Those who attract most devotion from others are those who are best able to suggest in their manner that they have no need of it, and from the urbanity of Hamlet to the sullen ferocity of Ajax, tragic heroes are wrapped in the mystery of their communion with that something beyond which we can see only through them, and which is the source of their strength and their fate alike. In the phrase which so fascinated Yeats, the tragic hero leaves his servants to do his "living" for him, and the center of tragedy is in the hero's isolation, not in a villain's betrayal, even when the villain is, as he often is, a part of the hero himself.

As for the something beyond, its names are variable but the form in which it manifests itself is fairly constant. Whether the context is Greek, Christian, or undefined, tragedy seems to lead up to an epiphany of law, of that which is and must be. It can hardly be an accident that the two great developments of tragic drama, in fifth-century Athens and in seventeenth-century Europe, were contemporary with the rise of Ionian and of Renaissance science. In such a world-view nature is seen as an impersonal process which human law imitates as best it can, and this direct relation of man and natural law is in the foreground. The sense in Greek tragedy that fate is stronger than the gods really implies that the gods exist primarily to ratify the order of nature, and that if any personality, even a divine one, possesses a genuine power of veto over law, it is most unlikely that he will want to exercise it. In Christianity much the same is true of the personality of Christ in relation to the inscrutable decrees of the Father. Similarly the tragic process in Shakespeare is natural in the sense that it simply happens, whatever its cause, explanation, or relationships. Characters may grope about for conceptions of gods that kill us for their sport, or for a divinity that shapes our ends, but the action of tragedy will not abide our questions, a fact often transferred to the personality of Shakespeare.

In its most elementary form, the vision of law (*dike*) operates as *lex talionis* or revenge. The hero provokes enmity, or inherits a situation of enmity, and the return of the avenger constitutes the catastrophe. The revenge-tragedy is a simple tragic structure, and like most simple structures can be a very powerful one, often retained as a central theme even in the most complex tragedies. Here the original act provoking the revenge sets up an antithetical or counterbalancing movement, and the completion of the movement resolves the tragedy. This happens so often that we may almost characterize the total *mythos* of tragedy as binary, in contrast to the three-part saturnalia movement of comedy.

We notice however the frequency of the device of making the revenge come from another world, through gods or ghosts or oracles. This device expands the conceptions of both nature and law beyond the limits of the obvious and tangible. It does not thereby transcend those conceptions, as it is still natural law that is manifested by the tragic action. Here we see the tragic hero as disturbing a balance in nature, nature being conceived as an order stretching over the two kingdoms of the visible and the invisible, a balance which sooner or later *must* right itself. The righting of the balance is what the Greeks called *nemesis:* again, the agent or instrument of *nemesis* may be human vengeance, ghostly vengeance, divine vengeance, divine justice, accident, fate or the logic of events, but the essential thing is that *nemesis* happens, and happens impersonally, unaffected, as *Oedipus Tyrannus* illustrates, by the moral quality of human motivation involved. In the *Oresteia* we are led from a series of revenge-movements into a final vision of natural law, a universal compact in which moral law is included and which the gods, in the person of the goddess of wisdom, endorse. Here *nemesis,* like its counterpart the Mosaic law in Christianity, is not abolished but fulfilled: it is developed from a mechanical or arbitrary sense of restored order, represented by the Furies, to the rational sense of it expounded by Athene. The appearance of Athene does not turn the *Oresteia* into a comedy, but clarifies its tragic vision.

There are two reductive formulas which have often been used to explain tragedy. Neither is quite good enough, but each is almost good enough, and as they are contradictory, they must represent extreme or limiting views of tragedy. One of these is the theory that all tragedy exhibits the omnipotence of an external fate. And, of course, the overwhelming majority of tragedies do leave us with a sense of the supremacy of impersonal power and of the limitation of human effort. But the fatalistic reduction of tragedy confuses the tragic condition with the tragic process: fate, in a tragedy, normally becomes external to the hero only *after* the tragic process has been set going. The Greek *ananke* or *moira* is in its normal, or pre-tragic, form the internal balancing condition of life. It appears as external or antithetical necessity only after it has been violated as a condition of life, just as justice is the internal condition of an honest man, but the external antagonist of the criminal. Homer uses a profoundly significant phrase for the theory of tragedy when he has Zeus speak of Aegisthus as going *hyper moron, beyond* fate.

The fatalistic reduction of tragedy does not distinguish tragedy from irony, and it is again significant that we speak of the irony of fate rather than of its tragedy. Irony does not need an exceptional central figure: as a rule, the dingier the hero the sharper the irony, when irony alone is aimed at. It is the admixture of heroism that gives tragedy its characteristic splendor and exhilaration. The tragic hero has normally had an extraordinary, often a nearly divine, destiny almost within his grasp, and the glory of that original vision never quite fades out of tragedy. The rhetoric of tragedy requires the noblest diction that the greatest poets can produce, and while catastrophe is the normal end of tragedy, this is balanced by an equally significant original greatness, a paradise lost.

The other reductive theory of tragedy is that the act which sets the tragic process going must be primarily a violation of *moral* law, whether human or divine; in short, that Aristotle's hamartia or "flaw" must have an essential connection with sin or wrongdoing. Again it is true that the great majority of tragic heroes do possess hybris, a proud, passionate, obsessed or soaring mind which brings about a morally intelligible downfall. Such hybris is the normal precipitating agent of catastrophe, just as in comedy the cause of the happy ending is usually some act of humility, represented by a slave or by a heroine meanly disguised. In Aristotle the hamartia of the tragic hero is associated with Aristotle's ethical conception of *proairesis,* or free choice of an end, and Aristotle certainly does tend to think of tragedy as morally, almost physically, intelligible. It has already been suggested, however, that the conception of catharsis, which is central to Aristotle's view of tragedy, is inconsistent with moral reductions of it. Pity and terror are moral feelings, and they are relevant but not attached to the tragic situation. Shakespeare is particularly fond of planting moral lightning-rods on both sides of his heroes to deflect the pity and terror: we have mentioned Othello flanked by Iago and Desdemona, but Hamlet is flanked by Claudius and Ophelia, Lear by his daughters, and even Macbeth by Lady Macbeth and Duncan. In all these tragedies there is a sense of some far-reaching mystery of which this morally intelligible process is only a part. The hero's act has thrown a switch in a larger machine than his own life, or even his own society.

All theories of tragedy as morally explicable sooner or later run into the question: is an innocent sufferer in tragedy (i.e., poetically innocent), Iphigeneia, Cordelia, Socrates in Plato's *Apology,* Christ in the Passion, not a tragic figure? It is not very convincing to try to provide crucial moral flaws for such characters. Cordelia shows a high spirit, perhaps a touch of wilfulness, in refusing to flatter her father, and Cordelia gets hanged. Joan of Arc in Schiller has a moment of tenderness for an English soldier, and Joan is burned alive, or would have been if Schiller had not decided to sacrifice the facts to save the face of his moral theory. Here we are getting away from tragedy, and close to a kind of insane cautionary tale, like Mrs. Pipchin's little boy who was gored to death by a bull for asking inconvenient questions. Tragedy, in short, seems to elude the antithesis of moral responsibility and arbitrary fate, just as it eludes the antithesis of good and evil.

In the third book of *Paradise Lost,* Milton represents God as arguing that he made man "Sufficient to have stood, though free to fall." God knew that Adam would fall, but did not compel him to do so, and on that basis he disclaims legal responsibility. This argument is so bad that Milton, if he was trying to escape refutation, did well to ascribe it to God. Thought and act cannot be so separated: if God had foreknowledge he must have known in the instant of creating Adam that he was creating a being who would fall. Yet the passage is a most haunting and suggestive one nonetheless. For *Paradise Lost* is not simply an attempt to write one more tragedy, but to expound what Milton believed to be the archetypal myth of tragedy. Hence the passage is another example of existential projection: the real basis of the relation of Milton's God to Adam is the relation of the tragic poet to his hero. The tragic poet knows that his hero will be in a tragic situation, but he exerts all his power to avoid the sense of having manipulated that situation for his own purposes. He exhibits his hero to us as God exhibits Adam to the angels. If the hero was not sufficient to have stood, the mode is purely ironic; if he was not free to fall, the mode is purely romantic, the story of an invincible hero who will conquer all his antagonists as long as the story is about him. Now most theories of tragedy take one great tragedy as their norm: thus Aristotle's theory is largely founded on *Oedipus Tyrannus,* and Hegel's on *Antigone.* In seeing the archetypal human tragedy in the story of Adam, Milton was, of course, in agreement with the whole Judaeo-Christian cultural tradition, and perhaps arguments drawn from the story of Adam may have better luck in literary criticism than in subjects compelled to assume Adam's real existence, either as fact or as a merely legal fiction. Chaucer's monk, who clearly understood what he was doing, began with Lucifer and Adam, and we may be well advised to follow his example.

Adam, then, is in a heroic human situation: he is on top of the wheel of fortune, with the destiny of the gods almost within his reach. He forfeits that destiny in a way which suggests moral responsibility to some and a conspiracy of fate to others. What he does is to exchange a fortune of unlimited freedom for the fate involved in the conseqeunces of the act of exchange, just as, for a man who deliberately jumps off a precipice, the law of gravitation acts as fate for the brief remainder of his life. The exchange is presented by Milton as itself a free act or *proairesis,* a use of freedom to lose freedom. And just as comedy often sets up an arbitrary law and then organizes the action to break or evade it, so tragedy presents the reverse theme of narrowing a comparatively free life into a process of causation. This happens to Macbeth when he accepts the logic of usurpation, to Hamlet when he accepts the logic of revenge, to Lear when he accepts the logic of abdication. The discovery or *anagnorisis* which comes at the end of the tragic plot is not simply the knowledge by the hero of what has happened to him—*Oedipus Tyrannus,* despite its reputation as a typical tragedy, is rather a special case in that regard—but the recognition of the determined shape of the life he has created for himself, with an implicit comparison with the uncreated potential life he has forsaken. The line of Milton dealing with the fall of the devils, "O how unlike the place from whence they fell!" referring as it does both to Virgil's *quantum mutatus ab illo* and Isaiah's "How are thou fallen from heaven, O Lucifer son of the morning," combines the Classical and the Christian archetypes of tragedy—for Satan, of course, like Adam, possessed an original glory. In Milton the complement to the vision of Adam on top of the wheel of fortune and falling into the world of the wheel is Christ standing on the pinnacle of the temple, urged by Satan to fall, and remaining motionless.

As soon as Adam falls, he enters his own created life, which is also the order of nature as we know it. The tragedy of Adam, therefore, resolves, like all other tragedies, in the manifestation of natural law. He enters a world in which existence is itself tragic, not existence modified by an act, deliberate or unconscious. Merely to exist is to disturb the balance of nature. Every natural man is a Hegelian thesis, and implies a reaction: every new birth provokes the return of an avenging death. This fact, in itself ironic and now called *Angst,* becomes tragic when a sense of a lost and originally higher destiny is added to it. Aristotle's hamartia, then, is a condition of being, not a cause of becoming: the reason why Milton ascribes his dubious argument to God is that he is so anxious to remove God from a predetermined causal sequence. On one side of the tragic hero is an opportunity for freedom, on the other the inevitable consequence of losing that freedom. These two sides of Adam's situation are represented in Milton by the speeches of Raphael and Michael respectively. Even with an innocent hero or martyr the same situation arises: in the Passion story it occurs in Christ's prayer in Gethsemane. Tragedy seems to move up to an *Augenblick* or crucial moment from which point the road to what might have been and the road to what will be can be simultaneously seen. Seen by the audience, that is: it cannot be seen by the hero if he is in a state of hybris, for in that case the crucial moment is for him a moment of dizziness, when the wheel of fortune begins its inevitable cyclical movement downward.

In Adam's situation there is a feeling, which in Christian tradition can be traced back at least to St. Augustine, that time *begins* with the fall; that the fall from liberty into the natural cycle also started the movement of time as we know it. In other tragedies too we can trace the feeling that *nemesis* is deeply involved with the movement of time, whether as the missing of a tide in the affairs of men, as a recognition that the time is out of joint, as a sense that time is the devourer of life, the mouth of hell at the previous moment, when the potential passes forever into the actual, or, in its ultimate horror, Macbeth's sense of it as simply one clock-tick after another. In comedy time plays a redeeming role: it uncovers and brings to light what is essential to the happy ending. The subtitle of Green's *Pandosto,* the source of *The Winter's Tale,* is "*The Triumph of Time,*" and it well describes the nature of Shakespeare's action, where time is introduced as a chorus. But in tragedy the *cognitio* is normally the recognition of the inevitability of a causal sequence in time, and the forebodings and ironic anticipations surrounding it are based on a sense of cyclical return.

In irony, as distinct from tragedy, the wheel of time completely encloses the action, and there is no sense of an original contact with a relatively timeless world. In the Bible the tragic fall of Adam is followed by its historical repetition, the fall of Israel into Egyptian bondage, which is, so to speak, its ironic confirmation. As long as the Geoffrey version of British history was accepted, the fall of Troy was the corresponding event in the history of Britain, and, as the fall of Troy began with an idolatrous misapplication of an apple, there were even symbolic parallels. Shakespeare's most ironic play, *Troilus and Cressida,* presents in Ulysses the voice of worldly wisdom, expounding with great eloquence the two primary categories of the perspective of tragic irony in the fallen world, time and the hierarchic chain of being. The extraordinary treatment of the tragic vision of time by Nietzsche's Zarathustra, in which the heroic acceptance of cyclical return becomes a glumly cheerful acceptance of a cosmology of identical recurrence, marks the influence of an age of irony.

Anyone accustomed to think archetypally of literature will recognize in tragedy a mimesis of sacrifice. Tragedy is a paradoxical combination of a fearful sense of rightness (the hero must fall) and a pitying sense of wrongness (it is too bad that he falls). There is a similar paradox in the two elements of sacrifice. One of these is communion, the dividing of a heroic or divine body among a group which brings them into unity with, and as, that body. The other is propitiation, the sense that in spite of the communion the body really belongs to another, a greater, and a potentially wrathful power. The ritual analogies to tragedy are more obvious than the psychological ones, for it is irony, not tragedy, that represents the nightmare or anxiety-dream. But, just as the literary critic finds Freud most suggestive for the theory of comedy, and Jung for the theory of romance, so for the theory of tragedy one naturally looks to the psychology of the will to power, as expounded in Adler and Nietzsche. Here one finds a "Dionysiac" aggressive will, intoxicated by dreams of its own omnipotence, impinging upon an "Apollonian" sense of external and immovable order. As a mimesis of ritual, the tragic hero is not really killed or eaten, but the corresponding thing in art still takes place, a vision of death which draws the survivors into a new unity. As a mimesis of dream, the inscrutable tragic hero, like the proud and silent swan, becomes articulate at the point of death, and the audience, like the poet in *Kubla Khan,* revives his song within itself. With his fall, a greater world beyond which his gigantic spirit had blocked out becomes for an instant visible, but there is also a sense of the mystery and remoteness of that world.

If we are right in our suggestion that romance, tragedy, irony and comedy are all episodes in a total quest-myth, we can see how it is that comedy can contain a potential tragedy within itself. In myth, the hero is a god, and hence he does not die, but dies and rises again. The ritual pattern behind the catharsis of comedy is the resurrection that follows the death, the epiphany or manifestation of the risen hero. In Aristophanes the hero, who often goes through a point of ritual death, is treated as a risen god, hailed as a new Zeus, or given the quasi-divine honors of the Olympic victor. In New Comedy the new human body is both a hero and a social group. The Aeschylean trilogy proceeds to the comic satyr-play, which is said to have affinities with spring festivals. Christianity, too, sees tragedy as an episode in the divine comedy, the larger scheme of redemption and resurrection. The sense of tragedy as a prelude to comedy seems almost inseparable from anything explicitly Christian. The serenity of the final double chorus in the St. Matthew Passion would hardly be attainable if composer and audience did not know that there was more to the story. Nor would the death of Samson lead to "calm of mind, all passion spent," if Samson were not a prototype of the rising Christ, associated at the appropriate moment with the phoenix.

This is an example of the way in which myths explain the structural principles behind familiar literary facts, in this case the fact that to make a sombre action end happily is easy enough, and to reverse the procedure almost impossible. (Of course we have a natural dislike of seeing pleasant situations turn out disastrously, but if a poet is working on a solid structural basis, our natural likes and dislikes have nothing to do with the matter.) Even Shakespeare, who can do anything, never does quite this. The action of *King Lear,* which seems heading for some kind of serenity, is suddenly wrenched into agony by the hanging of Cordelia, providing a conclusion which the stage refused to act for over a century, but none of Shakespeare's tragedies impresses us as a comedy gone wrong—*Romeo and Juliet* has a suggestion of such a structure, but it is only a suggestion. Hence while of course a tragedy may contain a comic action, it contains it only episodically as a subordinate contrast or underplot.

The characterization of tragedy is very like that of comedy in reverse. The source of *nemesis,* whatever it is, is an *eiron,* and may appear in a great variety of agents, from wrathful gods to hypocritical villains. In comedy we noticed three main types of *eiron* characters: a benevolent withdrawing and returning figure, the tricky slave or vice, and the hero and heroine. We have the tragic counterpart to the withdrawn *eiron* in the god who decrees the tragic action, like Athene in *Ajax* or Aphrodite in *Hippolytus;* a Christian example is God the Father in *Paradise Lost.* He may also be a ghost, like Hamlet's father; or it may not be a person at all but simply an invisible force known only by its effects, like the death that quietly seizes on Tamburlaine when the time has come for him to die. Often, as in the revenge-tragedy, it is an event previous to the action of which the tragedy itself is the consequence.

A tragic counterpart to the vice or tricky slave may be discerned in the soothsayer or prophet who foresees the inevitable end, or more of it than the hero does, like Teiresias. A closer example is the Machiavellian villain of Elizabethan drama, who, like the vice in comedy, is a convenient catalyzer of the action because he requires the minimum of motivation, being a self-starting principle of malevolence. Like the comic vice, too, he is something of an *architectus* or projection of the author's will, in this case for a tragic conclusion. "I limned this night-piece," says Webster's Lodovico, "and it was my best." Iago dominates the action of *Othello* almost to the point of being a tragic counterpart to the black king or evil magician of romance. The affinities of the Machiavellian villain with the diabolical are naturally close, and he may be an actual devil like Mephistopheles, but the sense of awfulness belonging to an agent of catastrophe can also make him something more like the high priest of a sacrifice. There is a touch of this in Webster's Bosola. *King Lear* has a Machiavellian villain in Edmund, and Edmund is contrasted with Edgar. Edgar, with his bewildering variety of disguises, his appearance to blind or mad people in different roles, and his tendency to appear on the third sound of the trumpet and to come pat like the catastrophe of the old comedy, seems to be an experiment in a new type, a kind of tragic "virtue," if I may coin this word by analogy, a counterpart in the order of nature to a guardian angel or similar attendant in romance.

The tragic hero usually belongs of course to the *alazon* group, an impostor in the sense that he is self-deceived or made dizzy by hybris. In many tragedies he begins as a semi-divine figure, at least in his own eyes, and then an inexorable dialectic sets to work which separates the divine pretence from the human actuality. "They told me I was everything," says Lear: " 'tis a lie; I am not ague-proof." The tragic hero is usually vested with supreme authority, but is often in the more ambiguous position of a *tyrannos* whose rule depends on his own abilities, rather than a purely hereditary or *de jure* monarch (*basileus*) like Duncan. The latter is more directly a symbol of the original vision or birthright, and is often a somewhat pathetic victim, like Richard II, or even Agamemnon. Parental figures in tragedy have the same ambivalence that they have in all other forms.

We found in comedy that the term *bomolochos* or buffoon need not be restricted to farce, but could be extended to cover comic characters who are primarily entertainers, with the function of increasing or focussing the comic mood. The corresponding contrasting type in tragedy is the suppliant, the character, often female, who presents a picture of unmitigated helplessness and destitution. Such a figure is pathetic, and pathos, though it seems a gentler and more relaxed mood than tragedy, is even more terrifying. Its basis is the exclusion of an individual from a group, hence it attacks the deepest fear in ourselves that we possess—a fear much deeper than the relatively cosy and sociable bogey of hell. In the figure of the suppliant pity and terror are brought to the highest possible pitch of intensity, and the awful consequences of rejecting the suppliant for all concerned is a central theme of Greek tragedy. Suppliant figures are often women threatened with death or rape, or children, like Prince Arthur in *King John*. The fragility of Shakespeare's Ophelia marks an affinity with the suppliant type. Often, too, the suppliant is in the structurally tragic position of having lost a place of greatness: this is the position of Adam and Eve in the tenth book of *Paradise Lost,* of the Trojan women after the fall of Troy, of Oedipus in the Colonus play, and so on. A subordinate figure who plays the role of focussing the tragic mood is the messenger who regularly announces the catastrophe in Greek tragedy. In the final scene of comedy, when the author is usually trying to get all his characters on the stage at once, we often notice the introduction of a new character, generally a messenger bearing some missing piece of the *cognitio,* such as Jaques de Boys in *As You Like It* or the gentle astringer in *All's Well,* who represents the comic counterpart.

Finally, a tragic counterpart of the comic refuser of festivity may be discerned in a tragic type of plain dealer who may be simply the faithful friend of the hero, like Horatio in *Hamlet,* but is often an outspoken critic of the tragic action, like Kent in *King Lear* or Enobarbus in *Antony and Cleopatra.* Such a character is in the position of refusing, or at any rate resisting, the tragic movement toward catastrophe. Abdiel's role in the tragedy of Satan in *Paradise Lost* is similar. The familiar figures of Cassandra and Teiresias combine this role with that of the soothsayer. Such figures, when they occur in a tragedy without a chorus, are often called chorus characters, as they illustrate one of the essential functions of the tragic chorus. In comedy a society forms around the hero: in tragedy the chorus, however faithful, usually represents the society from which the hero is gradually isolated. Hence what it expresses is a social norm against which the hero's hybris may be measured. The chorus is not the voice of the hero's conscience by any means, but very seldom does it encourage him in his hybris or prompt him to disastrous action. The chorus or chorus character is, so to speak, the embryonic germ of comedy in tragedy, just as the refuser of festivity, the melancholy Jaques or Alceste, is a tragic germ in comedy.

In comedy the erotic and social affinities of the hero are combined and unified in the final scene; tragedy usually makes love and the social structure irreconcilable and contending forces, a conflict which reduces love to passion and social activity to a forbidding and imperative duty. Comedy is much concerned with integrating the family and adjusting the family to society as a whole; tragedy is much concerned with breaking up the family and opposing it to the rest of society. This gives us the tragic archetype of Antigone, of which the conflict of love and honor in Classical French drama, of *Neigung* and *Pflicht* in Schiller, of passion and authority in the Jacobeans, are all moralized simplifications. Again, just as the heroine of comedy often ties together the action, so it is obvious that the central female figure of a tragic action will often polarize the tragic conflict. Eve, Helen, Gertrude, and Emily in the *Knight's Tale* are some ready instances: the structural role of Briseis in the *Iliad* is similar. Comedy works out the proper relations of its characters and prevents heroes from marrying their sisters or mothers; tragedy presents the disaster of Oedipus or the incest of Siegmund. There is a great deal in tragedy about pride of race and birthright, but its general tendency is to isolate a ruling or noble family from the rest of society.

The phases of tragedy move from the heroic to the ironic, the first three corresponding to the first three phases of romance, the last three to the last three of irony. The first phase of tragedy is the one in which the central character is given the greatest possible dignity in contrast to the other characters, so that we get the perspective of a stag pulled down by wolves. The sources of dignity are courage and innocence, and in this phase the hero or heroine usually is innocent. This phase corresponds to the myth of the birth of the hero in romance, a theme which is occasionally incorporated into a tragic structure, as in Racine's *Athalie*. But owing to the unusual difficulty of making an interesting dramatic character out of an infant, the central and typical figure of this phase is the calumniated woman, often a mother the legitimacy of whose child is suspected. A whole series of tragedies based on a Griselda figure belong here, stretching from the Senecan *Octavia* to Hardy's Tess, and including the tragedy of Hermione in *The Winter's Tale*. If we are to read *Alcestis* as a tragedy, we have to see it as a tragedy of this phase in which Alcestis is violated by Death and then has her fidelity vindicated by being restored to life. *Cymbeline* belongs here too: in this play the theme of the birth of the hero appears offstage, for Cymbeline was the king of Britain at the time of the birth of Christ, and the halcyon peace in which the play concludes has a suppressed reference to this.

An even clearer example, and certainly one of the greatest in English literature, is *The Duchess of Malfi*. The Duchess has the innocence of abundant life in a sick and melancholy society, where the fact that she has "youth and a little beauty" is precisely why she is hated. She reminds us too that one of the essential characteristics of innocence in the martyr is an unwillingness to die. When Bosola comes to murder her he makes elaborate attempts to put her half in love with easeful death and to suggest that death is really a deliverance. The attempt is motivated by a grimly controlled pity, and is roughly the equivalent of the vinegar sponge in the Passion. When the

Duchess, her back to the wall, says "I am the Duchess of Malfi still," "still" having its full weight of "always," we understand how it is that even after her death her invisible presence continues to be the most vital character in the play. *The White Devil* is an ironic parody-treatment of the same phase.

The second phase corresponds to the youth of the romantic hero, and is in one way or another the tragedy of innocence in the sense of inexperience, usually involving young people. It may be simply the tragedy of a youthful life cut off, as in the stories of Iphigeneia and Jephthah's daughter, of Romeo and Juliet, or, in a more complex situation, in the bewildered mixture of idealism and priggishness that brings Hippolytus to disaster. The simplicity of Shaw's Joan and her lack of worldly wisdom place her here also. For us however the phase is dominated by the archetypal tragedy of the green and golden world, the loss of the innocence of Adam and Eve, who, no matter how heavy a doctrinal load they have to carry, will always remain dramatically in the position of children baffled by their first contact with an adult situation. In many tragedies of this type the central character survives, so that the action closes with some adjustment to a new and more mature experience, "Henceforth I learn that to obey is best," says Adam, as he and Eve go hand in hand out to the world before them. A less clear cut but similar resolution occurs when Philoctetes, whose serpent-wound reminds us a little of Adam, is taken off his island to enter the Trojan war. Ibsen's *Little Eyolf* is a tragedy of this phase, and with the same continuing conclusion, in which it is the older characters who are educated through the death of a child.

The third phase, corresponding to the central quest-theme of romance, is tragedy in which a strong emphasis is thrown on the success or completeness of the hero's achievement. The Passion belongs here, as do all tragedies in which the hero is in any way related to or a prototype of Christ, like *Samson Agonistes*. The paradox of victory within tragedy may be expressed by a double perspective in the action. Samson is a buffoon of a Philistine carnival and simultaneously a tragic hero to the Israelites, but the tragedy ends in triumph and the carnival in catastrophe. Much the same is true of the mocked Christ in the Passion. But just as the second phase often ends in anticipation of greater maturity, so this one is often a sequel to a previous tragic or heroic action, and comes at the end of a heroic life. One of the greatest dramatic examples is *Oedipus at Colonus,* where we find the usual binary form of a tragedy conditioned by a previous tragic act, ending this time not in a second disaster, but in a full rich serenity that goes far beyond a mere resignation to Fate. In narrative literature we may cite Beowulf's last fight with the dragon, the pendant to his Grendel quest. Shakespeare's *Henry V* is a successfully completed romantic quest made tragic by its implicit context: everybody knows that King Henry died almost immediately and that sixty years of unbroken disaster followed for England—at least, if anyone in Shakespeare's audience did not know that, his ignorance was certainly no fault of Shakespeare's.

The fourth phase is the typical fall of the hero through hybris and hamartia that we have already discussed. In this phase we cross the boundary line from innocence to experience, which is also the direction in which the hero falls. In the fifth phase the ironic element increases, the heroic decreases, and the characters look further away and in a smaller perspective. *Timon of Athens* impresses us as more ironic and less heroic than the better known tragedies, not simply because Timon is a more middle-class hero who has to buy what authority he has, but because the feeling that Timon's suicide has somehow failed to make a fully heroic *point* is very strong. Timon is oddly isolated from the final action, in which the breach between Alcibiades and the Athenians closes up over his head, in striking contrast with the conclusions of most of the other tragedies, where nobody is allowed to steal the show from the central character.

The ironic perspective in tragedy is attained by putting the characters in a state of lower freedom than the audience. For a Christian audience an Old Testament or pagan setting is ironic in this sense, as it shows its characters moving according to the conditions of a law, whether Jewish or natural, from which the audience has been, at least theoretically, redeemed. *Samon Agonistes,* though unique in English literature, presents a combination of Classical form and Hebrew subject-matter that the greatest contemporary tragedian, Racine, also reached at the end of his life in *Athalie* and *Esther*. Similarly the epilogue to Chaucer's *Troilus* puts a Courtly Love tragedy into its historical relation to "payens corsed olde rites." The events in Geoffrey of Monmouth's British history are supposed to be contemporary with those of the Old Testament, and the sense of life under the law is present everywhere in *King Lear*. The same structural principle accounts for the use of astrology and other fatalistic machinery connected with the turning wheels of fate or fortune. Romeo and Juliet are star-crossed, and Troilus loses Criseyde because every five hundred years

Jupiter and Saturn meet the crescent moon in Cancer and claim another victim. The tragic action of the fifth phase presents for the most part the tragedy of lost direction and lack of knowledge, not unlike the second phase except that the context is the world of adult experience. *Oedipus Tyrannus* belongs here, and all tragedies and tragic episodes which suggest the existential projection of fatalism, and, like much of the Book of Job, seem to raise metaphysical or theological questions rather than social or moral ones.

Oedipus Tyrannus, however, is already moving into the sixth phase of tragedy, a world of shock and horror in which the central images are images of *sparagmos,* that is, cannibalism, mutilation, and torture. The specific reaction known as shock is appropriate to a situation of cruelty or outrage. (The secondary or false shock produced by the outrage done to some emotional attachment or fixation, as in the critical reception of *Jude the Obscure* or *Ulysses,* has no status in criticism, as false shock is a disguised resistance to the autonomy of culture.) Any tragedy may have one or more shocking scenes in it, but sixth-phase tragedy shocks as a whole, in its total effect. This phase is more common as a subordinate aspect of tragedy than as its main theme, as unqualified horror or despair makes a difficult cadence. *Prometheus Bound* is a tragedy of this phase, though this is partly an illusion due to its isolation from the trilogy to which it belongs. In such tragedies the hero is in too great agony or humiliation to gain the privilege of a heroic pose, hence it is usually easier to make him a villainous hero, like Marlowe's Barabas, although Faustus also belongs to the same phase. Seneca is fond of this phase, and bequeathed to the Elizabethans an interest in the gruesome, an effect which usually has some connection with mutilation, as when Ferdinand offers to shake hands with the Duchess of Malfi and gives her a dead man's hand. *Titus Andronicus* is an experiment in Senecan sixth-phase horror which makes a great deal of mutilation, and shows also a strong interest, from the opening scene on, in the sacrificial symbolism of tragedy.

At the end of this phase we reach a point of demonic epiphany, where we see or glimpse the undisplaced demonic vision, the vision of the *Inferno.* Its chief symbols, besides the prison and the madhouse, are the instruments of a torturing death, the cross under the sunset being the antithesis of the tower under the moon. A strong element of demonic ritual in public punishments and similar mob amusements is exploited by tragic and ironic myth. Breaking on the wheel becomes

Lear's wheel of fire; bear-baiting is an image for Gloucester and Macbeth, and for the crucified Prometheus the humiliation of exposure, the horror of being watched, is a greater misery than the pain. *Derkou theama* (behold the spectacle; get your staring over with) is his bitterest cry. The inability of Milton's blind Samson to stare back is his greatest torment, and one which forces him to scream at Delilah, in one of the most terrible passages of all tragic drama, that he will tear her to pieces if she touches him.

Myth and Drama

HAROLD H. WATTS

I

Every century—perhaps every decade—has its topics. In one sense, the effort to state the essence of tragedy and of comedy is one of our topics. This, unlike other topics that obsess us, is certainly not ours alone. Very nearly as long as men have possessed comedies and tragedies, they have labored to explain to each other what it was they possessed; it has never seemed "good enough" simply to luxuriate in the immediate pleasure which either tragedy or comedy affords. Thus, speculation on the natures of comedy and tragedy is a permanent as well as a twentieth century topic. But our accent, as we discuss these problems, is not the accent of other centuries. We are not very deeply impressed by the useful distinctions between the mechanics of the two forms; nor does the insight that one form moves us to tears and the other stirs us to laughter seem to take us to the heart of the question.

That the insights of earlier men into tragedy and comedy do not satisfy us may be an oblique reflection of a parlous condition; so be it. We have not the soundness and health to rest satisfied with the perceptions of difference that other men have found clarifying. With us, the tragedy-comedy difference has become not a question of dramaturgy or of surface-level psychology. It has become closely entwined with the religious question as it too is debated among us. Indeed, one of our recurrent suspicions is that the tragedy-comedy question is in fact the religious question. (This suspicion, I shall show, is part-right, part-wrong.) Such a suspicion once would have been termed sacrilegious since it mingles sacred and profane. It is a suspicion that now is inacceptable to some parties to the tragedy-comedy discussion for very different reasons; for it hints that there persists, for man, an area apart, an area of the sacred, on which tragedy and comedy impinge.

It is strange but true that to say that drama is closely allied with the

From *Cross Currents,* Vol. V (1955), pp. 154-70. Reprinted by permission of the author and the editors.

sacred stirs, in our times, resistance not from the clergy, who now draw freely on terms proper to dramatic discussion to cast light on religious mysteries; the resistance comes from hard-headed students of the drama who want to peg the discussion at a level that reflects Aristotle or that records "actual practice" or that traces the better-known and more obvious human responses to both tragedy and comedy. But these hard-headed efforts but prolong the confidence that drama is an utterly secular activity, one that has no tangential relations with religion—one that, in consequence, will be in no way illuminated by an association with religion, with myth and cult. This resistance, as it persists among us, is chiefly useful as astringent to all sorts of discussion of drama that hints or announces that the play and the theatre constitute one of the few sacred activities left to us. Criticism that refuses to trace analogies between drama and myth is certainly limiting, but it is certainly less misleading than an interpretation of the drama that finds it a valid surrogate for all that used to go under the name of religion.

Our relation to the drama, the drama's possible goods for us in this century, are described correctly by neither of the extremes just mentioned. A fair account of the situation of nineteenth and twentieth century man in relation to the drama is this: By the unfolding "logic" of Western intellectual growth, the forms of the sacred that seemed real and compulsive in many centuries—that indeed enabled earlier men to treat drama and other forms of art as manifestly secular—lost their power to stir the majority of cultivated minds. Thus, the present sense of many persons that drama, at least, is sacred and is in clear opposition to the emptiness of modern life is a sense which records an interesting shift in the meaning of the words *sacred* and *secular*. *Sacred* once referred to the portion of human life in which revealed truth, offered us by a church, made specific demands on us and gave us specific aids, and the secular was just that portion of life that seemed free of those demands and not dependent on those aids. This traditional division—once drama had reached the inn-yard or princely halls—definitely regarded both comedy and tragedy as secular creations. The drama was an amusement, a distraction, an activity on which the church did not "move in" except when stirred by excess of indecency or atheism. To us, this assignment of the drama to a secular realm seems less obvious. We partake of a general intellectual atmosphere in which the sacred (to put the matter mildly) is not hedged securely against the secular; the secular so occupies our waking thoughts that we may even regard the realm of the sacred as a pious fiction rather than as a going reality. And some of us find that the real sacred (if indeed it does exist) flourishes in an activity that men used confidently to regard as secular; we find the sacred in music or art or—as here—the drama with its power to light up our existence, to criticize or transform our secular boredom.

Those who find that drama is, for modern man, a locus of the sacred are a rather mixed company. Skeptics, workers in depth psychology, liturgists, ordinarily devout persons—these unlikely companions share what I have called a twentieth-century topical debate, the degree of sacredness in drama, and find they respond to the effects of drama—effects that they find peculiar and haunting. The traditional sacred is gone or—we suspect with varying emotions—is on the point of leaving us. We discover with relief that what we are about to lose is "really" available to us elsewhere—in the drama, for example.

Before we accept this discovery as fact, we ought to ask whether the relation between drama and religion, drama and myth, is one of essential identity or one of similarity. It is my feeling that the relation is one of similarity: a similarity that must be studied since it is deep-persistent, and illuminating to both drama and religion. Drama is no surrogate for myth and cult, but what it offers us finds partial explanation in what myth and cult have offered men.

II

So long as drama had, for its undoubted locus, the region of the secular, questions about tragedy and comedy, about their common root and their differences, were debated in what one must now regard as a dry, bright atmophere. There is something cold as well as competent, insensitive as well as clear, in the treatment Aristotle and others accorded the tragedy they knew. It is plain that many modern persons, skeptics as well as believers, find a more tremendous, more "sacred" import in tragedy than Aristotle found. (By extension, we find the same sort of import in comedy.) Rightly or wrongly, we are drawn by the dark uncertainties which drama embodies; and if this is our taste, we will experience no satisfaction when we read critics who wrote in other centuries and could reduce both tragedy and comedy to bright certainties, who looked to the playhouse for mechanically clever vehicles that enforced the moral platitudes of an era. Yet if both comedy and tragedy indeed do more, if they constantly draw us back toward their two Western sources of origin—the church chancel or the sacred grove—this covert filiation is a source of irritation to students who are willing to concede that drama is powerful and yet maintain that drama's "real" climate is certainly the climate of secular life: life untouched in any way by the sacred. Persons who feel that the "real" locus of drama has always been the sacred—or, the contention here, displays a close similarity to the sacred—turn from matters of construction, turn from the rise and fall of fashion in dramatic form, to the *effects* of viewed drama that pass beyond amusement and such superficial categories of criticism as realism, naturalism, and romanticism.

Yet is not this latter interest in drama, if uncritically followed, but a pursuit of surrogates for the conventional forms of the sacred: the church, its ritual, its body of organized dogma? Doubtless. We would not be impelled to isolate the sacred in drama did we not have some qualms about the conventional locus of the sacred. If we are devout, our study of drama is probably an attempt to win intellectual confirmation for truths that we still believe but which we find no longer self-confirming. And if we are skeptical, our study of drama proceeds with more passion still; drama does not just explain and validate the sacred —a religion that we persist in believing. Instead, drama *is* the sacred.

Both these approaches to the sacred—or, as I believe, the *resemblance* to the sacred—in the drama are partisan approaches. What is the sacred if we define it (as we now try to) not in terms of a church or a lapsed tradition? One ought to be able to define the sacred in terms of human action, or at least attempt to. The sacred is "created" —exists for us and probably becomes available to other persons who are in any way like us—by any gesture or word which makes a total assertion. Any word or gesture which offers, to our own awareness and the awarenesses that we are able to reach, some insight about what existence collectively *is*—this is a sacred word or announcement rather than a secular one. In contrast, a secular utterance concerns itself with some smaller portion of experience; neither actually nor by implication does it describe some aspect of the total act of existing. It is concerned with conveying facts, practical procedures under certain explicit circumstances, or—at its most ambitious—short-range predictions.

This distinction between what is sacred and what is secular does not rest on the authority of a particular revelation or the encrusted, polychrome prestige of a religious tradition. Rather do all churches and traditions rest on such a distinction; and all revolts against church and tradition are in essence (whatever they are accidentally, as *specific* protests) denials that the distinction between sacred and secular, between total assertion and what we may call partial assertion is a valid one. (The revolts usually express an understandable bitterness with some of the applications of the sacred, of total assertions; they do not usually envisage their own result: a denial that any total assertion whatever is valid. Yet this is the uneasy course that, in part, has created our present question.)

The peculiar twentieth century attitude toward drama, whether it is developed in a skeptic or a believer, is testimony that the distinction between total assertion, the sacred, and partial assertion, the secular, is one that, at least, haunts us. It is felt that one sort of gesture and assertion—here, drama—has an impact and validity different from another kind of gesture and assertion—say, a radio commercial praising a dentifrice.

So viewed, the contrast between the sacred and the secular makes little reference to church and tradition; the contrast rests on a juxtaposition of two sorts of direct experience. A sacred assertion—whether it be couched in myth, performed in rite, codified in dogma or (as some of us seem to suspect) enacted in significant drama—is a total assertion. It asserts what man's life is, and it cannot be demonstrated as true; it can be only accepted or rejected as true. A secular assertion is an observation of fact. It is a reference to a physical fact that can readily be checked; it makes—less clearly, we will admit if we are at all reflective—some observation about comparatively small phases of society, and offers us ways of seeming to manage "small" areas of human social and moral relations. When we are secularized, when we congratulate ourselves (if that is our mood) that the sacred has been driven from our lives, we believe that we are freed of the burden and the nonsense of making total assertions or of listening to discourses based on the total assertions that men "like us" have made in the past.

There are many reasons why such freedom is to be desired. For many decades, secular evangelists, working in the spirit of Lucretius, have impellingly pled with us to give up a frustrating taste for total assertion; man can (the evangel runs) live better by partial assertions. We can always check partial assertions, whether they be scientific laws or the little useful rules of thumb by which "actually" we conduct our societies and personal affairs. Yet we should never cease to observe—and this is what drives us back to drama or art or music as possible loci of the sacred—that secular evangelists offer us at least one total assertion, at least one *sacred* statement: that man *ought* to be willing to live by partial or secular assertions. Whether this one unavoidable, irreducible total assertion—the assertion that makes possible the cancellation of the sacred—is true, right, and correct we cannot say; faced with it, we are in as much doubt as we are when we face any of the other total, sacred assertions about man and his destiny. Perhaps we do well when we hesitate to accept it as bindingly true. At least, the current plunge into the depths harbored by comedy and tragedy may indicate that the sacred resembles proverbial truth: crushed to earth at a particular point, it rises vigorously elsewhere. But what would St. Augustine and other foes of secular spectacle think if they were to learn that a quasi-sacred light shines behind the theatrical proscenium?

III

Despite resemblances, it is stupid—it is, I believe, indefensible—to maintain that drama proffers to man *all* the effects of the sacred. Likewise, it is misleading to press too far the analogy between full religious activity, "pegged" to a myth, and the public performance of a play. Church-harbored rite and theatre-harbored drama have their rich similarities, similarities which I shall explore. But it is useless to wring final drops from perceived similarities that, say, draw *Oedipus Rex* and a religious rite toward each other. Music and art and drama *and* church-harbored rite may be akin since, in our terms, they all make inclusive rather than partial statements about life. But not all inclusive statements are the same statement. These various "statements," moreover, exist within unlike media, which make possible effects that are different although they may supplement each other intimately. Beethoven's Ninth may give us a feeling of transcendence (indeed, it does); it may give us the feeling that our ears have now listened to the music of the spheres and that our minds, for once, encompass the universe. But all this encompassing is not the precise encompassing that religious rite makes possible, when at a gesture from the priest we come forward to drink from a cup rather than—in response to Beethoven's invitation as celebrant—to immerse ourselves in a wonderful sea of harmony. Likewise, a retablo in a well-lighted art gallery is not a retablo in the Cathedral at Seville. A changed context has altered a powerful religious object into a powerful work of art; on the gallery wall, it has become something new, for, cut off from the gestures of the priest, the imprecision of cathedral light, and the mélange of cathedral odors pleasant and nauseous, the retablo addresses us in a different way. The way is still sacred since the effect the art-object, the retablo, creates is an inclusive one; it makes a total assertion. But it is not the inclusive effect to which it once contributed an essential note in a Spanish chapel.

The retablo's history can be our clue to the limitations we ought to impose on any discussion of the sacred in drama. Drama, let us concede, abounds in the sacred as here defined; it is indeed a sacred that can be studied in relation to the sacred of rite and myth. Modern criticism of drama abounds in over-assertions on this point; and these over-assertions but testify to a slightly frantic desire to offset religious *accidie*. No less than the Ninth Symphony and the Spanish retablo on the gallery wall does drama make total assertions. But they can never be identical with the assertions mediated to man by the complex of myth, rite, and dogma that makes up any "church." Consider the retablo on the gallery wall. It does not cease to make some of the total assertions it made in a chapel. But its assertions become involved in a different context of effect. The new context, let me insist, is not an unworthy one. (What is more essential to a full, even a sacred, existence than comprehension of the nuances and the mergings of styles of visual assertion that the skillfully displayed retablo offers us?) But it is not the same context. Vision is the "faculty" that the retablo always appealed to and always will appeal to. But a changed context—museum rather than chapel—has certainly altered the assertion that is mediated. In the chapel we "saw" this assertion: Existence finds its sum and center in a figure extended on several pieces of wood. In the gallery we "see" something like this: Existence finds its meaning in the competence of a creative and ingenious mind that is able to fuse—completely and for eternity—shades of color, given "real" objects (a body and a cross), and the lines that reproduce on a flat surface the colors and shapes of nature. This is not a contemptible fusion; it is, in my sense, sacred. But it is not the still more complex fusion that once took place in the Spanish chapel.

The analogy provided by the two states of the retablo is clear. Drama has great power, like the retablo in the museum, to remind us of what was, for many centuries, regarded as the sole locus of the sacred: the church, the temple-cave, the sacred grove. Drama rests on narrative, just as religious ceremonial rests on narrative (or myth). But we are too quick to say that drama gives to us—because of this and other resemblances—the essential of what has been, for "historical reasons," lost to us: the assertions that came to man in church or cave or grove. To insist on this perception of difference is not to attempt to discredit drama; it is the first step toward a precise definition of what drama does indeed make available to us.

If drama gives the sacred, it does not give the complete sacred assertion if our standard is (as it should be) the experience of the religious person rather than (as it often is) the experience of the person who feels religious while he is in the theatre. When this is the emphasis, it is drama that is teaching us (if we are interested) what religion is. Nor does it do this badly if we do not posit an identity between the two, if we do not suppose that one of the two (here religion) is expendable. (This is Cromwell's heresy toward drama in reverse.) At the present stage of our scrutiny of the topic (What is drama? What are the relations between tragedy and comedy?), there may be profit in sending drama to school to religion instead of religion to school to drama. (It is this latter relation that is set up when we say that the viable elements of religion "live on" in drama. It is the thesis of this essay that, whatever the resemblances, neither activity can hope to "live on" in the other.)

What do these two vehicles of total assertion have in common? Most strikingly, gesture and costume. Gesture and costume alike set the priest apart from his congregation and the personages of a drama from *their* congregations. Also in common, the two vehicles have a story. But the differences are at once apparent. How soon costume and gesture become inalterable in a "church," and how quickly the abundance of story that human fancy can supply becomes only one or two stories! And in drama—whatever its roots in old rite—how comparatively free is the range of costume and gesture, and how endlessly abundant—though this lies only on the surface—is the combination of represented event!

There are, however, differences just as immediate and striking. Religion "aspires" toward a state of fixity; drama exists—survives even—only by displaying a *superficial* ferment of change and innovation. How can we say that drama and religion are the same? A drama that does not produce new formulas dies, and a religion that lives in an unceasing ferment of innovation is (we usually judge) on its way to death. Let these differences be acknowledged then. For it is an acknowledgment that should make us quite humble about theories that "explain" the origin of the drama in religion; how could that which had to be conservative to survive (religion) "beget" that which has to be innovating to survive (drama)? Is not the history of Greek drama, conservative though it be by our standards, a series of innovations? Is not the failure of Greek religion, its tendency to respond to novel modes of thought, a negative testimony to the root-fixity of that sacred which we call religion?

But over and above this difference and beyond the similarity of gesture and costume that does not take our understanding very far, there is this resemblance that, first, casts a light on drama in general and, second, casts a most startling light on what has always been a key-question: the difference between comedy and tragedy. The resemblance is this: *Religion and drama both rest on narrative.*

What narrative is in drama we presume we know. That we may presume too much—that we may be too sure that we know what narrative "does" in a play—will not be clear to us until we make an attempt to be more precise about its religious analogue, myth. A myth is simply a narrative that a cult *happens* to employ for the purpose of making an over all assertion about man's experience of existing. Further, religion makes not one but two distinct uses of narrative material, uses that we will presently be explicit about. These two distinct uses are a sure clue to the two distinct sorts of drama, tragedy and comedy. This correspondence once perceived, we are far on our way to answering two questions: How are we to explain the coexistence of tragedy and comedy? (Answer: the coexistence is explained *by analogy* to the two uses made of narrative by cult.) How are we to explain the effects —often contradictory—of tragedy and comedy on us? How—to rephrase this second question—may we state, in some approximation to rational assertion, the permanently moving power of the logically contradictory all-over assertions that drama provides us with?

It is plain that in answering the question about the coexistence of comedy and tragedy we shall be explaining an effect in terms of its origin (an origin resembling if not identical with the two sorts of use of myth by religion that we shall identify). It is also plain that an explanation of the permanently moving power of the logical opposites, tragedy and comedy, must be a psychological explanation, an explanation that draws on one's insight into human reactions *now*. Yet the two answers are finally identical if one assumes—as I do—that there has been no great change in man himself—that the men whose expectations in a sense "created" the two forms, tragedy and comedy, are not altogether unlike the men who, in this century, continue to "demand" (if only in debased forms) both the laughable and the frightening.

IV

Let us, as lovers of drama or as esteemers of the *effects* of drama, seek to be instructed by the two uses of myth that we can observe in developed religions. For in these two uses are both the roots of comedy and tragedy and the rationale of their persisting appeal.

If religion has any distinguishing mark, it is this: it is an all-over assertion about the existence in which man is involved. (Magic is no such all-over assertion. It is not so much science before science as pragmatics before pragmatics.) Logically, one would expect that there would be, in religion, only one all-over assertion. But logic is a minor though not utterly absent element in religion and in drama; whatever their differences, both religion and drama must be faithful to existence first and only secondarily faithful to a pursuit of order. Thus, from the point of view of logic, a religious statement about the complete nature of reality, a statement made in terms of myth and cherished by cult, "ought" to make other statements of a similar nature impossible of assertion. Logic would suggest this question: if existence "at its heart" is thus and so, is it likely that the very same existence is "at its heart" something quite different? Yet developed religions make two such assertions, not one—assertions logically opposed to each other and cancelling.

One must, however, insist that religion does not proliferate uselessly contradictory statements about what is the total existence (its nature, its place for man) which we experience. But most developed religions find place for the following two (and contradictory) statements about existence. Logic would cancel one or the other, and we indeed find that systematizers of religion and secular systematizers of insights that have a religious origin if not at present a religious context struggle to cancel one of the two all-over statements as false or as an obscure form of the other statement. But these efforts overlook this truth: that both religion and drama are primarily records of man existing rather than of man trying to put his existence into comprehensible order. Religion and drama share this function; they enable man to *endure* existing, whereas philosophy and (in an often delusive way) science offer man the prospect of *comprehending* existence. Religion and drama are not interchangeable, despite certain present hopes. But one of the signs that they address themselves to the same task is that both are involved in advancing, at the same time, contradictory assertions about man and his existence. (That is, portions of a religious ritual make assertions that later portions cancel, logically. Comedy makes assertions about existence which tragedy always casts doubt on.)

Religion rests on a narrative. From the narrative may be drawn doctrines exceedingly abstract and indeed opposed to an esteem for narrative, for time-contained event, as the primary means of revelation (e.g., Buddhism). But what religion latterly becomes (and not all developed religions become the same thing) is not our interest here. Our interest must concern itself with how religion "began"—at least, "began" when it reached a point at which it supplemented its direct perceptions of numen—the wonderful, the pervasively compulsive—with narrative. The contrast between Greek religion, which richly supplemented its perceptions of the numinous with narrative and Latin religion which simply preserved, for several historical centuries, the perception of numen suggests that man did—at some unrecorded time in some civilizations—build into the structure of religion key-narratives that came to bear the great weight of religious superstructure—the weight of cult, rite, and dogma.

What were the two uses to which narrative was put at this point in the growth of religion—a point early, real, but mostly unrecoverable? They are sharply contrasting uses. They are uses that record two logically opposed insights which man came to have about his position in the world. Both insights are valid and real; they may be incompatible with each other, but they are not, by that circumstance, either to be disregarded or discredited. Man created and used mythological narrative for these two purposes: he asserted that existence, in its root organization, was *cyclic;* he asserted that existence—and this was an unconscious criticism of his cyclic assertion—was not what he had at first thought it but was, instead, *linear.*

We shall presently define and distinguish these two assertions. Let us grant at once the logical contradiction—indeed, to many, the puerility—involved in entertaining these two assertions simultaneously. It is plain that once the opposition between these two assertions is clearly perceived, many persons will judge that they have one more reason to dismiss the authority of religious experience. One may concede that such persons move in intellectual regions that are less demanding on the sympathetic imagination—regions that have their own sort of profit. But such persons are cut off from the profit that is the gift to man of religion and myth, and they are also in a poor position to measure the conflicting endowments, to man, of tragedy and comedy. These persons are not likely to see the significance of the likewise perplexing fact that tragedy and comedy are also logical incompatibles that coexist and that are intimately related in ways that vex and elude. Both tragedy and comedy are representations of experience; both mediate comprehension of experience. Are these two acts of comprehension so opposed to each other as to coexist only senselessly, as do random acts? Or do they have a supplementing function as they present their opposed visions of the universe? One form gives us the universe as a place suffused with laughter (*sustained* by laughter, we shall see); the other gives us the universe as a place falling in pieces, all props awry, "all coherence gone." Tragedy and comedy—the preliminary answer must be—constitute an uneasy unity: drama. But their coexistence *is* a unity and not an accident, not "random" coexistence, as above. And we can best understand the supplementary functions of these humanly contrived narratives—narratives that constantly vary on the surface—by seeking the analogy that links them with the two *uses* of myth that we discover in many developed religions.

As noted, what we present is an analogy only. Yet it is an analogy that (I believe) puts our ideas about comedy and tragedy in better order. Yet it is an analogy valid at only one point; it concerns only the two contrasting *uses* to which myth is put in religion and the two contrasting trains of reaction, of sensibility and induced comment, which the two forms of drama can stir in man. To make no mystery: comedy has its religious analogue in the *cyclic* assertions that myth enables religion to make, and tragedy finds its analogue in the noncyclic, *linear* assertions that myth sometimes supports. I would deny utterly the truth or usefulness of the analogy were it pushed beyond this point—were it argued that the myth that "asserts cycle" is comic *in substance* and the myth that asserts the linear perception tragic in substance. There is no comedy-tragedy contrast by which one can divide the abundance of myth. The *story* of Osiris and the *story* of Jesus—it has often been observed—resemble each other. Certainly the story of Osiris, a story that is the vehicle of a cyclic assertion, is not comic; it is quite as grim as the story of Jesus which, I judge, mediates a linear assertion. The story of Osiris "happened" to be "captured" by a religion which, at a particular time, needed to "assert cycle"; and the story of Jesus happened to be put to use as a narrative support to a linear, non-cyclic insight about existence. (The bulk of myth—of narrative that exists and functions to some degree in a religious context—asserts cycle. But the normal is not a binding norm; there is nothing abnormal about a story that a religion uses to express a linear insight about man's life. To my mind, the story of the "white god" Quetzalcoatl —the god who abandons his people *once* and promises a single return —asserts the linear almost as forcefully as does the narrative about Jesus.)

Deeper in drama, then—if the analogy I am drawing has real power to cast light—than the contrast between the laughable and the "weep-able" is this one: comedy is a representation of life that asserts cycle (as does the bulk of myth), and tragedy is that representation of life that asserts the linear, the non-cyclic. The laughter that, rightly, we associate with comedy is important but surface testimony to the fact that we have cause to rejoice when we contemplate the totality of existence as cycle; the tears that we shed for tragedy, the qualm that tragedy is said to stir, is a natural by-product of the perception that total existence is not cyclic at all—at least, not cyclic when it concerns us most intimately.

Comedy and tragedy, then, are secular purveyors—I mean no dis-respect by the word—of two all-over assertions about the root-nature of existence as man must experience it. (In *one* of these two ways he must experience it; he has no further choice.) The *materials* of comedy and tragedy do often differ much more than do the narrative materials that constitute the two sorts of myth. But, as often ob-served, what really distinguishes comedy from tragedy is the treatment accorded the materials that come to hand. It would not be impossible to alter *Oedipus Rex* into a knock-about farce, nor would it be dif-ficult to transform Malvolio into a figure of devastating import, par-ticularly were one writing a naturalistic or sociological tragedy. The imperfect religious analogue to all this is what we have already noted: that the narrative that becomes myth does not automatically proclaim whether it will be cyclic or linear; *that* is determined by the kind of existence it takes on in a specific religious context.

V

What are the distinguishing marks of these two all-over assertions, the cyclic and the linear?

Let us begin their precise definition thus. When we say that myth asserts two all-over insights into existence, we are concerned with existence collectively perceived and *not* discriminated. "Early man" had many of the powers of discriminatory judgment that we have; that is, he could look sensibly at *portions* of existence. Aspects of his arts, the bulk of his "civil law," and the conduct of his economy are sufficient records of this. But he—no more than can we—could not escape making a collective or all-over assertion about the world in which he was immersed. Nor is the "advance of human thought"—as modern drama, for one, obliquely testifies—from collective assertions to assertions that are more modest, more discriminated. Indeed, without a collective assertion of some kind, discrimination itself ceases; and this is just as true in a secular context as in a religious one. What we regard as the "advance of human thought" is simply a substitution of a later and more logically defensible collective assertion for an earlier one. The later assertion may be more valid, more soundly based. But that is not the point here. What we must perceive is that our "advance" has not freed our thought from the task of making total assertions not completely unlike the early religious cyclic and linear assertions.

Respect for them established, one may attempt a genetic explanation of the two mythological assertions that (I believe) casts great light on the way tragedy and comedy still function for us. A genetic explanation is not exhaustive; and, in this instance, it involves this bold hypothesis: that we can reproduce the intellectual and emotional growth of early man. What we say firmly on such a topic, we should also say modestly. But we need not abandon the effort; it is no more bold than the genetic efforts of literary scholars who speak of the formative attention of "Shakespeare's audience"—it is no more risky than the discourses on medieval piety that "explain" certain beautiful tensions at Chartres.

Man was first aware—and to this ancient scriptures are witness—of that which bore in on him from outside. He was aware of the great forces of nature as he saw them in wind and wave and weather; he was aware of his terrible dependence on the fertility of grass-land and arable field. And he was just as deeply impressed by the social forces that weighed on him: his family, his tribe, his tribal enemies. To assume as early man did that these outside forces—nature and the collective groups—made up each man's existence is to assume truly; it is also to assume incompletely, as religion after religion discovered at some point in its course.

Yet this incomplete assumption—that man's existence is composed of the awful natural and social forces that toss man about—"created" as its corollary an assertion made in terms of myth rather than, as here, in terms of abstract concept. Man employed myth for this reason: man must be more than the victim of the forces that are outside him; he must be their *imaginative* master. It is not enough to discriminate these external forces and come to a competent control of *some* of them. The nascent arts of agriculture did not free man from the need of myths about the forces of growth; the early and perhaps relatively satisfactory codes of law did not obviate the preservation of myths about the "origin" of law; and successful magic and medicine was never a threat to the inclusive assertions of religion. In short, all the practical control and knowledge of what bore in on man had to be supplemented by assertions that provided man *imaginative* all-over control. This control was provided by myths that, whatever their variety, were put to one task, the task of asserting cycle; they were man's warrant over and above his own observation for the recurrence of season and crop and for the persistence (despite the aging of all men and the death of leaders) of a given and experienced social form. It was myth and rite that could assure men that what man could not control was, in the long run, as much to be depended on as what he could control; natural and social phenomena would be exactly what man already knew them to be. Nature and society, myth testified, would always come full circle, would offer apprehensive man familiarity and not novelty. Man used, for example, the myth of Osiris to give himself this cyclic assurance. Osiris, we know, dies not once but many times; his scattered members are gathered by Isis in a basket again and again—in fact, year after year, so long as the society that uses the myth of Osiris persists. Mr. Joseph Campbell, in *The Hero with a Thousand Faces,* has revealed to us the impressive and yet monotonous use to which certain narrative materials were once put; the "thousand faces" are really the face of one hero. Beneath surface variety, the hero offers man the assurance of a *recurrent* salvation, of security in nature and in society that can never be really threatened by natural catastrophe or military invasion. The myth always repeats itself and is *cyclic.* If Osiris eternally dies and eternally is brought back to life, each man can feel secure: his plot of land will bear again, and the tribe or society to which he belongs will survive any temporary perils. Thanks to the myth, man is in calm imaginative control of what actually is beyond his just-nascent science and his non-existent sociology.

Is Christ Osiris? Is he too a vegetation god, a supporter of cycle? Not to those who cherished his story. Yet the bold outlines of his story are similar to the Osiris narrative; for this, some persons call him the last and most triumphant of the Asia Minor vegetation deities. On the basis of narrative materials, there is no utterly conclusive way of repudiating the similarity. But what one may deny—concerning Christ, concerning Quetzalcoatl as well—is that the Christ-story was put to the use the Osiris story was put to. A central Christian phrase refers to Christ as "our sacrifice once offered"; whatever the contradictory implications of certain Christian rituals, a sense that Christ did indeed die only once and rise only once remains at the heart of the Christian assertion and is opposed to the sense that lies at the heart of the Osiris mystery and similar mysteries.

Genetically speaking, what "begot" the Christian assertion? It was a second total perception of what existence was. After he had gained imaginative control of what lay outside him, man became aware of himself. He could express this awareness of himself only by uttering—with the aid of some myth—a total assertion that, logically but not actually, cancelled the cyclic assertion. (There are few developed religions in which the two assertions do not persist as peers.) When man turns to himself, he "knows" that what myth and cult have, to that point, told him either is not true or is very incompletely true. Nature and society are eternally dying and eternally reborn: let that stand. But man himself—man apart from the great processes that very nearly have him at their utter mercy—man is eternally dying and he never will be reborn.[1]

What is this second total assertion which the story of Christ, as well as other stories, implements? The assertion that man's existence is in time, historical. The assertion that to man *as man* (as opposed to man when he is plainly the creature of natural and social forces) the same event, the same choice, never comes round again. Man as man makes a choice among a series of events that follow each other in a non-repeating sequence; he has only one chance to make a certain choice since the time for a certain choice comes only once. As man, his experience is basically linear however much he may be, as an object, sub-

[1] It is beside the point to appeal to the developed dogma of Eastern religions which "work" this non-cyclic insight into the continuing assertion of cycle by elaborating theories of reincarnation and karma—and then absorb both the awareness of cycle and the "illusion" of linear existence into a superior awareness: Nirvana. That these complex adjustments had to be made is at least testimony to the existence and power, over man's will, of the insights that we now reconstitute. The synthesis called Nirvana is a witness to the painful tension created by the coexistence, in religious life, of the two ancient assertions that concern us. And Nirvana, as a theory, does not concern us, for it casts little light on either comedy or tragedy.

ject to the effects of natural and social cycle. As a cyclically oriented creature, man plants a crop at a certain time of the year and rethatches his house against the monsoons, and also prepares himself for the public fasts and the public rejoicings peculiar to his society. These come round again and again. But man comes to see that such preparations are not *all* his destiny or even a finally distinguishing part. He is, at the center of his nature, a creature of time, of *line;* and he and his forebears were, at the least, misled when they found the clue to human nature in what, in some sense, lay outside each separate man: in nature and the social group. The essential lies inside each man, in his experience of choice, of sequence; hence, the second total assertion, the one we have called the *linear* one.

The essential—we should observe when we watch *Hamlet* or *Oedipus* as well as when we savor the impact of the Christ-story—lies inside each man; it lies in man's experience of a horrid, sheerly linear necessity which no man, once he is aware of it, is ever able to evade. This is the necessity of choice; it is a necessity that gets no comforting "moral support" from the phases of the moon or the return of a season. Each human choice, at a certain time in a non-repetitive sequence of events, projects into future time only a certain portion of the past; each choice denies to the future significant developments of other portions of the past. This is human choice; it is also existence conceived in a linear fashion.

This all-over perception sought—and, of course, found—an august warrant. Not just the Jesus-myth itself but the whole body of what used to be called "sacred history" constituted a widely embracing myth that detached itself from the bulk of ancient myth and its cyclic assertions. The bulk of story that we may call the Christian myth—as well as groups of story that have some resemblance to it—braced man for the assertion that is just as essential to his health as is the earlier assertion of cycle. The linear assertion is, I believe, a record of a later, a more subtle, and certainly a more intimate reading of man's position in the world since it sees that man as a person, an individual, has an "economy" for which there are very few clues and models outside man. Why was this insight comparatively late in coming? Because what was outside man first rushed in on human awareness promising inclusive instruction. (And the cyclic instruction is one that man has never been able to dispense with.) But insofar as man has discovered individuality and personality, he has involved himself in myths that limit if they do not cancel the assurances of cyclic legend. A god that dies only once "answers" to man's more subtle analysis of the conditions of human action (as opposed to the conditions of natural event to which man was first eager to assimilate human action.) A god that dies only once, a god that does not enjoy the easy luxury of dying again and again, a god that traces the arc of choice only once—that god is a human god. His myth is a warrant for our most painful perceptions about what it is to be a human being rather than a tide that rushes up the shore or a society that persists even though its members unimportantly perish.

VI

The point of the analogy between cyclic and linear myth on the one hand and comedy and tragedy on the other now shapes up. Comedy, on a non-religious level, offers man the assurance that he can bank on the universe and its laws and, more importantly, on society and its structure. As does the myth that asserts cycle, comedy offers the individual the illusion that he exists and moves in a universe he can count on. This illusion, when it is effectively held, is a cause for rejoicing; it is a cause for *laughter*. It was in this sense that Dante wrote a *Comedy;* his poem was, at the last, an assurance of order—to be sure, an order of a complex kind. Even more ordinary comedy makes available to man some of the comforts that early man drew from religiously "asserting cycle." The comic narrative—in materials gulfs apart from the Osiris legend but in effect quite close to it—must, like *all* narratives, embody an upset, a threat to our sense of certainty. Farce or high comedy—the effect is the same. What is the archetypical plot? A shift of forces, a social realignment, threatens the security of the chief persons on the stage—threatens *our* security. Comedy, it appears, has its qualm as well as tragedy. But the qualm is allayed by a combination of strategies that dissociates comedy from tragedy. For it is soon clear that the threat is neither serious nor permanently effective. It is a trivial threat, no more, to the status quo—to what we would call in religious terms the continuance of cycle. And it is also soon clear that the persons involved are not full, real persons like ourselves. They are "comic"; in religious language, they have only that degree of reality that marks a cyclic interpretation of man's experience—they are not sufficiently alive to qualify or even shatter that view. Since the characters in a comedy are incomplete, they easily loom before us as quasi-ritual figures who march through the events of the comic play as unconcernedly as did the King of Egypt when he performed his yearly role of Osiris in the New Year festivals.

What is all that comedy offers us? It is certainly not a contemptible "all." It is simply an "all" that is inferior to the "all" that tragedy offers us, just as the "all" of Egyptian religion is at once valid and yet distinctly inferior to the gifts of a religion that has strong linear marks. In fact, all that comedy offers us is *a sense of regain.* The comic "qualm"—the "situation," the misunderstanding, the threat of someone's security—threatens the status quo in a way that is sometimes playful and sometimes serious. But very few comedies leave us with anything but a sense that the status quo has been essentially re-established. The happy ending reasserts the security of the important characters; much more important, their individual security amounts to a promise that well-known social forms will persist. The effect of cycle, put slightly in doubt, has, with the descent of the last curtain, been established more firmly than ever.

And as audience we have *regained* the security, personal and social, that the initial dramatic situation playfully threatened. We are, as characters, where we were at the commencement of the play, or where we deserved to be. The society to which we, as audience, imaginatively belong has been "established" more firmly than ever. In a popular farce, it is the most obvious sort of conventional standards which have been threatened by (say) adultery or sharp business practice and which are, in the last insincere minutes of the play, refounded; in a play of Shaw's like *Candida* it is the society of the Shavian elect. The differences are there, but they do not, in our connection, count. *Parlor, Bedroom, and Bath* and *Candida* function for their different audiences in exactly the same way. They mediate—in an obscure secular way, I admit—a counterpart of the cyclic religious assurance. They tell us that there is a secure, predictable, and even recurrent place provided for man in the universe. Further, they tell us that man can exercise imaginative control over this universe. The threats to this control—the situation that troubles Act I—always turn out to be delusive; and the comic drama always terminates with man more in imaginative command of his universe than before.

Not so tragedy. Tragedy, like the linear total assertion which it resembles, is no play for imaginative control of the world; it is a confession, sometimes noble and sometimes desponding, that man's "game" —the "game" utterly proper to him—lies somewhere else. It is a perception that, for man, imaginative control of the world that is distinctly external to him is beside the point. And when we regard comedy from the vantage-point of tragedy, we see that what it offers man is not so much a sense of regain as an *illusion* of regain. Comedy keeps man domiciled—and fairly securely domiciled—in a world that he does not live in properly unless he wills to live in a contradictory world at the same time. Comedy offers man an illusory paradise: the paradise of imaginative control of what is outside man. But man is driven from this paradise by his dismaying discovery that he does not entirely belong there. He is driven out not by any flaming sword but by his own nature whose destiny it is to exercise choice and thus deny or qualify all cyclically-based perceptions. For the reassuring continuum of cycle external to man, tragedy puts before us a discontinuity: man that chooses not to repeat, man that by his choice wills the unknown. Such a being is, from the cyclic point of view, a *lusus naturae,* one that taints and distorts the secure universe for which both Osiris and comedy stand. Were we to pair phrases, we might say that tragedy offers us a gift as permanent and pervasive as the comic sense of regain; it is a sense of loss, an awareness that man, in his most intimate activities, follows a line that leads only to darkness and an enigma—a line that will never curve back upon itself and so in the future confirm what it has been. The characteristic human act—that of choice—is closely allied with loss, even though we seem to choose to win something, to gain something. Choice, the specific linear activity, the activity that we see brought to sharp focus in Gethsemane and in the palace at Elsinore, always has for its ground-bass the note of loss. We turn our back on the joys we are certain of and might like to repeat, and we put ourselves in the trust of the future: a moment or an hour that we do not know but yet must count on—and we have willed to lose, if we must, the profit that can come to us from past moments: moments we have savored and could—did not choice intervene with its crucial break—still count on. Agony and death at some future time are but incidental marks of tragedy. The real agony, the real death, come at the moment when we choose; when, willing loss, we trust ourselves to an enigma; when we abandon the comic vein and cease counting on limited certainties. Not only is the crucifixion "a sacrifice once offered"; each crucial choice that marks a tragic drama is such a sacrifice, for it is loss of the world that the cyclic temper would preserve as man's great comfort and support. Whatever the upshot of tragic choice, whatever temporary palliatives and patent compensations may move toward us, the fact persists: we have given up or, at least, qualified a very useful insight into man's experience, the comic insight, the insight that we have compared with the cyclic assertions certain myths have made. In comedy the world we inhabit is but playfully threatened; by the end of the play, it is refounded more firmly than before. But in tragedy, as if in accord with its linear, non-reversible nature, choice threatens the world, the status quo, in deadly earnest. In choice, we do not know with much confidence what it is we shall create; we know with grim certainty what it is that we destroy: our happiness, our security—in short, our confidence in a future that follows—or seems to follow—cyclic laws.

Both tragic insight and the religious assertion that we call linear are not easy to endure, whether we arrogate to them exclusive truth or confess sadly that the comic or the cyclic insights are true also. Christians have permitted themselves the alleviation of encrusting their linear faith with recurrent ritual that prolongs, throughout the "Christian year," a necessary minimum of cyclic illusion. And, when we draw back from the blank that is choice and act in time, in linear succession, we may turn back to comedy which, in its way, represents our human lot if not our essential human lot. One way to endure tragedy, on the stage and off, is to listen to some of the things that comedy tells us when it speaks of "fundamental decency" and the recurrence of events and their correspondence to an understandable, definable order.

It is plain that there is nothing "wrong" with a penchant for comedy; tragedy is "truer" than comedy (it is a more penetrating comment on our lot) but it is less endurable. This relation between the truth of the two dramatic forms also gains light from the comparable religious tension. There is nothing "wrong" about the persistence of cyclic insights in a religion basically linear (e.g., the Christian). A perception that, at the centers of our being, we exist linear-wise can never cancel the truth that in relation to external forces we live under a cyclic dispensation. What is perhaps "wrong" is a reworking of the two religious insights that deprives either of its proper authority. This is the chief heresy that Western eyes find in Buddhism: the denial that both recurrence and unique event have high significance in man's life.

Finally, all that tragedy offers us in the audience is loss or deprivation: the possibility of becoming something that we have not yet been. If tragedy offers us a gain, it is a gain that is, unlike the comic gain, incalculable. If the tragedy we watch is real tragedy and not deterministic tragedy, which has the *events* of tragedy but the *certainty* of comedy, we live for a while lives from which the cyclic effects have fallen away or have receded into the background. Comedy occurs at any moment (it has the effect, if not the actuality, of being repeatable); tragedy occurs at only one moment: a moment that has come *this time* and that will never come again. It presents us with the spectacle of ourselves urged by the logic inherent in once-occurring events to make a choice. We cannot escape choice and responsibility for the choice which we make. Yet we make the choice without a full knowledge of the consequences. How can we, in a universe conceived in a linear way, have such knowledge? It is only in a cyclically conceived universe that we seem to have such knowledge. It is a knowledge which the other sort of drama strips from us.

For this reason, the tragic qualm—however purgation be explained—is never really purged. When we watch the acts of Oedipus and Hamlet and the results of those acts, the only comfort we draw is analogous to that which we get from a myth aligned with linear perceptions. Christ on the cross or Quetzalcoatl on his raft of serpents wrenches our eyes from a flattering and comforting view of our destinies as men. As men, we are apart from mountain and stream, we are apart from society collectively considered; we are—in all conventional or comic sense—apart from each other. We can find union only in the insight given to us by linear myth or by its analogue in tragic drama: that every moment is a crucifixion if we face it seriously. To do this we are most of the time incompetent. We would like to deny that we are Prince Hamlet. We would rather, along with Eliot's Prufrock, go to swell a crowd and there take refuge in sententious and (in our sense) "comic" remarks.

If we are correct, if the similarities between drama and religion are indeed striking, are we correct to oppose those who, directly or covertly, treat drama as a full surrogate for religious assertion? I think we are. The basic dissimilarity persists although it is not our duty here to study it. The religious context provides fixity and hence authority as the companions of the opposed total assertions, and drama provides a context of constant variety and change. This latter context will seem the correct and perhaps the only one to those who doubt that even the most sensitive and analytical attention to experience can win to binding answers. Such doubt is not hampering provided the doubter does not take the final step and observe that religion is really about the same thing as that which drama treats in two logically opposed ways. Religion, we should repeat, is "about" that which is sensed as permanently true; drama handles the permanently uncertain in what we see and recollect. All that the similarities we have traced here support is this observation: there are two sovereign ways of naming the impermanent and the fixed. Since these ways belong to both religion and drama, we are tempted to identify religion and drama. This we must refuse to do, for when we say "the same" we offer up, in the name of system and simplicity, discriminations rich, suggestive, and illogical that are a large part of the treasure that has been put into our hands.

The Psychology of the Paradox of the Fortunate Fall

HERBERT WEISINGER

In a paper titled, "Milton and the Paradox of the Fortunate Fall,"[1] Professor Arthur O. Lovejoy designated the thought expressed in lines 473-78 of Book XII of *Paradise Lost,* the paradox of the fortunate fall. It will be recalled that in this passage Adam has just been told by the Archangel Michael what his future will be and how man's fate is to be decided, and this prophecy of the Second Coming and of the Final Judgment so overwhelms him that he exclaims:

> O Goodness Infinite, Goodness immense
> That all this good of evil shall produce
> And evil turn to good . . .
> Full of doubt I stand,
> Whether I should repent me now of sin
> By me done or occasioned, or rejoice
> Much more that much more good thereof shall spring—
> To God more glory, more good will to men
> From God—and over wrath grace shall abound.

Such a view of the fall may well be termed a paradox because, while on the one hand, the fall of man was indeed the occasion of the most bitter sorrow—"sin by me done," yet on the other hand, without it, the subsequent history of man would be without meaning and purpose, the Incarnation and the Redemption could not take place—"more good thereof shall spring," and man could not look forward to the ultimate goal of creation, the Second Coming and the Final Judgment, when Christ shall reward his faithful and receive them into bliss—"over wrath grace shall abound," events of such cosmic transcendence, that, though they are projected into the future, they alone make possible the conception of a universe as understandable,

From *Tragedy and the Paradox of the Fortunate Fall,* 1953, pp. 19-30. Reprinted by permission of Michigan State University Press.

[1] Arthur O. Lovejoy, "Milton and the Paradox of the Fortunate Fall," *Essays in the History of Ideas* (Baltimore, 1948), pp. 277-95.

just, and good: "thus good of evil shall produce, and evil turn to good." For only under this divine plan can the good which Paul would do, be achieved, and the evil which he would not, be undone. Thus the fall of man is felt to be simultaneously harrowing and ecstatic, for at the very moment when man is thrown into the deepest despair, at that moment, and at that moment alone, he is made aware of the possibility of realizing the greatest good, and in this way, and only in this way, does good come out of evil. This idea, which comes from the innermost core of Milton's conviction that to be truly man, one must be capable of choice, and more, must be capable of bearing the burden of that choice, this idea, the progression from ignorance through experience to light, which at first glance seems so obvious a logical contradiction because it appears to contravene our own bitter experience of the irrationality and injustice of the world, transcends that experience in a leap which hurtles over the evidence of our senses to the creation of an intelligible pattern of human destiny capable of being held with the most profound conviction. Such a leap seems always to be made by those who, finding the notion of a universe as indifferent to man repugnant to them (and even Lucretius, though he rejected the Gods, could not bear to think of a meaningless universe), wrench experience into shape by forming a universe in which man enjoys, though at a bitter price, a transcendent rapport with himself, with nature, and with God. For Professor Lovejoy's purposes, it was enough for him to demonstrate how traditional and orthodox the paradox of the fortunate fall was by citing pertinent passages from Ambrose, Leo I, Gregory the Great, Augustine, the Easter Even hymn, the *Exultet, The Vision of Piers the Plowman,* Wyclif, Pererius, St. Francis de Sales, Du Bartas, and Giles Fletcher, and it was from the Easter Even hymn that he derived the classic expression of the idea as well as its name: *"O certe necessarium Adae peccatum, quod Christi morte deletum est! O felix culpa, quae talem ac tantum meruit habere redemptorem!"*

However, the idea of *felix culpa* has more than historical and theological interest; it possesses the power to attract, for, as the late Theodore Spencer testified, it produced in him an enlargement of experience, though he could afford no explanation of his experience.[2] Now, there are two ways by which the analysis of the paradox of the fortunate fall can be made: first, by the investigation of the psycho-

[2] Theodore Spencer, Review of Professor Lovejoy's *Essays in the History of Ideas, JHI,* IX (1948), pp. 439-46.

logical implications of the nature of religious contradiction which lies at the root of the paradox, a method suggested by Professor Lovejoy himself, and the second, by a consideration of the historical affinities of the idea. The first method I can only hint at, but some suggestions can be briefly indicated concerning its use and what it can be expected to accomplish. In a certain sense, the psychology of religious contradiction formed the central subject of James's *Varieties of Religious Experience,* for in that book he undertook to lay bare the state of mind of the "twice-born," as he called them, those ". . . sick souls who must be twice-born in order to be happy," to whom the world is a "double-storied mystery," which can be resolved only by the passage from one belief to another through conversion. This passage from belief to belief we can find movingly expressed in the Old Testament:

> And I will give them one heart, and I will put a new spirit within you; and I will take the stony heart out of their flesh, and I will give them a heart of flesh: that they may walk in my statutes, and keep mine ordinances, and do them: and they shall be my people, and I will be their God. (Ezekiel 11, 19-20.)

And again in the New Testament:

> Verily, verily, I say unto you, he that heareth my word, and believeth him that sent me, hath eternal life, and cometh not into judgement, but hath passed out of death into life. (John 5, 24.)

And in Paul's vivid words:

> But now we have been discharged from the law, having died to that wherein we were holden; so that we serve in newness of the spirit, and not in oldness of the letter. (Romans 7, 6.)

From death to life, from oldness to newness, these are the classic phrases to express that stirring movement from one state of mind to another, a movement which proceeds from despair to exultation in a victory of the spirit of man over the brute fact of meaningless existence. But the process of conversion need not be limited to religious conversion alone, as James was quick to see; he meant it to describe the conversion from one belief to another, and even from faith to scepticism as well. In any case, the process of conversion seems to consist of a repeated pattern of behaviour: first, irritation and frustration caused by the feeling that all is irrational, combined with an almost overpowering sense of chaos and meaninglessness leading to despair and instability of mind; then this state gives way when the pieces in the puzzle seem all at once to fit together under the impetus of conversion, and there is an almost overwhelming feeling of exhilaration which comes from the effect of strong conviction, and above all, the feeling of knowledge and power which comes from having ascended from ignorance to light, the recognition of order and design in the world which had hitherto seemed empty of them.[3]

Immediate and striking is the description of his conversion given by Augustine:

> Hastily therefore went I again to that place where Alypius was sitting; for there had I laid the Apostle's book whenas I rose from thence. I snatched it up, I opened it, and in silence I read that chapter which I had first cast mine eyes upon: Not in rioting and drunkenness, not in chambering and wantonness, not in strife and envying: but put ye on the Lord Jesus Christ; and make not provision for the flesh, to fulfil the lusts thereof. No further would I read; nor needed I. For instantly even with the end of this sentence, by a light as it were of confidence now darted into my heart, all the darkness of doubting vanished away.[4]

Hopkins has written how the power of conversion can turn the stubborn intractability of man against the will of God into the gentle acceptance of his ways:

> Thou art indeed just, Lord, if I contend
> With thee; but, sir, so what I plead is just.
> Why do sinners' ways prosper? and why must
> Disappointment all I endeavour end?
> Wert thou my enemy, O thou my friend,
> How wouldst thou worse, I wonder, than thou dost
> Defeat, thwart me? Oh, the sots and thralls of lust
> Do in spare hours more thrive than I that spend,
> Sir, life upon thy cause. See, banks and brakes
> Now, leavèd how thick! lacèd they are again
> With frettty chervil, look, and fresh wind shakes
> Them; birds build—but not I build; no, but strain,
> Time's eunuch, and not breed one work that wakes.
> Mine, O thou lord of life, send my roots rain.[5]

[3] My friend and colleague, Professor Arthur J. M. Smith, has called my attention to the description of the five stages in mysticism as stated by Evelyn Underhill: (1) Awakening or Conversion; (2) Self-Knowledge or Purgation; (3) Illumination; (4) Surrender, or the Dark Night; and (5) Union in *Mysticism* (London, 1923), pp. 205-6. But, as I believe, the process of conversion and illumination need not be confined to religion alone. See A. D. Nock, *Conversion* (Oxford, 1933), pp. 1-16.

[4] *St. Augustine's Confessions with an English Translation by William Watts,* 1631, ed. W. H. D. Rouse (London, 1912), I, p. 465.

[5] Gerard Manley Hopkins, "Thou Art Indeed Just, Lord" from *Poems.* Reprinted by permission of Oxford University Press. Copyright 1948.

He has done. Such is the power of illumination that it reveals in a flash the divine paradox of creation:

> O the sweet exchange, O the inscrutable creation, O the unexpected benefits, that the wickedness of many should be concealed in the one righteous, and the righteousness of the one should make righteous many wicked! [6]

James confined his illustrations of conversion to the area of religion, but conversion is a process of conviction found in all fields; and in our time, conversion is probably much more to be experienced in the area of social and political conviction than it is in religion, and the hero of Tolstoi's last novel, fittingly called *Resurrection,* is perhaps a more modern prototype than Augustine, though in both the process of conversion is strikingly the same.

But James did not try to account for conversion, nor did he intend to use the phrase "sick souls" in any pejorative sense, "sick" meaning merely the confusion and doubt which confront us all in the presence of the uncertain and the unclear. A possible explanation of the psychology of conversion may be found in Jung who distinguishes three mental levels: (1) consciousness; (2) the personal unconsciousness; and (3) the collective unconsciousness. The last he terms "a timeless and universal mind," the repository of "customary and eternally repeated facts" which, once having indelibly stamped their impress on the mind of man, everlastingly retain their potency to affect him. Concretized into permanent images, they become archetypes:

> . . . the formulated resultants of countless typical experiences of our ancestors. They are, as it were, the psychic residue of numberless experiences of the same type. . . . Each of these images contains a piece of human psychology and human destiny, a relic of suffering or delight that has happened countless times in our ancestral story, and on the average follows the same course.[7]

These configurations of images, small in number but basic to the constitution of the mind, account for our reaction to poetry, for these "basic, age-old patterns of central human experience . . . lie at the root of any poetry (or any other art) possessing special emotional

[6] *The Epistle to Diognetus,* ix, 5 in *The Apostolic Fathers,* tr. Kirsopp Lake (London, 1913), II, p. 371.

[7] C. G. Jung, "On the Relation of Analytical Psychology to Poetic Art," in *Contributions to Analytical Psychology,* tr. H. G. and Cary F. Baynes (London, 1928), p. 246.

significance." [8] Now, in her stimulating effort to link the Jungian psychology to the understanding of literature, Miss Maud Bodkin has shown that one such archetype is that of the rebirth pattern in which the conflict of emotional tendencies of opposite character is resolved in two ways simultaneously; through the assertive acts of the individual hero, and, through his death, the surrender of the ego to a greater power, that of the community consciousness. Such a process of rebirth, or of conversion, is made up of two succeeding movements: one downward and inward toward *statis* and death, the other upward and outward toward "reintegration and life-renewal." [9]

The problem of determining the origins of these archetypes Miss Bodkin cautiously avoided, but Jung had already attributed them to the racial consciousness, a concept which I suspect he obtained from elaborating on Freud's theory, first suggested in *Totem and Taboo,* and later and more fully, in *Moses and Monotheism,* but with political and racial implications which Freud had carefully kept out. Freud had suggested that the primeval history of mankind is a kind of recapitulation of the psychological history of the individual, and that the two cast a mutual light on each other. Thus there is effected a link, indissoluble and everlasting, between the most impressive experiences of man's past, which have bitten so deeply into the collective consciousness that they have become constituent parts of its very nature, and his contemporary consciousness at any time. "Early trauma-defence-latency-outbreak of the neurosis-partial return of the suppressed material: this was the formula," Freud wrote in *Moses* and *Monotheism,* "we drew up for the development of a neurosis." And he then assumed that what had happened in the life of the individual had happened in the life of the species itself: ". . . mankind as a whole passed through conflicts of a sexual-aggressive nature, which left permanent traces, but which were for the most part warded off and forgotten; later, after a long period of latency, they came to life again and created phenomena similar in structure and tendency to neurotic symptoms." [10] From the theory of repressed trauma reasserting itself at a later stage of development in a changed form, Freud derived his account of the early history

[8] Stanley Edgar Hyman, *The Armed Vision* (New York, 1948), p. 143. Cf. also the explanation of the theory of archetypes in Joseph Campbell, *The Hero with a Thousand Faces* (New York, 1949), pp. 17-19.

[9] Maud Bodkin, *Archetypal Patterns of Poetry* (London, 1934), pp. 4, 19-20, 81.

[10] Sigmund Freud, *Moses and Monotheism,* tr. Katherine Jones (London and New York, 1939), p. 126.

of man. Man in his original state lived in small hordes each dominated by a strong male who was ". . . the master and father of the whole horde, unlimited in his power, which he used brutally." The sons were deprived of all possessions, including women, and were therefore finally forced to band together to kill the father and eat him. In so doing, they exhibited a characteristic ambivalence: on the one hand, they feared and hated him, and therefore killed him; on the other hand, they respected his power and therefore partook of his body. Recognizing that internecine warfare would lead to endless slaughter, the brothers now created ". . . the first form of a social organization accompanied by a renunciation of instinctual gratifications," that is to say, the taboo of incest and the law of exogamy. And the memory of the father was perpetuated in the creation of the totem which, like the killed and eaten father it commemorated, was both revered and then slaughtered and eaten in the totem feast. In the course of time, the totems were humanized into Gods, ". . . but the memory of that first great act of sacrifice had proved to be indestructible despite all attempts to forget it." The son tried more and more to put himself in the place of the father but the sense of guilt occasioned by the primeval murder could not be allayed; it had to be expiated: "A Son of God, innocent himself, had sacrificed himself, and had thereby taken over the guilt of the world. It had to be a Son, for the sin had been murder of the Father." [11] Thus father and son are reconciled and, at the same time as the son makes his sacrifice, he takes over the rôle of the father.[12]

Here too, according to Freud, is the explanation of tragic guilt: the hero is the primal father and the primal murderer in one, and he takes upon himself that primeval guilt so as to free the members of the chorus from its taint:

> The crime foisted upon him, namely, presumption and rebellion against a great authority, is the same as that which in the past oppressed the colleagues of the chorus, namely, the band of brothers. Thus the tragic hero, though still against his will, is made the redeemer of the chorus.[13]

Something of the same idea, though less specific, is found in Professor Gilbert Murray's recognition of ". . . the strange, unanalyzed vibration below the surface" of such plays as the *Agamemnon* or *Electra*

[11] *Ibid.*, p. 136.

[12] Sigmund Freud, *Totem and Taboo*, tr. by J. Strachey (London, 1950), p. 145.

[13] *Ibid.*, p. 926.

or *Hamlet,* ". . . an undercurrent of desires and fears and passions, long slumbering yet eternally familiar, which have for thousands of years lain near the root of our most intimate emotions and been wrought into the fabric of our most magical dramas." [14]

The mystery of our response to tragedy, a response which is over and above such discernible factors as the Aristotelian categories, for example, with which we are accustomed to grapple for the secret of tragedy, is thus given a deeply rooted psychological basis which in its turn is found buried in the innermost layers of the group consciousness. That there are a basic few patterns in art which in various guises occur and re-occur, is, I think, without question, and Mr. Joseph Campbell has gone so far as to speak of the monomyth, which he describes as follows:

> The mythological hero, setting forth from his common-day hut or castle, is lured, carried away, or else voluntarily proceeds, to the threshold of adventure. There he encounters a shadow presence that guards the passage. The hero may defeat or conciliate this power and go alive into the kingdom of the dark (brother-battle, dragon-battle: offering, charm), or be slain by the opponent and descend in death (dismemberment, crucifixion). Beyond the threshold, then, the hero journeys through a world of unfamiliar yet strangely intimate forces, some of which severely threaten him (tests), some of which give magical aid (helpers). When he arrives at the nadir of the mythological round, he undergoes a supreme ordeal and gains his reward. The triumph may be represented as the hero's sexual union with the goddess-mother of the world (sacred marriage), his recognition by his father-creator (father atonement), his own divinization (apotheosis), or again—if the powers have remained unfriendly to him—his theft of the boon he came to gain (bride-theft, fire-theft); intrinsically, it is an expansion of consciousness and therewith of being (illumination, transfiguration, freedom). The final work is that of the return. If the powers have blessed the hero, he now sets forth under their protection (emissary); if not, he flees and is pursued (transformation flight, obstacle flight). At the return threshold the transcendental powers must remain behind; the hero re-emerges from the kingdom of dread (return, resurrection), the boon that he brings restores the world (élixir).[15]

This ideal version of the monomyth is substantiated in many ways by Lord Raglan's study of the myth of the hero, in which, from an analysis of the stories of Oedipus, Theseus, Romulus, Heracles, Perseus,

[14] Gilbert Murray, *The Classical Tradition in Poetry* (Oxford, 1927), p. 240. Cf. F. M. Cornford, "The Unconscious Element in Literature and Philosophy," in *The Unwritten Philosophy and Other Essays,* ed. W. K. C. Guthrie (Cambridge, 1950), pp. 1-13.

[15] Joseph Campbell, *op. cit.,* pp. 245-46.

Jason, Bellerophon, Pelops, Asclepios, Dionysos, Apollo, Zeus, Joseph, Moses, Elijah, Watu Gunung, Nyikang, Siegfried, Llew Llawgyffes, Arthur, and Robin Hood, he arrives at a pattern made up of the following incidents, all or most of which occur in the life of the hero:

1. The hero's mother is a royal virgin;
2. His father is a king, and
3. Often a near relative of his mother, but
4. The circumstances of his conception are unusual, and
5. He is also reputed to be the son of a God.
6. At birth an attempt is made, usually by his father or his maternal grandfather, to kill him, but
7. He is spirited away, and
8. Reared by foster-parents in a far country.
9. We are told nothing of his childhood, but
10. On reaching manhood he returns or goes to his future kingdom.
11. After a victory over the king and/or a giant, dragon or wild beast,
12. He marries a princess, often the daughter of his predecessor, and
13. Becomes king.
14. For a time he reigns uneventfully, and
15. Prescribes laws, but
16. Later he loses favour with the Gods and/or his subjects and
17. Is driven from the throne and city, after which
18. He meets with a mysterious death,
19. Often at the top of a hill.
20. His children, if any, do not succeed him.
21. His body is not buried, but nevertheless
22. He has one or more holy sepulchres.[16]

Lord Raglan rightfully suggests that the considerable number of coincidences points to a ritual pattern as the origin of the myth of the hero and he notes that the three principal incidents in the life of the hero, his birth, his accession to the throne, and his death, correspond to the three principal *rites de passage,* at birth, at initiation, and at death.

But it is not necessary, I think, to subscribe whole-heartedly to the theory of the monomyth (I am afraid Mr. Campbell rather over-does it) to accept the idea that there are, as I have said, a few basic patterns

[16] Lord Raglan, *The Hero* (Oxford, 1937), pp. 178-80. Compare, too, the lengthy "Annex II to V. C. (ii) (a)," titled "Christus Patiens," in *A Study of History* (Oxford, 1939), VI, pp. 376-439, in which Professor Toynbee uses the comparative method to demonstrate some eighty-seven points of similarity between the life of Christ and the lives of a number of pagan heroes. But his image of the pruner's knife and of the pollarded tree leads him to read history as a kind of relentless drive leading up to the making of Christ, at which point it abruptly stops, so that all subsequent events are but a dull and dispirited falling away from this one moment of great glory.

in art which, more than others, seem to possess much potency and such vitality that in whatever form we encounter them we respond immediately and intensely to them. I do not wish to minimize the differences which exist between the incidents in the lives of the heroes which Mr. Campbell and Lord Raglan tend to gloss over, but before we can deal with the differences, it is necessary first to take into account the similarities, for then we are in a sane and stable position to estimate the crucial matter of value which only the analysis of difference can make, and this is particularly true at the stage of literary development in which not the making of myth, but the use of myth, that is to say, at the conscious literary level, is our concern. Moreover, the emphasis on the monomyth alone fails to bring out with sufficient force the nature of the transformation of the hero; Mr. Campbell seems to see the story in the form of a rounded circle, the going forth, the encounter, and the return with the boon, but it is precisely the changed character of the hero on his return, a change which is fundamental and indeed dialectical in quality, as from a lower to a higher stage of development and with a corresponding insight and understanding, which gives the myth its power of illumination. From myth to literature there is as great a jump as from experience to myth.[17]

I have suggested that between experience and literature lies myth; in the same way, between myth and tragedy lies the paradox of the fortunate fall, a necessary intermediate step which translates the emotional overtones of myth into the conscious creation of tragedy. First, experience, the repeated primeval traumatic shocks ultimately crystallizing themselves into the archetype of rebirth; then, the myth and ritual mould of the ancient Near East, concretizing the archetype of rebirth into a pattern of behaviour and belief infused with conviction and faith; then, the paradox of the fortunate fall, summing up in brief the essence of the myth and ritual of the ancient Near East, sharper in its formulation, more ideological, yet, at the same time, carrying with it the emotional aura of the myth and ritual pattern; and finally, tragedy, the deliberate work of art, using the paradox of the fortunate fall as its ideological backbone, so to speak, but divergent in kind from the archetype of rebirth, from the myth and ritual of the ancient Near East, and from the paradox of the fortunate fall, yet partaking of the

[17] Richard Chase, "Myth as Literature," *English Institute Essays,* 1947 (New York, 1948), p. 10, seems to me to illustrate the failure to perceive this difference. See the sharp but sensible criticism of Chase's position by Stanley Edgar Hyman, "Myth, Ritual, and Nonsense," *The Kenyon Review,* XI (1949), pp. 455-75, which also contains a sound examination of Mr. Campbell's book.

force of each, and adding to them the conscious choice of materials and meaning which distinguishes art from the stuff out of which it is made. However, it is, as I have said, only with the transformation of the myth and ritual of the ancient Near East into the paradox of the fortunate fall that I shall be concerned here. And since we are dealing here with a pattern of thought which penetrates to man's most urgent needs, we can expect that this shape will necessarily undergo successive transformations, for, as man learns more, the more he attempts to retain what he already believes within what he keeps on learning; the pattern persists, but the forms it takes are almost endless in their variety. At the same time, I think we can also note a direction in the transformation of the form, for in its successive adaptations, it seems to move toward a greater refinement of significance; it becomes successively spiritualized, so that at the end its origins are almost completely concealed, and we are left within a pattern to which we respond without knowing why it is that we do respond. Thus, by returning to the sources, we revitalize the pattern, and, at the same time, we can look forward, we can see what further transformations it is capable of undergoing.

The Tragic Form

RICHARD B. SEWALL

A discussion of tragedy is confronted at the outset with the strenuous objections of Croce, who would have no truck with the genres. "Art is one," he wrote in his famous *Britannica* article,[1] "and cannot be divided." For convenience, he would allow the division of Shakespeare's plays into tragedies, comedies, and histories, but he warned of the dogmatism that lay in any further refining of distinctions. He made a special point of tragedy, which as usual was the fighting issue. No artist, he said, will submit to the servitude of the traditional definition: that a tragedy must have a subject of a certain kind, characters of a certain kind, and a plot of a certain kind and length. Each work of art is a world in itself, "a creation, not a reflection, a monument, not a document." The concepts of aesthetics do not exist "in a transcendent region" but only in innumerable specific works. To ask of a given work "is it a tragedy?" or "does it obey the laws of tragedy?" is irrelevant and impertinent.

Although this may be substituting one dogmatism for another, there is sense in it. Nothing is more dreary than the textbook categories; and their tendency, if carried too far, would rationalize art out of existence. The dilemma is one of critical means, not ends: Croce would preserve tragedy by insuring the autonomy of the artist; the schoolmen would preserve it by insuring the autonomy of the form.

But the dilemma is not insurmountable, as Eliot and a number of others have pointed out. There is a life-giving relationship between tradition and the individual talent, a "wooing both ways" (in R. P. Blackmur's phrase) between the form which the artist inherits and the new content he brings to it. This wooing both ways has been especially true of the development of tragedy, where values have been incremental, where (for instance) each new tragic protagonist is in some

From *Essays in Criticism,* Vol. IV, 1954, pp. 345-58. Reprinted by permission of the editors.

[1] Fourteenth edition, article "Aesthetics."

degree a lesser Job and each new tragic work owes an indispensable element to the Greek idea of the chorus. . . .

But we must first get a suitable idea of form. Blackmur's article[2] from which I have just quoted provides, I think, a useful suggestion. It is the concept of "theoretic form," which he distinguishes from technical or "executive" form. "Technical form," he writes, "is our means of getting at . . . and then making something of, what we feel the form of life itself is: the tensions, the stresses, the deep relations and the terrible disrelations that inhabit them. . . . This is the form that underlies the forms we merely practice. . . ." This (and here Croce's full concept of form is more adequately represented) is "what Croce means by theoretic form for feeling, intuition, insight, what I mean by the theoretic form of life itself." Discussion of the "form" of tragedy in this sense need be neither prescriptive nor inhibiting, but it may define a little more precisely a vital area of thought and feeling.

Here is the kind of situation in which such a discussion might be helpful: Two years ago, in *Essays in Criticism* (October 1952), Miss K. M. Burton defended what she called the "political tragedies" of Ben Jonson and George Chapman as legitimate tragedies, although non-Aristotelian. *Sejanus* was perhaps the clearest case in point. Herford and Simpson, in their commentary, had set the play down as at best "the tragedy of a satirist" a "proximate" tragedy, with no tragic hero and with no cathartic effect. "Whatever effect [Jonson] aimed at," they wrote, "it was not the purifying pity excited by the fatal errors of a noble nature." Miss Burton's reply lay in her concept of political tragedy. She saw Jonson's tragic theme as "the manner in which evil penetrates the political structure." The "flaw" that concerned him lay "within the social order," and whatever purifying pity we feel would come from contemplating the ordeal of society, not the fatal errors of a noble nature. The play for her had "tragic intensity"; it was both "dramatic, and a tragedy."

Whether one agrees with her or not, the question, despite Croce, is out: "Is the play a tragedy?" And many others follow. Can there be a tragedy without a tragic hero? Can "the social order" play his traditional role? Is catharsis the first, or only, or even a reliable test? In a recent article, Professor Pottle wrote, "I shall be told Aristotle settled all that." And added, "I wish he had." The disagreement on

[2] "The Loose and Baggy Monsters of Henry James: Notes on the Underlying Classic Form in the Novel," *Accent*, Summer, 1951; see also Eliseo Vivas, "Literature and Knowledge," *Sewanee Review*, Autumn, 1952.

Sejanus is symptomatic. F. L. Lucas once pointed out that (on much the same issues) Hegel thought only the Greeks wrote true tragedy; and I. A. Richards, only Shakespeare. Joseph Wood Krutch ruled out the moderns, like Hardy, Ibsen and O'Neill; and Mark Harris ruled them in.[3] The question arises about every new "serious" play or novel; we seem to care a great deal about whether it is, or is not, a tragedy.

I have little hope of settling all this, but I am persuaded that progress lies in the direction of theoretic form, as Blackmur uses the term. Is it not possible to bring the dominant feelings, intuitions, insights that we meet in so-called tragic writings into some coherent relationship to which the word "form" could be applied without too great violence? This is not to tell artists what to do, nor to set up strict *a priori* formulae, nor to legislate among the major genres. The problem of evaluating the total excellence of a given work involves much more than determining its status as a tragedy, or as a "proximate" tragedy, or as a non-tragedy. It involves, among other things, the verbal management within the work and the ordering of the parts. Furthermore, our discussion need not imply the superiority of tragedy over comedy (certainly not as Dante conceived of comedy) or over epic, although, if we look upon these major forms as presenting total interpretations of life, the less inclusive forms (lyric, satire) would seem to occupy inferior categories. But as we enter the world of any play or novel to which the term tragedy is at all applicable, we may well judge it by what we know about the possibilities of the form, without insisting that our judgment is absolute. If, set against the full dimensions of the tragic form, Jonson's *Sejanus* or Hemingway's *A Farewell to Arms* (for instance) reveal undeveloped possibilities or contrary elements, we can still respect their particular modes of expression.

In indicating these dimensions of tragedy, I shall be mindful of Unamuno's warning[4] that tragedy is not a matter, ultimately, to be systematized. He speaks truly, I think, about "the tragic sense of life." He describes it as a sub-philosophy, "more or less formulated, more or less conscious," reaching deep down into temperament, not so much "flowing from ideas as determining them." It is the sense of ancient evil, of the mystery of human suffering, of the gulf between aspiration

[3] F. A. Pottle, "Catharsis," *Yale Review*, Summer, 1951; F. L. Lucas, *Tragedy in Relation to Aristotle's Poetics*, N.Y., 1928; Joseph Wood Krutch, *The Modern Temper*, N.Y., 1929; Mark Harris, *The Case for Tragedy*, N.Y., 1932.

[4] *The Tragic Sense of Life*, tr. J. E. C. Flitch, London, 1921, pp. 17-18.

and achievement. It colours the tragic artist's vision of life (his theoretic form) and gives his works their peculiar shade and tone. It speaks, not the language of systematic thought, but through symbolic action, symbol and figure, diction and image, sound and rhythm. Such a recognition should precede any attempt to talk "systematically" about tragedy, while not denying the value of the attempt itself.

Two more comments remain to be made about method. The first is the problem of circular evidence,[5] the use of tragedies to define tragedy. I am assuming that we can talk meaningfully about a body of literature which reveals certain generic qualities and which can be distinguished from the body of literature called comedy, epic, satire, or the literature of pathos. My purpose is to isolate these qualities and to refer to the works themselves as illustrations rather than proof.

The second comment involves the problem of affectivism, which is the problem of catharsis: "This play is a tragedy because it makes me feel thus and so." As Max Scheler puts it, this method would bring us ultimately to the contemplation of our own ego. Thus, I would reverse the order of F. L. Lucas's discussion, which assumes that we must know what tragedy does before we can tell what it is: "We cannot fully discuss the means," Lucas wrote, "until we are clear about the ends." It is true that the usual or "scientific" way is to define natures by effects, which are observable. But rather than found a definition of tragedy on the infinite variables of an audience's reactions, I would consider first the works themselves as the "effects" and look in them for evidences of an efficient cause: a world-view, a form that "underlies the forms we merely practice." What are the generic qualities of these effects? Do they comprise a "form"? I think they do; and for convenience I shall use the term from the start as if I had already proved its legitimacy.

Basic to the tragic form is its recognition of the inevitability of paradox, of unresolved tensions and ambiguities, of opposites in precarious balance. Like the arch, tragedy never rests—or never comes to rest, with all losses restored and sorrows ended. Problems are put and pressed, but not solved. An occasional "happy ending," as in *The Oresteia* or *Crime and Punishment,* does not mean a full resolution. Though there may be intermittences, there is no ultimate discharge in that war. Although this suggests formlessness, as it must in contrast

[5] Cf. Max Scheler, "On the Tragic," *Cross Currents,* Winter, 1954. This is a selection from Scheler's *Vom Umsturtz der Werte,* vol. I (1923), tr. Bernard Stambler.

with certain types of religious orthodoxy or philosophical system, it would seem the essence of the tragic form. Surely it is more form than chaos. For out of all these tensions and paradoxes, these feelings, intuitions, insights, there emerges a fairly coherent attitude towards the universe and man. Tragedy makes certain distinguishable and characteristic affirmations, as well as denials, about (1) the cosmos and man's relation to it; (2) the nature of the individual and his relation to himself; (3) the individual in society.

1. *The tragic cosmos.* In using the term cosmos to signify a theory of the universe and man's relation to it, I have, of course, made a statement about tragedy: that tragedy affirms a cosmos of which man is a meaningful part. To be sure, the characteristic locale of tragedy is not the empyrean. Tragedy is primarily humanistic. Its focus is an event in this world; it is uncommitted as to questions of ultimate destiny, and it is non-religious in its attitude toward revelation. But it speaks, however vaguely or variously, of an order that transcends time, space and matter.[6] It assumes man's connection with some supersensory or supernatural, or metaphysical being or principle, whether it be the Olympians, Job's Jehovah, or the Christian God; Fate, Fortune's Wheel, the "elements" that Lear invoked, or Koestler's "oceanic sense," which comes in so tentatively (and pathetically) at the end of *Darkness at Noon.* The first thing that tragedy says about the cosmos is that, for good or ill, it *is;* and in this respect tragedy's theoretic opposite is naturalism or mechanism. Tragedy is witness (secondly) to the cosmic mystery, to the "wonderful" surrounding our lives; and in literature the opposite of tragedy is not only writing based upon naturalistic theory but also upon the four-square, "probable"[7] world of satire and rationalistic comedy. Finally, what distinguishes tragedy from other forms which bespeak this cosmic sense—for tragedy of course is not unique in this—is its peculiar and intense preoccupation with the *evil* in the universe, whatever it is in the stars that compels, harasses, and bears man down. Tragedy wrestles with the evil of the mystery—and the mystery of the evil. And the contest never ends.

But, paradoxically, its view of the cosmos is what sustains tragedy. Tragedy discerns a principle of goodness that coexists with the evil. This principle need be nothing so pat as The Moral Order, the "armies

[6] Cf. Susan Taubes, "The Nature of Tragedy," *Review of Metaphysics,* December 1953.

[7] The "wonderful" and the "probable" are the basic categories in Albert Cook's distinction between tragedy and comedy. (*The Dark Voyage and the Golden Mean,* Cambridge, Mass., 1949, chap. 1.)

of unalterable law," and it is nothing so sure as the orthodox Christian God. It is nearer the folk sense that justice exists somewhere in the universe, or what Nietzsche describes as the orgiastic, mystical sense of oneness, of life as "indestructibly powerful and pleasurable." It may be a vision of some transcendent beauty and dignity against which the present evil may be seen as evil and the welter as welter. This is what keeps tragedy from giving up the whole human experiment, and in this respect its opposite is not comedy or satire but cynicism and nihilism, as in Schopenhauer's theory of resignation. The "problem of the good" plays as vital a part in tragedy as the "problem of evil." It provides the living tension without which tragedy ceases to exist.

Thus tragedy contemplates a universe in which man is not the measure of all things. It confronts a mystery. W. Macneile Dixon[8] pointed out that tragedy started as "an affair with the gods"; and the extent to which literature has become "secularized and humanized," he wrote, is a sign of its departure from (to use our present term) the tragic form. While agreeing with him as to the tendency, one may question the wholesale verdict which he implies. The affair with the gods has not, in the minds of all our artists, been reduced to an affair with the social order, or the environment, or the glands. But certainly where it becomes so, the muse of tragedy walks out; the universe loses its mystery and (to invoke catharsis for a moment) its terror.

The terms "pessimism" and "optimism" in the view of the universe as conceived in the tragic form, do not suggest adequate categories, as Nietzsche first pointed out.[9] Tragedy contains them both, goes beyond both, illuminates both, but comes to no conclusion. Tragedy

[8] *Tragedy,* London, 1924. The extent of my indebtedness to this book, and to the other discussions of tragedy mentioned in this paper, is poorly indicated by such passing references as this. Since observations on tragedy and the theory of tragedy appear in innumerable discussions of particular authors, eras, and related critical problems, a complete list would be far too cumbersome. Among them would be, surely, the standard work of A. C. Bradley and Willard Farnham on Shakespearean tragedy; C. M. Bowra and Cedric Whitman on Sophocles; W. L. Courtney (*The Idea of Tragedy,* London, 1900); Maxwell Anderson, *The Essence of Tragedy,* Washington, 1939; Northrop Frye, "The Archetypes of Literature," *Kenyon Review,* Winter, 1951; Moody Prior, *The Language of Tragedy,* N.Y., 1947; and Herbert Weisinger, *Tragedy and the Paradox of the Fortunate Fall,* Michigan State College Press, 1953, which makes rich use of the archeological and mythographic studies of the origin of tragedy (Cornford, Harrison, Murray). I am indebted, also, to my colleague Laurence Michel for frequent conversations and helpful criticism.

[9] See also Reinhold Niebuhr, *Beyond Tragedy,* London, 1938.

could, it is true, be called pessimistic in its view of the evil in the universe as unremitting and irremediable, the blight man was born for, the necessary condition of existence. It is pessimistic, also, in its view of the overwhelming proportion of evil to good and in its awareness of the mystery of why this should be—the "unfathomable element" in which Ahab foundered. But it is optimistic in what might be called its vitalism, which is in some sense mystical, not earth-bound; in its faith in a cosmic good; in its vision, however fleeting, of a world in which all questions could be answered.

2. *Tragic man.* If the tragic form asserts a cosmos, some order behind the immediate disorder, what does it assert about the nature of man, other than that he is a being capable of cosmic affinities? What is tragic man as he lives and moves on this earth? Can he be distinguished meaningfully from the man of comedy, satire, epic or lyric? How does he differ from "pathetic man" or "religious man"? or from man as conceived by the materialistic psychologies? Tragic man shares some qualities, of course, with each of these. I shall stress differences in the appropriate contexts.

Like the cosmos which he views, tragic man is a paradox and a mystery. He is no child of God; yet he feels himself more than a child of earth. He is not the plaything of Fate, but he is not entirely free. He is "both creature and creator" (in Niebuhr's phrase)—"fatefully free and freely fated" (in George Schrader's). He recognizes "the fact of guilt" while cherishing the "dream of innocence" (Fiedler), and he never fully abandons either position. He is plagued by the ambiguity of his own nature and of the world he lives in. He is torn between the sense in common-sense (which is the norm of satire and rationalistic, or corrective, comedy) and his own uncommon sense. Aware of the just but irreconcilable claims within and without, he is conscious of the immorality of his own morality and suffers in the knowledge of his own recalcitrance.

The dynamic of this recalcitrance is pride. It sustains his belief, however humbled he may become by later experience, in his own freedom, in his innocence, and in his uncommon sense. Tragic man is man at his most prideful and independent, man glorying in his humanity. Tragic pride, like everything else about tragedy, is ambiguous; it can be tainted with arrogance and have its petty side; but it is not to be equated with sin or weakness. The Greeks feared it when it threatened the gods or slipped into arrogance, but they honoured it and even worshipped it in their heroes. It was the common folk, the chorus, who had no pride, or were "flawless." [10] The chorus invariably argue against pride, urging caution and moderation, because they know it leads to suffering; but tragedy as such does not prejudge it.

While many of these things, again, might be said of other than tragic man, it is in the peculiar nature of his suffering, and in his capacity for suffering and appropriating his suffering, that his distinguishing quality lies. For instance (to ring changes on the Cartesian formula), tragic man would not define himself, like the man of corrective comedy or satire, "I think, therefore I am"; nor like the man of achievement (epic): "I act, or conquer, therefore I am"; nor like the man of sensibility (lyric): "I feel, therefore I am"; nor like the religious man: "I believe, therefore I am." Although he has all these qualities (of thought, achievement, sensibility, and belief) in various form and degrees, the essence of his nature is brought out by suffering: "I suffer, I will to suffer, I learn by suffering; therefore I am." The classic statement, of course, is Aeschylus's: "Wisdom comes alone through suffering" (Lattimore's translation); perhaps the most radical is Dostoevski's: "Suffering is the sole origin of consciousness." [11]

This is not to say that only tragic man suffers or that he who suffers is tragic. Saints and martyrs suffer and learn by suffering; Odysseus suffered and learned; Dante suffered and learned on his journey with Virgil. But tragic man, I think, is distinguishable from these others in the nature of his suffering as conditioned by its source and locus, in its characteristic course and consequences (that is, the ultimate disaster and the "knowledge" it leads to), and in his intense preoccupation with his own suffering.

But to consider these matters in turn and to illustrate them briefly:

I have already suggested the main sources and locus of tragic man's suffering. He suffers because he is more than usually sensitive to the "terrible disrelations" he sees about him and experiences in himself. He is more than usually aware of the mighty opposites in the universe and in man, of the gulf between desire and fulfilment, between what is and what should be. This kind of suffering is suffering on a high level, beyond the reach of the immature or brutish, and for ever closed to the extreme optimist, the extreme pessimist,[12] or the merely indif-

[10] Cf. Arthur Miller, "Tragedy and the Common Man," *New York Times,* February 27th, 1949.

[11] *Notes from Underground,* tr. B. G. Guerney.

[12] Cf. William Van O'Connor, *Climates of Tragedy,* Baton Rouge, La., 1943.

ferent. It was Job on the ash-heap, the proto-type of tragic man, who was first struck by the incongruity between Jehovah's nature and His actions, between desert and reward in this life; and it was he who first asked, not so much for a release from physical suffering as a reasonable explanation of it. But above all, the source of tragic suffering is the sense, in the consciousness of tragic man, of simultaneous guilt and guiltlessness. Tillich called tragedy "a mixture of guilt and necessity." If tragic man could say, "I sinned, therefore I suffer" or "He (or They or God) sinned, therefore I suffer," his problem would be resolved, and the peculiar poignancy of his suffering would be removed. If he felt himself entirely free or entirely determined, he would cease to be tragic. But he is neither—he is, in short, a paradox and mystery, the "riddle of the world."

To draw further distinctions: The element of guilt in tragic suffering distinguishes it from the pathetic suffering of the guiltless and from the suffering of the sentimentalist's bleeding heart. On the other hand, tragic man's sense of fate, and of the mystery of fate, distinguishes his suffering from the suffering (which is little more than embarrassment) of the man of corrective comedy and satire. The suffering of the epic hero has little of the element of bafflement or enigma; it is not, characteristically, spiritual suffering. The Christian in his suffering can confess *total* guilt and look to the promise of redemption through grace.[13] The martyr seeks suffering, accepts it gladly, "glories in tribulation." Tragic man knows nothing of grace and never glories in his suffering. Although he may come to acquiesce in it partly and "learn" from it (a stage I shall discuss below), his characteristic mood is resentment and dogged endurance. He has not the stoic's patience, although this may be part of what he learns. Characteristically, he is restless, intense, probing and questioning the universe and his own soul (Job, Lear, Ahab). It is true that, from Greek tragedy to tragedy written in the Christian era (Shakespeare and beyond) emphasis shifts from the universe to the soul, from the cosmic to the psychological. But Prometheus had an inner life; Antigone, for all her composure, suffered an ultimate doubt; Oedipus suffered spiritually as he grew to understand the dark ambiguities in his own nature. And we should be mistaken if we tried to interpret the divine powers in the plays of Shakespeare simply as "allegorical symbols for psychological realities."[14]

[13] Cf. Karl Jaspers, *Tragedy is Not Enough,* tr. Reiche, Moore, Deutsch; Boston, 1952.

[14] Susan Taubes, *op. cit.,* p. 196.

Tragic man, then, placed in a universe of irreconcilables, acting in a situation in which he is both innocent and guilty, and peculiarly sensitive to the "cursèd spite" of his condition, suffers. What in the tragic view is the characteristic course of this suffering and what further aspects of tragic man are revealed by it? The tragic form develops, not only the partial outlines of a cosmology and a psychology, but of an ethic.

3. *Tragic man and society.* The tragic sufferer may now be viewed in his social and moral relationships. In the tragic world there are several alternatives. A man can default from the human condition—"Curse God and die"—and bring his suffering to an end: he can endure and be silent; he can turn cynic. Tragic man understands these alternatives, feels their attractions, but chooses a different way. Rising in his pride, he protests: he pits himself in some way against whatever, in the heavens above and in the earth beneath, seems to him to be wrong, oppressive, or personally thwarting. This is the hero's commitment, made early or late, but involving him necessarily in society and in action—with Prometheus and Antigone early, with Hamlet late. What to the orthodox mind would appear to be the wisdom or folly, the goodness or badness, of the commitment is not, in the beginning, the essence of the matter. In the first phase of his course of suffering, the hero's position may be anarchic, individual, romantic. Herein tragedy tests all norms—as, by contrast, satire,[15] comedy, or epic tend to confirm them. The commitment may even be expressed in what society knows as a crime, but, as with tragic pride (of which the commitment is in part the expression) tragedy does not prejudge it. Thus it is said that tragedy studies "the great offenders," and Dostoevski sought among criminals and outcasts for his greatest spiritual discoveries. But the commitment must grow in meaning to include the more-than-personal. Ultimately, and ideally, the tragic hero stands as universal man, speaking for all men. The tragic sufferer, emerging from his early stage of lament or rebellion (Job's opening speech; the first scenes of Prometheus; Lear's early bursts of temper), moves beyond the "intermittences" of his own heart and makes a "pact with the world that is unremitting and sealed." [16]

Since the commitment cannot lead in the direction of escape or compromise, it must involve head-on collision with the forces that would

[15] Cf. Maynard Mack, "The Muse of Satire," *Yale Review,* Spring, 1952.

[16] Wallace Fowlie, "Swann and Hamlet: A Note on the Contemporary Hero," *Partisan Review,* 1942.

oppress or frustrate. Conscious of the ambiguities without and within, which are the source of his peculiar suffering, tragic man accepts the conflict. It is horrible to do it, he says, but it is more horrible to leave it undone. He is now in the main phase of his suffering—the "passion." [17]

In his passion he differs from the rebel, who would merely smash; or the romantic hero, who is not conscious of guilt; or the epic hero, who deals with emergencies rather than dilemmas. Odysseus and Aeneas, to be sure, face moral problems, but they proceed in a clear ethical light. Their social norms are secure. But the tragic hero sees a sudden, unexpected evil at the heart of things that infects all things. His secure and settled world has gone wrong, and he must oppose his own ambiguous nature against what he loves. Doing so involves total risk, as the chorus and his friends remind him. He may brood and pause, like Hamlet, or he may proceed with Ahab's fury; but proceed he must.

He proceeds, suffers, and in his suffering "learns." This is the phase of "perception." Although it often culminates in a single apocalyptic scene, a moment of "recognition," as in *Oedipus* and *Othello,* it need not be separate in time from the passion phase. Rather, perception is all that can be summed up in the spiritual and moral change that the hero undergoes from first to last and in the similar change wrought by his actions or by his example in those about him.

For the hero, perception may involve an all-but-complete transformation in character, as with Lear and Oedipus; or a gradual development in poise and self-mastery (Prometheus, Hamlet); or the softening and humanizing of the hard outlines of a character like Antigone's. It may appear in the hero's change from moody isolation and self-pity to a sense of his sharing in the general human condition, of his responsibility for it and to it. This was one stage in Lear's pilgrimage ("I have ta'en too little care of this") and as far as Dostoevski's Dmitri Karamazov ever got. In all the manifestations of this perception there is an element of Hamlet's "readiness," of an acceptance of destiny that is not merely resignation. At its most luminous it is Lear's and Oedipus's hard-won humility and new understanding of love. It may transform or merely inform, but a change there must be.

[17] Cf. Francis Fergusson, *The Idea of a Theatre,* Princeton, N.J., 1949, chap. 1, "The Tragic Rhythm of Action." Fergusson translates Kenneth Burke's formulation "*Poiema, Pathema, Mathema*" into "Purpose, Passion, Perception." (See *A Grammar of Motives,* pp. 38ff.) Cf. also Susan Taubes, *op. cit.,* p. 199.

And it is more, of course, than merely a moral change, just as the hero's problem is always more than a moral one. His affair is still with the gods. In taking up arms against the ancient cosmic evil, he transcends the human situation, mediating between the human and the divine. It was Orestes's suffering that, in the end, made the heavens more just. In the defeat or death which is the usual lot of the tragic hero, he becomes a citizen of a larger city, still defiant but in a new mood, a "calm of mind," a partial acquiescence. Having at first resented his destiny, he has lived it out, found unexpected meanings in it, carried his case to a more-than-human tribunal. He sees his own destiny, and man's destiny, in its ultimate perspective.

But the perception which completes the tragic form is not dramatized solely through the hero's change, although his pilgrimage provides the traditional tragic structure.[18] The full nature and extent of the new vision is measured also by what happens to the other figures in the total symbolic situation—to the hero's antagonists (King Creon, Claudius, Iago); to his opposites (the trimmers and hangers-on, the Osrics); to his approximates (Ismene, Horatio, Kent, the Chorus). Some he moves, some do not change at all. But his suffering must make a difference somewhere outside himself. After Antigone's death the community (even Creon) re-forms around her; the "new acquist" at the end of *Samson Agonistes* is the common note, also, at the end of the Shakespearean tragedies. For the lookers-on there is no sudden rending of the veil of clay, no triumphant assertion of The Moral Order. There has been suffering and disaster, ultimate and irredeemable loss, and there is promise of more to come. But all who are in-

[18] Indeed, it has been pointed out that, in an age when the symbol of the hero as the dominating centre of the play seems to have lost its validity with artist and audience, the role is taken over by the artist himself, who is his own tragic hero. That is, "perception" is conveyed more generally, in the total movement of the piece and through all the parts. The "pact with the world" and the suffering are not objectified in a hero's ordeal but seem peculiarly the author's. This quality has been noted in Joyce's *Ulysses*; Berdiaev saw it in Dostoevski; Hardy, Conrad, Faulkner are examples that come to mind. At any rate, the distinction may be useful in determining matters of tone, although it is not clear cut, as distinctions in tone seldom are. But it is one way of pointing to the difference between the tragic tone and the Olympian distance of Meredithian comedy, the harmony of the final phase of Dantesque comedy, or the ironic detachment of satire. Nietzsche spoke of the difference between the Dionysian (or tragic) artist and "the poet of the dramatized epos . . . the calm, unmoved embodiment of Contemplation, whose wide eyes see the picture before them." (*Birth of Tragedy* in *Works,* ed. O. Levy, Edinburgh and London, 1909, III, p. 96.)

volved have been witness to new revelations about human existence, the evil of evil and the goodness of good. They are more "ready." The same old paradoxes and ambiguities remain, but for the moment they are transcended in the higher vision.

Tragedy and the Tragic Vision

MURRAY KRIEGER

> If there were no eternal consciousness in a man, if at the foundation of all there lay only a wildly seething power which writhing with obscure passions produced everything that is great and everything that is insignificant, if a bottomless void never satiated lay hidden beneath all—what then would life be but despair?
>
> Soren Kierkegaard, *Fear and Trembling*

Now of course the tragic is not the only vision projected by our serious literature and philosophy, nor is it necessarily the profoundest vision. But it is surely the most spectacular, and the most expressive of the crisis-mentality of our time. Consequently, it has won for those works obsessed with it the excited attention of our most stimulating critical minds. Perhaps in their excitement over the individual work they have neglected to define in general terms what this vision is—which is probably as it ought to be with the practicing critic. In any case there does not seem to be a systematic effort to say what is meant by the phrase and what, given this meaning, it has meant to recent writing.

It must be granted that, as with all terms of this kind, any meaning imposed upon it must be an arbitrary one that may or may not command agreement. But, agreed upon or not, it is valuable critically as it throws a consistently clear albeit diffuse light upon a broad enough and deep enough area in our literature. I propose here to create for the term a tentative definition that I have found most illuminating of modern literature and the modern mind, and in the balance of this volume to use it to conduct exploratory operations on a certain few novels of the last hundred or so years in order to demonstrate its incisive powers. Since I have some idea about where I shall come out, I must admit that my explorations will have all too much direction to

From *The Tragic Vision* by Murray Krieger, pp. 1-21. This essay is a slightly altered version of an article of the same title that appeared in *The Kenyon Review*, Vol. XX, 1958, pp. 281-99. Reprinted by permission of the author and Holt, Rinehart and Winston, Inc., Publishers.

them and that consequently they will somewhat mislead us about the total reality of the works in the interest of showing the widespread relevance of my definition. By way of defense I can plead only that the definition was empirical in its origin and that it followed my probings into the individual novels rather than the other way round; in other words, that the meaning I am trying to create for the term is one that in my reading of these novels I feel that I have discovered.

It is surely needless to add that the act of enclosing a number of literary works within the limits of a given definition hardly passes any judgment upon works on either side of the boundary. For a work not to qualify as an example of the tragic vision is hardly a mark against it. Indeed, in the eyes of many, it may be quite the contrary. Of course, the meaning I want to establish for the tragic vision—indeed, any that would be worth very much—will be far more restrictive than the general lay usage of "tragedy" or "the tragic," which somehow broadens out to synonymity with catastrophe, the sorrowful, that which stems from or leads to "pessimism." But how, if we limit ourselves to technical literary definition, can we find for the tragic any meaning beyond that of Aristotle? The answer is, by moving from formalistic aesthetics to what I would term "thematics." [1]

Thus it becomes necessary first to determine the extent to which we want the meaning of "the tragic vision" entangled with that of "tragedy," surely a term well enough defined in our critical tradition. The most obvious difference I would mark between the two is also a crucial one: "tragedy" refers to an object's literary form, "the tragic vision" to a subject's psychology, his view and version of reality. It is more than a difference between two extant approaches to the tragic. Rather, the second has usurped the very possibility of the first after having been born side by side with it. Perhaps it would be more accurate to say that the tragic vision was born *in*side tragedy, as a part of it: as a possession of the tragic hero, the vision was a reflection in the realm of thematics of the fully fashioned aesthetic totality which was tragedy. But fearful and even demoniac in its revelations, the vision needed the ultimate soothing power of the aesthetic form which contained it—of tragedy itself—in order to preserve for the world a sanity which the vision itself denied.

It is for these reasons that the reader who as a modern is obsessed with notions of the tragic ought in a way to find himself disappointed on turning for the first time to Aristotle's celebrated definition in the

[1] This is a term to which considerable discussion is devoted in my final chapter.

Poetics. We have been so accustomed to doing this treatise deference —and rightfully so from a formalistic point of view—that we can no longer approach it freshly and feel the letdown that should be ours as we glance over its superficial formal prescriptions that are to pass as a description of so sacred and reverenced a literary genre. All this about magnitude and completeness and catharsis—are these to do justice to the profound complex of metaphysical and psychological forces which the tragic unleashes? Or so, at least, we ought as moderns to say superciliously. But probably we should have expected no more than this from the *Poetics*. Perhaps it was not for the Greek theoretical consciousness—even in as late a representative as Aristotle—to be as self-consciously aware of the disturbing implications of the tragic mentality as it was of the formal requirements which transcended, or rather absorbed, this mentality and restored order to the universe threatened by it.

The cathartic principle itself, in maintaining that pity and fear are not merely to be aroused but to be purged, is evidence of the need in tragedy to have dissonance exploded, leaving only the serenity of harmony behind. As has often been noted, the peace of cosmic reconciliation is most explicitly insisted upon in the concluding portion of the *Oresteia*—the sublime *Eumenides*—or in the magnificent end of Oedipus' story at *Colonus*. Here is the restorative spirit of superhuman purgation at its most refined. Even in the less exceptional tragedies which do not conclude in such thorough and profound tranquillity—in those, that is, which end more "tragically" in the lay sense—there is often the touch of transcendent grace which saves the cosmos for us in the midst of the irrevocable devastation of human resources. It may, on rare and splendid occasions, be the pure shining thing of *Lear;* it may more often be little more than the matter-of-fact re-establishment of political order—an order, however, that reflects and is sanctioned by the cosmic order—which may be one of the reasons that it is so helpful to have tragedy concern itself with the fortunes of ruling princes.

But even if there were none of these, so long as tragedy remained a defined literary form, the fearsome chaotic necessities of the tragic vision would have to surrender finally to the higher unity which contained them. It is perhaps in this sense that we can speak of the formally sustained literary work ultimately coming to terms with itself. And from the standpoint of the audience—or at least the trained and sophisticated audience—even if there were no thematic elements of release for the passions aroused by the tragic performers, the disciplining and restricting demands upon aesthetic contemplation made by the rounded aesthetic whole would effect the catharsis demanded by Aristotle. The purging of dangerously aroused emotions, following as it does upon the satisfaction, the soothing grace, bestowed upon wayward materials by aesthetic completeness, uses form to overcome the threat of these materials and, consequently, these emotions. This roundedness, this completeness, carrying "aesthetic distance" with it as it brings us the assurances of form, presents us its formal order as a token, a security—something given in hand—to guarantee the cosmic order beyond the turbulence it has conquered. Thus it is that the cathartic principle *is* ultimately a purely formalistic one, even as tragedy, despite its foreboding rumblings, can remain a force for affirmation through its formal powers alone. Thus it is too that in the *Poetics* Aristotle rightly limits himself to formal considerations, leaving to later and less solvent generations the thematic implications of the vision which, so long as it is aesthetically framed in tragedy, is denied in its very assertion.

It is finally Hegel who, after many centuries during which no radically new approaches are made to tragedy—or at least none that are relevant to my interests here—takes up the task of explaining tragedy and catharsis in the thematic terms that Aristotle could afford to take for granted. Although it must be conceded that Hegel's analysis is clearly indebted to his metaphysic and his general philosophic method and although he does not concern himself with purely formal considerations, it is just this notion of reconciliation, of a final uniting or reuniting, that he emphasizes as the conclusive power of tragedy.[2] His insistence on the absoluteness, the wholeness, the indivisibility of what A. C. Bradley translates as "the ethical substance" is clue to Hegel's attempt to create a metaphysical equivalent for the unity of the Greek world—the unity which, translated into form, allowed tragedy to overcome the heretical defiance of its hero.

For Hegel the *hamartia* that defines the tragic hero always arises from his exclusive identification with a single moral claim, a claim which, however just within its own sphere, is, from the view of a total morality—that is, the ethical substance—merely partial, a too-assertive particular. Thus the hero's vision is necessarily destructive of

[2] For Hegel on tragedy, see his *The Philosophy of Fine Art,* trans. F. P. B. Osmaston (London, 1920), I, 272-313; II, 213-215; IV, 295-303, 308-326, 330-342. A. C. Bradley's is of course a brilliantly succinct and, by now, a classical summary of the Hegelian view ("Hegel's Theory of Tragedy," *Oxford Lectures on Poetry* [London, 1909], pp. 69-95).

the unity of the moral world, threatening with its monomaniac tendencies to produce an anarchy of unsupported metonymic leaps. And in defense of its absolute claims, the ethical substance must justly assert its oneness by ensuring the defeat of the hero whose nature it is, "at once his greatness and his doom, that he knows no shrinking or half-heartedness, but identifies himself wholly with the power that moves him, and will admit the justification of no other power." [3]

But this assertion of the ultimate unity of the moral order is what for Hegel leaves Greek tragedy with a final affirmation that transcends the carnage, "an aspect of reconciliation" that authoritatively seals the moral universe for even the most harshly devastated of its sacrificial victims, the bearers of the tragic vision. Here is a significant attempt to account thematically for the cathartic principle, to bring tragedy—for all its deadly turbulence—to the very threshold of a Wordsworthian "tranquil restoration." And who is to say that this restoration is not part of what may seem to be implied by the Aristotelian concept of *dénouement*—a falling action which does not usually stop with the hero's final destruction but leads to a quiet beyond the grave: to a resettling of things in acceptance of this destruction?

Of course it is this final inhibition of the tragic vision, this imposition of formal and moral order upon that which threatens it, that allows these dramas to be properly called classical in the best sense. And when the embracing frame is lost, the romantic tragic vision bursts forth unencumbered—often in merely melodramatic splendor—in no longer reconcilable defiance of traditional aesthetic as well as ethical order. Thus it may seem that Hegel, in assuming the virtues of the Greek world to be those of his own philosophic construct, is hardly representative of the self-conscious modernism that has dominated the last century and a half of our psychological history; the modernism that is characterized by fragmentation rather than by the ever-uniting synthesis which Hegel tried valiantly, if vainly, to impose upon it as its salvation. Can his or can any all-resolving "ethical substance" have validity for us as an absolute and claim our allegiance accordingly? Can it now claim the all-commanding universality that justly, though ruthlessly, imposes itself on the subversive tragic hero in its midst? Or is the tragic hero, as modern, fulfilling a proper human function and even a proper human obligation in standing with his integrity as an individual outside the universal? Which is another way of suggesting that whatever universals we may be left with do not deserve the obedi-

[3] Bradley, p. 72.

ence of the most daring of us. Hegel created a system whose universals, like those of the Greek world or even of the Elizabethan world as we find it reflected in Shakespeare, have a metaphysical sanction; whose social and political institutions have a cosmic sanction. How accurate an account is this of the shabby, Babbitt-like arbitrary things that must —if anything does—pass with our world as universals, given our secularized, hand-to-mouth versions of the claims of religion, of politics, of social morality? Surely the absolute is not to be found immanently within such as these. Justice, then, has passed from the universal to the rebellious individual; accordingly, our appropriate spokesman on matters relating the individual to the universal and the absolute is not the anachronistic system builder, Hegel, but that heterodox and unprofessional wrecker of the Hegelian universe, Soren Kierkegaard.

> Faith is precisely this paradox, that the individual as the particular is higher than the universal, is justified over against it, is not subordinate but superior—yet in such a way, be it observed, that it is the particular individual who, after he has been subordinated as the particular to the universal, now through the universal becomes the individual who as the particular is superior to the universal, for the fact that the individual as the particular stands in an absolute relation to the absolute.[4]

At what is for Kierkegaard the most crucial moment of man's existence—the moment of the leap to faith—the absolute is attainable only through the individual, the particular, the purely personal. It is denied to the universal. Here, unhappily enough perhaps, is the answer of modernism's "isolato" to the Hegelian attempt to restore the union of men within a congenial universe that sanctioned, indeed commanded, and fixed its divine blessing upon, this union. For Kierkegaard, the ultimate act—the act of faith—cannot be mediated, since only universals can mediate. Consequently, the paradox of faith is "inaccessible to thought" and cannot be verbally communicated, both thought and language—like reason, on which they largely depend—necessarily expressing universals. Further, it is the inaccessibility of faith to mediation that makes the Abraham who intended to sacrifice Isaac either a murderer or a "true knight of faith"—in my terminology, either a tragic visionary[5] or a religious visionary—but *not* the sacrificer

[4] *Fear and Trembling,* by Soren Kierkegaard, trans. Walter Lowrie (Princeton, N.J.: Princeton University Press, 1941), p. 82.

[5] In light of the shriveling of the tragic concept in the modern world and the reduction of a total view to the psychology of the protagonist, I believe that this protagonist is now more appropriately designated "tragic visionary" than he is "tragic hero."

of his individual self to the universal expressed in moral law. The latter individual would be the highest form of ethical man but, for Kierkegaard, something less than either visionary. And Kierkegaard's Abraham, whichever visionary he may be, repudiates the universal. Thus the "immediacy" of either the tragic or the religious vision eliminates the universal as a possible resting place for the errant, as a possible justification of what he has so privately dared to will. And we can never be sure which of the two visions he carries. Indeed, now beyond reason, how can he himself claim certainty? For the religious vision would be too easy for Kierkegaard if one could *know* its authenticity.

The categories which Kierkegaard can help us impose provide our insecure world with alternatives to the way of Greek tragedy as it is interpreted by Nietzsche as well as by Hegel. While Nietzsche is, like Kierkegaard, an unhappy epitome of modern man, an alienated creature who is close to being himself a tragic visionary, he is like Hegel in wistfully finding and admiring in early tragedy the elements of reconciliation that give order to elements of chaotic conflict. Nietzsche sees united in tragedy the Apollonian and Dionysian motives, appropriately named by him for their respective gods: the one the dreamlike, sublime, and gracefully measured order of the light principle, in the highest sense the civilizing principle; the other the primordial, ogiastic release of the natural principle—the "underground" reality probably related to Jung's "racial unconscious" or to Freud's "id"—the barbarizing principle.[6] Nietzsche sees these motives as akin to the forces represented by the creative and yet restrained Olympians and by the chaos-producing Titans, except, of course, that instead of the unreconcilable warfare between Olympians and Titans there is in Greek culture a perfect blending of the Apollonian and the Dionysian.

> The Greek knew and felt the terror and horror of existence. That he might endure this terror at all, he had to interpose between himself and life the radiant dream-birth of the Olympians. . . . out of the original Titan thearchy of terror the Olympian thearchy of joy gradually evolved through the Apollonian impulse towards beauty. . . . How else could this people, so sensitive, so vehement in its desires, so singularly constituted for *suffering*, how could they have endured existence, if it had not been revealed to them in their gods, surrounded with a higher glory?

[6] For this entire discussion, see "The Birth of Tragedy," trans. C. P. Fadiman, *The Philosophy of Nietzsche* (New York: Modern Library, n.d.), especially pp. 951-969, 992-1017.

Thus the Apollonian can so transform Dionysian terror "that lamentation itself becomes a song of praise."

Here is another thematic rendering of the principle of catharsis. But in order to make the formula work properly, both motives have to be maintained and maintained in equal strength. The Dionysian must be there for the Apollonian to transform, so that Apollonian radiance can retain its brilliance only by continually illuminating the Dionysian abyss. But it is an abyss which must not be denied, indeed must be acknowledged for what it is. Without the Dionysian, the Apollonian would seem to reflect a shallow, unearned optimism, a misreading of life that leaves the inescapable terror out of it. Thus Nietzsche can scorn the bland interpretations of "the serious and significant idea of Greek cheerfulness": "no matter where we turn at the present time we encounter the false notion that this cheerfulness results from a state of unendangered comfort." For the Apollonian cannot sustain itself in isolation; it can exist only in counterposition to the Dionysian. Otherwise it becomes perverted—as Nietzsche tells us it was perverted through Euripides—into the merely "Socratic," that moralistic denier of the Dionysian and consequently the destroyer of tragedy.

But what if we should find the Dionysian without the Apollonian? Here we would have life unalleviated, endlessly and unendurably dangerous, finally destructive and self-destructive—in short, the demoniacal. In effect it would be like tragedy without that moment in which the play comes round and the cosmos is saved and returned to us intact. It would be, in other words, the tragic vision wandering free of its capacious home in tragedy. The therapy produced by catharsis, which allowed the subversive elements to be healthily exposed and aesthetically overcome, would no longer be available. And the alienated members, now unchallenged, would be free to turn inward upon themselves to nourish their indignation in the dark underground. Nietzsche himself has told us:

> The tradition is undisputed that Greek tragedy in its earliest form had for its sole theme the sufferings of Dionysus, and that for a long time the only stage-hero was simply Dionysus himself . . . until Euripides, Dionysus never once ceased to be the tragic hero . . . in fact all the celebrated figures of the Greek Stage—Prometheus, Oedipus, etc.—are but masks of this original hero, Dionysus.

But picture a world into which Dionysus cannot be reabsorbed by way of the Apollonian with its final assertion of Greek "cheerfulness" and aesthetic form, a world in which the Appollonian and Dionysian—

long since torn asunder—must live in a lasting separation that causes each to pervert its nature, the Apollonian becoming the superficial worship of happiness and the Dionysian the abandoned worship of demonism. Our modern tragic vision is the Dionysian vision still, except that the visionary is now utterly lost, since there is no cosmic order to allow a return to the world for him who has dared stray beyond.

The Kierkegaardian spirit would rather characterize the tragic vision as "despair," perhaps finally much the same thing. It is despair which for Kierkegaard is both the most wretched and the most hopeful stage of man's sub-Christian existence. With some interpolation and considerable simplification on my part, the phenomenological pattern one may draw from Kierkegaard for the tragic visionary may be seen as something like the following sketch.[7] A man lives his day-to-day existence below the religious level, either "aesthetically," as an amoral or submoral hedonist, or "ethically," by easily subscribing, consciously or unconsciously, but for the most part automatically, to that hierarchy of moral values which enables him comfortably to function. If he is a self-conscious moralist, he is concerned with the discovery of order in apparent disorder; concerned, that is, with universal principles, but principles that are discoverable in and referable to the world of human relations.

While the ethical level is certainly an advance over the mindless complacency in the midst of an unperceived chaos found on Kierkegaard's "aesthetic" [8] level, nevertheless this ethical level, because it sees values—and the order constructed in terms of values—as immanent rather than as transcendent, must itself remain pragmatic in its dictates for action. The orderly and abstract principles, bounded by the

[7] In the interest of accuracy it must be acknowledged that Kierkegaard himself explicitly defines what he calls the tragic hero very differently from the way I am attributing to his view here. In *Fear and Trembling* he specifically claims that "the tragic hero still remains within the ethical." He sees the tragic hero as allowing himself to be embraced by the universal, his most cherished interests to be sacrificed to it. Perhaps here, as in so many other instances, Kierkegaard finds himself borrowing from the very Hegelianism he is bent on destroying. I believe that, as part of his dissatisfaction with the aesthetic in general, he never took this matter of the tragic as seriously as he might have taken it, that he never realized the revolutionary treatment of it that is promised by his other philosophic claims. It is thus, I hope, in the Kierkegaardian spirit, that I use Kierkegaard to support my own claims about the tragic though they run counter to his own occasional declarations.

[8] Whenever I use this term in the very special way of Kierkegaard I shall set it in quotation marks. Where it appears without them, it is being used in its common sense that pertains primarily to works of art and to our proper and limited responses to them as art.

uses of this world and resting on rationality, much resist the paradox or absurdity which for Kierkegaard characterizes the immediacy and subjectivity of Christian consciousness. Thus finally common-sense pragmatism must inhere in the ethical level.[9] And our ethical man, assuming the validity of his abstract and universal principles inasmuch as they are conducive to order, can make decisions cleanly, can act in accordance with these principles—as if they were the absolute—since they blink the possible existence of a true moral dilemma characterized by endless ambiguity. This is the farthest reach of Hegelian man.

But our man can undergo a cosmic "shock": he can one day, to use Kafka's metaphor, wake up and find himself irrevocably arrested "without having done anything wrong." Or an Ahab, living until then by the proper laws of seamanship, can one day lose his leg to the leviathan; a Lord Jim, living until then by a schoolboy's code of honor, can one day be paralyzed into inaction and be made to play the coward's role. Melville's Pierre, having dedicated himself at all costs to absolute righteousness, can discover in his righteousness a lust that has led to incest; Conrad's Kurtz, having dedicated himself through altruism to a missionary zeal, can discover in his zeal a worship of self and of gold that has led to blood sacrifice. Perhaps this shattering seizure is precisely what ethical man has had coming for assuming, as fallible individual, his identification with an ethical absolute. For the ethical is, by definition, the universal. And, however well meaning, the individual may very well be doomed to pervert the absolute he claims to represent, since he comes to it as individual and particular, and thus as unsanctioned.

In any case, with the shock our man is jarred loose. For "aesthetic"

[9] It is here, in his insistence that religion has dimensions beyond morality, that Kierkegaard strikes at the roots of that naturalistic humanism which would identify the two. Of course one may claim that Kierkegaard rather overdoes their separation since for him, it seems, the one (religion) can begin only where the other (morality) leaves off. I must, however, make it clear that, whenever speaking here of Kierkegaard's concept of religion, I mean only his version of Christianity. It must be conceded that in many places he refers to a pre-Christian, almost naturalistic religion, one in which the absolute is still immanent in the universal and which, consequently, still falls within the ethical. But if this stoical kind of religion can produce "the knight of infinite resignation," in its security it of course cannot begin to reach toward "the true knight of faith," who is rather a product of the loneliness and daring, the absurdity and subjectivity of Christian consciousness. It is only his notion of Christianity—defiant as it is of the ethical—to which Kierkegaard attributes absolute value, so that, to simplify matters, I have felt justified in speaking of it informally as his notion of religion in general, to the neglect of his other, inferior kind of religion.

man the oblivious evasions of hedonic existence will of course no longer do. And ethical man, confronted by a moral contradiction which resists the elimination of either pole as well as the synthesis of both, finds suddenly that the neatly ordered and easily enacted worldly rights and wrongs of his ethical assumptions are utterly inadequate to the data of his moral experience. Unless he yields to "infinite resignation" by blindly, if courageously, sacrificing himself to the implacable demands of ethical absoluteness—thus at all costs still remaining Hegelian man[10]—he must deny its authority forever. And then, hopelessly adrift from his or any other moorings, he can float into will-lessness and thus abdicate from tragic heroism, or he can surge toward the demoniac. If his rebellion has rendered him unfit for society and its necessary universals—its laws—it is because, at whatever price, he has seen beyond them. If his end, as tragic, must be condemned even as it is pitied by the trim categories of worldly morality, he may, prideful as he is, take further pride in the fact that he has defiantly looked upon those insoluble cosmic antinomies which have dictated his fall.

Someone like Conrad's Marlow, however—the sensible even if sensitive man—must, at whatever cost to his pride and his vision, finally rest in the ethical level, however sympathetic he may be to those who have renounced it to move into the realm of the tragic. Who is to say whether it is out of a "failure of nerve" or out of a special strength flowing from a profoundly tranquil vision, hardly known to us since the Greeks, that he has resisted the unmitigated tragic? It depends, very likely, on whether our view is Kierkegaard's or that of a less austere, less Protestant authority; on whether ours is the tragic vision or the classic vision.

On the other hand, our excommunicated ethical man, realizing the complete futility of human existence, cannot find a relationship with anything beyond it. His permanent forsaking of the universal seems to forbid it. This, the essence of the tragic vision, is "the sickness unto death," despair. It is the stage induced by the shock; the stage which, beyond the "aesthetic" and the ethical, yet falls short of Kierkegaard's version of the Christian. An advance over the first two, it is yet much more treacherous and, if one remains in it continually, far more miserable. If one can attain a break-through—a bravely irrational one unmediated by universals—he can reach the glories of transcendence; if

[10] This is in effect Kierkegaard's own definition of the tragic hero. He allows him to go no further; and this admission on my part indicates how far beyond him I have without authorization moved using his tools.

he fails, he must live in the contemplation of nothingness. Or, to put it more specifically, at best he can become a Kierkegaard, if we grant that Kierkegaard ever, or for very long, accomplished the leap of faith; if not, he must remain in the torments of the Zarathustrian Nietzsche or of a more consistent Heidegger who constantly and unblinkingly dares encounter the nothingness that has capriciously hurled him into momentary existence. But he can never again rest in the self-deceptions of our John Deweys: those of our insistent naturalists who, for all the hardheadedness of their religious disbelief, are yet naively optimistic believers in a structured social morality and in social progress. These are, from the Kierkegaardian standpoint, the men of little heart; those who, evading the atheist's existential obligation to confront nothingness and its frighteningly empty consequences, construct elaborate rational structures based on nothing else: who whistle in the dark as if all were light.

One may prefer to say that it represents a supreme act of human courage to create meaningful communal structures of value on a substructure of acknowledged nothingness. Perhaps, as humanists say, man's creating God *is* a more sublime act than God's creating man. Perhaps. But the honest existentialist—anxious to confront his ontological status—would see the naturalist's structure in the void as an evasive act of bravado, not a closing act of bravery.

In the Kierkegaardian universe, then, there are two authentic visions—those I have termed the tragic and the religious—that can be earned through crisis by being forged in what Dostoevsky spoke of as the "great furnace of doubt." The other I have referred to is in this sense an illusory one. For the cheerfully naturalistic vision, which, pampering its security, denies itself nothing despite the fearsome implications of its own metaphysical denials, which existentially shirks the void it must rationally insist upon, is a pre-crisis vision, an illusion of ethical man demanded by his comfort, but one the stricken man can no longer afford. Like Kurtz, the tragic visionary may at the critical moment search within and find himself "hollow at the core," but only because he has suddenly been seized from without by the hollowness of his moral universe, whose structure and meaning have until then sustained him. What the shock reveals to its victim—the existential absurdity of the moral life—explodes the meaning of the moral life, its immanent god and ground. And there can be no post-crisis meaning and god except in defiance of reason, in acknowledgment of the impossibly paradoxical nature of moral existence. But this is to go beyond the despair that defines the tragic visionary and to make the leap to the transcendent subjectivity of the only kind of religious vision that the Kierkegaardian Protestant world leaves to the stricken.[11]

On the other hand, the tragic visionary, in taking the alternative of defiance and seizing upon nothingness, is alone bold enough to take the existential consequences of his godlessness; and he takes them with pride, the very *hybris* that, in its sinfulness, moved him to godlessness rather than to transcendence. But he does not, like the naturalist, try to play both sides of the street to earn the prize of an ungrounded something: a world philosophically negated which is somehow made to yield the existential ease that would come if there were a meaning and purpose to be grasped. Sick of his pre-crisis delusion, the tragic visionary is God's angry man who will take only the real thing. He will refuse any longer to fool himself with the comfortable communal halfway houses of good works as a substitute for the absolute dedication of a religious faith which his inherited skepticism, issuing its curse, has denied him.

Of course, from a less severely Protestant point of view, other "authentic" visions would be sanctioned. One that concerned me earlier is what I called the classic vision, a vision that is of the world without being crass, that is universal and conducive to order without optimistically thinning moral reality as the superficially ethical man would. This vision is the all-embracing one of an older world and an older order.

[11] Although this issue may not seem germane to a discussion of the tragic vision, it is worth adding—in order to expose another favorite illusion of our naturalistic and anti-existential tradition—that the religious vision described here cannot in fairness be reduced to any so-called "failure of nerve." This phrase the Kierkegaardian would reserve for the ethical man who flees the impact of the shock, for the naturalist himself. The shock may indeed cause our nerves to quake, but they fail only with the failure of our inner strength to manage, from the depths of despair, the awesome leap that makes "the true knight of faith"—no easy accomplishment and hardly a soothing one. The earned religious vision must not be cheapened. It is a vision that runs quite counter to that implied by the Philistine claim that there were "no atheists on Bataan." No matter how devout the final protestations of these doomed souls, these protestations were all simply too comforting in their urgency, from the Kierkegaardian point of view, to have a claim to religious authenticity. Thus Kierkegaard comments on people who want to make an easy, escapist thing of faith:

> . . . these caricatures of faith are part and parcel of life's wretchedness, and the infinite resignation has already consigned them to infinite contempt. . . . They would suck worldly wisdom out of the paradox. Perhaps one or another may succeed in that, for our age is not willing to stop with faith, with its miracle of turning water into wine, it goes further, it turns wine into water. (*Fear and Trembling*, p. 50.)

It is what I have tried to talk about in discussing the formal and thematic triumph of tragedy over the errant tragic vision it contained within it. It is as if the security of the older order wanted to test the profundity of its assurances, its capacity to account for the whole of human experience, and thus bred within itself the tragic vision as its *agent provocateur*. And by having the rebellion incarnate in the tragic visionary finally succumb to a higher order which absorbs but never denies the "destructive element," by purifying itself through the cathartic principle, tragedy is asserting the argument a fortiori for the affirmation of its humanistic and yet superhumanistic values. Consequently, it can witness all that befalls its hero without sharing in his disavowal of the meaning of our moral life; without denying, with him, the sensibleness of the universe and of life despite the explosive terrors they can hold in store.

But human possibilities, reduced as they are by disintegrations within the world that produced a Kierkegaard as its spokesman, no longer can reach to so inclusive a vision. If the only appeal to universals, to order, is pre-religious as well as pre-tragic, then the path of the religious visionary is as solitary as the tragic visionary's. And the ethical once shattered, there is no higher return to community—although, of course, for the less daring there may always be a retreat. The tragic vision remains what it was, but it can no longer be made through tragedy to yield to an order and a shared religious vision. The ultimately absorbent power of tragedy, symbolic of the earned affirmation of universals, is gone, with the result that the solitary visionary is left unchallenged, except by the threats of uncomprehending and unsympathizing destruction at the hands of aroused ethical righteousness, the arm of social practicality. This is hardly the all-deserving antagonist the tragic vision once had, nor is it one that can command a satisfying aesthetic completeness any more than it can a moral-religious unity. Instead, in the Kierkegaardian universe, we now find for the aware and authentic existent an unresolvable disjunctive: either the way of nothingness or the way of transcendence, but both equally the way of utter solitude. The universals which must damn him have been left behind.

It is perhaps for these reasons that recent literature expressing an earned religious vision is hard to come by. For this kind of religious vision is primarily characterized by the fact that it cannot be shared. Equally subjectve, the tragic as the demoniac vision can at least be dramatized by being contrasted to the ethical with which it is at war and which, in defense of society, must seek to punish it—for good reasons and for bad. We can be shown the ambiguous nature of the values at stake in this struggle: the need for the insights provided by the tragic to advance our understanding beyond the unaccommodating caution of social necessity as institutionalized in the ethical; and yet the need to strike out at the visionary, to cling to the props society provides, at whatever cost to insight, since, man being a social animal, his struggle through daily drudgeries is a crucial and ordering activity that must not be threatened.

To sustain a balance and, consequently, an aesthetic tension between these antagonists, the author must resist identifying himself too thoroughly either with the tragic visionary or with the representative of the ethical. If he becomes one with his ethical man, he must dismiss the tragic realm too summarily, without granting its power—however costly—of revealing the full density of moral experience and the shallowness of the reasonable order it has been forced to cast off. And he must sell the vision short as vision, however quick he is to see it as tragic, or anyway as doomed, if not as at worst merely execrable or at best pathetic. Or if, on the other hand, the author becomes one with his tragic visionary, he so cuts himself off from man's communal need that, in surrendering to moral chaos, he surrenders also the only possibility left him to impose aesthetic form. Further, he shows himself to be too sure of the vision to acknowledge it as really tragic, however quick he is—in contrast to our too ethical author—to grant its value as a vision. Only within the balance, and the mutual qualifications it provides, can the vision be maintained both as tragic and as a vision worthy of our concern and our wonder. Thus, at the one extreme, in *Heart of Darkness,* for example, Conrad, through his alter ego Marlow, rejects Kurtz—indeed is utterly offended by the man—only in continual acknowledgment that his rebellion against decency, however odious, renders him in some way superior even to Marlow. And, at the other extreme, close as Gide comes to embracing the reckless passions of his hero in *The Immoralist,* the classical artist in him maintains enough distance to reveal to us honestly, and even with some condemnation, their destructive and self-destructive consequnces.

Even with the ethical and the tragic held in such balance, however, the ethical may seem finally to be treated superciliously and even as at least half blind to what really is going on. And since the tragic is from the ethical standpoint so dangerously evil, there would seem to be a need for some level beyond the ethical from which the tragic visionary would be judged absolutely—a level which would include his insight and with it soar beyond a parochial pragmatism, but one which would have passed beyond the rage of rebellion to a final, perhaps otherworldly affirmation. But this is to call once again for what we no longer have—for the transformations that only tragedy can perform. For how are we now to distinguish outwardly between the religious and the tragic, between the angelic and the demoniac, when both equally transgress the ethical and the universal? As Kierkegaard in such brilliant detail asks, how shall we tell the Abraham among us from the self-deceived, maddened infanticide? To stop short of the religious insight is of course to rest in demonism; yet to leap to the religious vision, itself a perilous undertaking, is not to deny the temporal and, of course, the dramatic validity of the tragic. In neither instance is a retreat to the ethical possible. And the balance of necessities between the tragic and the ethical must continue as the primary mode of dramatic conflict, with the inherent weaknesses of each—the moral failing of the one and the visionary failing of the other—poised against each other to create the unresolvable tension that must now replace tragedy's more sublime catharsis as the principle of aesthetic control.

By now I hope I have clarified the sense in which I have been speaking of the unrelieved tragic vision as a modern vision, which is to claim also that it is a Protestant vision and, in an obvious sense, a romantic vision. Further, in its seizing upon the particular and its denial of any totality it is an heretical vision; and in its defiance of all rational moral order it is a demoniac vision. Finally, in a very special sense it is a casuistic vision; and it is this characteristic, perhaps, that makes it especially accessible to literary portrayal. The tragic vision, a product of crisis and of shock, is an expression of man only in an extreme situation, never in a normal or routine one. Literature dealing with it frequently dwells on the exceptional man; and when it does choose a normal man it does so only to convert him, by way of the extremity he lives through, into the exceptional man. The tragic vision is, by my definition, a vision of extreme cases, a distillate of the rebellion, the godlessness which, once induced by crisis, purifies itself by rejecting all palliatives. And the tragic visionary, by the stark austerity of his ontological position and of his dramatic position in the fable, is the extremist who—despite his rich intermingling with the stuff of experience—finds himself transformed from character to parable.

The literary obsession with extremity, with the exceptional, may represent an attempt at realism ultimately more sincere and more authentic than the cultivation of the norm, of what Lionel Trilling celebrates as "the common routine." If one wishes to assume the Kierkegaardian version of the human predicament, he will insist that it does and that at all times it has represented the only authentic attempt at realism. Even without Kierkegaardian psychoanalysis, however, we must admit that, at least in our time, driven as it is by crises and "arrests" and blind as it is to the healing power and saving grace of tragedy, the tragic has come, however unfortunately, to loom as a necessary vision and—or so it seems to the sadder of us—as one that can be neither reduced nor absorbed. Or is it, perhaps, that the Kierkegaardian version is right and that our world has itself become the tragic visionary, in its unbelief using self-destructive crises to force itself finally to confront the absurdities of earthly reality—those which have always been there lurking beneath for the visionary who would dare give up all to read them? Which is to ask, fearfully and even unwillingly, whether we have not been beguiled by aesthetic satisfactions and whether the utterly stripped tragic vision may not after all be less illusory than the fullness which shines through tragedy.

Religious Drama and its Interpretation

H. D. F. KITTO

We have examined in detail the structure and style of certain classical Greek plays. We assumed that Aeschylus and Sophocles were in complete command of their own art, and had very good reasons for shaping their plays as they did; and we have, I think, found nothing to disturb that assumption. From this examination there has emerged the conception of "religious" drama, a form of drama in which the real focus is not the Tragic Hero but the divine background. This conception, if it is a sound one, gives rise to several considerations which it may be worth while to discuss briefly.

We may notice, in the first place, that the distinction between religious and secular drama is not a mechanical one. There is religious drama in which gods do not appear, and secular drama in which they do. There are no gods in the *Medea* or *Hecuba* for example, yet these plays must be regarded as religious drama: treated as tragic character-studies they fail, more or less disastrously; they make good sense only when we see that the real Tragic Hero is humanity itself.[1] On the other hand, the *Electra* and *Orestes* of Euripides are quite self-contained tragedies of character, even though gods do appear in them. The essential question is whether the play exists on one level or on two, whether the real focus lies in one or more of the characters, or somewhere behind them; in fact, what the field of reference is.

The next point is that the distinction is independent of the distinction which we were trying to establish . . . between constructive and representational drama. Religious drama is not peculiarly Greek, though the Greeks had their own way of presenting it. In fact, it will be argued . . . that *Hamlet* must be read as religious drama, in the sense in which we are using the term; and that much criticism of *Hamlet* fails, either wholly or in part, because this fact is not realised. Leaving

From *Form and Meaning in Drama,* 1956, pp. 231-45. Reprinted by permission of Methuen and Co., Ltd.

[1] See my *Greek Tragedy,* pp. 198-200, 219-221, 262.

this point for the moment, we may pass to a nearly related matter.

It may seem bold, even reckless, to suggest that good scholars and sensitive critics have missed a point of the first importance both in Greek drama and in at least one classical English play; nevertheless I think that this is the case, and there may be a very good explanation. Neither today nor for some centuries past have we been in immediate and imaginative contact with a religious culture—with its habits of mind, its natural means of expression.

We may reflect on what has happened to us since the Elizabethan Age. This was one which had by no means lost contact with the late Middle Age; and the drama of this age was played, literally, not on two levels but on three: Heaven, Earth and Hell, side by side. It was a drama with the very widest reference. But the succeeding Age of Reason was entirely out of touch with this; and, as we can see very clearly, it was out of touch with Shakespeare too, in certain important particulars. We know, for example, how Nahum Tate refashioned some of the Tragedies, and how Johnson approved:

> Shakespeare has suffered the virtue of Cordelia to perish in a just cause, contrary to the natural ideas of justice, to the hope of the reader, and, what is yet more strange, to the faith of the chronicles. . . . A play in which the wicked prosper, and the virtuous miscarry, may doubtless be good, because it is a just representation of the common events of human life: but since all reasonable beings naturally love justice, I cannot easily be persuaded, that the observation of justice makes a play worse; or, that if other excellencies are equal, the audience will not always rise better pleased from the final triumph of persecuted virtue. In the present case the publick has decided. Cordelia, from the time of Tate, has always retired with victory and felicity.[2]

One is reminded of Aristotle's remark, that in his own day those plays were preferred in which vice was punished and virtue rewarded—and the reason which he gives is *τὴν τῶν θεάτρων ἀσθενείαν*, "the debility of the audience." Debility is something with which one does not easily credit Johnson; but it seems clear that there was something in the lucid, orderly and essentially prosaic eighteenth-century mind which made it incapable not only of creating tragedy, but even of understanding it in some of its forms.

Nor did the Romantic movement bring any great amendment. True, it deposed the Rules of Art and exalted Imagination; but by now

[2] *General Observations on Shakespeare's Plays: Lear.*

individualism was rampant. The Hero, with his attendant personages, became the whole play; and it was only natural that in the actual theatre both the hero and the play should become confused with the transcendent genius of the Actor-manager. These excesses have gone, but our own age, though it has recreated a poetic drama, is hardly one which is instinctively attuned to religious modes of thought, so that it is not surprising if the wide outlook of an earlier age is one which we do not understand without some effort.

So far as the interpretation of Greek religious drama was concerned, the Aristotelian tradition reinforced rather than corrected contemporary secularism. It is necessary to examine the connexion between Aristotle's theory and the classical Greek tragedy, and to point out how very tenuous it is.

Aristotle places firmly in the centre of his ideal play the Tragic Hero, with his ἁμαρτία, the flaw in a character otherwise better than the average. In the best form of tragedy, the Hero will make his transit, his μετάβασις, from happiness to unhappiness by the logical working of the flaw, in the given circumstances; and the end is Pity and Fear—emotions which we feel because the hero is ὅμοιος, not unlike ourselves. To Aristotle (though not to the dramatists) the spectacle of a good man ruined by no fault of his own is μιαρόν, shocking, and not tragic. As for the gods, and their function in drama, Aristotle mentions them only once (1454 b 5), and then only to say: "We assume that the gods can see everything." That is, they are a dramatic convenience. These points we may consider one by one.

Our analysis of religious drama, if it is correct, shows that the centre of a play is not necessarily a Tragic Hero. It is meaningless to ask whether Agamemnon or Clytemnestra is the tragic hero of Aeschylus' play, and if we think of Ajax as an Aristotelian tragic hero, the structure of Sophocles' play becomes unintelligible. Aristotle's theory, as one would expect, is a perfectly consistent whole, so that what he says about the tragic hero cannot be separated from what he says about the tragic flaw. To how many of the heroes whom we have considered does this doctrine really apply? Agamemnon has indeed ἁμαρτία enough, but it is not presented as a flaw in a character otherwise admirable. What we are shown is practically nothing but his ἁμαρτία. It is true that the Watchman calls him "my well-loved master," and it may be that diligence might disclose one or two other scraps of information about other aspects of his character, but it is surely obvious that Aeschylus is not at all concerned to present him as a rounded character, better than the average in most respects, but ruined by one fault, so that at the end our cry is: "O the pity on't!" Effectively, he and Clytemnestra and Medea and perhaps Creon are nothing but ἁμαρτία. Prometheus may be said to show ἁμαρτία in his self-will, but if we try to make this the central feature of the play, we shall not get very far. Sophocles' Electra, like his Antigone, can be said to have a ἁμαρτία; but if Electra has one, it does not ruin her, and Antigone is destroyed because of her virtues, not her faults, if she has any. If we apply the doctrine to Philoctetes or to Neoptolemus, either the doctrine or the play breaks down. In any case, neither this play nor the *Electra* ends unhappily, nor is it a worse play in consequence.

Of how many of these characters is it possible or profitable to say that they are ὅμοιοι, "like us," though tending to the better rather than to the worse? Of some, undoubtedly. But when we read or witness the *Medea* or the *Ajax* or the *Electra,* to say nothing of the *Oresteia* or *Prometheus,* how much of the total impression that we receive comes from a feeling that we ourselves, in our modest way, resemble these heroes? That our mothers, wives and daughters think this when they contemplate Clytemnestra or Medea is doubtful; nor probably do the rest of us, when we tremble for Xerxes or Agamemnon or Orestes, fear περὶ τὸν ὅμοιον, "for one like ourselves." [3] It is arguable that every one of the plays which we have considered creates Pity and Fear, but it is certainly not the case that we always feel Pity and Fear for the tragic hero, nor that these are the most important of the thoughts or emotions aroused by the plays. Do we pity Sophocles' Electra and Orestes? Perhaps we do, but this is not the response that Sophocles is most anxious to stimulate in us; and any fear that we may experience on their behalf is discounted by the fact that Apollo stands over them; and it would be no convincing defence of Aristotle's doctrine to transfer our Pity and Fear, in this play, to the two murderers whom Electra and Orestes will destroy.

In fact, what this religious drama gives us is rather Awe and Understanding. Its true Catharsis arises from this, that when we have seen terrible things happening in the play, we understand, as we cannot always do in life, *why* they have happened; or, if not so much as that, at least we see that they have not happened by chance, without any significance. We are given the feeling that the Universe is coherent, even though we may not understand it completely. In this lies the true greatness of the *Tyrannus.* This is a play which Aristotle

[3] *Poetics* 1453 a 6.

treats as tragedy of character, and as such it is splendid enough; but how much more splendid is it when we see what Sophocles really meant: that although Life has been so cruel to Oedipus, nevertheless it is not a chaos; and that in his story there is no warrant for our abandoning allegiance to moral law and such prudent foresight as we may have. Pity and Fear are present in abundance, but even so they are overtopped by Awe and Understanding; they are in themselves emotions too personal to be the ultimate explanation of this religious drama.

Another part of Aristotle's theory is that "one must not represent good characters (τοὺς ἐπιεικεῖς) moving from prosperity to disaster, for this excites neither pity nor fear, but revulsion." The theory perhaps appears reasonable, but from dramatic theory we may turn to dramatic facts. We may contemplate what Aeschylus does with Orestes. To be sure, Orestes does not pass from happiness to unhappiness; he never was "happy," and as to what happens to him after his acquittal, whether "happiness" or not, Aeschylus is silent; the question is utterly irrelevant. But what we do see, in the play, is a man whose character, so far as it is revealed to us, is without blemish; yet he is in a cleft stick, and suffers anguish. Or we may think of Io, without fault, yet tortured. I will not mention Prometheus, because there are those who, although they belong to the human race, believe that Prometheus was at fault in preventing Zeus from destroying it; but what of King Pelasgus in the *Supplices?* At one moment he is, presumably, "happy"; at the next he is in the agonising position of having to choose between a dangerous war from which he and his city can gain nothing, and the afflictions that may descend on them all from the offended gods. It is possible, though I think not likely, that all came right for him in the end, but this does not alter the fact that we see this innocent man held fast in a cruel dilemma, and do not find the spectacle "revolting."

This matter is discussed by Macneile Dixon.[4] His argument is that the philosophers, from Plato to Schopenhauer, have been uneasy with Tragedy: the philosopher wants a fully rational or explicable universe, but the tragic poets know that the Universe is not such, since it will suddenly knock a man down for no just reason. Sometimes, says Dixon, the "tragic flaw" is in the Universe, and this is a possibility which the philosopher is reluctant to admit.

This may be true of some philosophers, and of some forms of tragedy, but it does not seem to be sufficient explanation of the discrepancy

[4] W. Macneile Dixon, *Tragedy* (London, 1924).

between the theory of Aristotle and the practice of Aeschylus and Sophocles. In the first place, both these poets were philosophers enough to believe in a world-order—even though Sophocles at least knew that it is not given to man to understand it fully. Both poets "believed in the gods"; and though this does not mean—though it certainly does not exclude—that they were endowed with a personal piety, it does mean that they believed in a Universe which is ultimately rational. When Aeschylus depicts a conflict between one god and another, which clearly is a sign of a disordered Universe, the reason is plain enough: he is depicting a world-order in the process of evolution. In the end, Zeus reigns without opposition. When Sophocles represents Oedipus as being destroyed though essentially innocent, he is not presuming a flaw in the Universe, but recognising that its majestic order may cut the thread of a single life and requite venial unwisdom with utterly disproportionate penalties, just as he recognises that when the insensibility of a Creon disturbs the path of Dikê, then an Antigone and a Haemon and an Eurydice may be destroyed. In these plays the innocent do suffer, and their suffering is not "revolting"; and the reason for this is that their suffering is seen to be part of a world-order, which though not always beneficent, is at least intelligible.

But Aristotle's theory, for whatever reason, takes no account of this religious drama. In this fact lies the explanation of our difficulty, that he, like Johnson, finds unmerited suffering "revolting." In the kind of tragedy which he is analysing it would be revolting—in a Tragedy of Character, in which our attention is focussed upon the hero, why and how he acts; and on the "inevitable or probable" way in which one error brings all to ruin. If in watching such a man, having our attention directed to nothing but his character, his situation, his actions, and their consequences; being made aware of no all-embracing world-order, but on the contrary finding a microcosm in the hero himself—if in a drama of this kind we were shown that the hero, guilty of no sin, no error of judgment, so acted that in the natural or inevitable course of events he worked his own damnation, we should certainly feel that the play was "revolting"; and we should feel this because it would imply that the Universe was unintelligible, even if not positively malignant.

Evidently, so far as religious drama is concerned, where Aristotle is right he is right by accident, and if his theory is drawn from dramatic practice and not evolved from philosophic prepossessions, it is from the practice of a contemporary kind of drama—unless indeed it is from a single play, the *Tyrannus*. Certainly it does not in the least fit any other extant play by Sophocles, to say nothing of Aeschylus. If it is based on a different drama—which perhaps we ought to assume, since Aristotle was something of a scientist, accustomed to the observation of facts—that drama would be one which we might call humanistic, or secular; if on the *Tyrannus,* then on the *Tyrannus* interpreted in a purely humanistic way, as the tragedy of a great man, with the divine background omitted. If we would frame a general theory of the classical Greek drama, it must be on lines already indicated, to this effect.

The tragic poet so constructs his play that the actions of the characters, being likely ones, combine to produce a result which is seen to be inevitable, either in prospect, as in the *Agamemnon,* or in retrospect, as in the *Antigone,* or both. This result may be said to display the validity of divine law in human affairs. The chief character or characters—for there may well be no single "tragic hero"—may themselves commit grave error which leads them to disaster, or they may, like Sophocles' Electra, Antigone, Philoctetes, be persons who are affected by, and resist, the wrongful actions of others, in which case the play may end, for them, "happily." These are all matters of indifference—whether there is one chief character or more, whether he is good or bad, and whether, in consequence, the play ends happily or unhappily. One thing is constant: the assertion of a world-order, symbolised by the presence or activity of the gods. Sometimes, as in the *Oresteia* and *Prometheia,* the poet shows this order in evolution. Sophocles shows it in operation. In Euripides it is often presented by implication rather than directly: it consists of a due balance of forces, such as for example of Aphrodite and Artemis, or Reason and Ecstasy, or the Rational and the Irrational, a balance which he will often call σωφροσύνη or "wisdom." Euripides is "the most tragic of the poets" because in his drama this balance, or order, seems the most unattainable.

That is to say, religious drama is a distinct kind, with principles of its own, different from those of tragedy of character, the form of tragedy that Aristotle analysed. These principles we have tried to find inductively, by observing the facts. We have seen that it is a form of drama which can use naturalism, but can and frequently does set it at defiance; that it can draw character sharply, but does not exist in order to study and display character; it can indeed almost entirely dispense with character-drawing. The individual, however vividly he may be drawn, however complex and delicate may be the relations between him and the other individuals in the play, never absorbs all our attention; he never, so to speak, grows in his creator's hand. Religious drama contains gods as well as men, and where gods are present they must take precedence. Only when the human drama in the foreground is seen against the background of divine action is the structure and significance of the play truly seen.

If we ask why Aristotle should have evolved a theory which so notably does not agree with the facts of the classical Greek drama, our answer can only be speculative; and perhaps it is well to remember that when we say "Aristotle" we mean, necessarily, Aristotle as revealed to us in the *Poetics*. Aristotle the man may have had a great love for Aeschylus; about this we can know nothing.

Wilamowitz suggested that Aristotle, as a foreigner from Stageira, did not understand "the pure Attic spirit." But perhaps the interval of time that separated him from Sophocles and Aeschylus was more potent than the interval of space that separated Stageira from Athens.

We may reflect on the extent and the swiftness of the change which came over the intellectual temper of Greece between say 450 B.C. and 400. It is roughly true to say that up to the time of Socrates and the Sophists, the poets had been among the profoundest and most active of the Greek thinkers. In the earlier part of the fifth century, poetry, religion, history, myth, philosophy, had not yet finally parted company, though the separation was becoming imminent. Herodotus, like any epic poet, says that one of his motives in composing his History was to preserve great deeds from oblivion. The word "history" means "enquiries," and with a splendid indifference Herodotus prosecuted and wrote into his book enquiries which we should distinguish as historical or geographical or archaeological or anthropological or biological [5] or something else—all this in a work designed "to preserve great deeds from oblivion," and suffused with a religious feeling. Specialism had not yet won the day. In a similar way, Aeschylus and Sophocles were considerable philosophers, but philosophers who gave out the results, not the processes, of thought, and expressed them in their art. But within the space of one generation the Greeks, always intelligent, became intellectualist. Problems of religion, conduct, philosophy, politics, became the subject of systematic and specialised enquiry, and so gradually ceased to be the material for art. The old intuitive approach to the truth no longer served; Socrates dismissed the poets because they could not answer his questions, which undoubtedly

[5] "Now I will describe the nature of the camel" (III, 103).

would not have been technical or aesthetic questions, but moral ones. As soon as matters of morality and conduct and the rest become the province of scientific philosophy, they cease to be the material for the poets. The sophist's radio-call, "it all depends what you mean by . . ." is the poet's warning; authority is being transferred from him to the systematic enquirer. Those wide regions which had been his natural home began to contract; the significant, constructive use of myth could not for long hold out against the new analytical spirit. A century after the death of Sophocles another considerable poet was making his appearance in the Greek world—Theocritus; but how much less intrinsically important were the themes which he handled! When Theocritus uses myth, in his Epyllia, it is only to make attractive poetry. He takes a theme which Euripides also had used—a woman in love: the second Idyll is a strong and beautiful poem, and a complete contrast to Euripides' treatment of Medea and Phaedra in this, that it has no wider reference. It is in fact the source of the poem's strength that it concentrates our attention on Simaetha—on her situation, not the human situation; on the particular moods and emotions which successively assail her. It is not, essentially, a question of better poetry or worse, but of a different attitude to poetry.

Signs of the change, as we have said before, appear in tragedy itself, in the later fifth century—in "romantic" drama like the *Iphigeneia in Tauris* or the *Ion*, and in high comedy like the *Helen*. What is the reason? War-weariness is often cited; the Athenian audience no longer had the stomach for profound and strenuous drama. Weariness no doubt played its part, but in all the arts, not in drama only, the current was setting strongly away from the old seriousness towards elegance or prettiness, and individualism or even sensationalism. One might refer to the individualism of early fourth-century sculpture, or the collapse of vase-painting into mere fussiness. The war does not seem to be a sufficient explanation. It was not the war that caused the sudden flowering of prose-literature which accompanied the decline of serious poetry. The old Greek world had known no real division between art, religion and philosophy; but that world was rapidly transforming itself into a new one, in which art and philosophy were each becoming autonomous, to the advantage, no doubt, of philosophy, but not of art.

As far as Tragedy is concerned, we have the testimony of Aristophanes, as well as the silent judgment of the Alexandrine critics who made the Canon, that Sophocles and Euripides left no worthy successors. In the circumstances, that is what might have been expected; the serious things were now being said in prose. Sometimes we hear it asserted that every age, as a matter of course, has its great artists, and if we do not see them the reason is that the great artist has to wait a generation for recognition; comforting doctrine, but as a general theory quite untrue. The greatness of Aeschylus and Sophocles, rather less so, perhaps, of Euripides, was fully recognised in their own time, and the succeeding centuries produced nothing to compare with them —though they did produce Plato and Aristotle and Zeno and Epicurus and a long line of mathematicians and scientists. We also hear today, from music critics, of "the tyranny of the Classics"; the indications are that fourth-century Athens similarly turned back to the fifth-century Classics—perhaps for a similar reason: they had had more important things to say.

Unhappily, we cannot have any more than a very general idea about the tragedy that was contemporary with Aristotle. We have one pointer in certain of the late plays of Euripides. There is perhaps another in the brief reference that Aristotle makes to the *Antheus,* by Euripides' younger contemporary Agathon: he says simply that the entire plot was invented by the dramatist. From this it is a likely inference that the play was of a romantic or melodramatic kind; a dramatist who had something of importance to say would hardly be tempted to abandon the weight and authority which established myth could confer on him.

We hear of rhetoricians, like Theodectes, who turned themselves into tragic poets, and wrote plays that were esteemed for their rhetorical qualities. We know, from Aristotle, that the cycle of myths used by the poets was now smaller; also that historical subjects began to reappear: Theodectes wrote a play about Maussolus, recently dead, and Moschion one about Themistocles, and possibly another, the *Pheraeans,* about the murder of Alexander of Pherae. These sound very like a species of Heroic Drama, reminding one of Dryden rather than of Phrynichus and Aeschylus.[6] Finally, there is great force in an incidental remark of Professor Fraenkel's, that Aristotle's dry and quite barren analyses of such things as the various ways of managing recognition-scenes faithfully reflect one of the chief interests of the contemporary theatre. It would be no new phenomenon, that in times when the

[6] If the recently discovered Gyges-fragment comes from a real play, and not from some "closet-drama," I should ascribe it without any hesitation to this or an even later period, certainly not to the early fifth century.

artists have nothing of great importance to say they give great attention to the means by which to say it. Certainly everything points to the conclusion that the fourth century was such a time, with the result that Tragedy, being driven in upon itself, became elegant and rhetorical, or sensational; in any case self-conscious, more concerned with its own technique than with anything that matters; a period of *pièces bien faites.*

There are strong resemblances between the *Aufklärung* of the late fifth and early fourth centuries B.C. and of the seventeenth and eighteenth centuries A.D. In each case the human mind seems to have achieved its new clarity by contracting its field of vision; in each case, a classical Tragedy, poetry at its most comprehensive, almost disappeared over the horizon; appreciated for its incidental merits, but not really understood; leaving as its successors Heroic or a rhetorical tragedy, and either witty or sentimental comedy. Aristotle was indeed not so much out of touch with the spirit of his classical tragedy as the run of eighteenth-century critics were with theirs; he would certainly not have approved if a fourth-century Nahum Tate had rewritten the last part of the *Antigone* in order to save Antigone from death and so bring the play into closer accord with poetic justice; and although his preferred type of tragic ending was not one of which the tragic poets themselves had thought very highly, and although his theory was incapable of accounting for plays like the *Trojan Women,* he did at least call Euripides "the most tragic of the poets," and despise, unlike Johnson, "the debility of the audiences." But the fact remains that if we would understand the spirit and the methods of the classical Greek Tragedy, we must study Aeschylus and Sophocles and Euripides in the appropriate way, without allowing ourselves to be deflected by the ideas natural to a "secular" age, whether that be the fourth century before Christ or the eighteenth or twentieth A.D.

An article in the *Contemporary Review*[7] illustrates the importance of understanding what the Greek dramatic poets meant by their divine background. The writer of this article takes the gods seriously, as one should, and at their face-value—their modern face-value: as a controlling element not only in the design of the plays, but also in the actions and sufferings of the characters. He argues that the human characters can do nothing but realise and reveal "the unalterable interweaving threads in the web of Fate," and that "any attempt to explain

[7] F. H. C. Brock: "Oedipus, Macbeth, and the Christian Tradition." (*Contemporary Review* CLXXVII, pp. 177ff.)

human fortunes in terms of human behaviour, or to establish any relationship between guilt and misfortune is entirely absent"—a remark which is indeed made specifically of the *Tyrannus*, but by implication of Greek Tragedy in general. Believing this, he quotes with approval something said by Mr. Ivor Brown, the dramatic critic, that it is difficult for the modern audience to maintain interest in "these fate-driven men"; and he draws the sharpest distinction between Greek tragedy, "ridden by the theological doctrine of Nemesis, and by the unscientific theory of determinism which that entails," and the Shakespearean tragedy, "in which human fortunes are not determined beforehand by a divine decree, in which the punishment of wrong-doing is not something immediate and particular, but in which the world means good, and will by its nature and the laws of its operation vindicate that principle against those who offend."

It is indeed difficult to imagine a presentation of Greek Tragedy which could be more exactly the opposite of the truth, or a description of the Shakespearean Tragedy which would more clearly bring out its resemblances to the Greek. "It [Greek Tragedy] was not content, as modern science is content, to regard the world as a framework of inexorable law within which mind, with free activities, could operate, playing upon these laws and bringing them into action, even manipulating them to its own ends"—because Fate, or the gods, have determined everything beforehand, and will intervene arbitrarily. To operate and exploit natural laws is of course no part of drama or of any other art; but in so far as scientific thought and Greek drama have a common element, it is well expressed in the foregoing sentence, if only we delete the negative. It is indeed disastrous to misconceive the function of the gods in this drama.

Divine activity, as I have tried to show, is a controlling element in this Religious Tragedy precisely because it represents "the framework of inexorable law," or, it may be, of inherent natural forces. Our business is to see that the divine activity neither controls human activity and suffering nor renders them merely pathetic, but is rather a generalised statement about them. The divine background holds up to us, so to speak, the system of co-ordinates against which we are to read the significance of what the human actors do and suffer. The gods are a controlling element in the plays, but not in what the actors do and suffer: that is entirely their own affair. The reason for saying that the divine element controls the play is this: the dramatist does not allow the human actors to do or suffer anything which does not have significance when it is read against the co-ordinates. The previous domestic history of Agamemnon and Clytemnestra is something that Aeschylus keeps out.

Hence comes, in the plays, the combination of lifelike vividness with that "constructiveness" which can be very far from "lifelike" or naturalistic: the persons and their actions must be real, true to life, not generalised into flabbiness, or they will not convince us of anything; they will naturally be vivid and sharp because (despite my mathematical metaphor) the dramatist was an artist, not a demonstrator; what he was seeking to communicate was communicated by sheer impact. But the vividness, the "truth to life," was restricted (for good artistic reasons) to what made immediate sense when the audience correlated it, as it instinctively would, with the universal co-ordinates in the background.

In this connexion we might quote a good passage by Thibaudet which Professor Gomme quotes in another context:[8] "L'histoire, telle que la propose Thucydide, unit et fait servir l'un à l'autre deux caractères qui, semble-t-il, s'excluent: la plus grande exactitude matérielle et la plus grand généralité. D'ailleurs, quand on croit qu'elles s'excluent c'est qu'on ne pense pas à l'art, qui les implique au contraire toutes deux et emploie l'une à la perfection de l'autre." If, in place of "la plus grande exactitude matérielle," we substitute what perhaps is its artistic analogue, vividness in the presentation of particulars, we can say that the tragic poets also combine two characteristics which may appear to be contraries but in fact serve and reinforce each other: sharpness of detail, and the greatest possible generality. The way in which Thucydides combined his two elements is not our present affair; of the means which the tragic poets used, the most important was the religious framework of their plays.

In [my] next chapter the structure of *Hamlet* will be examined, and the suggestion will emerge that this too is "religious drama"; that if we try to make the Tragic Hero the focus, the form of the play is not an artistic unity. Those who read this chapter will not need to be told that my knowledge of *Hamlet* criticism is much less than it should be. If therefore they think that it is an impertinence, I will add to the impertinence by blaming Professor Dover Wilson. It was his brilliant book on *Hamlet,* so stimulating, so very nearly persuasive, so entirely "secular," that impelled me for my own satisfaction to study

[8] A. W. Gomme, *The Greek Attitude to Poetry and History,* p. 139: A. Thibaudet, *La Campagne avec Thucydide,* p. 49.

Hamlet closely in order to see what would happen if the same critical methods were used on it as have been used here on Aeschylus and Sophocles. I have been encouraged to think that the results are worth putting into print.

The Implications of Tragedy

CLIFFORD LEECH

The gulf between the learned use and the popular use of the same word is nowhere better illustrated than in "tragedy." The term is used from day to day in referring to incidents of a distressful nature, and, in so far as it is popularly used as the name of a literary type, it is applied to any play or story with an unhappy ending. This is unfortunate, for the widespread vague use of the term makes it more difficult for students to clarify their ideas on the significance of *King Lear* and the *Agamemnon*: if our labels are smudged, we are forced to make a continual effort to remind ourselves of the contents of each package. Yet here we cannot blame the journalist for the blurring of the word's meaning, for the vague use of "tragedy" goes back to medieval times. Moreover, even those who have aimed at using the word precisely have not reached agreement concerning the nature of the literary type to which the word is, by them, applied.

The most famous definition of tragedy in medieval times is given by Chaucer in the Prologue to *The Monk's Tale*:

> Tragedie is to seyn a certeyn storie,
> As olde bokes maken us memorie,
> Of him that stood in greet prosperitie
> And is y-fallen out of heigh degree
> Into miserie, and endeth wrecchedly.

He adds that tragedies are commonly written in hexameters, but that "many oon" has been written in prose as well as in other metres. Similarly in his translation of Boethius he adds the gloss:

> Tragedie is to seyn, a ditee of a prosperitie for a tyme, that endeth in wrecchednesse.

It is evident that, in Chaucer's view, a tragedy need not be written in dramatic form. This arose out of the break in continuity between

From *Shakespeare's Tragedies and Other Studies in Seventeenth Century Drama*, London, 1950, pp. 3-20. Reprinted by permission of Chatto and Windus, Ltd. and Oxford University Press.

the drama of antiquity and the drama of the medieval church, and indeed most medieval references to tragedy similarly make no mention of dramatic representation. But this is not the only omission which strikes us in Chaucer's definition, for he indicates no cause for the fall from high degree. This, however, he had to consider when writing the "tragedies" of *The Monk's Tale*: he could not pen tales of woe without implying why the woe came about. In the opening lines of *The Monk's Tale* he averred that it was Fortune who was responsible for the change in a man's estate: capriciously she might turn her back, and man should steel himself for these methodless reversals. On the other hand, in some of the Monk's "tragedies" a totally different idea is put forward: man is there frequently robbed of his prosperity on account of sin: Adam, for example, is turned out of Paradise "for misgovernaunce." Chaucer, in fact, hesitates in his conception of tragedy in much the same way as do most people who tell sad tales: at times they believe that misfortunes come because they are merited, at times they feel that there is such a thing as bad luck: they waver between a planned universe of rewards and punishments and a chaotic universe in which chance operates without motive.

Yet if Chaucer's use of the term is the common one, we should recognize that literary theorists have been justified in trying to use the term more precisely. They have felt that certain pieces of dramatic literature are of a special kind, leaving an impression on our minds which is peculiar to themselves, and thus demanding a special label. Aristotle in Chapter VI of *The Poetics* produced a definition of tragedy which has served as a starting-point for every modern critic who has attempted to describe the effect of plays of this kind; and though the definition is obscure in the crucial point, that of *catharsis,* it provides clear evidence that Aristotle recognized tragic plays as constituting a special *genre*. At the same time Aristotle illustrates how difficult it is to be precise concerning the nature of his *genre:* in Chapter XIII he claims that the tragic hero, "a man not pre-eminently virtuous and just," should fall from prosperity to misery through a fatal flaw in his character or an error of judgment, and thus he defends the unhappy ending in tragedy; in Chapter XIV, however, he gives especial praise to that type of tragedy in which disaster is avoided at the last moment through the revelation of something previously unknown. The contradiction may well be due to the conflicting claims of philosophic theory and dramatic effectiveness. In any event, it may serve as a warning of the difficulty of achieving consistency in a theory of tragedy, and of deciding exactly which plays are to be accepted as tragic.

It is not my purpose here to consider the many explanations of *catharsis* that have been put forward from the time of the Italian Renaissance critics. In all likelihood Aristotle's notion was that tragedy served as a safety-valve, a means of freeing the mind from the pity and the fear that might otherwise enter public or private life, and Mr. F. L. Lucas may be right in his belief that Aristotle claimed this cathartic effect for tragedy as a defence against the charges of Plato.[1] But that the emotions of pity and fear are concerned in the tragic effect has not been disputed by any subsequent theorist. Dr. I. A. Richards, indeed, has seen these two emotions as opposing forces which tragedy brings into a state of equilibrium. For him the tragic effect is the achievement of a state of repose in the nervous system, a repose without inertia because it is the result of a perpetual opposition:

> Pity, the impulse to approach, and Terror, the impulse to retreat, are brought in Tragedy to a reconciliation which they find nowhere else, and with them who knows what other allied groups of equally discordant impulses. Their union in an ordered single response is the *catharsis* by which Tragedy is recognised, whether Aristotle meant anything of this kind or not. This is the explanation of that sense of release, of repose in the midst of stress, of balance and composure, given by Tragedy, for there is no other way in which such impulses, once awakened, can be set at rest without suppression.[2]

But the difficulty about this is that Dr. Richards does not tell us what it is that we feel an impulse to approach and a simultaneous impulse to retreat from. We feel pity—or perhaps sympathy would be the better word—with reference to the tragic hero and to other characters who are involved in disaster, but we are not terrified by him or them. Even where the tragic hero, like Orestes or Macbeth, causes fear to the other characters, we do not share their feelings. Our fear is aroused by the picture of the universe that the tragic writer presents, we are impelled to retreat from the contemplation of evil, we should like to shut our eyes if we could. If, therefore, the pity and the fear are aroused by different stimuli, it is difficult to see how any balancing of them can be other than fortuitous. Our sympathy with Hamlet is greater than our sympathy with Othello, because most of us find

[1] *Tragedy in Relation to Aristotle's Poetics,* 1927, p. 33.
[2] *Principles of Literary Criticism,* 1934, pp. 245-46.

Hamlet the more attractive character: yet it would be a rash assumption that the play of *Hamlet* arouses more terror than the play of *Othello*. Moreover, Dr. Richards's view of tragedy is weighted on the therapeutic side. He claims that it makes us feel that "all is right . . . in the nervous system," [3] but he neglects that part of our experience which is the recognition that the dramatist's view of the universe is terrible as well as strengthening.

Yet the idea that the tragic effect resides in an equilibrium of opposing forces does seem to correspond with our experience. After witnessing a successful performance of one of Shakespeare's four great tragedies, or of Webster's *The Duchess of Malfi,* or of the *Agamemnon,* our state of mind is active, and yet active to no immediate end: we are in a state of unusual stimulation, and yet we are more inclined to contemplate the experience than to plan our future conduct: we have seen a picture of evil, but it has neither palsied our faculties nor aroused us to struggle against it.

It is not surprising, therefore, that Professor Una Ellis-Fermor has also seen a balance of opposing forces in the effect of tragedy.[4] For her the balance is between the view that the world is controlled by an alien and hostile destiny and the view that somehow this apparent evil may be explained in terms of good. She points out that in the *Agamemnon* and the *Choëphroe* Aeschylus presents the evil of things through the actions and the words of the actors, and through the speeches of the Chorus suggests that outside the human world there is a divine organisation of things. In Shakespeare, she suggests, the fact that such characters as Cordelia and Kent can exist must lead to what she calls a "positive" interpretation—that is, an idea that the universe is under benevolent direction. Feeling, perhaps, that the indications of goodness are in some indubitable tragedies rather too slight, Professor Ellis-Fermor adds that the very principle of order apparent in the formal articulation of tragic plays acts as a counterpoise to the evil chaos that seems to prevail. Her view, in brief, is that the tragic equilibrium consists in the simultaneous holding in the mind of the two conflicting ideas: that the universe is divinely directed and that it is devil-ridden. She implies, however, that this equilibrium is impermanent, that the tragic writer may find his way beyond it to an acceptance of the idea of divine control, and she refers here to Shakespeare's final

[3] *Ibid.*, p. 246.
[4] *The Frontiers of Drama,* 1945, pp. 127-47.

romances as evidence that Shakespeare escaped from the dark vision of *Othello* and *Lear*.

The difficulty in Professor Ellis-Fermor's position is that the indications of a divinely controlled universe are in many tragedies scarcely sufficient to counterpoise the presentation of evil. It is not enough that in *Othello* we have characters who mean no harm: Othello and Desdemona are well-intentioned enough, but their disaster comes upon them through his credulity and her lack of directness: in view of the magnitude of the suffering that is brought about by these comparatively minor faults, it is difficult to see that their good qualities point to a divinely controlled universe. And the control of art need suggest nothing more than that man has a certain faculty for ordering part of his experience: it does not transform the nature of that experience, and it does not necessarily suggest that either he or a creator can control the totality of experience.

That there is an equilibrium of forces in the tragic effect I think we can admit, but Professor Ellis-Fermor has looked too far in trying to reconcile the tragic and the Christian pictures of life. We need to examine the tragic picture in more detail—to consider, banishing presuppositions as far as we can, the view of life offered to us by plays that we will all agree to have a similar effect on us, plays that we will not hesitate to call "tragic."

Not only are great evil and suffering presented in such plays but there is no comprehensible scheme of rewards and punishments suggested. Oedipus sins, as Aristotle puts it, through an error of judgment, yet he is led to a state of mind where even the thought of death is no escape from the horror; Othello is induced to murder his innocent wife and then to realise his mistake: only suicide offers itself as a way out; Desdemona and Ophelia are guilty of nothing more than weakness, yet they are destroyed; Lear is hot-tempered and foolish, yet no one will claim that he deserved to endure madness and the storm on the heath; Cordelia refuses to play her father's game, and is hanged for it; Gloucester begets Edmund, and his eyes are plucked out; Webster's Duchess of Malfi loves and marries her steward Antonio, and on that account is slowly tortured to death. Moreover, the plays frequently include a number of minor characters whose sudden and cruel deaths do not arise out of any fault of their own: Lady Macduff and her son, Polonius, Rosencrantz and Guildenstern, the brave servant in *King Lear* who tries to save Gloucester from blindness, the virtuous Marcello in Webster's *The White Devil*—all these can hardly be said to get their deserts. It is true that in some tragedies the final disaster springs from an evil act on the part of the hero—*Macbeth* and the plays of Marlowe come quickly to the mind—but even there we feel no satisfaction in the hero's punishment. Rather, we have a feeling that his initial conduct was hardly within his own control: Macbeth was singularly unfortunate in the joint temptation from the witches and his wife, and the witches' prophecy suggests from the beginning that his crime was predetermined; Marlowe's heroes are felt to act as they do because the world is what it is, a world which presents a perpetual challenge to the man of high courage. Thus we feel no desire to rejoice when the prepetrator of evil is brought to his doom, and at the same time we are aware that many characters in these plays are subjected to an evil for which they are in no way responsible.

Nor is there in great tragedy the suggestion that these things will be put right in another world. It is true that in comparatively minor works like Kyd's *The Spanish Tragedy* we are assured in an epilogue that the hero and his supporters will find their way to the Elysian Fields while their adversaries will know infernal tortures, but in *Othello* and *Lear* and *Macbeth* there is no such emphasis on a compensatory future life. Othello contemplates immortality only with horror:

> O ill-starr'd wench!
> Pale as thy smock! when we shall meet at compt,
> This look of thine will hurl my soul from heaven,
> And fiends will snatch at it. (V. ii.)

Cleopatra assumes a heavenly encounter with Antony, and fears that Iras will get to him first:

> This proves me base:
> If she first meet the curled Antony,
> He'll make demand of her, and spend that kiss
> Which is my heaven to have. (V. ii.)

Her speech is no consolation to the audience, who are made to feel only the strange limitations of this late tragic figure. In *Hamlet* heavenly joys are on occasion referred to: Horatio's

> Good night, sweet prince,
> And flights of angels sing thee to thy rest! (V. ii.)

and Laertes'

> I tell thee, churlish priest,
> A ministering angel shall my sister be,
> When thou liest howling. (V. i.)

are, however, pieces of embroidery on the situation of the moment rather than functional utterances in the play. Indeed, *Hamlet* is essentially a play of doubt concerning what happens after death, and we are likely to agree that in no Shakespearian tragedy are we made to think of the characters as emerging from their suffering into the beatific vision: the stresses they encounter are not preparations for a future life but are inescapable conditions of the only world in which they certainly have an existence. What may or may not happen after death is something that the tragic dramatist normally leaves out of consideration: on the rare occasions when he does consider it, as Marlowe does in *Faustus,* it is to see it as part of the evil which his tragic hero must endure.

Because of the apparent absence of a kindly or just disposition of things in the world and because of his disregard of a future life, the tragic dramatist inevitably sees the gods as remote, if not as beings actively hostile to man. Perhaps the remoteness of the gods is given most succinct expression in Webster's *The Duchess of Malfi,* where the Duchess is subjected to intense mental torture before she is finally killed. Hearing false news of the death of her husband and children, she cries out that she could curse the stars: Bosola, her enemies' instrument, let her tongue run on in grief for a few moments and then bids her look heavenward:

> Look you, the stars shine still. (IV. i.)

All seventeenth-century English tragedy is, indeed, marked by a feeling that, if there are gods who control the universe, they are far away from men, and indifferent to the individual's fate. Sometimes this sense of remoteness becomes sharpened into a belief that the gods are malicious, enjoying the impotence and the suffering in the world beneath them. Gloucester's cry in his despair:

> As flies to wanton boys, are we to the gods,
> They kill us for their sport. (IV. i.)

is almost paralleled by this piece of bitterness from *The Duchess of Malfi*:

> We are merely the stars' tennis-balls, struck and bandied
> Which way please them. (V. iv.)

But these are dramatic utterances, mere exclamations of the characters' despair, and are no more to be taken as expressing the totality of the playwright's attitude than are the words of Horatio and Laertes, already quoted, envisaging post-lethal joys. In the tragedies of the Greeks the gods intervene more directly than in Elizabethan tragedy, but there, too, there is no assurance of an evenhanded justice in the fates of men, and no suggestion that man can find his compensation in an after-life. When, as in the *Eumenides,* the dramatist tries to humanise the justice of the gods, the play becomes more of a civic pageant than a tragedy: the acquittal of Orestes through the casting-vote of Pallas answers no questions but diverts the spectators' emotions into a new, and non-tragic, direction. But when a play is consistently tragic, the Greek writer does not see a man's problems as solved by a mere appeal to the Gods.

Nevertheless, it is noticeable that tragedy does not necessarily or even normally present an indictment of the divine powers. Professor Ellis-Fermor is certainly right in claiming for the choric utterances in the *Agamemnon* an expression of faith in the divine plan: here, indeed, is a passage which simultaneously brings out the remoteness of Zeus and the divine guidance of man through suffering to wisdom:

Zeus, whoever He is, if this
Be a name acceptable,
By this name I will call him.
There is no one comparable
When I reckon all of the case
Excepting Zeus, if ever I am to jettison
The barren care which clogs my heart.

Not He who formerly was great
With brawling pride and mad for broils
Will even be said to have been.
And He who was next has met
His match and is seen no more,
But Zeus is the name to cry in your triumph-song
And win the prize for wisdom.

Who setting us on the road
Made this a valid law—
'That men must learn by suffering.'
Drop by drop in sleep upon the heart
Falls the laborious memory of pain,
Against one's will comes wisdom;
The grace of the gods is forced on us
Throned inviolably.[5]

[5] *The Agamemnon of Aeschylus,* translated by Louis MacNeice, 1936, pp. 18-19. Reprinted by permission of Faber & Faber, Ltd., and Harcourt, Brace & World, Inc.

Man thus has no certain knowledge even of God's name, and God is without pity in his hard discipline. So, too, it is remarkable that in *King Lear* there are repeated references to divine justice. When Albany hears that Cornwall was killed immediately after he had plucked out Gloucester's eyes, his comment is:

> This shows you are above,
> You justicers, that these our nether crimes
> So speedily can venge! (IV. ii.)

And the deaths of Goneril and Regan bring from him these words:

> This judgment of the heavens, that makes us tremble,
> Touches us not with pity. (V. iii.)

Most striking of all is Edgar's comment to his dying brother Edmund: he sees the misery of their father as springing from the dissolute begetting of Edmund, and pronounces that

> The gods are just, and of our pleasant vices
> Make instruments to plague us:
> The dark and vicious place where thee he got
> Cost him his eyes. (V. iii.)

This terrible sentence seems as outrageous to our moral sense as the hanging of Cordelia or the torture of Webster's Duchess. What kind of justice, we wonder, is this, which will seize on so small a fault and inflict so terrible a punishment? The "justice" of the gods, as seen in tragedy, is as terrible as their indifference: in fact, we shall not see tragedy aright unless we recognize that the divine justice mirrored in it is an indifferent justice, a justice which cares no whit for the individual and is not concerned with a nice balance of deserts and rewards.

This justice operates like an avalanche or an echo in an enclosed space. If an evil act is committed, no matter how trifling, it will bring consequences which are far more evil than the original act. Lear, vain and delighting in power and its display, indecently demands a public profession of love from his daughters: that leads to the events of the heath, the hanging of Cordelia, the loss of Gloucester's eyes, civil war, and Lear's own death. Thyestes seduces his brother's wife, and the long train of disasters begins for the house of Atreus. Sometimes, however, it is a neutral act which provides the starting-point: the marriage of Webster's Duchess to her steward Antonio shows only a mild disregard for "degree," but it releases the evil forces which have been stored up in the minds of her brothers. The justice of the gods consists simply in the natural law that every act must have its consequence and that the consequence will be determined by the act and its context. If the act is in any way evil or if the situation is one with evil potentialities, then a train of evil will be the result. The tragic writer believes in causation, in the doctrine that means determine ends, and in the powerlessness of the human will to interrupt a chain of disasters.

We may therefore easily understand why the revenge-motive is so common in Greek and Elizabethan tragedy: the blood-feud is the most obvious example of the kind of situation in which wrong inevitably succeeds to wrong.

In such a world-picture as the tragic writer presents to us, it may appear difficult to see how an equilibrium of forces can exist. The impact on our minds of such inhuman justice would at first sight appear only terrible and paralysing. Yet it remains true that our experience of tragic drama is not like that. When we think of Shakespeare's tragedies, of Webster's, of Marlowe's, or of modern tragedies like Mr. Eugene O'Neill's *Mourning Becomes Electra,* or Mr. Sean O'Casey's *Juno and the Paycock,* what we recall is made up of an indifferent universe and certain characters who seem to demand our admiration. Whether the characters are comparatively blameless, like Hamlet or Webster's Duchess, or deeply guilty, like Macbeth, we feel that they have a quality of mind that somehow atones for the nature of the world in which they and we live. They have, in a greater or lesser degree, the power to endure and the power to apprehend: ultimately they are destroyed, but in all their sufferings they show an increasing readiness to endure, an ever greater awareness. As the shadows gather around them, they stand up the more resolutely, they see the human situation with clearer eyes. Webster's Duchess is at the beginning of the play merely an attractive and enterprising woman, but it is when she cries, in the midst of torment: "I am Duchess of Malfi still," that we recognise her full stature. Lear develops even more remarkably from a vain, hot-tempered tyrant to a man who sees the omnipresence of social wrong and the bodily distress of the poor. So, too, our attitude to Electra and Orestes and Oedipus is inevitably one of growing admiration. Because, moreover, the dramatist has made it clear that his tragic hero is human, a man with weaknesses like our own, we feel not merely admiration but pride:

we are proud of our human nature because in such characters it comes to fine flower. In a planned but terrible universe we see man justifying his existence.

Thus the equilibrium of tragedy consists in a balancing of Terror with Pride. On the one hand, we are impelled to withdraw from the spectacle, to try to forget the revelation of evil methodised; on the other, we are roused to withstand destiny, to strive to meet it with the fortitude and the clear eyes of the tragic figure. This feeling of Pride comes into full existence when the hero knows his fate and contemplates it: it is essentially distinct from the *hubris* which he may display, but which we cannot share in, before his eyes are opened.

The tragic picture of the universe postulates a limited free will. Man cannot determine the pattern of event, but he is frequently responsible either for the initiation of an evil chain or for the release of evil forces latent in a situation. Moreover, his thoughts and feelings, his attitude to the enveloping situation, are in his own control: like Orestes, he can see the horror of the matricide he must commit; like Macbeth, he can recognise his own weakness and ultimately his own insignificance in the universal scheme. Some degree of free will is, indeed, essential in tragedy, for we could hardly feel proud of an automaton.

Because of its closer approximation to the everyday appearance of things, there seems to be a greater degree of free will in Elizabethan than in Greek tragedy: it seems as if Hamlet could deflect the course of the action at almost any point if he wished, while clearly Orestes and Oedipus are bound to an established pattern. But Shakespeare and his contemporaries have gone out of their way to make us realise that the pattern is preordained for their characters too: in some plays Shakespeare uses supernatural devices to indicate the course of future events—for example in *Macbeth, Julius Caesar* and *Antony and Cleopatra*—and always he draws his characters in such a way that there is clearly only one line of conduct possible for them in the particular situation in which they find themselves: for them it is the doom-in-the-character rather than the doom-on-the-house. Hamlet must be killed because Hamlet in his particular situation can have no other end: his fate is as inevitable as that of a man lost in the heart of a desert.

Dr. E. M. W. Tillyard has put forward an idea of tragedy that must be considered. This has, indeed, often been suggested by writers who have tried to dilute the element of Terror in tragic plays, asserting that in tragedy, as in real life, we see how man can learn and be redeemed through suffering. Dr. Tillyard's presentation of this idea is linked up with his view of the *Oresteia* and of Shakespeare's final romances. He sees tragedy as a picture of life disturbed by the intrusion of a disruptive evil force, the apparent triumph of that force, and then the reassertion of a normality which has been strengthened through trial.[6] He points to Othello's last speech, to Lear's wider sympathy near the close of his drama, to Shakespeare's own passage through the despondency of *Timon* to the serenity of *The Tempest*. Certainly our pride in Lear grows as the play proceeds, he emerges as a great figure through the increasing darkness of the situation, but this is not to say that normality resumes her reign, all the better for the testing-time. Lear dies, defeated: that is the essential reason for our Terror; our Pride comes from his acceptance and full knowledge of the situation. The potentialities of evil and suffering are as strong as ever, the gods as ruthless, man's will as powerless. At the end of a Shakespearian tragedy, as at the end of Marlowe's *Faustus* or of *Oedipus at Colonus*, we have a quiet close: words of peace are spoken, and we are conscious that the evil situation no longer exists: the forces of evil have worked themselves out: Hamlet and all his kin are dead. There is nothing reassuring in the new situation, no promise that a new chain of evil will not quickly ensue, no lesson that men or the gods have learned. No message of hope for the future has been brought. The tragic situation, it is implied, is recurrent in human life: that is why we feel Terror; because we have seen men like ourselves yet stronger than we could expect to be, we feel also Pride.

Thus the tragic picture is incompatible with the Christian faith. It is equally incompatible with any form of religious belief that assumes the existence of a personal and kindly God. For that reason we should not be surprised at the rarity of tragedy. Chaucer's view of it as a story of a fall from prosperity to wretchedness, either at the bidding of Fortune or through divine retribution, is a mixture of unconscious paganism with Christian tradition: we cannot expect to find true tragedy anywhere in the Middle Ages, except here and there in early times when literature was not thoroughly Christianised. We can indeed recognize something of the tragic spirit in English poetry before the Conquest, from *Beowulf* to *The Battle of Maldon*. But we should not look for tragedy in the drama of seventeenth-century Spain, for al-

[6] *Shakespeare's Last Plays*, 1938, pp. 16-18.

ways there the spirit of religion burned brightly: Calderón and Lope de Vega might show evil in their plays, but it was an evil which attended on divine forgiveness or on an acceptable retribution; they might show suffering, but with them indeed it was the suffering of purgatorial fire. Nor should we look for tragedy in the classical drama of India: the gods there are seen as close to man, as his friends and teachers, ready to test human beings but ultimately to reward virtue wherever it should show itself. We can, however, find tragedy in those European countries which were brought most fully under Renaissance influences, with a weakening of medieval faith and some return to stoicism. In the atmosphere of comparative toleration under Elizabeth and James, English tragedy was especially free to develop. In seventeenth-century France, Racine could write tragically, though the form of his plays makes them appear almost like careful exercises in imitation of the classics: there is a lack of immediacy, of direct relation to the life around him, which perhaps made both the author and his audience feel safer: there was no compulsion for them to take too seriously the tragic view of things there presented. But from the seventeenth century until comparatively recent years the tragic form has been exceedingly rare, not because of a revival of religious faith, but because in these years men have not often combined a sharp sense of evil, a faith in man, and a sense of the impersonality of divine justice. In later days it is the faith in man that has been most difficult to come by, though tragedy has made an occasional appearance in modern European and American drama, and the tragic spirit has not infrequently found non-dramatic expression in the modern novel.

But whenever tragedy has come into being, its customary and right dress has been poetry. The equilibrium of Pride and Terror is, as we have seen, an opposition of persistent forces, and consequently the tragic play is characterised by strong tension. An appearance of casualness in the play will weaken the tension, and contradict the implication of a preordained pattern of event. Moreover, in order that the spectator's mind may more fully respond to the vision of evil and of human strength in defeat, the language must be finely turned. The medium of tragedy must be poetry, or at least a kind of prose which in its formal properties is clearly distinguished from the prose of the everyday, haphazard situation—not because the beauty of the words will atone for the presentation of evil, soothing our nerves and dulling our perceptions, but because only by a co-ordination of our faculties can we reach a full realisation of any complex picture of the world. Tragedy offers us a view of things which aims at comprehensiveness, and thus in its scope resembles the great religions of east and west. Like them, therefore, it needs all the resources of language for communication with men.

The Presuppositions of Tragedy

I: J. C. MAXWELL
II: CLIFFORD LEECH

I

The question whether Shakespeare's tragedies spring from, or are compatible with, a Christian view of life has been much canvassed in recent years. In the first part of his *Shakespeare's Tragedies and other Studies in Seventeenth Century Drama,* and especially in the opening chapter, "The Implications of Tragedy," Professor Clifford Leech has argued that "the tragic picture is incompatible with the Christian faith." On the other side, the term "Christian" has been freely applied to Shakespeare's tragedies, sometimes by those who may be under some suspicion of having a confessional axe to grind, but also by others (including the present writer) who are not guilty at least on that score. A reading of Professor Leech's chapter has suggested certain very simple considerations that seem to me important in tracing some of the reasons for disagreement.

It is taken for granted by Professor Leech that there is something that can be called "the tragic picture" (p. 18),[1] and, still more unequivocally, "the tragic view of things" (p. 19). I confess that this seems to me a paradoxical assumption. For one thing, it places tragedy on a separate footing from the other main literary forms. It would not, I think, be claimed that there is an epic or a comic view of things in anything like the same sense. Shakespeare, after all, wrote comedies, and the most it would seem reasonable to claim is that in these the tragic view of things was left in abeyance. To suggest that it is replaced by a "comic view of things" would sound curiously ponderous, and, indeed, any such idea would really detract from the seriousness which a "tragic view of things" is supposed to confer on tragedy. It would appear something of a pose if it were only a suit of clothes from a writer's wardrobe of *Weltanschauungen.* If we are to have a "tragic

From *Essays in Criticism,* Vol. V, 1955, pp. 175-81. Reprinted by permission of the editors.

[1] Page references are to the original source.—Ed.

view of things" at all, it must be *the* view of things with which the tragic author identifies himself, even if he may prescind from it in some non-tragic compositions. Only so can it be of sufficient weight for its compatibility or incompatibility with Christianity or any other religion to be a proper subject of discussion.

Is there such a view? It often seems to be assumed that tragedy cannot have adequate seriousness unless there is. But this is by no means self-evident. It may readily be admitted that certain philosophies of life can be so trivial or shallow that it is impossible to imagine tragedy springing from them or co-existing with them. But this would be because they are blind to, or wantonly deny, some of the facts about life which a tragedy has to present, not because these facts, as seen by the tragic writer, necessarily impose a specific "view of life."

Again, the fact that great tragedy is as rare as it is, and that it is never produced for very long at a time, suggests that it requires an unusual combination of conditions. But whether these conditions include a specific "view of life" needs to be argued. Professor Leech himself notes the shortness of the period during which almost all the best English tragedies were produced, and it is hard not to see something forced in his attempt to correlate this with a specific "phase in the current of Elizabethan thought" (p. 29).[2] He makes no claim that the writers of this period deliberately and consciously held the "tragic view"—indeed the briefness of the great period is in part attributed to "the dramatists' imperfect comprehension of their own achievement." The whole theory seems to rest on very shaky foundations. Moreover, if the "tragic view" is one that has been held only in a few specially favoured periods, and even then, as often as not, without full consciousness, is not the wide appeal of tragedy to men of different ages and creeds hard to understand? In the very process of exalting tragedy, Professor Leech is in danger, paradoxically, of making it appear something esoteric and specialized.

I turn to the more particular question of incompatibility between tragedy and Christianity. Here it must be admitted that Professor Leech can claim some support from Christian critics, writing as Christians. This is a subject he deals with most directly in his chapter "Rymer on Othello," in which he discusses Rymer's demand for poetic justice in tragedy, quoting his interesting contention that, according to the Greeks,

[2] He regards as secondary the other conditions he refers to: those connected with the "development of playhouse technique" (p. 44).

> a *Poet* must of necessity see *justice* exactly administred, if he intended to please. For, said they, if a World can scarce be satisfi'd with God Almighty, whose holy will and purposes are not to be *comprehended;* a *Poet* (in these matters) shall never be pardon'd, who (they are sure) is not *incomprehensible;* whose *ways* and *walks* may, without *impiety*, be penetrated and examin'd (pp. 102-3).

As Professor Leech notes, "Rymer was not so blinded as to think that such justice was to be found in actuality" (p. 102), and his demand turns on supposed requirements of the literary medium. None the less, Professor Leech, quoting Rymer's question about *Othello,* "If this be our end, what boots it to be Vertuous?" describes it as showing that "Rymer realized far more clearly than most critics that *Othello* and Shakespeare's other great tragedies present a view of the world that cannot be reconciled with Christianity."

This is very precipitate. Let us admit that Christian critics more profound than Rymer—first and foremost Dr. Johnson—have made this demand for poetic justice, but was it on the ground that tragedies in which it is not observed "present a view of the world that cannot be reconciled with Christianity"? Not in any straightforward sense. We have just seen that Rymer's objection to tragedies of this sort is not that they are not true to life. It remains a tenable view that the possibility of events such as those in *Othello* is *in fact* incompatible with the truth of Christianity. But at least Christians (including Rymer and Johnson) who have not lived an abnormally sheltered existence have contrived to believe in Christianity in the face of such facts. It was a rather complicated—very likely a confused—combination of literary and moral principles that none the less prompted their demand for poetic justice. It may well be that this demand undermines the foundations of tragedy as a literary form, and that Rymer and Johnson ought to have concluded that tragedy had no place in a Christian society. But this is by no means to say that a tragedy *cannot* be the product of the imagination of a Christian conscious of what his own creed implies.

I have tried to keep this note as free as possible from speculations about the nature of tragedy and, in general, from anything that can be called theorizing. My purpose is purely to express scepticism. The point of view put forward by Professor Leech, and implied by a good many other writers, seems to me so paradoxical that the whole onus of proof lies on its supporters. Of the not very large number of great tragedies in existence, a good many are the work of men writing for

Christian audiences, and, to put it no more strongly, not overtly rejecting a Christian outlook. It is not at all obvious that these tragedies are so closely linked with, say, Greek tragedy, that we must posit a "view of things" characterizing them as tragedies, and cutting them off from Christianity. Any such thesis needs to be proved, not presupposed.

II

As his note was written before the appearance of Professor Richard B. Sewall's article "The Tragic Form" [*Essays in Criticism,* IV (October 1954), 345-58], I have no means of knowing whether Mr. J. C. Maxwell is yet convinced, whether in fact a reply from me is in any measure required. Yet there are certain things he has said that do perhaps call for challenge.

He does not think it would be claimed that "there is an epic or a comic view of things in anything like the same sense" as has been claimed for tragedy. This is surprising indeed. On epic the light has been darkened, doubtless, by Aristotle's near-equation of the form with tragedy, but that should not in these days blind us to the basic differences in attitude: the epic poet moves away from the world around him to a world in which man can from moment to moment act or fail, and always in the grand manner; the tragic writer may use remote settings and characters difficult to approach, but he sees life as a process, not as a series of juxtaposed incidents or achievements. The distinction has perhaps been put most compellingly by Professor Emil Staiger in the section on epic in his *Grundbegriffe der Poetik* (Zürich, 1946, pp. 89-153). Of course the human vision is not constant: as Sir Maurice Bowra has pointed out, there is a momentary feeling of the tragic in *The Iliad* when Hector dies (*Heroic Poetry,* 1952, pp. 77-8), and *Hamlet* may at times approach the epic in its elaboration of the particular incident. But to deny a constancy of viewpoint is not to deny the inherent congruence of certain viewpoints and certain Kinds.

The comic and the tragic points of view are, of course, closer than those of tragedy and epic. It needs only some diminution of terror, some (at times inevitable) doubt of man's stature, to transform the tragic into a comic presentation. When this happens from time to time in tragedy but with the sense of terror and the sense of exaltation dominant in the work as a whole, we feel that the tragic Kind has been preserved and enriched. When, however, the scepticism is stronger, the terror subdued through the lethargy of custom, we have the chance that *The Cherry Orchard* or *Troilus and Cressida* may emerge. I would agree, it appears, with Mr. Maxwell that better-humoured comedies come into existence only through a measure of deliberate exclusion. It should, however, be clear why the writer of tragedies may write comedies as well—particularly if he is often productive.

The human inconstancy of attitude should explain, too, why tragedy, though a-Christian in its implications, may be written by Christians and may please a predominantly Christian audience. For most men religious opinions are not equally powerful on every day of the year or the week. We know what amounts to nothing of Shakespeare's or Webster's religious views, but we know that our thoughts are not directed to God and His purposes when we have come to an end of reading *Othello* or *The Duchess of Malfi*. Indeed, Mr. Graham Greene, while affirming his Catholicism, can claim that his writing must be free to run counter to a sentiment and a doctrine to which, as a non-writer, he gives a general assent (*Why do I write? An Exchange of Views between Elizabeth Bowen, Graham Greene and V. S. Pritchett*, 1948, pp. 31-2). Of course, with so determined an affiliation as Mr. Greene's, the independence is necessarily limited: hence the concluding hints of "reconciliation" that modify the tragic impact in *The Heart of the Matter* and *The Living Room*. Hence, too, though slighter in stress and in effect, the suggestions that things will be well again in Scotland and in Malfi which we find at the ends of *Macbeth* and Webster's *Duchess*. And hence, perhaps, the dissolving of the tragic attitude in *The Oresteia* when Pallas, the city's patron, is physically present as supreme arbitress in the judgment of Orestes: this is strongly contrasted with the allusion to the arbitrarily named, the unknowable Zeus in the first part of the trilogy. The tragic attitude is not, to use Mr. Maxwell's terms, "esoteric and specialized," but it is hard to maintain throughout the writing of tragedy. Indeed, in modern times a tragic attitude presented uniformly through a play or novel, unmodified by comic dubiety or a polite or wishful inclination to the Christian scheme, is likely to arouse some incredulity in us, to make us feel that the writer is protesting too confidently his faith in Man, his independence of God: he wears, we think, with too much ease a mantle that should be heavy for the strongest shoulders. That may appear in Hardy or in *Bussy d'Ambois*. Perhaps tragedy is at its most powerful when it is achieved reluctantly or without full consciousness. If so, we must recognize a likelihood of inconsistency.

Of course Mr. Maxwell is right in denying an equation of Greek and Jacobean tragedy. Yet there were historical links, through Seneca and perhaps, as Professor J. A. K. Thomson (*Shakespeare and the Classics*, 1952, pp. 242-54) has suggested, through Plutarch. More important is the approach to identity in the total effects of, say, *Lear* and *Oedipus*. It would not be denied, one presumes, that these plays aim at giving an inclusive view of the nature of human life, and in neither of them is the concept of divine justice congruent with Christian feeling. No more than *Oedipus* does *Lear* contain a hint of salvation or divine suffering. That the world presented in Jacobean tragedy is more various than in Greek tragedy, that often in Shakespeare and his contemporaries the picture is complicated by the measure of automatic adherence to the Christian scheme, the medieval and Tudor concepts of social order—these things contribute to the total effect but do not prevent us from feeling that the Jacobeans and the Greeks were at their best when working within the limits of the same Kind.

Shakespearian Tragedy

A. P. ROSSITER

Can we arrive at a conception of Shakespearian Tragedy? The easy way is *a priori:* not to arrive *at,* but to arrive *with* one ready-made; to start with previous notions derived from the Greek, from Aristotle (or from Bradley, whom many still mistake for a pseudonym for Aristotle). If we take the Aristotelean previous notion, there is nothing to add to what Mr. Trotter says in Shaw's *Fanny's First Play:*

> If you had been classically educated . . .
> *Fanny:* But I have.
> *Trotter:* Pooh! Cambridge! If you had been educated at Oxford, you would know that the definition of a play has been settled exactly and scientifically for two thousand, two hundred and sixty years.[1]

As I was not educated "classically," I find that unacceptable.

The testing of Shakespearian drama by the *Poetics* is recognizably a consequence of the eighteenth century: part and parcel of their demonstrations of how much that is "classical" was to be found in this apparent Goth. This is not to say that Shakespearian tragedy cannot be seen more clearly by contrasting Greek and English, on the basic assumption that tragedy is a rare literary product, cast up only in *some* cultures or cultural stages; and that there is (if no more) a "tragic sense" in common between Sophocles, Racine, Ibsen, Pirandello and Shakespeare. But it cannot be assumed that Aristotle's generalizations are relevant to Elizabethan-Jacobean tragic writing. There is no evidence that Sidney knew the *Poetics.* There is apparent evidence that Shakespeare did not know much about Aristotle, who is mentioned twice: once as pre-Homeric (*Troilus and Cressida,* II. ii.); once by Tranio as the opposite to Ovid. And only once does any Elizabethan mention *catharsis:* and then only to mock at it.[2] All this (so far as Eliza-

Published with the permission of Theatre Arts Books, New York, from *Angel with Horns* by A. P. Rossiter, edited by Graham Storey, © 1961 by Longmans, Green & Co., Ltd.

[1] Reprinted by permission of the Public Trustee and The Society of Authors.

[2] Robert Peterson in *Galateo of Manners and Behaviours,* 1576: see J. W. H. Atkins, *English Literary Criticism of the Renaissance,* 1947, pp. 223-24.

bethan popular stage-writing goes) can be dismissed with Dryden: "It is not enough that Aristotle has said so, for Aristotle drew his models of tragedy from Sophocles and Euripides; and, if he had seen ours, might have changed his mind." [3]

The other way—*a posteriori*—is to find out what the Elizabethans (including Shakespeare) had to say about tragedy; and to add to that by inference from their practice, whether with words or with the names of plays.

Shakespeare uses the word *tragedy* eleven times: once in mere jest (*A Midsummer-Night's Dream*); twice merely descriptively (*Hamlet*); of the eight occasions left, only one usage, in *Henry V,* is later than *Richard III. Tragic* (eight times) and *tragical* (five times) add another thirteen usages, of which eight are in early plays. Thus of twenty-four occurrences, fifteen are as early as *Richard III,* and three are in jest (*A Midsummer-Night's Dream*). We can say, then, that over 70 per cent are very early; the three usages in *Hamlet* only concern the Players' repertoire; and that leaves but three for plays anywhere near the Tragedies in time of composition. *Othello* is the only tragedy in which any of the three words is found; and "the tragic loading of this bed" did not mean, to the Elizabethans, anything as weighty as we feel from it.[4]

Tragedy, in Shakespeare's own usage, seems to mean "an alarming calamity, usually bloody, and often determined by the plotted designs of someone." When not plotted, it means simply "a calamitous fall"; and can be applied to defeat in battle (as used by, e.g., Warwick at Towton, or the Archbishop of Canterbury on the Black Prince in France). It is associated with "dire induction" and "prologue"; and "this scene of rude impatience" is the same as "an act of tragic violence" (Queen Elizabeth in *Richard III,* II, ii. 39). In short, it seems to refer exclusively to the kind of "tragic" of Kyd: not to modern critical associations at all (although the newspaper-sense is represented: Salisbury [*1 Henry VI*] is shot by cannon—has his eye out and his cheek missing—and that is "this woeful tragedy"). The only usage with any hint of wider, more philosophical implications is in *Titus Andronicus:* Titus asks why Nature made "so foul a den" as the place where Lavinia was ravished, "unless the gods delight in tragedies."

The next place to try is the Stationers' Register, where the names

[3] *Heads of an answer to Rymer's Remarks on the Tragedies of the last Age.*
[4] Cf. the "stern and tragical" look of Winchester in *1 Henry VI,* where "tragical" means "murderous."

of plays were entered before legitimate printing. It is arguable that the players would be reasonably careful to put down the right titles, and that (though Shakespeare may have had no hand in it) what we can read *was* what the plays were called.[5] The Stationers' Register has *Richard III* and *Richard II* both down as tragedies; *Hamlet* (1602: Robertes's entry) is "the Revenge of Hamlett Prince Denmarke"; *King Lear* (1607), the "history of Kinge Lear"; *Antony and Cleopatra* (1608), "a book called Antony and Cleopatra"; *Othello* (in the Register of 1621), "The Tragedie of Othello, the moore of Venice."

If we consult the early Quartos, printed during Shakespeare's lifetime, we find the same uncertainty. *Romeo and Juliet* (Q2: 1599) is the "most Excellent and lamentable Tragedie"; but *Hamlet* (1604) "The Tragicall Historie" (as was Q1), and *King Lear* (1608) the "true chronicle Historie." In the Folio we have not only the presence of *Troilus and Cressida* between the Histories and Tragedies (which may be explainable), but also *Cymbeline* as a tragedy, fully entitled.[6]

Now we might *guess* from all this, that by *c.* 1599 Shakespeare was aware that he was writing something different from what had *been* "tragedy" at the time when he most used the word in his plays, five to ten years earlier. Accordingly, he avoided the word in his Tragedies. This is only a guess; but better than supposing that he had no conception of tragedy, or only a crude one. He must at any rate have been perfectly aware that he was writing something totally unlike the most respected kind of tragedy; the highbrow kind that imitated Seneca directly (or at one remove), with a Chorus and at least a compromise with the neo-classical principles which required that the time represented should be as near as possible to a single day, that the scene should remain as far as possible one and the same throughout, and that scenes of violence should be described rather than presented (in keeping with the Horatian *Ne pueros coram populo Medea trucidet*). About this kind of tragedy there is no lack of first-hand Elizabethan information; in fact, most of the contemporary tragedy-criticism is about *form*. Sidney and Jonson give representative comments; and their main relevance to Shakespeare is that they show what he must have known he was *not* attempting to do.

Not that Jonson was the strict pedant he is often supposed to be.

[5] With the Folio we can be certain of no such thing. The date is 1623; and the editors are commited to their tripartite division of the canon.

[6] The very least I can infer from that, is that it was never called a comedy (conceivably it was a "true chronicle Historie," and analogy with *King Lear* did the rest: both being stories of ancient Britain).

In "To the Readers," before *Sejanus,* he admits the play's classical deficiencies (in the unity of time, and there being no Chorus), but continues that it is not "needful" nor perhaps "possible in these our times, and to such auditors as commonly things are presented, to observe the old state and splendour of dramatic poems, with preservation of any popular delight." Webster says much the same, but ill-temperedly, in *The White Devil.* It would be no good his offering "the most sententious tragedy . . . observing all the critical laws": the breath of the "uncapable multitude" would poison it. And he quotes Horace's Epode about the horrid garlic—*O dura messorum ilia*—and rounds off the paragraph with a further civility about giving pigs what is meet for pigs.

I mention both these views (1) because Webster is a dramatist of the "school of Shakespeare"; (2) because there is nothing to show that Shakespeare was dissatisfied with what he was making of the changing "tragic-history" form; and (3) to emphasize that there were two forms of tragedy,[7] and that Shakespeare's choice was consistently for the *lower.* Consistently: because there is no sign that he ever tried to tighten his form in tragedy; for his last tragedy (*Antony and Cleopatra*) and his greatest triumph (*King Lear*) are the loosest-woven of all. What "lower" means is shown by a passage of 1604. Anthony Scoloker is writing an "Epistle" as preface to his *Daiphantus.* He wants it to please all; and, to express this, he uses first an allusion to highbrow reading, and then turns to something more vulgar and popular: something which appealed to those who were not up to Sidney's *Arcadia.* This is how he puts it:

> It should be like the *Neuer-too-well read Arcadia,* where the *Prose and Verce* (*Matter* and *Words*) are like his *Mistresses* eyes, one still excelling another and without Corriuall: or to come home to the vulgars *Element,* like *Friendly Shakespeares Tragedies,* where the *Commedian* rides, when the *Tragedian* stands on Tip-toe: Faith it should please all, like Prince *Hamlet.*

But though Shakespeare worked in "the vulgars Element," that does not mean he therefore abandoned what high-sententious tragedy had to offer. What that was, to the Elizabethans, Sidney and Jonson can tell us; and I see no reason to suppose that Shakespeare could have taken an entirely different view of what tragic writing included

[7] I.e. excluding Latin performances and unstageworthy sedulous apings of them.

(the most important differences concern what orthodox tragedy would *exclude*).

Jonson includes among the "offices of a tragic writer," "truth of argument, dignity of persons, gravity and height of elocution, fulness and frequency of sentence" (*Sejanus:* "To the Readers"). In modern terms we should say: a veracious *plot;*[8] great or distinguished *characters;* seriousness and elevation of *style;* and a richness of sound moral teaching, memorably expressed.

Sidney is relevant, for all that he does not write for "the vulgars Element." In his *Apologie for Poetrie* he has three main criteria of tragedy: (1) In his criticism of *Gorboduc:* it should keep the classical forms (i.e. the unities), and should teach morality "most delightfully"—that being "the very end of Poesie," i.e. "the end of well dooing and not of well knowing onely." (2) it "maketh Kinges feare to be Tyrants, and Tyrants manifest their tirannicall humors"; (3) it "teacheth the uncertainety of this world" by "sturring the affects of admiration and commiseration": i.e. it makes *felt* the "mutability-ethic" of the Middle Ages, and especially through *exempla* of men-of-power (cf. his quotation from Seneca's *Oedipus: Qui . . . duro imperio regit/ Timet timentes, metus in auctorem redit*).

The first of these principles adds nothing to what we have had from Jonson. Modern inquiries have shown that there is far more "notable moralite" in *Richard III, Julius Caesar, Macbeth, Coriolanus,* than used to be supposed. But the moral framework of the Histories (Order, degree, the magical King-figure, the order of the State as a branch of Natural Order) is less than the *moral pattern* of *Macbeth;* and in *Hamlet* and *King Lear* the extractable Elizabethan morality is trivial beside the total effect of the play: even if we do not feel that this total

[8] I say "a veracious plot" to avoid the difficult question of what was regarded as "truth of argument" in a play. Jonson presumably means the same as "my integrity in the story," which he "shows" by footnote-quotations from Latin historians. It is obvious that Shakespeare attempted no such historical accuracy; and that he must often have been aware of how he altered alleged records of fact (e.g., in *Macbeth* and *Coriolanus*). It is arguable that he was conscious, in this, of his own efforts to reach at a higher, more general human truth, obscured by chroniclers and historians: what Sidney called the "golden" world of poetry, as compared with the "brazen" that Nature gives us. But it seems quite certain that the *audience* knew of no such refinements. The poets may have had their own "philosophical" standard of "truth"; but their hearers in the theatre assumed that the staged events really happened. As Hamlet told the Court, "This play is the image of a murder done in Vienna . . . the story is extant, and writen in very choice Italian."

effect *runs contrary* to what we suppose an Elizabethan would take for its moral teaching.[9]

The second is slightly comical, if we think of a row of stalls full of kings being shown what happens to tyrants. It might apply to *Richard III,* but is too crude for *Richard II.* "Tyrants" manifesting "tirannicall humors" is more promising—if translated. "Tyrant" is a Senecan word, and by it Sidney means the kind of character (Atreus, Oedipus, Lycus, Eteocles) who is, to Stoics, an *exemplum* of tyrannic *"passion"* (will-to-power; will to revenge; passionate will, as in Phaedra; madness).

> The overgrowth of some complexion
> Oft breaking down the pales and forts of reason

might well be applied to Othello (and to Iago too?), to Coriolanus, and perhaps to Romeo and to Antony: all are in some sense obsessed or infatuated men. So is Timon: victim of two consecutive and opposite obsessions. But the view (Masefield's) that the tragedies are tragedies of obsession is again too crude: though it does show how easily Sidney's Senecan-extracted fear of passion can be made Christian for those who are neither Senecan nor Stoical. If Shakespeare started with some such conception of tragedy, he not only went far beyond it by 1600: he was doing so even in *Richard III,* where that very sardonic humorist has (for all his naked villainy) an engaging gusto and a daring resoluteness which run counter to the moralists' requirements. Sidney's "tirannicall humors" does not signify anything at all like the sarcastic, grimly ironical, often profane sense of humour which Richard displays. The Senecan "tyrants" are, in fact, if not mad, as humourless as madmen.

Sidney's last principle is the widest and the best. "The uncertainety of this world," the demonstration of what weak foundations gilded roofs may rest on: that touches the old primitive distrust of Nature. Both Stoic and Christian have capitalized it as "world-contempt," yet it remains primitive still. There is a murmur behind calamity which tells us, in the words of Lafeu, that "we have our philosophical persons to make modern [commonplace] and familiar things supernatural and causeless." And what follows? "Hence is it that we make trifles of terrors, ensconcing ourselves into seeming knowledge, when we should submit ourselves to an unknown fear." [10] That "unknown fear" visits

[9] One has to guess. But I cannot see that *King Lear*—seen from the Elizabethan moral point of view—says anything very different from what *Gorboduc* did. Both are about kings who split up the State, destroyed the magic bond of subordination, and let loose unnaturalness upon themselves, their children and their people.

[10] *All's Well,* II. iii. 1-6.

us in our own catastrophes. "Why this, to me?" "Why should it happen as it did? Why just then?" And the *sense* of tragic poetry is there, though the words are lacking: "I am a man/ More sinned against than sinning."

It is a manifest quality of Shakespearian tragedy that it visits us with such unknown fears, and in almost as high a degree as if the fates of imaginary creatures were our own. All the tragedies deal with men and women caught in traps of circumstance: though the degree of mere "accident" varies enormously (e.g., as between Romeo and Macbeth or Coriolanus). So too does the extent to which the hero has made the circumstances in the first place. Hamlet does not make his at all. Richard II has apparently made his. Antony, Macbeth, perhaps Lear, we watch making theirs, almost absolutely. Othello we watch having the circumstances made about him: he stands somewhere between Hamlet and Macbeth. The heroes' characters are partially determinants of their sufferings and destructions; but their ends are either so *different* from their intentions as to *seem* unjust (Romeo, Brutus, Hamlet, Othello), or so entirely excessive in misery that there is no question of "seeming" about it (Lear, Gloucester). The two most arguably "just" ends are those of Macbeth and Coriolanus: Macbeth, only if we keep our eyes strictly on the hero (*not* on the ruins around him); in *Coriolanus,* the hero is the only real sufferer.

I take occasion to quote Bradley here. He labours to believe that the gods *are* just: that a moral principle re-establishes itself at the end of *King Lear;* and yet he writes: "to assert that he deserved to suffer what he did suffer is to do violence not merely to language but to any healthy moral sense." [11] On the next page he says: "Let us put aside the ideas of justice and merit . . ."; and I have used Sidney's tragic principles as an approach to Shakespeare, because it seems to me that what Shakespeare had to do was to put aside those ideas, in order to become a Shakespearian, not an Elizabethan, *tragedian:* a writer of genuine tragedy, not "moral-tragicall" Histories.

Set beside Elizabethan tragical principles (as in Sidney), Shakespeare's tragedies have rejected the "Tudor-Christian" conception of a moral and just world. I do not mean that their author has "accepted" the opposite of that conception: only that it is distanced—like a hypothesis, not a faith. The *personae* themselves, in their suffering and uncertainty, try to jump to superstitious or pessimistic conclusions; and we may be tempted to accept them emotionally: "There is a

[11] *Shakespearean Tragedy,* p. 32.

divinity that shapes our ends";[12] "The time is out of joint"; "It is the very error of the moon"; "It is the stars"; "The wheel is come full circle"; "As flies to wanton boys"; "O, I am fortune's fool!"; "the false housewife Fortune."

But these are not philosophic utterances. "I see men's judgements are/ A parcel of their fortunes," Enobarbus says. The "uncertainety of this world" is not only its hidden threats of terrible consequences following from human actions which seemed right (or, at least, quite safe); but the blind, explosive "spread" of retribution. Witness the fates of Ophelia, Desdemona and Cordelia. Fools, knaves and innocents go the same way, though we feel less about them than about the heroes. County Paris, Polonius, Rosencrantz, Roderigo, Oswald (a servant rather maligned in the interests of sound morality), all die. Cassius, much more on terms with evil than Brutus, shares his fate (and suffers less). Hamlet is destroyed with Claudius, Othello with Iago; Cassio (of doubtful "daily beauty") escapes; Emilia is killed. This alarmingness of circumstance is only evaded by the theory of "tragic flaw" or "tragic weakness." The theory (extracted from Aristotle) says that the hero's nature is "flawed" and his fate follows from this excess or deficiency. Its effect is to shift all blame from the universe (or to give that consoling impression),[13] and it is popular enough: both because of the ease with which "tragic weaknesses" can be diagnosed (or devised)—when we know how the story ends; and, again, because it re-establishes the comforting belief that the universe is moral, and the fates of tragic heroes somehow just.

Take *Othello*. Critics jump to conclude that Othello *was* "one not easily jealous"; or that he "loved not wisely, but too well"; or (with Bradley) that "credulousness, excessive simplicity" must go in the list of "marked imperfections or defects" which begins with "irresolution, precipitancy, pride," and ends with "excessive susceptibility to sexual emotions." [14] "Credulousness, excessive simplicity" look all right in the list, till I turn to my texts. I find:

> The Moor is of a free and open nature
> That thinks men honest that but seem to be so;

[12] Or "There is a special providence in the fall of a sparrow," which comes in the very scene where Hamlet says: "I am constant to my purposes [which he is *not*]; they follow the King's pleasure" (which is true. Claudius *is* being the divinity that shapes his end).

[13] It only gives an impression, because it does not even attempt to answer the question: 'Is there any cause in nature that makes these hard hearts?'

[14] *Shakespearean Tragedy*, pp. 34-5.

And will as tenderly be led by th' nose
As asses are (I. iii. 393-6);

and remember:

He, being remiss,
Most generous, and free from all contriving,
Will not peruse the foils; (*Hamlet*, IV. iii. 134-6)

and:

A credulous father! and a brother noble,
Whose nature is so far from doing harms
That he suspects none; on whose foolish honesty
My practices ride easy! (*King Lear*, I. ii. 170-3)

Why are these qualities in Othello, Hamlet, Edgar, to be called "evil" —even "in the wide sense of the word"? [15] When Bradley adds, "Evil exhibits itself everywhere as something negative, barren, weakening, destructive, a principle of death. It isolates, disunites, and tends to annihilate not only its opposite but itself,[16] I have to say that the noble frailties in his list are not "evils" at all. He is right enough about the quality of evil in Macbeth or Iago or Goneril; but with the others he has turned a nobility (generosity of mind) into an "evil," to evade the issue, and to avoid the embarrassing position of Auden's schoolmistress, "giving the Universe nought for conduct."

I do not think it an exaggeration to say that to press these patterns of "tragic weakness" is to destroy tragedy.[17] They reintroduce the Elizabethan moral machinery under various disguises; and, so to speak, go back to *Richard III* and Sidney against the current which took Shakespeare from *Hamlet* to *Macbeth* and *Lear*. The play, in fact, to which the "tragic weakness" pattern applies neatest, *Timon*, is the most ignored of the later tragedies; and the next nearest to it, *Coriolanus* (where Shakespeare does alter Plutarch to increase Coriolanus's recalcitrant pride), is not commonly bracketed with *Antony and Cleopatra* as "Shakespeare's most assured artistic success." None the less, there does seem to be a problem here. Shakespeare wrote these two

[15] Bradley, *ibid.*, p. 35.

[16] *Ibid.*

[17] There is an English complacency which evades the hurting contemplation of misfortune or misery by finding that the victim is to blame (as he may be): to blame for *all* of it. Coleridge knew this very well in Wordsworth, settled, married and a man of propriety and property. If he could have brought that knowledge alive into his criticism of tragedy, "hamartia-hunting" might have been strangled at birth.

plays, either before *Antony and Cleopatra* or between that and *Cymbeline* and the Romances. It is possible that they represent a going-back from the tragic conception of *Lear* towards something more moral, simpler and less terrifying: towards the Histories, in fact. Both Timon and Coriolanus are alienated from a *social* world: the universes of Macbeth and Lear shrink to a πόλις. Their passions are more like the "ruling passions" of the eighteenth century.

Shakespeare's conception of tragedy plainly and constantly concerns the man who *is* "passion's slave"—in the extended, Senecan sense of "passion." Hence the distinguishing mark of his emotional effects: that even among his violent contemporaries he is a past-master at scenes of pain. He gives us not only the pure pathos of Lear kneeling before Cordelia, utterly humbled ("If you have poison for me I will drink it"), or the rages of Othello, Lear, Antony, Coriolanus; but the immense variety of "on the torment of the mind to lie/ In restless ecstasy" in Brutus, Hamlet, Othello, Macbeth. Suffering beyond solace, beyond any moral palliation, and suffering because of a human greatness which is great because great in passion: that, above everything else, is central to Shakespeare's tragic conception. "The man who is not passion's slave" gets his passage in Hamlet's mouth, and the invitation to make Horatio a paragon of animals is duly accepted by your even-tempered Christian. But before we make too much of that, we should call in those others to whom the term applies: Bolingbroke, Octavius, for example; and perhaps we should ask whether, if cool self-management is a virtue, we can exclude Claudius and Iago?

If, then, "distinction" is Shakespeare's tragic subject—*passional* distinction, and as much *through* suffering as despite it—a phrase of Bradley's casts an immediate light on one essence of that tragic quality. He says that the hero is so circumstanced that his greatness is fatal, adding: "To meet these circumstances something is required which a smaller man might have given, but which the hero cannot give." [18] And if you ask what quality that implies in the hero, the answer is *pride:* Renaissance pride, seen as self-greatness. Hence such heroes as Richard III and Macbeth, distinguished in flat defiance of their time's morality; hence too the approach *towards* being tragic figures of all the History kings. The Shakespearian tragic universe is such that mediocrity is pretty safe, for all that "some innocents escape not the thunderbolt" (as Cleopatra said). I see no sign that Shakespeare has any conception of bourgeois tragedy: to him, I suppose, *Arden of*

[18] *Shakespearean Tragedy,* p. 21.

Feversham (or *Women Beware Women*) was not tragic; for his heroes go beyond something greater than the Common Law, the trap of retribution in domestic crimes.

Much rather, he offers adumbrations of a fundamental antinomy. The universe produces human greatness, which is therefore *natural* to it; and yet it is antagonistic to distinction. If we approach the tragedies through the Histories, then we must see that, in so far as cosmic order still appears, it has become the *antagonist*. In *Julius Caesar, Macbeth* and *Lear,* this is so explicitly. In the Roman plays, the world seems to be conceived as a polity, in which there is, at most, room for one great man—*and,* it would appear, for only certain sorts of greatness (not, for example, for that of Brutus or of Antony). By its destruction and the calm that ensues—if Bradley is right—greatness seems *unnatural* to this world. Virginia Woolf said the same of *The Mayor of Casterbridge:* "Henchard is pitted, not against another man, but against something outside himself which is opposed to men of his ambition and power." I had rather she said it of Captain Ahab and *Moby Dick,* but that makes no odds here. We cannot "accept" this apparent "unnaturalness" of the qualities we are moved by and admire; and that contradiction is at the root of the "sense of mystery" which all critics agree to find in Shakespearian tragedy. The emotional experiencing of this universal antinomy is what Aristotle called φόβος: the tragic fear which is not self-regarding.

If this view is acceptable, then *Hamlet* ceases to be an awkward and perplexing aberration—as it is, if approached through the Histories. For though Prince Hamlet has had a King-father murdered and a throne usurped, he *never* refers to cosmic order, Divine Kingship or curses on State and posterity. Hamlet is a cosmic non-conformist. If seen as the good mind in an evil world, as alien to it—as *all* the heroes are alien—I see no problem. And indeed *Hamlet's* evil world-frame follows logically on the collapse of the ideal pattern of cosmic order in *Troilus and Cressida.*

I do, however, find the greatest difficulty over Bradley when he tells us (p. 23) that the central tragic feeling is the impression of waste; and then (p. 37) that, by the end of a tragedy, "it [the moral order] has lost a part of its own substance—a part more dangerous and unquiet, but far more valuable and *nearer to its heart*[19] than that which remains,—a Fortinbras, a Malcolm, an Octavius." I feel the "waste"; but my difficulties over that "nearer to its heart" are insuperable, unless

[19] Not Bradley's italics.

I conclude that the "moral order" has a *double* heart: i.e. that the universe is quasi-Manichean, and that human greatness (which is *one* God's "good") is the evil of the *other* God (i.e. the God of order and degree). I cannot think Bradley meant this. Yet such a view can result from seeing Renaissance *virtu* superimposed on Christian order: *Virtu contra Ordinem.* If I do make myself accept Bradley's Hegelian terms, I find myself irreverently remembering Peer Gynt, when he is marooned in Africa and suddenly sees the yacht that has dropped him blow up: "Ah! God *is* a Father to me after all . . . but He's not what you'd call economical about it!"

But that is not the whole picture. Not only is the vulnerability to fortune of human distinction Shakespeare's theme: its special liability to intense suffering and destruction. He also emphasizes the precariousness of its very *quality* of greatness: of its right to regard, respect, admiration, awe. A regular concomitant of his tragedies is that the pettier and less dignified aspects of heroes and heroines are insisted on; and, more than that, that comic and even farcical scenes, persons and effects are thrust against the main figures and episodes.

I turn back to Jonson and Sidney, and take up my point about "what orthodox tragedy would *exclude*." It is what Sidney called "mungrell Tragy-comedie": the thrusting in of "Clownes by head and shoulders, to play a part in majesticall matters," clean contrary to the orthodox principle of "strict separation." It is, again, what Scoloker meant with his "*Friendly Shakespeares Tragedies,* where the *Commedian* rides, when the *Tragedian* stands on Tip-toe."

This insistence on the *comic* is entirely absent in *Richard II;* nearly so in *Julius Caesar;* fumbled or uncertain in *Titus Andronicus* and *Romeo and Juliet:* but from *Hamlet* to *Antony and Cleopatra* it is always there, though never constant. It is by no means entirely dependent on conventional clowns. So, although the traditional clown explains its *evolution* as a factor in true-English tragedy, it cannot be argued that Shakespeare included it simply because the clown had to have a part. Hamlet mad,[20] Ophelia mad and bawdy, Iago cynical, Cleopatra raging or mocking Antony till he looks ridiculous, Menenius, Enobarbus: none of those are clowns' parts.

Again, as can be shown from the Fool's part in *Lear,* the characteristically Shakespearian effects are far less ludicrous than *grotesque.* They *might* be laughable, if they could be noted with a heart devoid

[20] "In his shirt" appears to have been the Elizabethan idea: too much for Olivier, that!

of sympathy, but by an intelligence keenly aware of their immense incongruity and of the mocking wit which seems to have devised them. They somewhat resemble tragic irony, of the kind where a man's words seem as if malevolently mis-designed for him, by a witty spirit which foreknows how true they are,[21] but in a sense quite other than he imagines in uttering them:

Macbeth: Is't far you ride? . . . Fail not our feast.
Banquo: My lord, I will not.

Or *Othello:*

If it were now to die,
'Twere now to be most happy; for I fear
My soul hath her content so absolute
That not another comfort like to this
Suceeds in unknown fate.

But in these comic ironies is more of a spirit of witty *rascality:* a sly derisiveness, which not only emphasizes men's blind ignorance of their ends, but seems (by mocking it) to question their intrinsic value—their very quality of distinction. This mockingly *critical* function, which criticizes by making game of what men respect, admire, feel sympathy towards or are drawn to, is expressed in Goethe by Mephistopheles. "*Der Geist der stets verneint*" ("the spirit that ever denies") he calls himself. But before the Lord Almighty, in the Prologue, his comic-derisive quality of "rascality" is at once stated, and by the Lord himself. To Mephistopheles' "Dust shall he bite, ay, lick it up with zest," the Lord replies:

Ich habe deinesgleichen nie gehasst:
Von allen Arten Geisten, die verneinen,
Ist mir der Schalk am wenigsten zur Last.

(In that you also have a dispensation.
Your kindred never had my hate or scorn:
Of all the spirits of negation
The scamp is least of burdens to be borne.)[22]

There the resemblance ends: for Goethe cannot write tragedy, and his spirit of negation must "toil to serve creation, though a devil."

As an example, take the element of bawdry in Ophelia mad, which

[21] Or, of course, how ridiculously *false,* when all the truth (of later events or latent natures) is known. *Coriolanus* has much of this irony: e.g., Aufidius at I. II. 19 27, or Coriolanus himself at I. i. 231. "Tragic irony" is really verbal *peripeteia.*

[22] Philip Wayne's translation. Penguin, 1949. Reprinted by permission.

tends to *negate* the suffering by rousing (Elizabethan) hilarity.[23] Or Hamlet at the grave-side, quibbling on mortality, ignorant that it is Ophelia's grave. The Clown's "You lie out on't, sir," is a sardonic jest with three edges to it. It is another, that Hamlet talks of *equivocation:* for all he says to the Gravedigger is equivocal, and death is creeping up behind him while he prattles. How comical a set-up for a Chaplin! Othello in the "brothel-scene," treating Emilia like a professional bawd, has moved towards the pure grotesque. This has a quality of horrifying absurdity, because Othello is playing to a "Desdemona" only of his diseased imagination; and yet playing the scene to caricature-like excess before Desdemona herself. This equivocal quality also appears in the coarse parallels of Bianca and Emilia, not to Desdemona herself, but to what Othello imagines as "Desdemona." Bianca *is* a whore; Emilia not over-scrupulous, given her price; and Iago's Desdemona, and Roderigo's too, are similar "light" illusions.

It is a wide jump: but in *Twelfth Night* the grotesque delusion of Malvolio, in love with an illusion called Olivia, is a parallel instance of this kind of malevolent gulling. Few things undermine dignity more than a display of ridiculously misplaced confidence in a man's own misjudgment. There is a beautiful example of it in *Coriolanus,* in Menenius's mission to the Volscian army (v. ii.). The Sentinels bar his way, and then—when Coriolanus appears—the old man tells them what they have let themselves in for: "Behold now presently, and swoon for what's to come upon thee." But it is he who is left near swooning: utterly snubbed; allowed to say two words only ("How! away!"); and abandoned to the Sentinels' mockery. If funny, it is also moving—with that strange pathos of the Clown's tragedy, which only the greatest comedians understand.

"Ridiculously misplaced confidence in a man's own misjudgment": the phrase might also be applied to *some* of Shakespeare's tragic patterns. Richard III (setting aside his diabolic sense of comedy) does set to work on a programme summarized in Queen Margaret's curse. But though he hears the curse, it never crosses his mind that he is fully "working to rule," and that *he* is last on the list. Othello sets out to prove his love false; and does. Coriolanus would stand as if a man were author of himself and knew no other kin; by the end, he has achieved the total separation this implies; and the intolerable word "traitor" is true of him *vis-à-vis* both Rome and Corioli. Lear, having

[23] Experimental producers might attempt inserting contemporary smutty songs to try out a genuine Elizabethan effect?

made his everything turn on the truth of his youngest daughter's love, having staked all his force of passion on it, has to play to that stake. He wins; and it costs him everything.

All these simplified patterns suggest a view in which "Fate" has taken the hero, the magnificent egotist, at his word; only "Fate" is a sardonic *farceur* who "gives with subtle confusions," and deals out supple equivokes. The same outline-patterns could create comedies (a commonplace, I know, but not the flat truism people seem to think it). I mention those four plays, because critics have exaggerated the amount of inner conflict in them. Some would exclude *Othello*. But here too we should contrast *Hamlet, Macbeth, Antony and Cleopatra*—and the first wavering hero, Brutus. The point is that all these "patterns" repeat the inverting effect of so-called comic relief.

It is impossible to do more than touch on the comic-ironic grotesque in *Lear*. Nothing elsewhere approaches the phantasmagoric quality of the "Farmhouse-scene," the trial of Goneril and Regan. But let two points suffice. First, the Fool. His loyalty and his half-dazed sufferings are only *one* side to him; for the other, no Spirit Ironic from Hardy could more wittily strike Lear and us on the raw than the Fool, "Lear's shadow," does with his pitilessly clear-sighted *comical* statement of what Lear's folly has done, and is. Bradley is uninterested in such comic effects. Then, for a more grotesque example of a heartless and comic aptness in words, take the scene where the blinded Gloucester meets Lear, mad and "every inch a king," inveighing against sexual hypocrisy, simpering dames. Lear offers him money for civet.

> *Gloucester:* O, let me kiss that hand! . . . Dost thou know me?
> *Lear:* I remember thine eyes well enough. Dost thou squiny at me? No, do thy worst, blind Cupid; I'll not love. Read thou this challenge; mark but the penning of it.
> *Gloucester:* Were all thy letters suns, I could not see one.

That is the Shakespearian grotesque. Utterly unlaughable, it has all the wit of a malevolent commentator as pitiless and well-informed as the records of the Day of Judgment. "Blind Cupid" for Gloucester: bastard Edmund's father, who tells us "yet was his mother fair; there was good sport at his making." The only possible comment is Edgar's:

> I would not take this from report. It is,
> And my heart breaks at it.

There remains the problem of *Macbeth*. Looking ahead, we find belittling and half-derisive commentaries, similar to those we have already examined, in Menenius and Enobarbus. The effect of much they both say is to call in question, with witty common-sense or cynicism, the heroic qualities of Coriolanus, Antony, Cleopatra. But in *Macbeth* there is only the Porter, finely equivocal in a play about nothing else *but* equivocation; otherwise an absence of these witty, malevolent sidelights which do more than catch the hero off his guard. There seem to be two possibilities to explain this. The first is that Macbeth is a hero too precariously heroic to stand this biting comic irony. This is true both of Richard II and of Brutus. It "explains" why Mercutio dies when he does.[24] The mordant force which undermines the value of passionate sexual love is *bawdry:* light-hearted, witty derision of the whole undignified business which young men make such a fuss about. Mercutio is an expert at that form of masculine amusement. His commentary would wreck the delicate, sentimental catastrophe; and therefore, to keep the play together, either he must stop being Mercutio, or he must cease altogether. Shakespeare stopped him.

The second explanation is this. *Macbeth* is a heavily cut text. It may just be that the figure of the "giant's robe upon a dwarfish thief" represents an element in the play as Shakespeare *wrote* it. That it represents an element in Shakespeare's true *conception* of Macbeth himself seems to me quite certain. In Dr. Caroline Spurgeon's words, the imaginative picture is of "a small, ignoble man encumbered and degraded by garments unsuited to him"; and she calls attention to the use of this appearance by comedians. It may be that this devaluation and comic aspect was marked by other comic scenes in the uncut play, which have vanished as a result of abbreviating it for Court-production. It would be pure Shakespeare to give here too an *aspect* of the hero—especially the power-hero—which, by itself, would belittle him. We know, from the report of an eye-witness in April 1611, that in the Banquet-scene "the ghoste of Banco came and sate down in his cheier be-hind him. And he turninge About to sit down Again sawe the goste of banco, which fronted him so, that he fell into a great passion of fear and fury."[25] This is an undeniable detail of Elizabethan production; and one that no modern producer dare attempt, because it would seem funny.

These examples sum up the last essential of the Shakespearian conception of tragedy: that the tragic includes its seeming opposite. The

[24] As Dryden saw.
[25] Simon Forman: *The Bocke of Plaies.*

final alarmingness is not loss of life (with no promise of any after-life); nor the injustice of excessive or too widespread retribution: but the threat of indignity, of the loss of heroic *existence,* by the mocking devaluation of those very qualities by which the hero commands our admiration. Here it is that the commonplace about tragedy and comedy conjoining at their limits is demonstrable. In that generalization to which Coleridge was so excessively and profoundly attached, "extremes meet." We can see from the performance of half a dozen Elizabethan dramatists that tragi-comedy was the distinctive *English* practice; and it is a practice for which no Aristotelean or classical precedent can possibly be invoked. The other great tragic qualities of Shakespeare can be paralleled. This alone is uniquely his.

And why? Because of the immense value of human dignity to Renaissance man. That "sense of vertiginous insecurity" which has been called the true "tragic qualm" [26] was not, for Shakespeare's age and mind, evoked by the threat of suffering or death. Imaginatively at least, the Elizabethan owed it to himself to die in the grand manner: as Caesar and Antony and Cleopatra do, and Othello (to Mr. Eliot's annoyance). And many real Elizabethans did indeed die like that: like stage-heroes. But the full tragic qualm, the image of the terrifying uncertainty of human actions and human fate, could *only* be rendered through the illusions of the theatre by the hint that all the heroic gestures, all human distinction and greatness, might be played by strutting, fretting humans against a vast cosmic background which made them small, "full of sound and fury,/ Signifying nothing."

To sum up. Shakespeare's tragic conception of *order* is medieval and Christian; his conception of human *greatness* verges towards the antithesis of goodness in that order, and includes much of what his age called *virtu:* a complex ideal of self-sufficiency, pride and will, derived *via* Marlowe from Seneca read by English candle-light, but with much Italian illumination added. Just as those two principles are antithetical, so again is the clash between the pathetic or passional aspect of the heroic, and the comical or derisive. Here the whole hangs between two poles: "We that are great, our own self-good still moves us"—and Isabella's

> But man, proud man,
> Dress'd in a little brief authority,
> Most ignorant of what he's most assur'd,
> His glassy essence, like an angry ape,

[26] Prosser Hall Frye, *The Idea of Greek Tragedy.*

Plays such fantastic tricks before high heaven
As makes the angels weep.

And the angels (she continues) would "laugh mortal," *if they could.*

Somewhere in his *Tragedy,* W. Macneile Dixon quotes Garibaldi: "Let those who wish to continue the war against the stranger come with me. I offer neither pay, nor quarters, nor provisions. I offer hunger, thirst, forced marches, battles and death." And he goes on to say, "Explain to me the force of this appeal, why it warms and not chills the heart, and I will listen when you speak of tragedy." [27] My own answer would be something like this: "It appeals because it implies that those who *can* hear those words are men enough to meet and face the worst, and with open eyes; and also that (unlike those others whom these facts of war intimidate) they are 'free men.' Even if free will is a delusion and were scientifically exploded, they would still have more degrees of freedom than those others have."

Garibaldi offered strength to overcome the world, if only in will. But only the tragically aware, the open-eyed, are aware how uncertain that greatness is—not only in its *fate,* but at its very centre in the mind of man: that centre which Shakespeare's tragedy touches, not only with the fear of the proud man's blindness, but with the other (and opposite) apprehension of his potential littleness, in the comic obverse of his pride.

[27] P. 159.

Some Limitations of a Christian Approach to Shakespeare

SYLVAN BARNET

Broadly speaking, we can distinguish in our intellectual history two sharply opposed attitudes toward death: either it is an end, or it marks a beginning. "A man that is in his wits," writes Plutarch, "cannot be ignorant that he is . . . born to this very end that he must die." And to this pagan quotation we may contrast the message of Christ: "Verily, verily, I say unto you, Except a corn of wheat fall into the ground and die, it abideth alone: but if it die, it bringeth forth much fruit."

Eminent English and American scholars have, in the last few decades, emphasized the close relation of the Middle Ages to the Renaissance. The approach has yielded profitable results, but, like many theories, it has been overworked, and too often secular Elizabethan writings are analyzed against a religious medieval background. Tragic drama, and Shakespeare's work especially, has suffered from a subtle spiritualizing, and plays about fallible men are frequently studied as *exempla* in the sermon to which, it is implied, the Elizabethan was continually exposed, even when he deserted his shop for a visit to the theaters on the Bankside.

Shakespeare as Christian appears most subtly and most persuasively in the pages of Messrs. E. M. W. Tillyard and G. Wilson Knight, but he is also to be found in numerous books and articles by less sophisticated scholars and critics who have adopted the method, and lopped off or stretched out the tragedies to fit the Procrustean bed. Thus a recent contribution to Shakespearean scholarship sees God's love and mercy manifest throughout the tragedies, and asserts that Shakespeare's tragic heroes live in the most friendly of universes, for they act "within the boundaries of a beneficent and divine order," where "the wheels of retribution move irrevocably, quickly, impartially,

From *ELH*, Vol. XXII, 1955, pp. 81-92. Reprinted by permission of The Johns Hopkins Press.

but compassionately." [1] Knight and Tillyard look more closely at the plays and pay more attention to the characters in the dramas, but they, too, supply their own backdrop against which they examine the *dramatis personae*. Shakespeare, it is argued, was a Christian, and his audience thought in Christian terms. Now as St. Paul realized, the heart of Christianity is the resurrection, for if Christ is not risen, faith is a foolish hope, and death is not succeeded by life. The Christian pattern moves from weakness to strength, from death to life, from sin to bliss. Its form is therefore comic, and Dante writes a *Commedia* because he knows that a tragedy begins quietly and ends in horror, while a comedy begins harshly but concludes happily. Though Dante himself spoke of his poem merely as a comedy, the Tenth Epistle makes clear his view that a "divine" poem cannot be constructed in a tragic form. But Knight and Tillyard insist that Shakespeare's plays are written in accordance with Christian thinking, and that the tragedies no less than the comedies are sermons and moralities. The plays are seen to follow the Christian movement from death or catastrophe to regeneration, and Shakespeare's late romances are invoked to show that the total structure of his dramatic thought is one of happiness following close upon disaster, with death turning into life. Knight suggests that the romances embody not Shakespeare's response to the demands of a new audience and a new (for Shakespeare) theater, but the dramatist's final vision of life. Shakespeare adds, Knight says in *The Crown of Life* (p. 30), his Paradiso to his other works.

Tillyard's theory runs close to Knight's: whatever tragedy is, it ultimately embodies the idea of regeneration, and the tragic hero quits the world a better man for his sufferings. Tillyard insists that *King Lear* and *Othello* follow this principle, and that the plays depict "through the hero not only the destruction of an established way of life, but the birth of a new order. Othello in his final soliloquy is a man of a more capacious mind than the Othello who first meets us." [2] Elsewhere Tillyard suggests that *Hamlet* is not a tragedy because the idea of regeneration is not present. The social order has been purged of its evil, and the hero has suffered greatly, but because his sufferings do not enlighten him and reorganize his personality, the play is not tragic.[3] Putting aside the problem of whether or not Hamlet be-

[1] Carmen Rogers, "Heavenly Justice in the Tragedies of Shakespeare," *Studies in Shakespeare,* ed. Arthur D. Matthews and Clark M. Emery (Coral Gables, Florida, 1953), pp. 117, 125.

[2] *Shakespeare's Last Plays* (London, 1938), p. 16.

[3] *Shakespeare's Problem Plays* (London, 1950), pp. 12-17.

comes an enlightened avenger who is unsullied by base motives, we may for a moment inquire into the source and validity of Tillyard's definition of tragedy. He is, of course, influenced by traditional Christian teaching, but also by the anthropology of the last sixty years. Drawing chiefly upon the work of Maud Bodkin, he finds that ritual frequently enacts the idea of renewal through destruction. Primitive rituals (at least according to Frazer and Jung) thus parallel Christian beliefs, and since the drama had its beginnings in the church, what could be more natural than to examine tragedy in the light of its origins and analogues? But to do so, however methodically, is to engage in the reductive fallacy and to see the product as containing no more than the source. Furthermore, the claims of early anthropologists that the study of primitive (usually defined as non-literate) drama illuminates the drama of urban societies, we now realize, is ill-founded, for primitive people have their own history, and are not merely representatives of earlier stages of our past. Nor can we regard Elizabethan tragedies as ritual dramas. Though a study of early Christian rites sheds some light on the first stages of English drama, tragedy must be recognized as qualitatively different from ritual, containing themes not necessarily identical with those of its antecedents. Elizabethan drama can be traced back to church ceremonies, but only in a crude sense may we say that liturgy flowered into tragedy. We can trace most of the steps in the secularization of drama, but not even by hindsight can we detect the embryo of tragedy in medieval plays. Elizabethan tragedies, then, are not necessarily related to ritual dramas of other cultures; nor are they merely artistic refinements of an earlier native ceremony.

Christianity is optimistic in its assertion that with God all things are possible; and it is consummated in man's union with the love that moves the sun and other stars, or with the affirmation of the boys in *The Brothers Karamazov*. The crucifixion itself, viewed properly, is an occasion for happiness, and St. Anselm wrote that he felt joy when he thought of the benefits it brought.[4] But where is the note of rejoicing in the tragedies of the master dramatists? The Greeks, though deprived of Christianity, knew a good deal about tragedy, and they seem not to have required the theme of regeneration. Aristotle is silent on the subject, and though Aeschylus sometimes ends his plays on a note of life, Sophocles and Euripides are, for the

[4] See Theodore Spencer, *Death and Elizabethan Tragedy* (Cambridge, Mass., 1936), p. 19.

most part, content to end merely with a choric summary of the catastrophe. The "quiet ending" of Greek tragedy has helped to give rise to the belief that tragedy ends happily, but the theme of renewal is, in fact, absent from most of Sophocles and Euripides. *Oedipus the King* concludes grimly enough, and were it not for *Oedipus at Colonus,* written twenty years later, few critics would see in the exiled stumbling hero the suggestion of a purified man beginning a new life. Euripides' plays are even more clearly lacking in the idea of renewal. Medea leaves Corinth, and Jason—about whom we are not greatly concerned—is left to live out a barren life until the day when a rotted timber will strike him dead. *Hippolytus* concludes with only the promise of more horror: Artemis will destroy a favorite of Aphrodite's, and Theseus lives on futilely to lament his error.[5]

A survey of the work of Shakespeare's contemporaries (playwrights and critics) reveals not that the Elizabethans demanded that the final catastrophe be alleviated, but, on the contrary, that they conceived of a tragedy as a play which concluded with the death of the hero. A. C. Bradley, who generally interpreted Shakespeare's tragedies without reference to Christianity, saw hints of regeneration in them and concluded, influenced probably by Hegel, that a tragedy suggests, among other ideas, that "if we could see the whole, and the tragic facts in their true place in it, we should find them, not abolished, of course, but so transmuted that they had ceased to be strictly tragic." [6] In a footnote to this passage he introduced the problem of the relevance of Christianity to the plays. He concluded that the idea that tragic facts are not irreducible facts would, if too dominant, "confuse and even destroy the tragic impression. So would the constant presence of Christian beliefs. The reader most attached to these beliefs holds them in temporary suspension while he is immersed in a Shakespearean tragedy." [7] Now, Christianity is dramatic, but it is not tragic, for, as historians from Raleigh to Hegel have realized, Christian teleology robs death of its sting. The numerous scholars who compare tragedies

[5] About one-third of the extant Greek tragedies do not end with death, and Aristotle, of course, recognized that many conclude with an "averted catastrophe"; but he clearly indicated his preference for the unhappy ending, and in chapter 13 of the *Poetics* he characterized it as the most truly tragic.

[6] *Shakespearean Tragedy* (London, 1950), p. 324.

[7] Twenty years later I. A. Richards recorded the same idea, and, like Bradley, seems to echo an aspect of Coleridge's esthetic. "Tragedy is only possible to a mind which is for the moment agnostic or Manichean. The least touch of any theology which has a compensating Heaven to offer the tragic hero is fatal" (*Principles of Literary Criticism* [London, 1925], p. 246).

to Elizabethan sermons invariably cramp the meanings of the great plays, and end with a saved hero or a damned villain, rather than a tragic man. We pick up Henry Hitch Adams' provocatively titled book, *English Domestic or Homiletic Tragedy,* only to find that Mr. Adams is not talking about tragedy at all, but about morality plays which show us adulterous wives who repent and are thus ensured of a place in heaven. In these plays the endings are frankly optimistic, for the women go and sin no more, and heaven is achieved. But advocates of Christian tragedy (if there is such a genre) assert that Shakespeare's dramas, too, have their note of regeneration. *Lear* and *Othello,* these critics suggest, follow the Christian pattern and portray divine justice dispensing new life to the heroes. De Quincey was correct in maintaining that *Paradise Lost* does not require *Paradise Regained,* for it contains within itself the note of rebirth, and, like *Samson Agonistes,* ends with nothing for tears. Milton scholars have agreed with his view, yet they have suggested that *Samson* is no less tragic than its Greek models or Elizabethan tragedies. But the choral comment at the end of *Samson* announces that all is well and fair,[8] while a typical choral comment in Shakespeare's tragedies emphasizes the picture of destruction, and the irreparable ruin. Horatio summarizes the happenings at Elsinore:

So shall you hear
Of carnal, bloody, and unnatural acts,
Of accidental judgments, casual slaughters;
Of deaths put on by cunning and forc'd cause,
And, in this upshot, purposes mistook
Fall'n on the inventors' heads.

Death stands at the end of each of Shakespeare's tragedies, and in none of these plays is death the beginning of life, for "the rest is silence." The point will be discussed below with the examination of Christian interpretations of *Lear* and *Othello,* but a few more general observations must first be made.

Shakespeare's plays have been analyzed not merely in ethical terms,

[8] The concluding lines of *Samson Agonistes* are, I think, a poor summary of the play. The drama is tragic, but the chorus tries, at the end, to reconcile the action with Christian thinking, and thus insists that the piece is not really tragic. Milton is giving his version of Aristotle's doctrine of purgation, but it is one thing to say that *we* are purged, and quite another to suggest that the hero's death is a victory. Miltonists, including Tillyard, have tried to counteract Milton's chorus by insisting that we remember not the words of comfort, but the fallen hero. The choral comment, however, is clearly intended as a general summary and interpretation of the action.

but in terms of Christian theology. The procedure is harmful because the business of tragedy, unlike that of a religious system, is not to explain the world, but to portray an aspect of it. Tragedy does not claim to offer the whole truth, nor does it require an act of faith to be believed. It sets forth a kind of experience which every man knows, presenting suffering and death as the hard facts which most men feel them to be. If it presented the death of a good man in medieval Christian terms, i.e., the release of a man from this realm to his eternal reward, it would cease to be tragic.

Shakespeare was a writer of, among other things, tragedies, and his tragedies show the material fall of heroes. In the great plays this fall is generally accompanied by an increased awareness of the nature of life, but such profit is gained at the expense of life. Shakespeare had an Anglican education,[9] and the ethics in the plays partake of Christian ethics, but they are not based, as Christian ethics in fact are, upon the eschatology of the Christian system. Shakespeare finds such virtues as love and honor good, and such vices as hatred and cheating bad, but he does not concern himself with the fortunes of his lovers and haters in the next world, nor does he insist that the meek shall inherit the earth. Furthermore, his tragic heroes are heroic. Princes, kings, and generals, they are duly concerned about their strength and reputation, and have little in common with the heroes of Christianity, with Peter the fisherman, with Mary Magdalene, or with Jesus, the Son of God who humbled Himself. Altering Alcuin, we might well ask, "*Quid enim Othello cum Christo?*" Shakespeare employs, of course, Christian imagery and terminology, and presents ecclesiastical personages. *Romeo and Juliet* has a Friar Laurence, and the heroine is, in the hero's eyes, a "bright angel." But the play is not a Christian drama (although it might have been, had Shakespeare followed his source more closely), for the supernatural power seems to be not God but Fate, and though the lovers are rash and, more important, suicides, we cannot believe that Shakespeare sends them in a sixth unwritten but clearly imagined act to the seventh circle of Dante's Inferno.

Christian sentiments abound in Shakespeare's dramas, especially in the history plays, but when Guy Boas says that Desdemona is meek, and implies that the meek are assured of a Christian heaven,[10] he is reconstructing the play and shaping it into something with which

[9] See T. W. Baldwin, *William Shakespeare's Petty School* (Urbana, 1943).
[10] "Shakespeare and Christianity," *Shakespeare Review,* I (1928), p. 91.

Shakespeare probably would have agreed but did not himself write. Othello exclaims that Desdemona's look

> will hurl my soul from Heaven,
> And fiends will snatch at it,

but the ending of the play announces that Othello was "great of heart," and the bodies of Desdemona and the Moor are "the tragic loading of this bed." Othello is a great man, but he performs an abominable deed. Aware of his crime, he enjoins the public to remember his honorable deeds (an action which, from a Christian point of view, might seem to show undue pride), and then kills himself. What is the moral? Is the play merely a parable acted out? Does Shakespeare draw a simple moral? Does he even wish us to draw one?

The scholars who wish to apply Christian thinking to Shakespeare's plays insist that the dramas do not end with the heroes' death, but should be acted out to Judgment Day and for eternity. Mr. Kenneth Myrick, for example, asserts that Othello is not damned, for the Moor is repentant and contrite.[11] Othello's suicide, of course, presents a problem to the Christian interpreter, but Mr. Myrick nevertheless concludes that the hero and heroine will join hands in the realm of the blessed. Othello has, however, despaired of grace, and such a state of mind would preclude salvation, though Myrick suggests that his last words imply "repentance" and "contrition." But, as Dante points out (Inferno XXVII), one cannot will a sin and simultaneously repent it, and Othello's suicide must be viewed as a deadly sin. However, for Myrick an Elizabethan audience would be sure that Hamlet is saved, Claudius damned, Laertes and the Queen granted an audience before God, yet it would not regard Ophelia as damned, though a *felo-de-se,* and would willingly overlook Othello's self-slaughter. The latest study of *Othello,* G. R. Elliott's *Flaming Minister,* interprets the play as a tragedy of that deadly Christian sin, pride, but similarly suggests that Othello, despite his suicide—which would not, according to Mr. Elliott, be of great importance to the audience—is a worthy tragic hero and is saved at last. But it is perfectly obvious that if the spectators have been conscious of the play as a morality, and regard the characters as figures or representations of hell, various vices, Christ, and so forth, they will not suddenly transpose their thinking to a secular level merely in order to allow the hero to escape the flames of hell. The

[11] "The Theme of Damnation in Shakespearean Tragedy," *SP,* XXXVIII (1941), p. 244.

truth is that Shakespeare does not treat suicide in a consistent Christian manner. In the Roman plays it is clearly not a sin, and these dramas are not outside the pattern of Shakespearean tragedy. We do not distinguish between Shakespeare's pre-Christian and Christian plays, nor can we separate the secular from the religious ones.

The Everlasting, as Hamlet knew, had fix'd his canon 'gainst self-slaughter, and though a few suicides were traditionally numbered among the saints, these were very special persons whose deaths had been dictated by God and redounded to His glory. Obviously Othello is entitled to no special dispensation, and the sanguine view of Myrick and Elliott runs contrary to the Christian meaning which they have superimposed upon the first four acts. Even G. Wilson Knight's more modest statement, that "the Iago spirit never envelopes him, masters him, disintegrates his soul," is suspect, if the rest of the play is as theological as he suggests.[12] A whole-hearted commitment to a Christian interpretation of Shakespeare must insist, I should suppose, that Othello is damned, and Paul Siegel and S. L. Bethell elect to sacrifice esthetics to theology.[13] Mr. Bethell damns Othello for his suicide, but Mr. Siegel insists that his fate is sealed even before he kills himself. Othello attacks Desdemona and "loses his own claim to God's mercy. . . . Emilia pounds on the locked door to tell Othello of the attempted assassination of Cassio, who, escaped from death, can help the truth be revealed, but it is indeed too late: Othello's soul is lost." The truth is finally revealed to the Moor as "he realizes that he is indeed damned" and "knows his irrevocable fate." [14] But why, we may ask, is his fate irrevocable, and how has he forfeited his claim to God's mercy? The possibility of repentance yet remains, and Siegel is so anxious to interpret the tragedy as "The Damnation of Othello" that he prematurely introduces the Black Cherubim.

Having damned Othello, Siegel goes on to announce that Roderigo, too, will go down to the fiends' abode, though Desdemona will have the company of Emilia in heaven as on earth.[15] Here is the modern scholarly version of Mary Cowden Clarke's *Girlhood of Shakespeare's Heroines.* Not the youth, however, but the second life of the characters is sketched according to the critic's fancies. Siegel cites not only the

[12] *The Wheel of Fire* (London, 1949), p. 118.

[13] Paul N. Siegel, "The Damnation of Othello," *PMLA,* LXVIII (1953), 1068-78; S. L. Bethell, "Shakespeare's Imagery: The Diabolic Images in *Othello,*" *Shakespeare Survey 5,* ed. Allardyce Nicoll (Cambridge, 1952), pp. 62-80.

[14] "The Damnation of Othello," pp. 1071-72.

[15] *Ibid.,* pp. 1074-77.

Christian references in the play, but Christianizes the action, so Desdemona, "reminiscent of Christ" (p. 1068), and a paragon of Christian ethics (here Mr. Boas anticipated him by a quarter of a century), will be saved, and when Othello's married life is cut short, "he loses an earthly paradise" (p. 1069). The Moor is damned, and we have witnessed God's justice, "terrible and pitiful" (p. 1077). In a footnote on the same page Siegel alludes to "the theology depicted in Dante and inherited by the Elizabethans," but he has apparently forgotten that, under the tutelage of Vergil, Dante learned that human pity for the damned is presumptuous and incompatible with Divine Justice:

> Ancor sei tu de li altri sciocchi?
> Qui vive la pietà quan'd è ben morta.
> Chi è più scellerato che colui
> Che al giudicio divin passion comporta?
> (Inferno XX, 27-30)

Bethell, who has made valuable contributions to the study of Elizabethan dramaturgy, and a less valuable one to the study of imagery, also interprets the tragedies (to say nothing of the last plays) in terms of Christian theology, although he concedes that *King Lear* portrays a world prior to Christian revelation.[16] Such a concession, however, does not prevent him from writing, in a more recent study, that "Lear, after being bound upon his fiery wheel in this life, attaining humility and patience, . . . is fit for heaven." [17]

Four years earlier Oscar James Campbell published an article entitled "The Salvation of Lear," [18] wherein he suggested that the drama was "a sublime morality play" which might be understood by reference to medieval and Elizabethan sermons about the road from sin to salvation. Because Mr. Campbell also discusses Lear as the tragedy of an unstoical man, his article is somewhat less theologically oriented than its title indicates, but on the whole he sees the play as a Christian picture of regeneration: "The real redemption of Lear

[16] *Shakespeare and the Popular Dramatic Tradition* (London, 1944), p. 54. Myrick, too, exempts *Lear* from his view of Shakespearean tragedy as Christian drama, as though *Lear* were an entirely different sort of play. Bethell suggests that Christianity enters at the end of the play. "The gods are often called on, but God only once ('God's spies' [*Lear,* V.iii. 17]) when Lear's purgatorial struggle is completed" (*Shakespeare,* p. 54). But T. M. Parrott, in "God's or gods' in *King Lear,* V.iii. 17," *SQ,* IV (1953), 427-32, demonstrates that the correct reading is "gods'."

[17] "Shakespeare's Imagery," p. 78.

[18] *ELH,* XV (1948), pp. 93-109.

comes when he awakens from the delusions of his frenzied mind to discover Cordelia and her unselfish enduring love. The mere sight of her 'kills the great rage' in him, the unstoical emotional turmoil from which all his sins and sufferings have sprung. Now he is calmly receptive to the healing power of Christian love." [19] Just why her love is specifically Christian, in a play set in pre-Christian days, is not explained, and the assertion that unstoical emotion causes sins would be, I think, acceptable neither to Stoics (who did not talk about sin) nor to Christians (who talk much about sin but not about the evils of unstoical emotion). Campbell continues, however, and suggests that Cordelia, like Christ, is hanged so that mankind might be saved, but he fails to explain just how her death saves the king, and why it is necessary when her mere presence had (as Campbell says) already restored health of soul to the king. Lear's agonized ravings over the dead Cordelia are explained away as mere preludes to his "blessed discovery that Cordelia is not dead after all, that the breath of life still trembles on her lips. . . . In the joy of this discovery the old man's heart breaks in a spasm of ecstasy. For only to earthbound intelligence is Lear pathetically deceived in thinking poor Cordelia alive. Those familiar with the pattern of the morality play realize that Lear has discovered in her unselfish God-like love the one companion who is willing to go with him through Death up to the throne of the Everlasting Judge." [20]

But Cordelia is very dead, and Lear's discovery is a mistake, not the poet's allegorical statement that love is eternal. The king dies joyfully, as Bradley pointed out, but his joy is the product of an error, and the audience feels not merely relief for his death but also horror for his ultimate false perception. George Orwell refused to grant that Lear is a whit better at the end of the play than at the beginning,[21] but if this is too bold a conclusion, we can at least say that although Lear learns humility through suffering, at the conclusion he is still capable of the misconceptions and "unstoical emotion" which are the stuff of tragedy.

The rigidly Christian interpretation forces a tragedy to fit ideas which Shakespeare doubtless held but did not dramatize. It is of value in explicating some puzzling lines and in emphasizing the moral tone pervading the plays. But it turns Othello into a villain (at

[19] *Ibid.*, p. 106.
[20] *Ibid.*, p. 107.
[21] "Lear, Tolstoy and the Fool," *Shooting an Elephant and Other Essays* (New York, 1950), pp. 32-52.

least in Bethell's and Siegel's view), and it gives a comic ending to every tragedy, for it insists that the good are rewarded and the bad are punished. It shifts the focus from this world to the next, muting the conflict of the tragic hero. It assumes that if he acted wrongly, he could have acted rightly or at least repented, and so is justly damned. Such interpretations are not based on a total appreciation of the tragedy, but on individual lines which are related to a preconceived context. Shakespeare presents such full worlds that it is possible, with a little ingenuity and effort, to find in him almost any theory which the researcher wishes to discover. It is perhaps better to accept the immediate impressions yielded by the plays, and to see in these dramas not explicit eternal theological verities, portrayed on a canvas stretching from hell-mouth to heaven, but a picture of man's achievements and failures, hopes and fears, life and death.

The Possibility of a Christian Tragedy

LAURENCE MICHEL

I

The nature of this subject almost demands that we concern ourselves, in large part, with definitions and distinctions, an invidious procedure. But in the hope of escaping the dead ends into which the usual approaches to tragedy seem always to lead, one is free also to adopt an inductive, exploratory method which resolutely avoids being committed to a definition. The reading of many tragedies would undoubtedly spell Tragedy, but they will not define it for us. Nor is Aristotle a help, in the main. We will salvage three things of his for use later on: the tremendously fertile notion of an Action of which the concrete work of art is an imitation; pity and terror, which Aristotle did not define, but Stephen Dedalus did; and catharsis. Beyond these, I believe, with Macneile Dixon, that Aristotle, the ethician, makes mischief; he is a reductionist; the doctrine of *hamartia* "runs counter to the poets." [1] At the outset, perhaps it would be best to set down some descriptive phrases, adjectival rather than nominative, the tragic rather than tragedy.

Here, then, are some phrases, or counters, which various artists have forged in the heat of the imaginative act: And God saw everything that He had made, and behold it was very good. . . . And God looked upon the earth, and behold, it was corrupt. From the gods who sit in grandeur, grace comes somehow violent. With bitter drugs men purge out bitter bile. What message of disaster from that sweet-throated Zeus? The arrows of the Almighty are within me. Woe unto you that desire the day of the Lord! To what end is it for you? The day of the Lord is darkness, and not light. . . . Even very dark, and no brightness in it. . . . Woe to them that are at ease in Zion. Vanity of vanities, and all is vanity. Without the shedding of blood there is

From *Thought,* Vol. XXXI (1956), pp. 403-28. Reprinted by permission of the editor.

[1] *Tragedy* (London, 1938), pp. 126-39; p. 137.

no remission. It is a fearful thing to fall into the hands of the living God. Created sick, commanded to be sound; What meaneth Nature by these diverse laws? Is there any cause in nature that makes these hard hearts? As flies to wanton boys are we to the gods: they kill us for their sport. Ripeness is all. Cover her face. Mine eyes dazzle. She died young. Everyone is responsible to all men for all men and everything. There is a wisdom that is woe; but there is a woe that is madness.

Here are some which various sensitive people have struck out in the heat of the imaginative response: Patterns of death in life. The spirit of inquiry meets the spirit of poetry. The search for the best by the worst. Salvation through action as suffering. The dead tragic hero is at last equal to the occasion. The freedom of the whole is the destiny of the part. A grasp of the majesty of the ungraspable. Piety in the face of the enigmatic and afflicting. Tragedy is consummated when the dream of innocence is confronted by the fact of guilt, and acquiesces therein.

It is this last formula, concocted out of a phrase of Leslie Fiedler's,[2] that seems to be applicable, in some fashion or other, to the greatest number and variety of situations or forms which invite scrutiny by a putative "tragic sense of life." The "Dream" stands for all those characteristics and attitudes we are accustomed to applaud in the tragic hero at the beginning of his action: his vision of the good, his rebellion against his vision of evil, his pride, his drive, articulateness, resilience; champion-ship; the aspiration, the forward look, the yearning, the vision which inspires his protagonism; and the creativeness, the purposiveness of his response to what he finds enigmatic and afflicting; the thesis. It also includes that piety which binds him to the "Other" he is seeking. "Innocence" is inclusive of the urge to be free, to escape the inhibitions of mortality and mutability and evil, of finiteness and contingency and competition and waste and shame; to be one's own self, to fulfill one's potential, to be man par excellence, to be like God. The "confrontation" provides for action, conflict, tension, predicament, dilemma, antagonism; peripety; modification or qualification of purpose, tarnishing of the dream; suffering, the hard loss of personality and self-satisfaction; the antithesis (or hypothesis?),[3] bringing the action

[2] In "Our Country and Our Culture," *Partisan Review,* May-June 1952, 298.

[3] See the writings of John Courtney Murray, S.J., *passim,* for this concept; also Augustin Leonard, "Religious Tolerance and Civil Liberty," *Cross Curents,* V (1955), 16, 20; nn. 10, 55. It might be illuminating to recast, for the tragic rhythm, the Hegelian triad into "thesis-hypothesis-synthesis"; or to say that

of the hero into a condition of *pathos*, of being acted upon. The "fact" represents that amount of reality which is reached; anagnorisis; the tears of things, the human condition, the apple of knowledge. "Guilt" means failure, unworthiness, defeat, collapse, being a fool, a sinner, being a part, a prisoner; death. "Acquiescence" tries to include the relevant notions of perception, salvation, recognition, reconciliation, atonement; catharsis, exhaustion, calm, peace; Yea-saying, assent, Amen; being quiet in the face of the mystery brought to epiphany, the present deity; synthesis. This is the formula I should like to use for the action of which tragedies are imitations.

Then there are the effects, which may properly be used as an after-the-fact touchstone[4] (to use Stephen Dedalus' amplification of Aristotle): Pity is the feeling which arrests the mind in the presence of whatsoever is grave and constant in human sufferings, and unites it with the human sufferer. Terror is the feeling which arrests the mind in the presence of whatsoever is grave and constant in human sufferings and unites it with the secret cause.[5] Or, to try a variation: Tragic pity is the only attitude which can satisfactorily confront "undeserved" (unexplainable) suffering; tragic terror is the only attitude which can satisfactorily confront "undeserved" (unexplainable) pressure. Note that the word is "terror," not "fear" or "horror": the former is too general, and slights the element of awe-fulness, the mysterious; the latter is on the slippery slope to the pathological.

To complete the dossier from which it is proposed to extract the tragic, there are two things: something I should like to call, with acknowledgments to Harry Levin,[6] the "overplot." Francis Fergusson

---

tragedy really gets started when the hypothesis (which we *can* live with) is seen as an antithesis (which the tragic hero *cannot* live with). Thesis is distinguished from hypothesis in logic, from antithesis in rhetoric; synthesis, in grammar, is a figure by which a sentence is constructed according to the sense, in violation of strict syntax. There is no neat formula here, but some kind of handle useful for grasping parts of the tragic experience might be forged out of the terms.

[4] But not, as is so often tried, as materials for a definition; to wit: *Othello* is a tragedy because audiences have always been shocked and have wept at Desdemona's death; Satan is the hero of *Paradise Lost* because he was a hero to Shelley, and Shelley was a satanist; Falstaff's "humanism" is the authentic note of *Henry IV* because humanists since Elizabeth I have established a gleeful empathy with him. This is relativism, and confusing effects with causes; it blurs Roy Morrell's otherwise well-focused paper on "The Psychology of Tragic Pleasure" (*Essays in Criticism,* V, 1956).

[5] James Joyce, *A Portrait of the Artist as a Young Man,* Ch. V. (Signet Books No. 664), p. 159.

[6] See *The Overreacher* (Harvard University Press, 1952), p. 67.

calls it the "anagoge";[7] a vision, apprehended more through the emotions and music and the protagonist's *pietas* than through mind, that tragedy is an "affair with the gods," that it is concerned more with Man and God than with man and man; that the attempt "to make the heavens more just" involves the risk (as Empson puts it) of finding that the gods are fools, too.[8] This is very helpful in ruling out of our discussion the whole recalcitrant business of modern, naturalistic claims to tragedy—from Ibsen on down.[9] It provides for the largeness, the emancipation of the spirit, the "swing towards greatness," amplitude, which helps make man's suffering meaningful and worthwhile, and generates the terror. And it provides an object for that dynamic af-filiation, composed of fear and love, which I have called "piety." It is akin to the *pietas* of Aeneas, but has a larger object of reverence. We see it in Abraham; in Job, who calls it his Integrity, and who denounces his wife as a fool when she tells him to curse God; in Prometheus, when he insists on a closer walk with Zeus even though he hates him—he is not lukewarm, like the chorus; in Electra and Antigone, willing to be goddess-like, even if they are to share the fate of Niobe; in Iô and Kassandra, who make the god's heart hot with love, to their own shattering destruction; in Oedipus, spiritual child of Good Luck and brother to the years, who, when Jocasta exults: "The oracles are dead, hurrah!" answers sorrowfully, "The oracles are dead, alas"; in Lear and Cordelia and Kent, who preserve the inviolateness of the holy cords, even at the risk of finding out that the gods too are old, and foolish, whose pleasures are horrible, who pour a deadly incense upon our sacrifices; in Venus-preyed-upon Phèdre, who dies to purify her bloodthirsty divinity; in Ahab, who holds fast to his "patriotism," even though his country is hell-seeming rather than the heaven of Father Mapple with its transcendent delight; in Ike McCaslin, who learns to share responsibility for what God "Himself had done in order to live with Himself in His lonely and paramount heaven." The word is an early form of "pity"; it connotes *com*-passion; *with*-feeling; empathy; sympathy; the affective, anti-Cartesian criterion for fullness of being: I feel, therefore I am; a source of energy

[7] See *The Idea of a Theater* (Princeton University Press, 1949), p. 175; also *Dante's Drama of the Mind* (Princeton University Press, 1953).

[8] William Empson, "Fool in Lear," *Sewanee Review*, LVII (1949), 178-412; this is also a chapter of *The Structure of Complex Words* (New York, 1951).

[9] Fergusson, *The Idea of a Theater*; and William F. Lynch, S.J., "Confusion in our Theater," THOUGHT, XXVI (1951), 342-60, make the case against the naturalists in a way quite satisfactory to me.

transcending the intellectual, an irrational bond; a yearning to feed the Other with one's own life-blood: the pious and piteous pelican. "It is with fiction as with religion," says Melville; "it should present another world, and yet one to which we feel the tie." [10] The Mass for the Dead everywhere softens the dread of "that day" with the rewards of piety: *quia pius es.*

And finally, a distinction, made by Harold Watts,[11] between the comic and the tragic on the basis of the circular versus the linear: comedy promises a return to the familiar; tragedy is exigent—the choice opted for looks to the future, but in the dark; a leap into the unknown, the unpredictable, the irrecoverable.

You will have noticed one quality running through all these approximations: that of dualism, ambiguity. This is important, as a check, from the side of form; for we find the dialectic rhythm, the oscillatory dance one does on the horns of a dilemma: agons; strophe, antistrophe, epode; purpose, passion, perception; withdrawal and return; peripety and anagnorisis; thesis, antithesis, synthesis: almost invariably as the incarnation, the objective correlative, of the idea. Man, in the tragic view, is an amphibian. His amphibiousness lays him open to both possibilities and dangers. He can refuse the gambit, and go back into the organic, astigmatic fish-world; or he can grow lungs from gills and legs from fins and binocular vision, and gradually evolve toward what he has the capacity for being, thus, even though it be a long, arduous, homesick process, avoiding the distortions of Father Lynch's Gnostic fish-out-of-water;[12] or he can try to grow up too fast, and in his radical effort suffocate, or be crippled for life, or go blind with overmuch sunlight. The first of these alternatives is outside our subject; the second can stand for a religious view of man's nature and destiny; the third for a tragic view.

II

In the interests of economy of presentation, I should like, in the following exploration of the common ground which I think religion and tragedy cover, to use the Old Testament as exemplar for all

[10] Herman Melville; cited in *The American Treasury,* ed. C. Fadiman and C. Van Doren (New York, 1955), "Teller of Tales."

[11] "Myth and Drama," *Cross Currents,* V (1955), 154-70.

[12] "Theology and the Imagination," THOUGHT, XXIX (1954), 68.

"Western" non-Christian religious manifestations, for one thing because it provides us with literary documents, artistic forms. I hope to make it do duty for the "religious instinct," for "the numinous," for myth and ritual, for the still imperfectly assimilated fact that Greek tragedies grew out of Dionysian rites and Eleusinian mysteries, for all post-Renaissance, homeless and orphaned mysticisms, up to and including the Jungians and Koestler's "oceanic feeling." [13] All this is said under correction, and craving such special dispensations as ignoring the fact that the Scriptures were inspired, that their profound truth is in their typology, and that there are elements of the un-tragic therein—the lyrical parts, the proverbs and wisdom literature, etc. The failure to distinguish between the Old Testament and the New vitiates, I think, the whole controversy arising out of Daiches Raphael's BBC talk on "Tragedy and Religion";[14] and *his* lumping them together as "the religion of the Bible" is in itself fatal to his purpose. I will try here, first, a rather special and "literary" interpretation of Genesis.

St. John tells us, in the preamble to his Gospel, that "In the beginning was the Word, and the Word was with God, and the Word was God." He goes on to say that "All things were made by Him, and without Him was not any thing made that was made." And he relates further, that "the Word was made flesh, and dwelt amongst us"; that the sublime result of this incarnation and this indwelling was that "as many as received Him, to them he gave power to become the sons of God."

This masterpiece of compression we may call history, if we like; but it is on a scale larger than any we are accustomed to, for it includes time, aforetime, and aftertime: it is not only history, but prehistory and eschatology. It stems from a philosophy of history which is appropriate to the New Covenant which, in Christ's words, is not only New but Everlasting, for the central fact of this story is the intersection of eternity and time, the Word made flesh, and in it the temporal condition of man is viewed under the aspect of eternity. Consequently, it is the Gospel, Good News, Glad Tidings of Great Joy, which shall be to all the people. The Christian life is to be full of paradoxes, but without irony. The Cross is the central symbol, yet this yoke is sweet,

[13] *Darkness at Noon* (Penguin Signet No. 671), pp. 181-85. Koestler is, of course, citing Freud.

[14] Printed in *The Listener,* 2 Sept. 1955, pp. 36-61. Commenting letters follow in the issues of 9, 23, and 30 Sept., and Raphael replies in the issues of 16 Sept. and 14 Oct.

this burden light; men are provided with the Way, the Truth, the Life; Our Father has established for us mansions in our home, heaven is our destination. We are to lift up our hearts; for the faithful life is to be changed, not taken away; there is no place for fear, no time for tragedy.

All this was possible because St. John was given ("vouchsafed" is the traditional and more precise word, with its overtones of comfort) knowledge and assurance about God's nature and His love, outside of the world and time: for example, that there was society as well as being from the beginning, for the Word was with God, and was God too. But no such overarching framework was made available to the writers of the Old Testament. Its opening words are identical with those of the Evangelist, but, whereas St. John's Gospel describes a state of being, "In the beginning was . . . ," Genesis announces a happening: "In the beginning God created the heaven and the earth." God is there, to be sure, and His abiding existence and presence and Lordship are to be the central fact of this history, but His nature as God is given, although not as Triune. He does, and He commands; and for this historian creation is the true beginning, for then was born time as well as the world. These two dimensions form the arena for man; and his life will consequently demand mobility and tenacity upon space, and urgency and endurance in his days.

Let us return, then, to "the beginning," and submit ourselves to the story of creation from this general point of view. We might say that the "action" is: To bring the world and man into being, *as we know them*. Immediately we are confronted with actuality and existence, with the word "good," and in very short order with life, knowledge of good and evil, commandments, sorrow, fear, sin, death. But I would dwell on a point of ambiguity which comes through, more in the "literary" way than explicitly; a dualism which is present from the beginning. Creation is the action, but it requires, seemingly, for its fulfillment, multiplication; and this involves that form of activity —separation, divisiveness—which is normally felt to be destructive. As C. S. Lewis puts it, "Evil is fissiparous, and could never in a thousand eternities find any way to arrest its own reproduction. If it could, it would be no longer evil: for Form and Limit belong to the good." [15] This buttresses his ingenious argument for God's essential mercifulness in creating a fixed Hell; but here we may feel something of the drama and "danger" of creation, in which God permits evil

[15] *The Pilgrim's Regress* (New York, 1944), p. 233.

because of the greater good to which evil is attached, for He allows the fissiparous process up to the point at which He desires to set His limits. Great and noble things are possible, in this universe, but they are not achieved pusillanimously or without "risk."

Order presupposes unification of multiplicity; order and positiveness somehow presuppose synthesis and connection. To be sure, Light was created, and it was good; but immediately thereafter it was *divided* from the darkness. And the waters were *divided* from the waters, and the dry land was *divided* from the water, and the day was *divided* from the night. And the river in Eden *parted* into four heads. And Adam was made *out of* the dust of the ground, and he was put *aside* and *above* the rest of creation, to *subdue* it and *have dominion over* it, and it was to him for meat; and there was no creature fitting for Adam; and to make up this deficiency God *separated* a part from Adam himself; and the mystic union which resulted from this fission was henceforward to be maintained at the expense of a man's *leaving* his father and his mother. So, in the very beginning and creative *élan* there seems to be built in forebodings of what we call, for want of a better expression, "metaphysical evil"—separateness, competition, finitude. And yet, God saw that the results were good, and indeed at last very good, and blessed.

I do not want to run this approach into the ground; perhaps we may leave it here with some such formulation as this: To have a world imitative of the simple perfection of God one must have multiplicity and diversity of goods. Various evils and contraries will be found in it and, therefore, physical evils will exist. From the very outset, in a creative act there are elements of destruction and danger and hardship; but somehow at the end there is life abundantly, and blessedness, and rest. And this is a view of things in which the tragic sense of life can flourish.

On the sixth day of creation, "God saw every thing that he had made, and behold, it was very good." And by the time of Noah, "God looked upon the earth, and, behold, it was corrupt. For all flesh had corrupted his way upon the earth." Evil had somehow irrupted into the creation, and it had come through the best of God's creatures, and through his distinguishing excellency of intellect and will whereby he was made in the image and likness of God. *Corruptio optimi pessima;* and the goods of creation themselves were apparently ambiguous—they were at least potentially dangerous, because of their very goodness. There was knowledge, for instance, tied in mysteriously with death: the fruit of the tree was good for food, and pleasant to the eyes, and to be desired to make one wise; so man looked and desired and ate: and was cursed. Let us put ourselves again for a moment into the context of Genesis, and try to feel the impact of this perilous good, knowledge.

Unfortunately, its shock is largely absorbed in our English translations, because our language alone seems to have discarded a basic distinction between two kinds of knowledge: the distinction maintained by the words *savoir* and *connaître, wissen* and *kennen, scire* and *cognoscere*. Milton undoubtedly felt the force of this dichotomy running through the prototypes of his story of the Fall, and he does his best to supply the deficiencies of English by using "knowledge" as a basic metaphor throughout his poem. He explores all its tributary meanings, he lays down provisional distinctions, such as that between discursive and intuitive reasoning, and calls on all the resources of word play and assonance to express the simultaneously different and alike nature of the two, when he has Raphael counsel Adam to use his intelligence to be lowly wise, or himself comments that Adam and Eve will be happiest if they "know to know no more." Very simply, it is the difference between knowing about something, knowing *that* it is so, at a distance; and knowing it by contact, by experience, through immediate and intimate acquaintance. We know that fire is hot, and stings and consumes; when we touch a glowing coal, we are acquainted with fire: the burnt child will recognize the hot stove with his fingers.

Now, the first chapters of Genesis are pervaded by this double-edged-ness of the nature of knowledge, as a glance at the Vulgate will show. I cannot claim that the distinction is maintained consistently, either therein or in the originals from which the Vulgate was translated;[16] but I rather welcome this fact than am distressed by it, for I am looking for a feeling, the proper characteristic of which is spontaneity. The Vulgate uses the verb *scire,* or some derivative of it, to talk about God's knowing, and the phrase *lignum scientiae boni et mali* for the receptacle of the inclusive and composite thing itself. The serpent, of course, lied: he had said that men would become as gods, knowing (*scientes*) good and evil. By extension, we might perhaps say that Adam and Eve knew about (*sciebant*) the tree, because God told them about it; but they knew it with knowledge and experi-

[16] The point is canvassed with regard to the Hebrew by Charles Hauret, *Beginnings: Genesis and Modern Science* (Dubuque, 1955), pp. 160-61.

ence (*cognoverunt*) indeed, when they looked, and touched, and tasted.

But a change takes place immediately after the act of eating. *Cum cognovissent se esse nudos,* says the Vulgate, "When they knew they were naked," they hid themselves. Before, they had been able to observe the fact that they had no fur like the animals, and "they were not ashamed"; but now their eyes were opened, and they knew—felt, realized, were intimate with, had become accomplices of—their nakedness, and they knew it to their shame and passion and fear. And God asked, "Who told you that you were naked?" There is no answer, because nobody told them so, they merely knew it, in the flesh.

"How in the world can knowledge be bad?" rhetorically asks Satan, the rationalist. "Depends on what you mean by knowledge," ruefully replies post-lapsarian Adam. "It seems that there are more things in heaven and earth, counsellor, than are defined in your dialectic."

And so man let evil into God's good world, by what was essentially the first step in a tragic career: pride, dissatisfaction with the *status quo,* an urge to get above himself, in a word, to be like unto God, to have dominion over all things as God has. The trouble was, of course, that man's creativeness *is* godlike in its initial phase; but man does not have the braking power with respect to the effect of his choice; his free will can loose but it cannot bind, and once he has started the wheels turning he cannot stop them. So man suffered the immediate divisive results of his contamination with evil: enmity, hostility, curses; he hid himself *from* the presence of the Lord God, and he was *sent forth* and *driven out* from the garden, and disjoined from the tree of life by a flaming sword.

Now indeed the burning question was, After *such* knowledge, what salvation? Although hints are given, that sorrow and thorns and sweat and death are to be the medicinal penalty, the promise is oracular and cloudy; and the at-one-ment which alone can finally defeat the powers of darkness, which are evil, is to be achieved only in the fullness of time. But here and now the beginnings are made, the journey is started. There is to be nothing automatic about it: God's spirit will strive with man, and it will at times grieve Him at His heart; the people will build Babels and golden calves, and their original one-ness will have to be scattered abroad upon the face of the earth. But little by little a man, a tribe, a people, a race are Chosen and Covenanted to start carving God's kingdom from the corrupted world.

Another image illustrates the inextricability of the good and evil in this covenant relationship: the cloud and the bow. God will indeed bring clouds over the earth—the gathering wracks of deluge—but the rainbow will henceforward be seen therein. And the mystery of it is that the bow is not only in, or against, the cloud, but *of* the cloud; the very color and form and beauty of it could not exist without the destructive wateriness and the impending and precipitant imminence of its darkness.

I submit here, as a kind of hypothesis, that two conditions, among others, are necessary for a tragic view, and that both are present in the Old Testament: in the background, but impinging on the actuality of events, and somehow affected or invoked by earthly events, there is the inscrutability of God; in the foreground there is plenty of what may be called "actual" or "moral" evil. Now, lacking a sense of the former, the story would lose its power, and degenerate into a kind of ethicism; lacking the latter, the story escapes from the human realm, and becomes an abstract intellectual speculation. What I have called the actuality of events normally falls in the second sphere: and, for most modern sensibilities moral evil means "man's inhumanity to man." In the Old Testament the materials are often, to be sure, those of competition between men: Cain slew Abel, Jacob defrauded Esau, David coveted Uriah's wife: but the important aspect of these actions is that they are not only evil or dangerous, but sinful. God is the Lord; unrighteousness is *lèse-majesté*. What counts is how a man acts in the eyes of the Lord. God is good, He is all-powerful, He is all-wise—but He is inscrutable. No sin is a little thing, because of *God's* greatness. And it is here that the Hebrews, unlike their contemporaries, took the step that allows their history to be seen tragically: Having abandoned God they caused their own penalty and woe. Therefore, Moses followed the promulgation of the Commandments with an insistence on the inseparability of the fear and the love of the Lord, "that it may be well with us all the days of our life." The world man inhabits, and must move and act in, is a moral universe. Man cannot escape his responsibility therein, for he is a free agent. His great glory, and his great peril, lie in the fact that he has been called, chosen, elected; he must also acknowledge the election, respond to the vocation, he too must choose to be chosen. "Thou shalt fear the Lord thy God . . . The Lord our God is one Lord . . . Thou shalt love thy Lord thy God with thy whole heart . . . The Lord thy God hath chosen thee, to be his peculiar people . . . the Lord [is] joined unto you . . . because the Lord hath loved you . . . the Lord thy God is in the midst of thee, a God mighty and terrible." Man must act on his own, often perplexed in the extreme, and he must pay heavily for his transgressions; but, if his spirit does not fail, he may also speak with God, and speak for God, and be raised up to be a savior of his people. A synthesis of some kind can be achieved, a coming to terms, a temporary, precarious balance. But because the whole scheme is being worked out in the world and time, there can be no abiding solution; and this provides room for the tragic response. The big men are representative, but they must act as individuals, and at their peril, and in the midst of their yearning, their lack of comprehension, their sorrow, their loss. Their proper attitude is responsiveness, questioning, action; their reward is that of having been used, and used up; their final statement is "Yea, Lord; Amen; Blessed be the Name of the Lord."

* * * *

Fallen man had the limitations of his nature and of his fall; yet God chose man to be his agent in the world, to conquer it (as it were) for Him from the powers of darkness, to bring it into the realms of light. And, to come down from the ideal to the immediate, God chose certain men to take possession of and to hold, for Him, that land and those ways of life which should be his City, his citadel, in the midst of the corrupted world. I cannot deal with the mystery of God's love for man, nor of His seeming "dependence" upon man once man had been given free will: what this concept can do for us here is to light up man's role in this relationship—that somehow he was chosen to be God's champion; and that it was this destiny which endowed him with grandeur and immense potentialities, and at the same time laid on him an almost intolerable burden. We said that the great advance of the Hebrews over other early peoples was in their recognition that this is pre-eminently a moral universe, in the concept of "ethical monotheism." But God can at least be approached, spoken to, remonstrated with, by those like Job who have the courage; some *modus vivendi* can be worked out, even if not understood. Salvation in this context has to be worked out, not thought out: the protagonists were presented with the task not merely of understanding, but of living with God and their destiny: it is a tragic, not a philosophic, question. The Creation and the Fall have been the prologue to the play; now the struggle begins, down on earth, the struggle for the real-ization of the God-like in man.

And it seemed to come to pass, at various times. God said to Satan, the heavenly prosecuting attorney, "Hast thou seen my servant Job? There is none like him on the earth, a man perfect and upright, one that feareth God and avoideth evil." Ah, but prove it, says the Adversary—let me work on him, "and he will blaspheme Thee to Thy face." God allows the evil to hit, and, from Job's point of view at least, tragedy results.

It is, of course, in Job that we come closest to a complete tragic action, and it is uncompromisingly grounded in religion; it is *about* religion. All Job's physical and material evils are correlatives to his vision of spiritual evil: he knows that his Defender liveth, his piety is strong and ardent, the spirit of God is in his nostrils, and yet the arrows of the Almighty are within him. God keeps away and will not answer him. Job is God's champion, against the essentially impious comforters as well as against Satan; he is as much concerned with theodicy as is Prometheus or as Aeschylus himself. His purpose is to cry out loud and long, and not be silenced; his passion is to argue down his comforters, at the imminent danger of sinning by mere vehemence with his mouth; and he actually succeeds in talking God down out of His heaven, he hears the voice from the whirlwind. His perception is a grasp of the majesty and power and wisdom of his God, and that it transcends our ideas of righteousness and justice and retribution. And he subsides under the terms of the action: "How shall I answer Thee? I lay my hand upon my mouth . . . I had heard of Thee by the hearing of the ear, But now, mine eye hath seen Thee; Therefore, I repudiate . . . And repent on dust and ashes." It has been, from start to finish, an affair with God; whatever questions are raised about the secret cause remain secret. God comes down, the theology of suffering is begun to be manifested but there is no incarnation and no sacrament. The rectitude of Job's life has been vindicated. Job has made his point, and has been equal to his occasion; but it will all have to be done over again by every man for himself. This is good Tragedy.

Ecclesiastes is another matter. Here is a vision of evil, powerfully and comprehensively stated: everything cancels out; God seems to hide Himself from us, keeping from us the solution to the problem. He has tried it all, says the Preacher, on the basis of what God has endowed us with, and nothing avails, the pit awaits all alike. He sees both the possibility of evil and the actuality of moral evil—and he sees the connection between them. Job's God is, he knows, all-powerful and all-wise, but what good does the knowledge do him?

There is nothing availing unto salvation—*all* is vanity, that is, momentary, unenduring. Ecclesiastes is near the end of the great Hebrew "pilgrimage"—someone has described his threnody as "The Second-Century Blues"; and he was certainly tainted with pessimism. But his tragic vision of evil is undiluted, uncompromised. Melville calls him "true," because he has more of sorrow than joy in him, like the ocean, "which is the dark side of this earth, and which is two thirds of this earth . . . Ecclesiastes is the fine hammered steel of woe." [17] This may fall short of tragedy, but it is centrally and powerfully tragic.

Tragedy and "religion," then, are not incompatible—indeed, they both insistently concern themselves with man's urge and desire to become god-like, with the fact of the numinous; both feed on piety; both ultimately find the key to all problems in the question of immortality; both come to terms with death.

III

But, there is religion, and there is Christianity. And the central point of this paper is that there is a radical and immitigable difference as well as distinction between Christianity and all other religions, past, present, or possible. I need do no more than state it baldly: Christ was and is God; He became man, instituted the sacraments, died for our sins, rose from the dead, and reopened the gates of heaven. This act was unique and will remain inimitable. The consequences of recognizing it as such are very great, for our purposes. For example: The "neo-realist" Protestant theologians—the Niebuhrs, Calhoun, Bennett, even Barth—going back to Kierkegaard, keep insisting on the essential "*discontinuity* between the . . . highest human goodness . . . , and the goodness of God" [18] on God's will and sovereignty as paramount; that the resolution of these discrepancies and incompatibilities is *beyond* history; that, while sin can be forgiven, guilt cannot; that man cannot make himself pure in the eyes of the most holy; that, since man exists simultaneously in time and eternity, since "what existence requires on the one level is forbidden by existence on the other," human life is possible only as existence in tragedy, fear and trembling, dread, anxiety, despair, the absurd. It is interesting to note that Reinhold Niebuhr,

[17] *Moby Dick*, Chapter XCVI.

[18] Mary F. Thelen, *Man as Sinner* (New York, 1946), p. 114; q.v. for all these attributions, and an analysis of the whole "theology of crisis" position. Cf. Drucker, below, pp. 243, 248.

whose book of "sermonic essays" *Beyond Tragedy*[19] has a wistful chapter on "Christianity and Tragedy," derives nine-tenths of his illustrative material from the Old Testament.

But how easily is this impressive tragic doctrine undercut! Jaspers,[20] Brunner, Daniélou, Graham have merely to point out that Our Lord's death was "the crucial point of time, the act of reconciliation with God"; that "history is not a closed circle, but a straight line"; the believer has a present: "charity is of the same nature as eternity, which is the true present";[21] that "humanity is substantially saved . . . the irreversible character of salvation . . . Christian hope is the awaiting of entrance into the *joy* of an already acquired good";[22] that "sin *is* the greatest of evils, but it is a moral, not an ontological, disorder." [23] Josef Pieper, raising the interesting question of the "negative" element in the philosophy of St. Thomas Aquinas, ends by pointing out that, although "truth and unknowability belong together," Aquinas denies the *intrinsic* unknowability of something real.[24] Maritain has done the same thing for many quasi-tragic aspects of Aquinas' thought—"metaphysical evil," knowledge by connaturality, existentialism, etc.[25]—and the proto-realism of St. Thomas' theology always can serenely resolve the gloom of the "neo-realistic" theology. The hope-structure of epistemology, Pieper calls it; and "hope is closer to the Yes! than to the No!" Perhaps this is enough to indicate the theoretical consequences of taking the reality of the Incarnation seriously.

There is no intention here of slighting the sincerity and importance of the Neo-realist theologians, even though Guardini can amusingly account for the "theology of crisis" as the product, "not of Christian severity, but only Nordic exasperation." [26] Their insights show that

[19] New York, 1937.

[20] Karl Jaspers, *Tragedy is Not Enough* (Boston, 1952), trans. K. W. Deutsch (a chapter of *Von der Wahrheit*).

[21] Emil Brunner, "The Christian Sense of Time," *Cross Currents,* I (Fall 1950), 27; 29; 33.

[22] Jean Daniélou, "A Dialogue with Time," *Cross Currents,* I (Winter 1951), 79.

[23] Dom Aelred Graham, *Catholicism and the World Today* (New York, 1952), p. 158.

[24] "The 'Negative' Element in the Philosophy of Thomas Aquinas," *Cross Currents,* IV (Fall 1953), 46-56.

[25] Jacques Maritain, *St. Thomas and the Problem of Evil* (Milwaukee: Marquette University Press, 1942); *Existence and the Existent* (New York, 1948); *True Humanism* (New York, 1938).

[26] Romano Guardini, "The Legend of the Grand Inquisitor," *Cross Currents,* III (Fall 1952), 64.

there *is* a somber side to Christianity—not peace but the sword; the opposite of Sin is not easy Virtue but hard-kept Faith; the Crucifixion as well as the Eucharist is part of the Church, and will continue to be re-enacted until the *parousia*. Tragedy and Christianity are allies in combating rationalism and the Power of Positive Thinking and Mr. Brooks Atkinson's feeling of betrayal by *The Living Room*.[27] But I cannot find that the tragic theologians have a radical and consistent theoretical foundation. Max Scheler makes what I think is a profound distinction, between moral, or "guilty" guilt, which "is based on the act of choice," and "tragic or unguilty guilt, which is based on the *sphere* of choice." Under the Christian dispensation, the guiltiness of the "sphere" has already been atoned for, purged away—all now is in the realm of moral guilt, which provides for "objectively guiltless possibilities." On the other hand, "the tragic hero 'becomes guilty' while doing a guitless thing . . . he 'falls into guilt.' "[28]

What else, then? The doctrine of sin and grace (prevenient grace, sufficient though not always efficacious grace, etc.) I will just mention, trusting that its implications will be apparent. What of the Calvinistic doctrine that man is radically incapable of being loved by God, because he is so impure, so guilty, so vitiated by Original Sin—"Earth ails from the prime foundation"? The answer is in one of our most frequent prayers: ". . . that we may *be made* worthy of the promises of Christ"; or, as Dom Aelred Graham puts it, "God does not treat his children *as if* they were lovable in His sight: He makes them so by infusing His own regenerative love into them." "Theology and ethics depend, not on God's nature or truth or essence, but on His sovereignty."[29] Dante had said much the same thing: *In la sua voluntade è nostra pace;* it is a bond of the will, of love, not of "thinking that makes it so." Any number of the Mass prayers pierce through the supposed dilemma: the Preface for the Mass for the Dead; the Offertory prayer with *mirabiliter* followed by *mirabilius;* the "dies nostros *in* tua pace disponas." What of the blood of martyrs, the Communion of Saints, the treasury of Christ's merits?

What of the Sacraments—Incarnation on a human scale—God's coming down, and *staying down,* accommodating Himself to us, effecting the tragically supposed impossible marriage of the spirit and the flesh?

[27] See his review, *The New York Times,* 18 November 1954.

[28] "On the Tragic," *Cross Currents,* IV (Winter 1954), 190-1 (part of *Vom Umsturtz der Werte,* Vol. I, Leipzig, 1923).

[29] *Op. cit.,* p. 159.

What of God within our breasts, grace in our bowels, but grace not violent, not arrowy as in Job; no distorted Iô's or shattered Kassandra's? What of the whole edifice of morals, based upon the Natural Law, which the Christian mystery allows to be built up? And of the fascinating concept of Hopkins and Father Lynch,[30] of Christ the Athlete? The "Christic" grappling with the actual, using man-ness as the path through the finite into the infinite, even staring down death, certainly does defeat the evasions of both Manichean naturalism and Cartesian angelism. But in spite of Father Lynch's recognition of the exigency of death, he has complete confidence that not only Christ the Tiger Himself can make the muscular leap, but even the least of us, by bringing through analogy this athleticism into the daily human imaginative act, can walk the path on the boundary between the two worlds. In Father Lynch's scheme, the voice is often the voice of Tragedy, but the hands (or feet) are those of Epic.

But I think the point can best be made by contrasting, with our exemplary Old Testament, what I take, under correction, to be the crux and distinguishing mark of Christianity. We cited Genesis and Ecclesiastes, early and late phases of the Hebrew vision (and it has been said that Ecclesiastes is a "meditation on the undeveloped implications of Genesis"); what does St. Paul say?

First, and easiest: "By a man came death, and by a man the resurrection of the dead. And as in Adam all die, so also in Christ all shall be made alive." Actually, this is enough; but to some it perhaps lacks a middle term, a recognition of the in-between-time, the anguished cry of Ecclesiastes, "*All* is vanity, all go down alike into the pit." But Paul knows about death and vanity too: "*If* there be no resurrection from the dead, and *if* Christ be not risen again, then *is* our preaching vain, and your faith is also vain. . . . For you are yet in your sins. . . . *But* now Christ *is* risen from the dead . . . And the enemy death shall be destroyed last . . . I die daily. That which thou sowest is not quickened, except it die first . . . And when this mortal hath put on immortality, . . . O death, where is thy sting? *Therefore,* be ye steadfast and unmoveable, always abounding in the work of the Lord, knowing that your labor is *not in vain* in the Lord . . . But all things are of God, who hath reconciled us to Himself by Christ; and hath given to us the ministry of reconciliation." [31] All is vanity—yes, all would be

[30] "Theology and the Imagination," THOUGHT, XXIX (1954), 73-5. Also, Part II, "The Evocative Symbol," THOUGHT, XXIX (1954), 346-7. See, e.g., G. M. Hopkins' *The Windhover*.

[31] I Corinthians 15.

vanity, unless death were defeated. All things *are* of God, and we *have* the ministry of reconciliation. It could have been bad, but it is not. The Thing has happened, God be praised. *O felix culpa.*

IV

Since my purpose has been to set up a discussion of the *possibility* of a Christian tragedy, I shall conclude with only a tentative classification of things that have been called that, by various people. But there remain a few more distinctions, within which I think a discussion of the actual should contain itself. First, we should recognize that while a study of the times, the *Zeitgeist,* can often explain the *absence* of fully articulated tragedy (one thinks immediately of the end of the Roman Empire, the middle ages, the eighteenth and nineteenth centuries, the first quarter, at least, of the twentieth), it can do little, confidently, to account for the efflorescence when it does come. Secondly, we should recognize two possible though not equally cogent interpretations of "Christian tragedy": (1) tragedy written since the beginning of the Christian era: (2) tragedy about Christianity. The latter will come closest, I believe, to fulfilling the "possibility," only to find itself at the last minute undercut by the latent impossibilities we have described. The former is what causes all kinds of confused and inconsequent criticism. Mr. Auden states the position well: that the authors of this "Christian tragedy"—specifically, Shakespeare and Melville—"do not necessarily believe in the dogmas, but their conception of man's nature is, historically, derived from them." [32] One can see what a proliferation and dilution this leads to: people immediately start talking of "the tragedy of" this or that: Auden, who does better with the "religious hero" in *The Enchafèd Flood,* opts for "Christian tragedy" as "the tragedy of possibility," as opposed to Greek which is "the tragedy of necessity." We find Henri Peyre identifying *Phèdre* as "the tragedy of passion," in the same volume with Reichardt's "Ibsen, the tragedy of idealism" and Louis Martz's "The saint as tragic hero"; [33] Mark Harris goes so far as to call for a "tragedy of determinism." [34] In another connection I have found it necessary to question "the pro-

[32] W. H. Auden, "The Christian Tragic Hero," *New York Times Book Review,* 16 December 1945.

[33] *Tragic Themes in Western Literature,* ed. Cleanth Brooks (Yale University Press, 1955).

[34] *The Case for Tragedy* (New York, 1932), p. 178.

priety of such terms as 'political tragedy' in distilling out of various kinds of serious literature that which will distinguish the genuinely 'tragic' from something else. The terms have a kind of understandability, along with such other formulations as the Tragedy of Revenge, the Tragedy of Blood, Domestic Tragedy, Heroic Tragedy, what might be called Monk's Tale Tragedy, even [in desperation] Shakespearean Tragedy and something called 'the Jonsonian variety'; we should add, I suppose, a possible Problem Tragedy—Comical-Historical-Pastoral Tragedy. But these are dangerous in that their common assumption of the *noun,* the very name of the thing itself, so dilutes or distorts that thing by the multiplicity of the adjectives it is made to support, that the important business of ascertaining—and ultimately, properly responding to—the underlying form and essence of tragedy is obstructed rather than fostered." [35] The term "Christian Tragedy," then, used as the starting point for this sort of thing, leads also to all manner of Coleridgean, Bradleyan, or parsonical misconceptions about Shakespeare, is a misnomer, and does not grapple with the Tragic properly so-called. Mr. Leech has, I think, effectively answered those who try to make too much of the formal, lip-service, automatic adherence to "the Christian scheme, the medieval and Tudor concepts of social order" found in Elizabethan drama: "The human inconstancy of attitude can explain . . . why tragedy, though a-Christian in its implications, may be written by Christians and may please a predominantly Christian audience. For most men religious opinions are not equally powerful on every day of the year or the week. We know what amounts to nothing of Shakespeare's or Webster's religious views, but we know that our thoughts are not directed to God and His purposes when we have come to the end of reading *Othello* or *The Duchess of Malfi.*" [36] He could have added *Macbeth, Hamlet,* and *King Lear.* And, *mutatis mutandis,* this will serve for such other putative "tragedies in the Christian context" as the work of Ibsen, Conrad, Hardy, O'Neill, Arthur Miller, and Tennessee Williams.

What, then, are some of the data we have to deal with? The story of Christ's passion? He suffered, sweat blood, felt the sense of heaven's desertion, died, and descended into hell. But He was the Victim, He

[35] "Yardsticks for Tragedy," *Essays in Criticism,* V (1955), 84-5. I have attempted to apply some of the implications of this essay in "Shakespearean Tragedy: Critique of Humanism from the Inside," *Massachusetts Review* (Summer 1961), 633-50; and "Hamlet: Superman, SubChristian," *Centennial Review,* VI (1962), 230-44.

[36] *Essays in Criticism,* V (1955), 179-80.

did it willingly, He descended in triumph and rose in glory, and He knew He was going to, all the time. Anyone who watches a representation of the Passion has got the perception ahead of time. There is no tragedy, nor can there begin to be.

Are there other serious treatments of man's plight and his destiny, under the Christian aegis? Boethius gets consolation and satisfaction from philosophy, imagining that he pierces the mystery of predestination and free will. Dante writes a comedy. Chaucer, who translated Boethius, has his Monk tell pedantically and indiscriminately the "tragedies" of Lucifer, Adam, Samson, Hercules, Nero, Ugolino of Pisa, and Croesus, but they only annoy the merry company of pilgrims, "for litel hevynesse Is right ynough to muche folk, I gesse," and the Nun's Priest restores equanimity and mirth with the tale of Chaunticleer. Everyman feels the pressure of God's agent, Death, and the pathos of the failure of things under the sun, but the angel waits for him on the other side of the little door; and he is even accompanied by his Good Deeds: no discontinuity here! Spenser, graveled by the fact of Mutabilitie (another name for mortality), works it out, at the end of his moral epic, in a neat punning paradox: "O that great Sabbaoth God, graunt me that Sabaoths sight." That is, Thou art both God of hosts and God of peace; even though I cannot understand how, I shall take it on faith, through the mystical, poetic at-one-ment of Thy Name. Marlowe's *Faustus*? Greatly planned, perhaps, as Goethe said; but it disintegrates under the incompatibility of the ingredients. *Romeo and Juliet* is not a tragedy, it is an opera, an aria, a perfect *Liebestod* two hundred years before Wagner.

Milton is tragedy superseded and overwhelmed by Calvinism and epic; *O felix culpa. Samson:* autobiography, Greek, Old Testament, heroically finishing a life heroic—nothing is here for tears; spasmodically tragic, anything but Christian. Corneille: curious combination of *gloire* and martyrdom—Christian, but not tragic. Racine is another matter, nor do I believe that the humanistic attempt to discount his ingrained Jansenism has been successful. Insofar as Gnosticism, Manicheanism, Calvinism, Jansenism are religions, they do indeed provide a powerful support for tragedy, and Richards would be right in saying that "tragedy is only possible to a mind which is for the moment agnostic or Manichean" [37] if he restricted it to the *initial* moment. And, when Racine wrote religious tragedies *per se*, on commission, he went back to the Old Testament, and the powerful typological Christ-figures in

[37] I. A. Richards, *Principles of Literary Criticism* (New York, 1945), p. 246.

Athalie are tragic because they can see the future only darkly, like Eliot's Simeon.

Dostoevsky certainly plunged into the depths of a tragic world, investigated the dilemma of guilt and atonement under the aspect of crime and punishment, knew that wisdom comes only through suffering, plumbed the abyss of the divided heart and soul of modern man; and he presented a vision of social evil which had to be seen ultimately as "the religious question," the question of God and the devil and immortality, and an equally forceful vision of the claims of Sodom and the Madonna on human nature. He makes us go through what he himself called a "powerful negation." He brings to bear on the tragic problem the insights of Zossima, who knows about weeping and about the seed dying and about everybody being responsible for everybody else and everything, and that though all men are Karamazov (with its baseness), all men too are brothers, under the fatherhood of God. But again, it is unsatisfactory: Sonia's Lazarus-solution intrigues Raskolnikov, but does not convince him, at least "not in this story"; Zossima dies out of his book, and Alyosha's own story, deferred to another time, never gets told; the other brothers all fail to go the tragic distance. Dostoevsky's tragico-religious insights were strongly based on the Book of Job, which he read when eight years old and never forgot. His Christianity was curiously tied up with pan-Slavic Russian messianism, and the Orthodox Russian monk; Guardini has shown that, even if we take the Christ-figure of the "Grand Inquisitor" legend as Dostoevsky's instead of Ivan Karamazov's (which is temerarious, at best), it is strangely different from the Christ the rest of the Western world knows.[38] Berdyaev and de Lubac, both Christians, tragedy-lovers and Dostoevsky-ites, end by telling us to beware of lingering too long in this apocalyptic whirlpool.[39]

[38] *Op. cit.*

[39] Nicholas Berdyaev, *Dostoievsky* (New York, 1934), pp. 220-24; Henri de Lubac, *The Drama of Atheist Humanism* (London, 1949), pp. 200ff. Martin Jarrett-Kerr, C.R. (*Studies in Literature and Belief,* New York, 1954) touches, with tantalizing unevenness, upon our subject; he is especially good on Dostoievsky. He can recognize (speaking of Calderón) that "the Christian hero has the card of immortality and beatitude with which he can trump the last tricks of his opponents, Paganism and Death . . . what seems to be agony is unreal because it is willed, not undergone—the victim remains in control." Exactly; but in the next paragraph he presents us, summarily, with what is apparently the opposite deduction. "Briefly: only in a world where real tragedy is possible is redemption also possible. Perhaps the reverse is also true: only in a world where redemption—and therefore damnation too—is possible, is tragedy also possible. Thus it is not true that there can be no genuine Christian tragic drama (one

What of the American Puritans? Hawthorne's figures are reincarnations of Satan, Adam, and Eve; Dimmesdale fears and loves Jehovah, not Christ; and he and Hester "have ransomed [themselves] with all [their] woe." Melville's was the dark and true tragic vision, and enigmatic enough about the "evil-ness of God" to stir a controversy which is still raging; but Ahab does oscillate from the orphic to the sultanic, and madly breaks himself to pieces, like Macbeth; Father Mapple, who has the right answer, deriving "top-gallant delight" from his ability to recognize Christ the savior in the story of Jonah, appears briefly, and ineffectually, at the beginning of the story. The Quakers bow out of the action. Job, Ecclesiastes, King Ahab; Queequeg's Ramadan idol, the fiend Fedallah; the great Leviathan himself—these are the gods and prophets who steer the tragic ship to its destruction. And at the end who are left? Rachel, weeping her loss, and finding some sort of consolation in the salvation of the outcast of Genesis, Ishmael.

Faulkner works out his torturous scheme of expiation through what Claude-Edmonde Magny calls an "inverse theology," [40] and his world is the world before the Incarnation—the temple violated—without the prophecy of the Messiah. His highest reach is a Stoical, pre-Christian endurance, a forlorn hope that man "will prevail" (over what, we are not told, nor unto what); and a topsy-turvy un-incarnation which can only be called a Fable.

Mr. Martz has made out a case for Shaw's Saint Joan and Eliot's Becket as tragic-hero saints[41]—but he, too, is unsatisfactory, because he avoids the question, What *is* a saint, and the destructive implications, for tragedy, of maryrdom. The Shavian saint is nothing but the perennial Shavian heroine, who is exceptional (in this case) because she takes religious manifestations seriously—no more. There is really more of a genuine idea of the tragic in the epilogue and, of course, the preface, than in the play. Eliot, as usual, tries to get in everything at once: Greek chorus and furies, *Everyman* dialogue, the renaissance, the present day. Again, as usual, his protagonist is split: it is the chorus who, illegitimately, undergo the tragic "action"; the saint is not a tragic

---

would prefer to say, no genuine tragic drama within and compatible with a Christian metaphysic); on the contrary, all genuine tragic drama is material for Christian understanding." I surmise that it is the fatally easy to adopt phrase, "real tragedy," that causes the trouble; as usual, it begs the question.

[40] "Faulkner's Inverse Theology," *Cross Currents*, IV (Spring-Summer 1954), 204-22.

[41] Louis L. Martz, "The Saint as Tragic Hero," in *Tragic Themes in Western Literature* (see note 33 above).

hero but a martyr. It is instructive of Eliot's honorable failure to make Christianity and tragedy go together that the Greek play with most affinities to *Murder in the Cathedral* is *Oedipus at Colonus,* the exceptional, end-of-his-life, *Tempest*-like Sophoclean play; his other attempt, *The Cocktail Party,* takes as exemplar *Alcestis,* Euripides' tragi-comedy. *The Family Reunion* is a self-confessed failure to make anything out of Aeschylus' Orestes and his Furies. Christianity is intransigent to tragedy; tragedy bucks and balks under Christianity.

Finally, what of those radical gropers, as often as not converts to Catholicism, who boldly investigate the thing itself under the aegis of the tragic sense: Graham Greene, Mauriac, Bloy, Bernanos? I must remain tentative about this latest development. Is a genuine Christian tragedy possible for the saint of the dark night of the soul? *Can* Bernanos be a "pessimistic Catholic," as Hatzfeld calls him, without falling over into Jansenism? [42] Perhaps, but on the whole it is doubtful. Greene hit his highest point with *The Heart of the Matter:* an amazing feat of balancing the "two holocausts of Scobie"—of fear and damnation—up to the very end. And maybe it will stand, a tour de force, on its vanishing point. But the signs of imbalance are there already. Scobie's pity is so radically exigent as to appear inhuman, diseased, an obsession, and to drown out the tragic terror. And Greene has since gone on into what might almost be called a fascination with the pathology of sin. Historically, it is reminiscent of Shakespeare's probing the fringes, the frontiers, of tragedy in *Antony, Troilus, Timon. He* purged himself of it, and wrote the "final plays." But tragedy after him collapsed into the Jacobean nightmare.

This brings us up to date and the moment for summarizing my position.[43] Profound ambiguity in the presence of evil; human life as a predicament; standing under judgment; assurances called into question—these things generate the tragic frame of mind, the tragic sense of life. For the religious person, the problem of evil, which is the root of tragedy, becomes the conviction of sin; the tension, the qualm, the psychomachia, the agon-izing, all result from "the dream of innocence confronted by the fact of guilt." Thus tragedy can get a start in a religious vision of human life, and of the cosmos, which is "Jewish" or Manichean. But Christians believe in the efficacy of the Incarnation

[42] Helmut Hatzfeld, "Under the Sun of Satan," *Cross Currents,* II (Winter 1952), 57.

[43] Much of this paragraph was printed in a communication by the author to *The Commonweal,* 17 July 1953, 370-71.

and the Resurrection and the Redemption: that the hegemony of the devil was destroyed once and for all. The Gordian tragic knot has been cut. Sin remains, although the *devastating* effect of Original Sin has been removed, and each man must work out his salvation with diligence, if not in fear and trembling; but his life is no longer in the proper sense a predicament or a dilemma. In whatever theological, philosophical, cultural, or pragmatic terms Christian optimism expresses itself, it is grounded in enthusiasm not for the natural powers of man but for the supernatural fact of redemption. At the root of the question of living in a vale of tears, then, there is a basic incompatibility between the tragic and the Christian view. And nothing has yet come forward which can be called, without cavil, both Christian and Tragedy at the same time.

The Christian Tragic Hero: Contrasting Captain Ahab's Doom and its Classic Greek Prototype

W. H. AUDEN

Moby Dick is at once an heroic epic like the *Iliad,* an heroic tragedy like the *Oresteia,* an heroic quest like the legend of the *Golden Fleece,* and an allegorical religious quest like *Pilgrim's Progress;* it is also a nineteenth century American novel. Even if it were not the great book it is, it would therefore be of unusual interest to the critic who would compare the values believed in and the attitudes held at different stages in Western civilization. I propose in this article to consider only one of them, the concept of the Tragic Hero in Greece and in Christendom. Most of the characteristics one observes in Melville's hero can also be seen in, say, the heroes of Shakespeare's tragedies, but Melville's choral asides make them more explicit in his own case.

To sum up in advance, the conclusions I shall try to demonstrate are these: first, Greek tragedy is the tragedy of necessity; i.e., the feeling aroused in the spectator is "What a pity it had to be this way"; Christian tragedy is the tragedy of possibility, "What a pity it was this way when it might have been otherwise"; secondly, the hubris which is the flaw in the Greek hero's character is the illusion of a man who knows himself strong and believes that nothing can shake that strength, while the corresponding Christian sin of Pride is the illusion of a man who knows himself weak but believes he can by his own efforts transcend that weakness and become strong.

In using the term Christian I am not trying to suggest that Melville or Shakespeare or any other author necessarily believed the Christian dogmas, but that their conception of man's nature is, historically, derived from them.

As an example of Greek tragedy let us take *Oedipus Rex.* As a young man, Oedipus learns from a prophecy that he is fated to murder his father and marry his mother. Believing that his foster parents are his

From *The New York Times Book Review,* 16 December 1945, pp. 1, 21. Reprinted by permission of the author and the publisher.

real parents he leaves Carthage [*sic*]. He meets an old man on the road; they quarrel about who shall give way to the other, and Oedipus kills him. He comes to Thebes, saves it from a monster, and is rewarded by the hand of its Queen, Jocasta. Thebes is stricken with plague, and the Oracle declares the cause to be the undetected presence of a criminal. Oedipus undertakes an investigation and discovers that the criminal is himself. In expiation of his crime he puts out his eyes, and Jocasta hangs herself.

A modern reader, accustomed to the tragedy of possibility, instinctively asks, "Where and when did he make the wrong choice?" and as instinctively answers, "He should not have listened to the prophecy in the first place, or, having done so, then he should never have struck the old man or anyone else, and should never have married Jocasta or anyone else." But such thoughts would never have occurred to Sophocles or his audience. Macbeth and Captain Ahab are wrong to listen to the prophecies about them, because they are equivocal, and each reads into his a possibility he is wrong to desire; the prophecy Oedipus hears is not only unequivocal but something he is right to wish to avoid. When he kills the old man he feels no guilt, neither is he expected to feel any, and when he marries Jocasta there is nothing the matter with the relation as such. It is only when it turns out that, as a matter of fact, the former was his father and the latter is his mother that guilt begins.

The tragedy is that what had to happen happened, and if one asks what was wrong with Oedipus, that such a terrible fate should be assigned to him, one can only say that it is a punishment for a hubris which was necessarily his before he learnt of the prophecy at all; i.e., had he not had such a character, the prophecy would never have been made.

Other Greek heroes are faced with the tragic choice between two evils: Agamemnon must either sacrifice his daughter or fail in his duty to the Greek Army; Antigone must be false either to her loyalty to her brother or to her loyalty to her city.

The tragic situation, of learning that one is a criminal or of being forced to become one, is not created by the flaw in the hero's character, but is sent him by the gods as a punishment for having such a flaw.

The pessimistic conclusion that underlies Greek tragedy seems to be this: that if one is a hero, i.e., an exceptional individual, one must be guilty of hubris and be punished by a tragic fate; the only alternative and not one a person can choose for himself is to be a member of the chorus, i.e., one of the average mass; to be both exceptional and good is impossible.

How does "Moby Dick" compare with this?

The hero, Captain Ahab, far from being exceptionally fortunate, is at the beginning, what in a Greek tragedy he could only be at the end, exceptionally unfortunate. He is already the victim of what the modern newspaper, which is Greek in this respect, would call a tragedy; a whale has bitten off his leg. What to the Greeks could only have been a punishment for sin is here a temptation to sin, an opportunity to choose; by making the wrong choice and continuing to make it, Ahab punishes himself. To say that a character is tempted means that it is confronted by possibility, that it is not a fixed state but a process of becoming: the possibilities are not infinite; i.e., Ahab cannot become Starbuck or Pip or Ishmael or anyone else except Ahab, but the possibilities are eternal; the past is irrevocable but always redeemable now.

Thus we can at every moment answer the question, "What should Ahab do now?" Before the story opens he has suffered and made his first wrong choice. He was not wrong to make Moby Dick into a symbol of all the inexplicable suffering in the world; on the contrary, the capacity to see the universal in the particular is the mark of human greatness, and it is only Flask, the Philistine trimmer, who says, "A whale is only a whale"; he was wrong, however, to insist on his own explanation, that the motive behind the whale's act and behind all suffering is personal malevolence. Once he has done so, he can still be saved, but he has made his salvation a much harder task, for he is now required to forgive the whale personally, in contrast, for instance, to Captain Boomer, who, like Ahab, has been deprived of a limb by Moby Dick, but in his pragmatic English way explains the whale's ferocity as mere clumsiness which is easier to forgive than malice.

In Greek tragedy are two kinds of characters, the exceptional hero and the average chorus, and neither can become the other; in Christian tragedy there is not only an infinite variety of possible characters, varying all the way from Ahab, the captain, who defiantly insists on being absolutely unique, down to Pip, the cabin boy, who is too afraid to claim even his own name, but overshadowing them all is the possibility of each becoming both exceptional and good; this ultimate possibility for hero and chorus alike is stated in Father Mapple's sermon, and it is to become a saint—i.e., the individual who of his own free will surrenders his will to the will of God. In this surrender he does not become a ventriloquist's doll, for the God who acts through him can only do so by his consent; there always remain two wills, and the saint, therefore (unlike the late Greek conception of the undramatic Sage who is good by necessity because he knows), never ceases to be tempted to obey his own desires.

Of this possibility Ahab's career is at every point a negative parody.

The saint does not ask to be one, he is called to become one, and assents to the call. The outward sign that Ahab is so called, is the suffering which is suddenly intruded into his life. What he is called to become, we do not, of course, know for certain—all we know for certain is that he rejected it—but we can guess that he was called to give up hunting whales—i.e., the normal cannibalistic life of this world, a life which is permitted, for instance, to Queequeg (who, though sinless, is not a saint, but the innocent man before the fall) but no longer to Ahab once he has been made uniquely conscious of the suffering it inflicts. Of the others, less is required: of Starbuck that he face evil instead of superstitiously avoiding it, of Stubb that he face his fears instead of whistling in the dark; but of Ahab alone is required, because he alone has the necessary heroic passion, to become a real and not a merely respectable Quaker.

Ahab is not deaf; he hears the call and refuses it with all the passion with which he might have accepted it; like the saint he wills one thing, to kill Moby Dick. For this he leaves his wife and child; for this his first act in the book is to throw away his pipe, his last physical addiction, his last relation with the element of earth; for this he destroys the ship's quadrant, its relation to the element of air so that the Pequod can only know the universe through compass and line in terms of the dualistic antagonism of fire and water.

The saint, knowing his will to be weak, may express his external resolve by a temporal or bodily ritual act, but his vow and his act concern his own will alone. Ahab attempts to use ritual as a magical means of compelling the wills of others, as when he forces the crew to swear on their harpoons, and finally even to compel lifeless things, as when he baptizes a harpoon itself.

Just as the saint never ceases to be tempted to forsake his calling, so, vice versa, Ahab is never free from the possibility of renouncing his refusal. Divine grace offers itself, now in the nostalgic beauty of fine weather, now as Gabriel, the mad idolater of the whale, an unlovely reflection of himself, and finally, in its strongest and least disguised form, as the cry for help of a friend in distress when the Pequod meets the Rachel, and it is only after he has refused this last offer that his doom becomes necessary. Melville portrays this decisive change with great subtlety. For it is at this point that Ahab places the idiot Pip in his cabin and, in a grotesque parody of the saint as the servant of servants, takes for himself the humble position of lookout on the mast which is the negative image of the martyr's cross. Instead of gaining a martyr's crown, however, his hat, the badge of his authority, is snatched from his head by the Jovian eagle, and from this moment Fedallah, the slave, the projection of Ahab's will, seems suddenly to have taken charge of his creator, or rather his summoner. Fedallah is clearly intended by Melville, I think, to represent the demonic, i.e., that which (unlike Ahab, who is tempted by suffering) tempts itself and denies for the sake of denying, and about which, therefore, nothing historic can be said; we are only told his religion.

So Ahab, refusing life, goes unrepentant, like all of Shakespeare's tragic heroes, to the unnecessary death he has chosen, dragging with him all his companions, and the only survivor is, as in Greek tragedy, the Chorus, the spectator, Ishmael. But Ishmael is not, like the Greek Chorus, the eternal average man, for he isn't a character at all. To be a character one must will and act, and Ishmael has no will, only consciousness; he does not act, he only knows, and what he knows is good *and* evil, i.e., possibility. He cannot die because he has not yet begun to live, and he ends the book as a baby, reborn from the sea in Queequeg's coffin, thrust back into life as an orphan with his first choice still to make.

The Unfashionable Kierkegaard

PETER F. DRUCKER

I

The Kierkegaard boom of the last few years is showing the first signs of fatigue. For Kierkegaard's sake I hope it will burst soon. The Kierkegaard of the literary boom is a fellow wit and fellow modern, distinguished from the other members of the smart set mainly by his having lived a hundred years earlier. But this Kierkegaard of the psychologists, existentialists and assorted ex-Marxists bears hardly any resemblance to the real Kierkegaard who cared nothing for psychology or dialectics (save to show them to be inadequate and irrelevant) but concerned himself solely with religious experience. And it is this real Kierkegaard who is meaningful for the modern world in its agony. We have neither Saint nor Poet to make whole the shards of our experience; in Kierkegaard we have at least a prophet.

Like all religious thinkers, Kierkegaard places in the center the question: How is human existence possible?

All through the Nineteenth Century this question—which before had been the core of Western thought—was not only highly unfashionable; it seemed senseless and irrelevant. The era was dominated by a radically different question: How is society possible? Rousseau asked it, Hegel asked it, the classical economists asked it. Marx answered it one way, liberal Protestantism another way. But in whatever form it is asked, it must always lead to an answer which denies that human existence is possible except in society.

Rousseau formulated this answer for the whole era of progress: whatever human existence there is; whatever freedom, rights, and duties the individual has; whatever meaning there is in individual life—all is determined by society according to society's objective need of survival. The individual, in other words, is not autonomous. He is determined by society. He is free only in matters that do not matter.

From *The Sewanee Review,* Vol. LVII, 1949, pp. 587-602. Reprinted by permission of the author and the editor.

He has rights only because society concedes them. He has a will only if he wills what society needs. His life has meaning only in so far as it relates to the social meaning, and as it fulfills itself in fulfilling the objective goal of society. There is, in short, no human existence; there is only social existence. There is no individual; there is only the citizen.

It is hardly possible to exaggerate the differences between Rousseau's "General Will," Hegel's concept of history as the unfolding of ideas, and the Marxian theory of the individual's determination through his objectively given class situation. But they all gave the same answer to the question of human existence: there is no such thing, there is no such question! Ideas and citizens exist, but no human beings. What is possible is merely the realization of ideas in and through society.

For if you start with the question, How is society possible?, without asking at the same time, How is human existence possible?, you arrive inevitably at a negative concept of individual existence and of freedom: individual freedom is then what does not disturb society. Thus freedom becomes something that has no function and no autonomous existence of its own. It becomes a convenience, a matter of political strategy, or a demagogue's catch phrase. It is nothing vital.

To define freedom as that which has no function is, however, to deny the existence of freedom. For nothing survives in society save it have a function. But the Nineteenth Century believed itself far too secure in the possession of freedom to realize this. Prevailing opinion failed to see that to deny the relevance of the question, How is human existence possible? is to deny the relevance of human freedom. It actually saw in the question, How is society possible? a key to the gospel of freedom—largely because it aimed at social equality. And the break of the old fetters of inequality appeared equivalent to the establishment of freedom.

We now have learned that the Nineteenth Century was mistaken. Nazism and Communism are an expensive education—a more expensive education, perhaps, than we can afford; but at least we are learning that we cannot obtain freedom if we confine ourselves to the question, How is society possible? It may be true that human existence in freedom is not possible; which is, indeed, asserted by Hitler and the Communists as well as, less openly, by all those well-meaning "social engineers" who believe in social psychology, propaganda, re-education, or administration, as a means of molding and forming the individual. But at least the question, How is human existence possible? can no longer be regarded as irrelevant. For those who profess to believe in freedom there is no more relevant inquiry.

I am not trying to say that Kierkegaard was the only thinker during the Nineteenth Century who saw the direction in which Rousseau was leading the Western world. There were the Romanticists, some of whom, especially in France, sensed what was coming. There was the futile and suicidal revolt of Nietzsche—a Samson whose gigantic power pulled down nothing but himself. There was above all Balzac, who analyzed a society in which human existence was no longer possible, and who drew an Inferno more terrible than Dante's in that there is not even a Purgatory above it. But although they all asked, How is human existence possible? none but Kierkegaard answered.

II

Kierkegaard's answer is simple: human existence is possible only in tension—in tension between man's simultaneous life as an individual in the spirit and as a citizen in society. Kierkegaard expressed the fundamental tension in a good many ways throughout his writings—most clearly and centrally when he described the tension as the consequence of man's simultaneous existence in eternity and in time. He took his formulation from St. Augustine; it is the intellectual climax of the *Confessions*. But Kierkegaard gave to the antithesis a meaning that goes far beyond St. Augustine's speculation in dialectical logic.

Existence in time is existence as a citizen in this world. In time, we eat and drink and sleep, fight for conquest or for our lives, raise children and societies, succeed or fail. But in time we also die. And in time there is nothing left of us after our death. In time we do not, therefore, exist as individuals. We are only members of a species, links in a chain of generations. The species has an autonomous life in time, specific characteristics, an autonomous goal; but the member has no life, no characteristics, no aim outside the species. He exists only in and through the species. The chain has a beginning and an end, but each link serves only to tie the links of the past to the links of the future; outside the chain it is scrap iron. The wheel of time keeps on turning, but the cogs are replaceable and interchangeable. The individual's death does not end the species or society, but it ends his life in time. Human existence is not possible in time, only society is possible in time.

In eternity, however, in the realm of the spirit, "in the sight of God," to use one of Kierkegaard's favorite terms, it is society which does not exist, which is not possible. In eternity only the individual does exist. In eternity each individual is unique; he alone, all alone, without neighbors and friends, without wife and children, faces the spirit in himself. In time, in the sphere of society, no man begins at the beginning and ends at the end; each of us receives from those before us the inheritance of the ages, carries it for a tiny instant, to hand it on to those after him. But in the spirit, each man is beginning and end. Nothing his fathers have experienced can be of any help to him. In awful loneliness, in complete, unique singleness, he faces himself as if there were nothing in the entire universe but him and the spirit in himself. Human existence is thus existence on two levels—existence in tension.

It is impossible even to approximate eternity by piling up time; mere time, even infinitely more time, will still only be time. And it is also impossible to reach time by subdividing eternity; eternity is inseparable and immeasurable. Yet it is only as simultaneous existence on both planes, existence in the spirit and existence in society, that human existence is possible. St. Augustine had said that time is within eternity, created by eternity, suspended in it. But Kierkegaard knew that the two are on different planes, antithetic and incompatible with each other. And he knew it not only by logic and by introspection, but by looking at the realities of nineteenth-century life.

It is this answer that constitutes the essential paradox of religious experience. To say that human existence is possible only in the tension between existence in eternity and existence in time is to say that human existence is only possible if it is impossible: what existence requires on the one level is forbidden by existence on the other. For example, existence in society requires that the society's objective need for survival determine the functions and the actions of the citizen. But existence in the spirit is possible only if there is no law and no rule except that of the person, alone with himself and with his God. Because man must exist in society, there can be no freedom except in matters that do not matter; but because man must exist in the spirit, there can be no social rule, no social constraint in matters that do matter. In society, man can exist only as a social being—as husband, father, child, neighbor, fellow citizen. In the spirit, man can exist only personally—alone, isolated, completely walled in by his own consciousness.

Existence in society requires that man accept as real the sphere of social values and beliefs, rewards and punishments. But existence in the spirit, "in the sight of God," requires that man regard all social values and beliefs as pure deception, as vanity, as untrue, invalid, and unreal. Kierkegaard quotes from Luke 14:26, "If any man come to me, and hate not his father and mother, and wife and children, and brethren and sisters, yea and his own life also, he cannot be my disciple." The Gospel of Love does not say: *love* these *less* than you love me; it says *hate*.

To say that human existence is possible only as simultaneous existence in time and in eternity is thus to say that it is possible only as one crushed between two irreconcilable ethical absolutes. And that means (if it be more than the mockery of cruel gods): human existence is possible only as existence in tragedy. It is existence in fear and trembling; in dread and anxiety; and, above all, in despair.

III

This seems a very gloomy and pessimistic view of human existence, and one hardly worth having. To the Nineteenth Century it appeared as a pathological aberration. But let us see where the optimism of the Nineteenth Century leads to. For it is the analysis of this optimism and the prediction of its ultimate outcome that gave Kierkegaard's work its vision.

It was the very essence of all nineteenth-century creeds that eternity can and will be reached in time; that truth can be established in society and through majority decision; that permanence can be obtained through change. This is the belief in inevitable progress, representative of the Nineteenth Century and its very own contribution to human thought. You may take the creed of progress in its most naive and therefore most engaging form—the confidence that man automatically and through his very sojourn in time becomes better, more nearly perfect, more closely approaches the divine. You may take the creed in its more sophisticated form—the dialectic schemes of Hegel and Marx in which truth unfolds itself in the synthesis between thesis and antithesis, each synthesis becoming in turn the thesis of a new dialectical integration on a higher and more nearly perfect level. Or you may take the creed in the pseudo-scientific garb of the theory of evolution through natural selection. In each form it has the same substance: a fervent belief that by piling up time we shall attain eternity; by piling up matter we shall become spirit; by piling up change we shall become permanent; by piling up trial and error we shall find truth. For Kierkegaard, the problem of the final value was one of uncompromising conflict between contradictory qualities. For the Nineteenth Century, the problem was one of quantity.

Where Kierkegaard conceives the human situation as essentially tragic, the Nineteenth Century overflowed with optimism. Not since the year 1000, when all Europe expected the Second Coming, has there been a generation which saw itself so close to the fulfillment of time as did the men of the Nineteenth Century. Certainly there were impurities in the existing fabric of society. But the liberal confidently expected them to be burnt away within a generation or, at the most, within a century by the daily strengthening light of reason. Progress was automatic. And though the forces of darkness and superstition might seem to gain at times, that was only a momentary illusion. "It is always darkest just before the dawn" is a truly liberal maxim (and one, incidentally, as false in its literal as in its metaphorical sense). The apogee of this naive optimism was the book which the famous German biologist, Ernest Haeckel, wrote just before the turn of the century—the one which predicted that all the remaining questions would be finally and decisively answered within a generation by Darwinian biology and Newtonian physics. It is perhaps the best commentary on the fate of the nineteenth-century creed that Haeckel's *Weltraetsel* sold by the millions in the generation of our grandfathers (and still hides out on old bookshelves) at the very moment when the universe of Darwinian biology and Newtonian physics was completely disintegrating.

To those whom the optimism of liberalism or Darwinism failed to satisfy, Marx offered the more complicated but also infinitely more profound vision of a millennium that had to come precisely because the world was so corrupt and so imperfect. His was a truly apocalyptic message in which the impossible, the attainment of the permanent perfection of the classless society, is promised precisely because it is impossible. In Marx the nineteenth-century optimism admits defeat—only to use defeat as a proof of certain victory.

In this creed of imminent perfection, in which every progress in time meant progress toward eternity, permanence, and truth, there was no room for tragedy (the conflict of two absolute forces, of two absolute laws). There was not even room for catastrophe. Everywhere in the nineteenth-century tradition the tragic is exorcised, catastrophe suppressed. A good example is the attempt—quite popular these last few years—to explain so cataclysmic a phenomenon as Hitlerism in terms of "faulty psychological adjustment," that is, as something that has nothing to do with the spirit but is exclusively a matter of techniques. Or, in a totally different sphere, compare Shakespeare's *Antony and Cleopatra* with Flaubert's *Madame Bovary,* and see how the essentially tragic "eros" becomes pure "sex"—psychology, physiology, even passion, but no longer a tragic, i.e., an insoluble, conflict. Or one might, as one of the triumphs of the attempt to suppress catastrophe, take the early Communist explanation of Nazism as "just a necessary stage in the inevitable victory of the proletariat." There you have in purest form the official creed that whatever happens in time must be good, however evil it is. Neither catastrophe nor tragedy can exist.

There has never been a century of Western history so far removed from an awareness of the tragic as the one that bequeathed to us two world wars. Not quite two hundred years ago—in 1755 to be exact—the death of 15,000 people in the Lisbon earthquake was enough to bring down the tottering structure of traditional Christian belief in Europe. The contemporaries could not make sense of it, they could not reconcile this horror with the concept of an all-merciful God, they could not see any answer to a paradox of catastrophe of such magnitude. For years now we have learned daily of vastly greater destruction, of whole peoples being starved or exterminated. And it is far more difficult to comprehend these manmade catastrophes in terms of our modern rationality than it was for the Eighteenth Century to comprehend the earthquake of Lisbon in the terms of traditional Christianity. Yet our own catastrophes make no impression on the optimism of those thousands of committees that are dedicated to the belief that permanent peace and prosperity will "inevitably" issue from today's horrors. To be sure, they are aware of the facts and duly outraged by them. But they refuse to see them as catastrophes. They have been trained to deny the existence of tragedy.

IV

Yet however successful the Nineteenth Century was in suppressing the tragic, there is one fact that could not be suppressed, one fact that remains outside of time: death. It is the one fact that cannot be made general but remains unique, the one fact that cannot be socialized but remains personal. The Nineteenth Century made every effort to strip death of its individual, unique, and qualitative aspect. It made death an incident in vital statistics, measurable quantitatively, predictable according to the actuarial laws of probability. It tried to get around death by organizing away its consequences. Life insurance is perhaps the most significant institution of nineteenth-century metaphysics; its proposition "to spread the risks" shows most clearly the nature of the attempt to consider death an incident in human life rather than its termination. And the Nineteenth Century invented spiritualism—an attempt to control life after death by mechanical means.

Yet death persists. Society might make death taboo, might lay down the rule that it is bad manners to speak of death, might substitute "hygienic" cremation for those horribly public funerals, and might call grave diggers morticians. The learned Professor Haeckel might hint broadly that Darwinian biology is just about to make us live permanently; but he did not make good his promise. And so long as death persists, the individual remains with one pole of his existence outside of society and outside of time.

So long as death persists, the optimistic concept of life, the belief that eternity can be reached through time, and that the individual can fulfill himself in society, must have only one outcome—despair. Suddenly every man finds himself facing death; and at this point he is all alone; all individual. If his existence is purely in society, he is lost—for now this existence becomes meaningless. Kierkegaard diagnosed the phenomenon and called it the "despair at not willing to be an individual." Superficially, the individual can recover from this encounter with the problem of existence in eternity; he may even forget it for a while. But he can never regain his confidence in his existence in society. Basically he remains in despair.

Society must make it possible for man to die without despair if it wants him to be able to live exclusively in society. And it can do so in only one way—by making individual life meaningless. If you are nothing but a leaf on the tree of the race, a cell in the body of society, then your death is not really death; you had better call it a process of collective regeneration. But then, of course, your life is not a real life either; it is just a functional process within the life of the whole, devoid of any meaning except in terms of the whole. Thus as Kierkegaard foresaw a hundred years ago, an optimism that proclaims human existence as existence in society leads straight to despair. And this despair can lead only to totalitarianism. For totalitarianism—and that is the trait that distinguishes it so sharply from the tyrannies of the past—is based on the affirmation of the meaninglessness of life and of the nonexistence of the person. Hence the emphasis in the totalitarian creed is not on how to live, but on how to die; to make death bearable, individual life had to be made worthless and meaningless. The optimistic creed, that started out by making life in this world mean everything, led straight to the Nazi glorification of self-immolation as the only act in which man can meaningfully exist. Despair becomes the essence of life itself.

V

The Nineteenth Century arrived at the very point the pagan world had reached in the late Roman Empire. And like antiquity, it tried to find a way out by escaping into the purely ethical—by basing virtue on man's reason. The great philosophical systems of German idealism—above all Kant's, but also Hegel's—dominated the age because they identified reason with virtue and the good life. Ethical culture and that brand of liberal Protestantism that sees in Jesus the "best man that ever lived," with its slogans of the Golden Rule, of the "categorical imperative," and of the satisfaction of service—these and related ethical formulae became as familiar in the Nineteenth Century as most of them had been in antiquity. And they failed to provide a basis for human existence in modernity just as they had failed two thousand years before.

In its best representatives, the ethical concept leads indeed to moral integrity and moral greatness. Nineteenth-century humanism—based half on Plutarch, half on Newton—could be a noble thing. (We have only to remember the great men of the last nineteenth-century generation, such as Woodrow Wilson, Masaryk, Jaures, or Mommsen.) Kierkegaard himself was more attracted by it than he realized. Though fighting every inch of the way, he could never quite free himself from the influence of Hegel; and Socrates, symbol of the ethical life, remained to him the apogee of man's natural history.

But Kierkegaard also saw that the ethical concept, while it may give integrity, courage, and steadfastness, cannot give meaning—neither to life nor to death. All it can give is stoic resignation. Kierkegaard considered this position to be one of even greater despair than the optimistic one; he calls it "the despair at willing to be an individual." And only too often the ethical position does not lead to anything as noble and as consistent as the Stoic philosophy, but turns into sugar coating on the pill of totalitarianism. This is, I feel, the position of many an apologist for Soviet Russia; he hopes that man will find individual fulfillment in the ethical attempt at making his neighbor happy; and that this will suffice to offset the reality of totalitarianism. Or the ethical position becomes pure sentimentalism—the position of those who believe that evil can be abolished and harmony established by good intentions.

And in all cases the ethical position is bound to degenerate into relativism. For if virtue is to be found in man, everything that is accepted by man must be virtue. Thus a position that starts out—as did Rousseau and Kant a hundred and seventy-five years ago—to establish man-made ethical absolutes, must end in the complete denial of absolutes and, with it, in the complete denial of the possibility of a truly ethical position. This way there is no escape from despair.

Is then the only conclusion that human existence can be only existence in tragedy and despair? Are the sages of the East right who see the only answer in the destruction of self, in the submersion of man into the Nirvana, the nothingness?

Kierkegaard has another answer: human existence is possible as existence not in despair, as existence not in tragedy—it is possible as existence in faith. The opposite of Sin (to use the traditional term for existence purely in society) is not Virtue; it is Faith.

Faith is the belief that in God the impossible is possible, that in Him time and eternity are one, that both life and death are meaningful. Faith is the knowledge that man is creature—not autonomous, not the master, not the end, not the center—and yet responsible and free. It is the acceptance of man's essential loneliness, to be overcome by the certainty that God is always with man; even "unto the hour of our death."

In my favorite among Kierkegaard's books, a little volume called *Fear and Trembling,* he raises the question: What distinguished Abraham's willingness to sacrifice his son, Isaac, from ordinary murder? If Abraham had never intended to go through with the sacrifice, but had intended all the time only to make a show of his obedience to God, then Abraham indeed would not have been a murderer, but he would have been something more despicable: a fraud and a cheat. If he had not loved Isaac but had been indifferent, he would have been willing to be a murderer. Yet Abraham was a holy man; God's command was for him an absolute command to be executed without reservation; and we are told that he loved Isaac more than himself. The answer is that Abraham had faith. He believed that in God the impossible would become possible—that he could carry out God's command and yet retain Isaac.

Abraham was the symbol for Kierkegaard himself, and the sacrifice of Isaac the symbol for his own innermost secret, his great and tragic love—a love he had slaughtered although he loved it more than he loved himself. But the autobiographical allusion is only incidental. The story of Abraham is a universal symbol of human existence which is possible only in faith. In faith the individual becomes the universal, ceases to be isolated, becomes meaningful and absolute; hence in faith there is a true ethic. And in faith existence in society becomes meaningful, too, as existence in true charity.

The faith is not what today is so often glibly called a "mystical experience"—something that can apparently be induced by the proper breathing exercises or by prolonged exposure to Bach. It can be attained only through despair, through suffering, through painful and ceaseless struggle. It is not irrational, sentimental, emotional, or spontaneous. It comes as the result of serious thinking and learning, of rigid discipline, of complete sobriety, of humbleness, and of the self's subordination to a higher, an absolute will. The inner knowledge of one's own unification in God—what St. Paul called hope and we call saintliness—only a few can attain. But every man is capable of attaining faith. For every man knows despair.

Kierkegaard stands squarely in the great Western tradition of religious experience, the tradition of St. Augustine and St. Bonaventura, of Luther, St. John of the Cross, and Pascal. What sets him apart, and gives him this special urgency today, is his emphasis on the meaning of life in time and society for the man of faith, the Christian. Kierkegaard is "modern," not because he employs the modern vocabulary of psychology, aesthetics, and dialectics—the ephemeral traits which the Kierkegaard boom ballyhoos—but because he concerns himself with the specific disease of the modern West: the falling apart of human existence, the denial of the simultaneity of life in the spirit and life in the flesh, the denial of the meaningfulness of each for the other.

Instead, we have today a complete divorce, the juxtaposition of "Yogi" and "Commissar"—the terms are of course Arthur Koestler's—

as mutually exclusive possibilities: an either-or between time and eternity, charity and faith, in which one pole of man's dual existence is made the absolute. This amounts to a complete abdication of faith: the "Commissar" gives up the entire realm of the spirit for the sake of power and effectiveness; the "Yogi" assigns human existence in time, that is social life, to the devil, and is willing to see millions lose their lives and their souls if only his own "I" be saved. Both are impossible positions for any religious man to take, but especially for a Christian who must live in the spirit and yet must maintain that true faith is effective in and through charity (i.e., in and through social responsibility).

But at least both are honest positions, honestly admitting their bankruptcy—in contrast to the attempt at evading the problem by way of the various "Christian" political parties in Europe, Protestant and Catholic, or the movement for "Social Christianity" still powerful in this country. For these attempts substitute morality and good intentions for faith and religious experience as mainsprings of action. While sincere and earnest, while supported and sometimes led by good, even by saintly men, they must not only be as ineffectual in politics as the "Yogi" but must also fail, like the "Commissar," to give spiritual life; for they compromise both, life in time and life in eternity. That Austrian cleric and Catholic party leader who, in the Thirties, came out for Hitler with the argument "at least he is opposed to mixed bathing," was a ghastly caricature of the Christian moralist in politics; but he caricatured something that is ever present where morality is confused with faith.

Kierkegaard offers no easy way out. Indeed it could be said of him —as of all religious thinkers who focus on experience rather than on reason and dogma—that he greatly over-emphasizes life in the spirit, thus failing to integrate the two poles of human existence into one whole. But he not only saw the task, he also showed in his own life and in his works that there is no escape from the reality of human existence, which is one in tension. It is no accident that the only part of Kierkegaard's tremendous literary output that did not originally appear under a pseudonym but under his own name was the *Edifying Discourses*. Not that he wanted to conceal his authorship of the other works—the pseudonyms could not have fooled anybody; but the "edifying" books alone translate faith into social effectiveness and are thus truly religious and not just "Yogi." It is also not an accident that Kierkegaard's whole work, his twenty years of seclusion, of writing, thinking, praying, and suffering, were but the preparation for the violent political action to which he dedicated the last months of his life—a furious one-man war on the Established Church of Denmark and its high clergy for confusing morality and tradition with charity and faith.

Though Kierkegaard's faith cannot overcome the awful loneliness, the isolation and dissonance of human existence, it can make it bearable by making it meaningful. The philosophy of the totalitarian creeds enables man to die. It is dangerous to underestimate the strength of such a philosophy; for, in a time of sorrow and suffering, of catastrophe and horror (that is, in our time), it is a great thing to be able to die. Yet it is not enough. Kierkegaard's faith, too, enables man to die; but it also enables him to live.

Aristotle on Catharsis

GERALD F. ELSE

49b21-31

περὶ μὲν οὖν τῆς ἐν ἑξαμέτροις μιμητικῆς καὶ περὶ κωμῳδίας ὕστερον ἐροῦμεν · περὶ δὲ τραγῳδίας λέγωμεν ἀπολαβόντες αὐτῆς ἐκ τῶν εἰρημένων τὸν γινόμενον ὅρον τῆς οὐσίας. ἔστιν οὖν τραγῳδία μίμησις πράξεως σπουδαίας | καὶ τελείας μέγεθος ἐχούσης, ἡδυσμένῳ λόγῳ, χωρὶς ἑκάστῳ τῶν εἰδῶν ἐν τοῖς μορίοις, δρώντων καὶ οὐ δι' ἀπαγγελίας [[δι' ἐλέου καὶ φόβου περαίνουσα τὴν τῶν τοιούτων παθημάτων κάθαρσιν]]. (λέγω δὲ ἡδυσμένον μὲν λόγον τὸν ἔχοντα ῥυθμὸν καὶ ἁρμονίαν [καὶ μέλος], τὸ δὲ χωρὶς τοῖς | εἴδεσι τὸ διὰ μέτρων ἔνια μόνον περαίνεσθαι καὶ πάλιν ἕτερα διὰ μέλους.)

49b21

Well then, about the mimetic art that works in hexameters, and about comedy, we shall speak later; let us now discuss tragedy, picking out of what has been said the definition of its essential nature that was emerging in the course of its development. Tragedy, then, is an imitation of an action which is serious, | complete, and has bulk, in speech that has been made attractive, using each of its species separately in the parts of the play; with persons performing the action rather than through narrative [carrying to completion, through a course of events involving pity and fear, the purification of those painful or fatal acts which have that quality]. (By "speech that has been made attractive" I mean speech that has rhythm and melody [and song] attached to it; and by "each of its | species separately" I mean that some sections of the play are carried forward by verses alone and some the other way round, by song.)

Enough of epic and comedy for a while; we turn to tragedy. The famous definition appears to be put forward as "emerging (Bywater: "resulting") from what has been said." But this involves assuming a hyperbation (*ἐκ τῶν εἰρημένων τὸν γινόμενον ὅρον* for *τὸν ἐκ τ. ε. γ. ὅρον*)[1] and an awkward catachresis of *γινόμενον*. Definitions do not "grow"

Reprinted by permission of the publishers from Gerald F. Else, *Aristotle's Poetics: the Argument,* Cambridge, Mass.: Harvard University Press, 1957, pp. 221-32, 423-25, 436-46.

[1] See Gudeman *ad loc.;* Vahlen, *Poet.*³ 117, 184-85.

out of things said, in Aristotle's world, however natural the metaphor may seem to us. The clue to the participle is rather in 4. 49a13-14, ὅσον ἐ γ ί γ ν ε τ ο φανερὸν αὐτῆς; *ibid.* 15, ἔσχε τὴν αὐτῆς φύσιν; and the implication which we uncovered in 5. 49b9-10, ἡ μὲν οὖν ἐποποιία τῇ τραγῳδίᾳ . . . ἠκολούθησεν. Tragedy became itself in the development which was outlined in chapters 4 and 5; and the allusion here is to that process of becoming: "Let us talk about tragedy, (first) picking out from what has been said the definition of its essence as it was (which was, which we saw in process of) becoming." The present participle represents precisely the imperfect ἐγίγνετο.

This not only clarifies the present construction but supplies another proof that the "history" in chapter 4 was indeed intended as a record of tragedy's γένεσις εἰς οὐσίαν. And this in turn facilitates our review of the items in the definition: they are in fact taken both from the systematic chapters 1-3 and from the "history."

Μίμησις was introduced in chapter 1, but attained its first significant realization in Homer (4. 48b34, μάλιστα ποιητής, = μάλιστα μιμητής) and its final one in tragedy (49a15, ἔσχε τὴν αὐτῆς φύσιν, which as we saw meant (1) the victory of dialogue over choral odes and (2) adoption of the appropriate verse-form).

Πράξεως. Poetry was said to imitate πράττοντας, 2. 48a1. The implication inherent in the participle, which will later be formulated in explicit terms (50a16, μίμησίς ἐστιν οὐκ ἀνθρώπων ἀλλὰ πράξεως καὶ βίου κτλ.), was likewise adumbrated by Homer: 48b35-37, μιμήσεις δραματικὰς . . . δραματοποιήσας, and even before him, in the first serious improvisations, 48b25, τὰς καλὰς ἐμιμοῦντο π ρ ά ξ ε ι ς κτλ. Moreover the words used to designate the object of imitation have tended from the beginning to be neuter more often than masculine:[2] Aristotle has been thinking all along of actions more than of men.

Σπουδαίας has been said before (2. 48a2), but when put, as now, in direct connection with πράξεως, makes it clearer than before that the business of tragedy is not simply to represent moral elevation. A shift of meaning has set in which is parallel to that actually stated for comedy in 5. 49a32: μίμησις φαυλοτέρων μέν, οὐ μέντοι κατὰ πᾶσαν κακίαν.

Τελείας was more evidently *not* anticipated in any of the preceding chapters. It was at best implied in the "norm of length" passage, 5.

[2] Ἕτερα, 1. 47a17; 2. 48a8; τὰ αὐτά, 3. 48a20; ἅ, *ibid.* 25; τὰ σπουδαῖα, 4. 48b34; τὸ γελοῖον, *ibid.* 37; 5. 49a34; σπουδαίων (probably neuter), 5. 49b10.

49b12-14—how, we shall see when we come to chapter 7. The concept is part of a fabric of thought that will not be finished for some time yet.

Μέγεθος was stated explicitly in 5. 49b10 as a point of likeness between tragedy and epic.[3] There it was not attached to the action, but was an attribute of "tragedy" and "epic" as such. Why it must belong specifically to the action is again something that will have to grow clearer as we proceed.[4]

Ἡδυσμένῳ λόγῳ again introduces no new element, but makes explicit the hierarchical relation which emerged in the course of the "history" among the three media, speech, melody, and rhythm. In chapter 1 they seemed to figure as equals, marrying and divorcing with apparent freedom. But even there we found that poetry was really the realm of speech. Its two great divisions were those of "speech used bare" and speech combined with melody and rhythm.[5] Here at last speech takes its due place at the center, in explicit terms, and is distinguished according as it is "sweetened" by rhythm alone (the spoken verses, *μέτρα*, b30) or by rhythm and melody (the songs, *μέλος*, b31).[6] This is at the same time a ranking: speech is the basic food, rhythm and melody are the frosting on the cake.[7] Again we were prepared for this estimate by Aristotle's "history," which ignored melody[8] and took effective cognizance of the poetic medium only *qua* verse, that is, *qua* rhythmical speech. Moreover the crucial fact about

[3] The customary reference to ἔτι δὲ τὸ μέγεθος, 4. 49a19, is not in place, even if our athetesis of that passage should be wrong, since there the word almost certainly implies "grandeur," "solemnity," and here it almost certainly does not.

[4] A formal distinction between terms previously mentioned or virtually mentioned—e.g., *μέγεθος* (in *μεγάλη* and *μήκει*, 5. 49b10-12) and those not so mentioned, like *τελείας* would be artificial and misleading. "Catharsis" is different; see below.

[5] As we saw, *τῷ δὲ τὸ μέτρον ἁπλοῦν ἔχειν*, 5. 49b10, summarized and implied this dichotomy.

[6] *Καὶ μέλος* is a gloss (*del.* Victorius) on *ἁρμονίαν*, by someone who had 1. 47b25 (*ῥυθμῷ καὶ μέλει καὶ μέτρῳ*) in mind. In b31 *μέλος* is song, the compound of words, rhythm, and melody; it cannot at the same time be one of its own components, or be "had" by λόγος. See above on 1. 47b25.

[7] Aristotle betrays the limitations of his literary sensibility in *ἡδυσμένῳ λόγῳ*. The expression may be borrowed from Plato, *Rep.* 10. 607a, but there it refers to all the wanton enticements of poetry, not merely its music and rhythm. When all is said and done, Aristotle's attitude toward style is basically that of the *Rhetoric*, 3. 1. 1404a11: *ἀλλ' ἅπαντα φαντασία ταῦτ' ἐστὶ καὶ πρὸς τὸν ἀκροατήν.*

[8] After its first mention, 4. 48b20.

the culmination of the development was the emergence of speech or dialogue as the "protagonist," under Aeschylus.[9]

Χωρὶς ἑκάστῳ[10] τῶν εἰδῶν. Ἢ χωρὶς ἢ μεμιγμένοις was the principle of division of the media in chapter 1 (47a23), and we saw that χωρίς there did not mean each medium singly: that it referred to their use in pairs. Moreover, under the rubric μεμιγμένοις, which denoted the use of all three media, tragedy belonged to the class which used them κατὰ μέρος (47b28). Χωρὶς ἑκάστῳ τῶν εἰδῶν ἐν τοῖς μορίοις is a re-statement of (πᾶσι τοῖς εἰρημένοις) κατὰ μέρος. Fortunately Aristotle has spelled out his meaning in this case (a29-31) and made it clear that he regards the play as falling into just two alternating[11] "parts," the verses (dialogue) and the songs.[12]

Δρώντων is the new formulation of the principle (ἔστι μιμεῖσθαι) ὡς πράττοντας καὶ ἐνεργοῦντας τοὺς μιμουμένους, 3. 48a23. We saw that the long subsequent note, 48a24-b2, betrayed a new special interest on Aristotle's part in the term δρᾶμα; that in fact, so far as we can see, he is the originator of the concept "drama." But this concept already appeared full-fledged in the new terms δραματικάς and δραματοποιήσας, 4. 48b35-37, a passage which we saw no reason to diagnose as "late." Δρώντων likewise belongs to the original stock of Aristotle's theory, indeed it seems to represent the germinal idea of "drama."

So far we have found no term, or at least no concept, which was not either stated or prepared for in chapters 1 to 5. The exact word or phrase was not there in every case; but it is a matter of ideas, not words. Aristotle's definition is not assembled mechanically out of phrases previously employed; it represents the essence which was in process of realization in the history as he summarized it.

Δι' ἐλέου καὶ φόβου περαίνουσα τὴν τῶν τοιούτων παθημάτων κάθαρσιν. This part of the definition has certainly *not* been prepared for. Nothing in chapters 1 to 5 gives us the slightest clue to anything in it. It

[9] 49a17; cf. *ibid.* 23, λέξεως . . . γενομένης.

[10] Tkatsch's defense of ἑκάστου as genitive absolute, 2. 75-76, is not convincing in the absence of an ὄντος. The parallel τὸ δὲ χωρὶς τοῖς εἴδεσι, b29-30, is decisive.

[11] Καὶ πάλιν ἕτερα διὰ μέλους.

[12] That is, he pays no attention to the *interlacing* of spoken verses and songs (κομμοί, ἀπὸ τῆς σκηνῆς), the operatic tendency which, especially in Euripides, tended to break down the clear division between the two "kinds." The handling of these matters in the spurious chapter 12 is quite different; see below *ad loc.*

is not merely that the terms are new, but that nothing has been said with which we could possibly associate them. The difference in this respect between the clause and the rest of the definition is complete.

The isolation and difficulty of the catharsis-clause are indeed notorious; for the word κάθαρσις does not occur again in the *Poetics*.[13] But critics and philologists are not the men to be daunted by lack of evidence: the mass of writing about δι' ἐλέου . . . καθαρσιν is almost in inverse proportion to the extent of the visible material. The controversy over catharsis has revolved—for some periods, "spun" would be a better term—on its own axis for so long, and with so little determinate result, that one sometimes wonders whether it should not be declared officially closed or debarred. Certainly it would be quixotic to try to deal with it as a whole here. Even a full survey of the literature on the subject would require a book in itself.[14] All that we

[13] Except in one passage (17. 55b15) which has nothing to do with "catharsis."

[14] There is no full survey in print of the voluminous literature on the catharsis question. An unpublished North Carolina dissertation by Duane W. Robertson, Jr. (Chapel Hill, 1937), gives *A Preliminary Survey of the Controversy over Aristotle's Doctrine of the Tragic Catharsis.* Unfortunately the only *Jahresbericht* on Aristotle published in this century devotes only five pages to the whole *Poetics* (Paul Gohlke, *Burs. Jahresber.* 220 [1929] 323-28). The most useful summaries of the standard interpretations of catharsis are still those of Susemihl and Hicks, *The Politics of Aristotle, Books I-V,* London, 1894, 641-56, and Bywater, 152-61, 361-65. Butcher's chapter (VI, pp. 240-73) professes to accept the medical interpretation, but builds on top of it a precarious structure of other ideas ("refining or clarifying of emotion"; connection with the theory of the universal) which really have nothing to do with it. The prevailing "medical" interpretation is of course that of Jakob Bernays, *Grundzüge der verlorenen Abhandlung des Aristotles über Wirkung der Tragödie,* Breslau, 1857; reprinted in *Zwei Abhandlungen über die Aristotelische Theorie des Drama,* Berlin, 1880 (anticipated by Henri Weil, "Ueber die Wirkung der Tragödie nach Aristoteles," *Verhandlungen der* 10. *Versammlung deutscher Philologen und Schulmänner in Basel 1847,* Basel, 1848, 131-40, and in effect by Tyrwhitt and others as far back as the Renaissance: see Bywater, *loc. cit.*), according to which "catharsis" is a purgation, accompanied by a pleasurable sense of relief, from accumulating emotional tendencies, especially tendencies to pity and fear, which would otherwise poison our mental health. Bernays' interpretation has been corrected or refuted on several major points, e.g., by Bonitz, who showed ("Aristotelische Studien, V. Über πάθος and πάθημα im Aristotelischen Sprachgebrauche," *Sitzungsber.* Vienna 55 [1867] 13-55) that Aristotle makes no essential distinction between πάθος and πάθημα. Nevertheless it has dominated most thinking on catharsis since its publication, and still remains, with minor variations in detail, what one might call the vulgate. The most determined attack upon Bernays' theory was made by Heinrich Otte in a series of publications beginning with *Kennt Aristoteles die sogenannte tragische Katharsis?* Berlin, 1912, and ending with *Neue Beiträge zur Aristotelischen Begriffsbestimmung der Tragödie,* Berlin, 1928, and "Noch einmal κάθαρσις τῶν παθημάτων," *Philol. Wochenschrift* 50 (1930) 1165-66 (for the rest see the Cooper-Gudeman *Bibliography of the Poetics of Aristotle,*

are attempting to do is to analyze Aristotle's argument as it moves forward, leaving the general *Katharsisfrage* to come up later.

It will assist in clarifying our interpretation, however, if we begin by summarizing the presuppositions that are shared by all or most of the writers on the subject:

1. They almost all [15] agree that Aristotle is talking about a change of feeling, or even of character, which tragedy brings about (effectuates: *περαίνουσα*) in the spectator.

2. They all assume (implicitly) that this effect is automatic and is produced by all "tragedies."

3. They almost all [16] presuppose that *παθημάτων* means "feelings" or "passions."

4. Most of them take *ἐλέου καὶ φόβου* as likewise denoting the spectator's emotions: pity and fear are aroused in him and subsequently purified or purged. Others, however,[17] read *δι' ἐλέου καὶ φόβου* as equivalent to *δι' ἐλεεινῶν καὶ φοβερῶν*, the pathetic and fearful *events* of the play.

5. Most of them translate *τῶν τοιούτων* by "such" (*dergleichen, de ce genre, talium*, etc.)—a translation which if pressed would force one to admit that there are other "such" emotions (i.e., tragic emotions) besides pity and fear. Others take *τῶν τοιούτων* as meaning in effect *τούτων*, pity and fear being the only tragic emotions.[18]

[*Cornell Studies in English*, 11], New Haven, 1928, 167). My own interpretation is akin to Otte's (summarized briefly in *Neue Beiträge* 9-10) in some respects, but was arrived at independently and differs in important particulars.—The Cooper-Gudeman *Bibliography* and its continuation by M. T. Herrick (*AJP* 52 [1931] 168-74) list 147 books, dissertations, and articles since 1856 whose titles clearly indicate that they deal specifically with catharsis; and to that figure one must add of course all the major editions of the *Poetics* and many of the general books on the *Poetics* and Aristotle. I confess that I have not tried to master this flood of publications, few of which are of more than ephemeral importance. But those of the last fifteen years are summarized in my report in *CW* 48 (1954-55) 73-82. See also Pohlenz *Trag.*[2] 487-89, Erläut.-band 195-198; and cf. H. Flashar, *Hermes* 84 (1956) 17-18.

[15] Except Otte.

[16] Again excepting Otte.

[17] E.g., Rostagni (= Valgimigli): "mediante (una serie di) casi che suscitano pietà e terrore"; Fyfe: "with incidents arousing pity and fear, wherewith to accomplish its catharsis. . . ."

[18] So Bernays himself, Butcher, Gomperz, Rostagni. On the importance of the phrase see Otte, *Neue Beiträge* 8; for a refutation of its equivalence to *τούτων*, J. I. Beare, "Anaphoric *ὁ τοιοῦτος* in Aristotle," *Hermathena* 18 (1914-19) 116-35. Recent explanations of the construction of the genitive by F. Dirlmeier, "*Κάθαρσις παθημάτων*," *Hermes* 75 (1940) 81-92; Max Kommerell, *Lessing u. Ar.*

6. Almost all of them understand Aristotle to say that the emotional change designated by τὴν τῶν τοιούτων παθημάτων κάθαρσιν is brought about *by* (by means of, δι') pity and fear: the pity and fear aroused in the spectator somehow purge or purify themselves.

7. As to the change itself (κάθαρσιν), a majority of interpreters in the last century follow Bernays and Weil in understanding it to be a "purgation"; though the older idea of "purification" still has some supporters.[19]

It will be seen that notwithstanding the controversy over κάθαρσιν itself ("purgation" vs. "purification"), most of the interpreters agree on a series of understandings as to the other terms in the passage. The sum or mean of these understandings can be suitably represented by Butcher's translation: "through pity and fear effecting the purgation of these emotions." In particular it has been taken for granted, without argument, that the catharsis-clause, whatever it means, has to do with the emotional reaction of the spectator (no. 1 above).[20] So deep-seated is this prejudice ("prejudice" in the root-sense) that a challenge to it is not very likely to receive a full hearing. It is like the unspoken prejudice that 5. 49b12-14 deals with the alleged duration of the poetic action, and perhaps it will do more good here than there to point out that Aristotle does not *say* anything of the kind: that the reigning assumption is based entirely on a particular interpretation of terms which are capable of other meanings.

In the present case, since we cannot fall back on anything that has been said by Aristotle up to this point, we shall have to break our rule of method and lean more heavily on what he says later; for in

---

(*Frankfurt. Wiss. Beiträge zur Kult.-wiss.* 2), Frankfurt, 1940, 262-72; R. Schottlaender, "Eine Fessel der Tragödiendeutung," *Hermes* 81 (1953) 22-29.

[19] Spengel, for example, sustained it against Bernays. Actually it is an oversimplification to reduce the alternatives to two, purgation and purification, since there are a number of other possibilities. Cf. A. Dyroff's complaint (*Berl. Philol. Wochenschrift* 38 [1918] 615-17) against Bernays for insisting on a strict alternative, "lustration" (religious) *or* "relief" (medical). But in fact, since Bernays, there have been two main lines of interpretation of "catharsis," one holding to the medical sense (purgation or relief of the spirit *from* the emotions) and insisting on the "autonomy" of art, the other explaining the word in various ways but tending towards an ethical concept (purification *of* the emotions). The latter view has been on the wane; but Rostagni, for example, though professing to accept the medical sense, combines it with the "orgiastic" and arrives at an eclectic moral theory: catharsis is the reduction of the passions to measure and reason. See his Introd. XLIII-LIV, and, for a similar interpretation, Louis Moulinier, *Le pur et l'impur dans la pensée des grecs d'Homère à Aristote* (*Études et Commentaires,* 12), Paris, 1952, 410-19.

[20] See Otte, *op. cit.* 11-12.

contradistinction to Bernays and the cathartic school I believe that there is adequate material later in the *Poetics* to define his meaning here.[21] That material is mainly in chapters 13 and 14. We will do no more at present than to show by means of it that the catharsis clause *can* have a different meaning from the one usually ascribed to it; the full analysis of the matter will be reserved till later.

Δι' ἐλέου καὶ φόβου need not necessarily mean "through, by means of" pity and fear. A good many unprejudiced observers have questioned [22] how pity and fear can be purged or purified—whichever it is —by themselves. Some critics have therefore tended to reinterpret "pity and fear" as "pathetic and fearful incidents" (= δι' ἐλεεινῶν καὶ φοβερῶν). That is sound enough so far as it goes, but it does not solve the problem. The reason why the notion of pity and fear being purged by pity and fear has persisted is that no other agency has been visible in the sentence through which the catharsis could be brought about. But there is such an agency, as we shall see in a moment.

"The purification (or purgation) of such emotions." It is natural to refer παθημάτων to ἐλέου καὶ φόβου, since the latter stand so near. But the reference involves us in another ineluctable difficulty; for then either (1) τῶν τοιούτων must = τούτων, or (2) there must be other tragic emotions besides pity and fear. But (1) τῶν τοιούτων is *not* simply = τούτων,[23] and (2) there is no plausible case for any other tragic emotion, much less a series of them.[24] The solution is not difficult, but it involves reading παθημάτων in the sense which is defined in 11. 52b11: πάθος δέ ἐστι πρᾶξις φθαρτικὴ ἢ ὀδυνηρά.[25] It is clear that Aristotle thought the *pathos* the basic, indispensable "part" of the tragic plot, since (1) peripety and recognition are limited to complex plots while the *pathos* is not, and (2) the calculations of the tragic

[21] One considerable weakness of Bernays' theory, though one which has seldom been pointed out, is that although it draws on the *Politics* (particularly, of course, 8. 7. 1341b32-42a16), Plutarch, Aristides Quintilianus, Iamblichus, and Proclus, but neither explains nor is supported by anything in the *Poetics* itself. See below, pp. 269-70.

[22] Most recently Maria T. Cardini in *Studi di filosofia greca,* Bari, 1950, 302 n. 1, and Schottlaender, *op. cit.*

[23] See Beare, *op. cit.*

[24] Not that others are not possible, but that Aristotle never speaks of them. 'Ὁ μὲν γὰρ κτλ., 13.53a4ff., clearly excludes any third factor (ὁ μέν and ὁ δέ, "the one" and "the other"). Τό φιλάνθρωπον, in the same passage, is not a distinct emotion but a low-grade variety or sub-form of pity; see below *ad loc.*

[25] Παθημάτων is normally used for the genitive plural, instead of παθῶν, without any difference in meaning: Bonitz, *op. cit.* (above, n. 14), esp. 53n. 16. It appears in precisely the sense suggested here in 24. 59b11-12.

quality of a play (14. 53b14ff.) are based upon the way the *pathos* is brought about, revealed, averted, etc.[26] The purpose of Aristotle's survey there is to determine which of the *συμπίπτοντα* (that is, the *pathê*: 53b20) are pitiable and fearful. There are in fact *pathê* which are bloody or painful enough but which do not arouse either pity or fear, or not in the desired amount.[27]

These parallels supply us with an unexceptionable meaning for *τῶν τοιούτων*. "Such *pathê*" are *pathê* which are such as to have tragic quality, i.e., to arouse pity and fear.[28] Aristotle makes it amply clear, 53b19, under what general condition they have that quality, or the possibility of it: namely when the destructive or painful events in question take place *within the bounds of family ties* (ἐν ταῖς φιλίαις). Τῶν τοιούτων παθημάτων, then, will be *pathê*—a murder or intended murder, etc.—involving father and son, brother and sister, or the like. (Once again, we are not trying to settle the whole catharsis problem here, but simply to show another possible meaning for the catharsis-clause. The final decision must wait until we have analyzed chapter 14).

To return now to δι' ἐλέου καὶ φόβου: the preposition can perfectly well mean "through (a sequence of), in the course of," referring not to an emotional end-effect with which we leave the theater, but to pity and fear as they are incorporated in the structure of the play by the poet.[29]

Περαίνειν, usually translated "effect, accomplish," has from its root (πέρας) the sense "carry through, bring to completion": said of something that takes a while to complete, and emphasizing the duration.[30] Naturally this is especially the case in the progressive tenses (πεπεράνθαι means either "to be finished" or "to be bounded"). Above all it is profitable to notice the other two occurrences of the word in the

[26] See below *ad loc.*

[27] E.g., the killing of an enemy, 53b17.

[28] The reference to ἐλέου καὶ φόβου is close and easy, and since the *pathê* are not themselves emotions but have emotional quality, we are rid of the awkwardness about *τοιούτων*. When I say, "If you want to arouse pity and fear you have to look for such incidents (incidents of that kind)," it will not occur to anybody that "such" includes more emotions than the two I have just mentioned.

[29] "Built into the events," i.e., woven into the plot, 14. 53b13.

[30] E.g., *Phys.* 4. 14. 222b6, τῶν κινήσεων τῶν ἅμα περαινομένων; *De Part. An.* 3. 4. 666b14, περαίνονται (sc. αἱ κινήσεις) διὰ τοῦ ἕλκειν καὶ ἀνιέναι; *Hist. An.* 1. 15. 494a24, ἵνα περαίνηται τὸ ἐφεξῆς; cf. Pl. *Prot.* 353b, πέραινε ὥσπερ ἦρξω ("carry on as you have begun"); *Laws* 9. 864c, περαίνοντες τὴν θέσιν τῶν νόμων; and the common expression ὁ συλλογισμὸς περαίνεται, "the syllogism is completed (synonym τελειοῦται, cf. *Anal. Pr.* 1. 7. 29a30-34). See Bonitz, *Index* 579b17-25.

Poetics: 24. 59b27, *πολλὰ μέρη ἅμα ποιεῖν περαινόμενα,* "to 'compose' many 'parts' at (as of) the time[31] they are happening, being carried on"; and three lines below our own sentence, 49b30, *διὰ μέτρων ἔνια μόνον περαίνεσθαι,* "that some are carried on (forward)[32] by verses alone. It seems at least possible, in view of these facts, to take *περαίνουσα* as denoting a process which goes forward throughout the play, rather than simply an end-result which accrues to the spectator.

What, now, "carries forward" the purification through the course of the play? Not the text, as a body of words, or the performance of the text in a theater, but the *process of imitation* which tragedy essentially is. Tragedy, which imitates action, is itself an action. According to Aristotle's analysis, which is put forward and strongly emphasized later in this same chapter, this action is represented by the plot: the plot *is* the imitation of it.[33] Plot is the *ἀρχὴ καὶ οἷον ψυχή* of tragedy: i.e., its principle of motion, its soul, as it were.[34] The purification, then, is carried forward by the plot, the "structure of events" which is the poet's own indispensable contribution to the play. What this means cannot be seen clearly or fully until we have studied chapters 13 and 14. But there is a corollary that can be seen at once: this reading makes catharsis a process, not an end-result, and *a process operated by the poet through his "structure of events."* It follows that some tragedies will accomplish it supremely well, others less well, still others, it may be, not at all. If catharsis depends on the constructive activity of the poet, it ceases to be a standard result, automatically attained by any play called "tragedy."

As for *κάθαρσιν* itself, we shall have to reserve our explanation of it also till later.[35] Again, however, one fact is clear at once. If the *παθημάτων* are incidents or actions rather than emotions, then *κάθαρσιν* must mean purification of some kind, not purgation: for the incidents are certainly not to be purged out of the play.

I submit that this interpretation of the catharsis clause is possible, does full justice to every word, and is not dogged by the paradoxes and inconsistencies that we have noticed in the current theory.[36] Its

[31] See below *ad loc.* for this interpretation of *ἅμα*.

[32] "Verlaufen," Gomperz. Not "are rendered" (Butcher), "are worked out" (Bywater).

[33] 50a3-4.

[34] 50a38.

[35] Below on 14. 53b37-54a9.

[36] The chief strength of Bernays' theory was that it fit the passage in the *Politics* (8. 7. 1341b38ff.) so well; its chief weakness was its inadequacy vis-à-vis the present clause, which it was supposed to explain. Conversely, the chief

final justification remains to be seen. Again, however, there is a corollary which must follow if our analysis has had any virtue at all. Howald and his pupil Lienhard [37] have put forward the thesis that the catharsis clause belongs to an early, in fact the original, stage of the work: that when Aristotle began he was concerned above everything else with the ethical and emotional *effect* of tragedy. If there is any virtue in our analysis so far, Howald would seem to be wrong. The catharsis clause must be, if anything, later than the rest of the sentence, for three reasons:

1. Unlike the rest of the definition, there is not a syllable in it which has been said or anticipated in the foregoing chapters.

2. Παθημάτων (πάθος) is used in a sense which was not likely to be understood unless one had read or already knew the contents of chapters 11 to 14.

3. Περαίνουσα is felt in close connection with μίμησις: a connection which is much easier to imagine if Aristotle wrote δι' ἐλέου κτλ. as a subsequent note, with his eye directly on μίμησις,[38] than if he wrote it in its present place, separated from μίμησις by so many subordinate elements.[39]

For these reasons I have ventured to show the clause in double brackets. But once more it should be borne in mind that marking a clause as "subsequent" does not necessarily make it "late" or identify

---

weakness of my hypothesis is that it does not fit the *Politics* passage. I hope that it has the compensating virtue of according with the *Poetics*, including the crucial passages in chapter 14. Ἄμεινον τὰ μὲν οἴκοι καλῶς ἔχειν . . .— Otte was right, I think, on the main point, that the clause has to do with how the poet shapes his plot (*op. cit.* 9); in taking παθημάτων to denote events or actions rather than feelings as such; and in seeing that περαίνουσα refers to something *going on* throughout the play, not merely delivered as a product at the end (the same point is made by E. P. Papanoutsos, *Eranos* 46 [1948] 77-93). He went astray, on the other hand, in insisting that the purification is achieved *by pity and fear* and in making τῶν τοιούτων refer all the way back to πράξεως σπουδαίας (*op. cit.* 22-46). Moreover he established no really organic link between the catharsis clause and the crucial remarks in chapter 14, although he saw that there must be a connection.

[37] Ernest Howald, "Eine vorplatonische Kunsttheorie," *Hermes* 54 (1919) 187-07, esp. 188, 196; *id., Philol.* 76 (1920) 215-22; Max K. Lienhard, *Zur Entstehung und Geschichte von Ar. Poetik* (diss.), Zurich, 1950, esp. 17-21.

[38] Later, when it was copied into the text, the note of course lost this immediacy of connection.

[39] We can add a fourth argument; that λέγω δὲ ἡδυσμένον κτλ. is a trifle abrupt as it stands, referring back over the intervening words, but is very natural if most of the latter are a subsequent addition. The same must be said of the following sentence also (ἐπεὶ δὲ πράττοντες κτλ.): it refers back to δρώντων in a matter-of-fact way which is easier if the catharsis-clause was originally not there.

it with a "late stratum" in the work. Such a note might have been written at any time after the first draft had "hardened" slightly.[40]

Howald and Lienhard seem to be wrong on another count also. According to them catharsis belongs to the original stock of the *Poetics* but was later incorporated—inorganically—into a new scheme which emphasizes the concept of "structure of the plot" (σύστασις τοῦ μύθου, τῶν πραγμάτων). If our approach to the matter is at all correct, catharsis is on the contrary a function of the structure of the plot and cannot therefore be earlier than that concept—which, be it noticed, need not be "late."

* * * *

It is at this point, I believe, that we can take up the problem of catharsis again. In analyzing the catharsis-clause in the definition of tragedy[41] we established certain tentative theses: (1) that the purification was a purification of the *pathos,* that is, of the fatal or painful act which is the basic stuff of tragedy; (2) that it was not brought about "by pity and fear" but "through (a course of) pity and fear," that is, in the course of a sequence of pathetic and fearful incidents; and (3) that the agent of the purification was the "imitation," that is, the plot. Since then we have accumulated a good deal of material, some of it tending to confirm those theses, some of it supplying additional concepts which appear to be parts of the same complex. Thus: (1) the *pathos* has emerged as a well-marked, fundamental element in the tragic structure, and the limits within which it can be tragic have been closely defined; (2) we have seen "pathetic and fearful events" substituted for "pity and fear" in the definition of what the tragic imitation imitates (9. 52a2-3; 13. 52b32; cf. 11. 52a38-b1, ἔλεον . . . φόβον, οἵων π ρ ά ξ ε ω ν ἡ τραγῳδία μίμησις ὑπόκειται); and (3) the crucial role of the imitation, i.e., the plot, as the agent of the emotional "work" of tragedy has been explicitly affirmed, 14. 53b12: διὰ μιμήσεως.

But even more important are the new concepts which have been introduced, above all the dyad *hamartia*-recognition. It has become clear that the best tragic plot must be complex and based on a *hamartia,* an ignorance or mistake, and a mistake as to the identity of a "dear one." The *hamartia* is the precedent condition, the premise upon which the (complex) dramatic structure is predicated; and conversely the working out of the tragic potential which lies in the *hamartia*-situation

[40] See further below, on 9. 52a1ff.
[41] See above on 6. 49b27.

is operated by the recognition. The fulcrum upon which this emotional system balances is the *pathos*. The *pathos* in itself, merely *qua* act of violence or destruction, has only low emotional quality. It rises to the genuine tragic level only when it involves "dear ones," and to the highest level only when the act is based on a *hamartia* (i.e., would not be performed except for the *hamartia*).

To this complex of ideas the mention of the μιαρὸν in our passages adds what seems to be to be the final clue for a solution of the catharsis problem. In assessing μιαρόν in chapter 13 (52b36) we said that its meaning there could not be the original or fundamental one. The passage now before us bears this out. The moral shock we feel at the plunge of a virtuous man into misery is a pale and derivative thing compared to our revulsion at the murder of a father or mother or son or brother. Whether this feeling is appreciably weaker among us moderns than it was among the Greeks is a point we need not argue. Neither do we need to point out what a large role was played in the history of Greek religion, law, *and poetry* by the concept of pollution for the killing of blood-kin. The story is familiar in all its ramifications: its roots in the primitive solidarity of the family;[42] the preoccupation, not to say obsession, of archaic Greece with means of purification, especially for the spilling of kindred blood;[43] the connection of all this with new ideas (actually old ideas revived) about the survival of the dead;[44] the flourishing concept of the Erinys or Erinyes, especially those excited by the murder of kindred;[45] the very large share which these preoccupations had in the rise of Delphi to a place of commanding importance;[46] the tardiness and hesitancy of the state in taking over responsibility for the direct prosecution of homicide, especially the mur-

[42] G. Glotz, *La solidarité de la famille dans le droit criminel en Grèce,* Paris, 1904.

[43] See most recently E. R. Dodds, *The Greeks and the Irrational* (*Sather Class. Lects.* 25), Berkeley and Los Angeles, 1951, esp. 35-37 (with notes), 44-48, and Index *s. vv.* "catharsis," "miasma," "purity"; M. P. Nilsson, *Gesch. d. gr. Religion* (*Handb. d. Alt.-wiss.*), 1, Munich, 1941, 88-92. The most complete and lucid survey of the whole range of concepts involved is that by Pfister, art. "Katharsis," PW Suppl. 6. 146-162; the most exhaustive treatment is that of L. Moulinier, *Le pur et l'impur dans la pensée des Grecs d'Homère à Aristote* (*Études et Commentaires,* 12), Paris, 1952.

[44] E. Rohde, *Psyche*^{8}, London, 1925, 174-182 and notes.

[45] Rapp, art. "Erinys" in Roscher's *Lexikon,* 1. 1310-1336.

[46] Nilsson, *op. cit.* 599-604. T. Dempsey, *The Delphic Oracle,* Oxford, 1918: see pp. 149-63 (no more than a provisional compilation; see Nilsson 592n. 2); Parke, H. W., and Wormell, D. E. W., *The Delphic Oracle,* Oxford, 1956, 1. 303-307, 362-64, 382-83.

der of blood-kin;[47] the special provisions (as to both courts and procedure) for handling such cases, even in fully developed Greek law;[48] and, finally, the literary precipitate of all these fears and taboos in Attic tragedy, particularly that of Aeschylus (above all in the *Oresteia,* but also in other trilogies and in individual plays).[49]

This, I submit, is the background we require for Aristotle's concept of the "purification of tragic acts."

* * * *

To return to our question, then: what will be the judgments and the feelings of a normal spectator or hearer or reader when confronted with a tragic story? First of all, so far as the plot as a whole is concerned, if it is to gain his sympathy and ultimately his fear and/or pity, he must make two judgments (one or the other, and, for the best effect, both): (1) that the hero is "like himself," and (2) that he does not deserve his misfortune. These judgments are not after-effects of the spectator's feeling, they are the prerequisites to it, the conditions which must be satisfied *before his psyche* (that is, the rational element in his soul) *will allow the emotions to be felt.*

The analogy between these judgments and those which an Athenian was called upon to make in a murder trial becomes much closer when we bring the question down to the specific issues that are before us in chapter 14: those, namely, that cluster around the tragic act. Before us is a person—Oedipus, Alcmeon, Medea, Heracles—who has killed

[47] It is well known that even in the fourth century the prosecution for murder still lay upon the relatives of the slain man, the state limiting itself to seeing that the relatives did take action: Glotz, *op. cit.* 304-306, 372-76, 425-27. Plato, *Laws* 9. 871b, permits any citizen to institute prosecution if the relatives are derelict in their duty. Glotz remarks, 321, that the most fearful crime of all, parricide, is not mentioned in the code of Draco: not because it was condoned, but because its punishment was left solely and entirely to the family.

[48] See above, c. 13, n. 52, on the five Athenian homicide courts. Our chief ancient source for them is the speech of Demosthenes *Against Timocrates,* 65-81. —One of the most important documents from outside Athens for the fourth-century view of all matters involving purity and impurity is the so-called sacral law of Cyrene (last published in *Suppl. Epigr, Graec.* 9 [1938] 31-34, with bibliography).

[49] Notably in the Theban trilogy of which the *Seven Against Thebes* was the last play; see esp. *Sept.* 682, οὐκ ἔστι γῆρας τοῦδε τοῦ μιάσματος; 694. We do not know whether the murder of their bridegrooms by the Danaïds, which must have occurred in the middle play (*Egyptians*?; see Schmid 1. 2. 198) of the trilogy which began with the *Suppliants,* led to their pollution and some form of purification, but it does not seem likely that Aeschylus would have avoided it. On his blood-polluted Telephus who journeyed to Mysia in search of purification see above on 13. 53a21.

or is about to kill a "dear one": father, mother, children. In itself the act, or even the intention, is impure and abhorrent in the highest degree. We have seen in what solemn and special tones Plato dealt with such crimes against one's own blood, and with what horror they were still regarded, what taboos and perils still surrounded them, even in the relatively enlightened Athens of the fourth century. Such outrages against god and nature are fearful, there can be no mistake about that. But under what circumstances can I bring myself to pity the murderer or would-be murderer? I can pity him if I judge that *he did not intend the parricide, matricide, or whatever, as such:* in other words, if it is established to my satisfaction that he performed or intended the fearful act δι' ἁμαρτίαν τινά, because of some error.

Let us be precise. The category "slaying of a close blood-relation because of ignorance of his identity" did not appear as such in Plato's code. Book 5 of the *Ethics* showed us Aristotle striving for a closer definition than Plato's of those cases of wrong-doing (including homicide) which lie between full intent and mere unforeseeable accident. Similarly in book 3 he defined the deed which rates pity and forgiveness, instead of reprobation, as the one performed out of ignorance of details. Beyond these specific parallels lies the general fact of the development of the sense of equity (ἐπιείκεια) in the fourth century—a concept to which Aristotle explicitly attached his discussion in book 5. This is the sphere in which we are moving in tragedy. The deeds or intended deeds before us are such as comported the full horror of blood-pollution and stirred even Plato to a severity which was inconsistent with his own ideas. But they are also deeds caused (not merely accompanied) by ignorance, and therefore having a claim upon our sense of equity and pity. The claim might not lie in a court of law, but it will suffice here because we are sitting in judgment as a court of fellow human-beings, fallible and exposed to misfortune as the hero is. We must and do judge, but as men, not ministers of the law.

I would argue, then, that the spectator or reader of the play is the judge in whose sight the tragic act must be "purified," so that he may pity instead of execrating the doer. But again let us be precise. The spectator or reader[50] does not *perform* the purification, any more than the judges at the Delphinion or in Plato's state did so. The purification, that is, the proof of the purity of the hero's motive in performing an otherwise "unclean" act, is *presented* to him, and his conscience accepts

[50] I keep adding "or reader" because whatever the catharsis is it must be accessible to him also; see below.

and certifies it to his emotions, issues a license, so to speak, which says: "You may pity this man, for he is like us, a good man rather than a bad, and he is καθαρός, free of pollution."

But this is not enough either. The hero, who comes before us with hands dripping with his father's or mother's blood, is not merely presented to us by the dramatist on a platter bearing the label "pure." The question is how the catharsis is operated, and the answer is that it is operated ("carried forward, brought to completion": περαίνουσα) by the *plot* (the μίμησις). To some extent this is achieved by all that we see and hear about the hero in the play. All that we see of Oedipus assures us that he is a strong-willed, excitable, hot-tempered man, but also a kind, loving, and public-spirited one. Such a person cannot, we feel, have killed his father and married his mother in cold blood. But these reassurances are not enough. Aristotle himself tells us in book 3 of the *Ethics* (3.2. 1110b19, 1111a20) what it is that guarantees the innocence of motive of the person who has done wrong δι' ἄγνοιαν: it is his remorse when the truth is discovered. And the complex plot offers precisely this kind of certification, in the recognition and the hero's subsequent behavior. It is Oedipus' self-blinding, his transport of grief and remorse when he learns the truth, that finally assures us of his "purity" and releases our tears.[51] Thus recognition is the structural device which makes it possible for the hero to prove that he did indeed act δι' ἁμαρτίαν τινά and so deserves our pity. For the *Oedipus*[52] the sequence would be: (*pathos*, i.e., deed of horror, inherently μιαρόν but performed in ignorance→)[53] steady augmentation of the horror as the climax approaches→recognition, undoing (reversing) the ignorance→ grief and remorse of the doer, certifying the ignorance as cause of the deed and the deed therefore as οὐ μιαρόν→pity (→tragic pleasure).[54]

[51] It is evident that if the fear in the *Oedipus* is diffused throughout the play, rising to a climax just before the recognition, the pity is concentrated in the final scene.

[52] It should be emphasized that no generalized chart can be drawn for all plots, even all complex plots. Thus in the *Iphigenia in Tauris* the interrelation and sequence of the elements is quite different. Here the *pathos* lies before instead of behind us at the beginning of the play, pity and fear are aroused more or less concurrently, and the recognition and the consequent averting of the *pathos* turns our feelings off in a different channel. On the possible reasons why Aristotle found this ultimately superior to the play with tragic ending, see below.

[53] The parentheses signify that in this case the *pathos* takes place before the drama begins.

[54] This time the parentheses indicate that we cannot be sure just how the "pleasure peculiar to tragedy" operates. See below.

Thus the catharsis is not a change or end-product in the spectator's soul, or in the fear and pity (i.e., the dispositions to them) in his soul, but a process carried forward in the emotional material of the play by its structural elements, above all by the recognition. For the recognition is the pay-off, to use a vulgar but expressive modernism; or, in more conventional figure, it is the hinge on which the emotional structure of the play turns. The catharsis, that is, the purification of the tragic act by the demonstration that its motive was not μιαρόν, is accomplished by the whole structure of the drama, but above all by the recognition.

This interpretation makes catharsis a transitive or operational factor within the tragic structure itself, precedent to the release of pity, and ultimately of the tragic pleasure, rather than the be-all and end-all of tragedy itself. By so much, it robs our aesthetic vocabulary of one of those "Prachtausdrücke," as Bernays put it, "die jedem Gebildeten geläufig und keinem Denkenden deutlich sind." The great virtue, but also the great vice, of "catharsis" in modern interpretation has been its incurable vagueness. Every variety of moral, aesthetic, and therapeutic effect that is or could be experienced from tragedy has been subsumed under the venerable word at one time or another. Thus, to cite one obvious example out of many, in Butcher's essays on *Aristotle's Theory of Poetry and Fine Art*—which for all their shortcomings are still the best whole treatment of the subject—catharsis rises to the universal plane and ultimately means or implies a notion of "universalising the emotions and ridding them of an intrusive element that belongs to the sphere of the accidental and individual." [55] Bernays' own explanation, for all the revolution it brought in the assessment of Aristotle's doctrine as a whole, was at one with the rest in assuming that catharsis is the "work" or end, the τέλος, of tragedy. But Aristotle nowhere says or implies this, even in the definition in chapter 6. He speaks repeatedly of the need for tragedy to arouse pity and fear, and he alludes three times (14. 53b12; 23. 59a21; 26. 62b14) to the special pleasure it is to give; but nowhere is catharsis said or implied to be the τέλος.

Actually, as is well known, Bernays' explanation was not drawn from the *Poetics* at all, but from the 8th book of the *Politics* and certain utterances of Proclus and Iamblichus[56] which may or may not

[55] P. 268. Butcher is aware (same sentence) that this is a modern idea which we have no strict warrant for attributing to Aristotle. But he pleads that "it is at least the natural outcome of his doctrine; to this conclusion his general theory of poetry points."

[56] Most conveniently available in the "Fragmenta" of the *Poetics* in Bywater, pp. 94-95.

have anything to do with the case. It had the corresponding virtue of explaining or fitting (with some discrepancies and unevenesses) the passage in the *Politics*. But what we have to explain before everything else is the *Poetics;* and neither Bernays' explanation nor any of the others has ever shed any light on the *Poetics* itself or linked catharsis with any other crucial part of Aristotle's theory.[57] And there is another objection to Bernays' interpretation, which would long since have been recognized as fatal if the authority of the *Politics* passage had not been accepted as beyond dispute. His interpretation, no matter how adapted or refined, is inherently and indefeasibly *therapeutic*. It presupposes that we come to the tragic drama (unconsciously, if you will) as patients to be cured, relieved, restored to psychic health. But there is not a word to support this in the *Poetics,* not a hint that the end of the drama is to cure or alleviate pathological states. On the contrary it is evident in every line of the work that Aristotle is presupposing *normal* auditors, normal states of mind and feeling, normal emotional and aesthetic experience.

There is still another fatal objection to Bernays' theory, and to any theory which is based like his on the concept of the *musical* catharsis:[58] that the musical part of tragedy is precisely the one that Aristotle minimizes, not to say ignores, in his theory of tragedy. If the catharsis is in any sense a musical experience, the *Poetics* is the work that least provides a place and mode of operation for it. Connected with this is another deficiency in the reigning explanations of catharsis, not only in that of Bernays but in all the others. They all assume—tacitly, for the most part—that the catharsis is an experience which comes *in the theater*.[59] But Aristotle insists again and again, not merely that tragedies can be read with pleasure or profit, but that "the capacity of tragedy [i.e., its capacity to do its 'work,' produce its effect] exists even without a competition [= actual performance] and actors" (6. 50b18); that the plot should be so constructed that one who merely hears it (i.e., not the full play) will feel pity and fear.[60] If catharsis has anything to do with the emotional side of tragedy—and we cannot doubt

[57] Except Otte's (see above on 6. 49b27), which did at least take into account Aristotle's general theory of the pleasure we get from imitation (4. 48b8ff). But Otte never managed to connect catharsis with the doctrine of the tragic plot.

[58] E.g., Jeanne Croissant's subtle and highly instructive book *Aristote et les mystères* (*Bibl. de la Fac. de Philos. et Lettres de l'Univ. de Liège,* fasc. 51), Liège and Paris, 1932; see esp. pp. 103-111. Mlle Croissant's results are important and relevant, but to the *Politics,* not the *Poetics*.

[59] If it is anything of a musical nature, this must obviously be the case.

[60] See above on 14. 53b3ff.

that it has—then it, like the tragic emotions and the tragic pleasure, must be "built into" the plot and thus made available to a reader in the same way, on the same terms, as it is to the spectator in the theater.

The strengths and weaknesses of my explanation are the converse of those of the traditional explanations, including Bernays'. What it does, first and foremost, is to interpret the *Poetics* out of the *Poetics*. In so doing it puts catharsis in the center of a nexus of concepts with which it is organically connected: *pathos, hamartia,* recognition, pity and fear, and (perhaps) the tragic pleasure. Its most obvious weakness, on the other hand, is that it does not explain the catharsis passage in the *Politics;* for I can see no direct bridge leading from the structural-objective concept of the *Poetics* to the therapeutic-subjective concept of the *Politics*. More specifically, it does not explain Aristotle's promise in *Politics* 8. 7. 1341b38: "what we mean by the 'catharsis' we will explain now in general outline, and later more clearly [i.e., in greater detail] in the discussions on poetry."

To this objection there are various things to be said. First, and most important, is the question of method. If an interpretation of a detail in a given work is solidly based on the rationale and argument of that work, if it fits firmly into place in a system of thought along with other concepts which it helps to explain and which help to explain it, then it cannot be refuted *merely* by appealing to a reference in another work which seems to imply a different concept, especially if that reference is obscure or controversial in itself. It does seem clear that "catharsis" in the *Politics* means some kind of purgation of the subject's emotions, or at least some kind of therapeutic treatment of them. And the reference to τὰ περὶ ποιητικῆς would naturally lead one—did in fact lead Bernays and others—to expect a similar catharsis in the *Poetics*. But the reference (which is the only overt link between the two works)[61] is capable of explanation in a number of other possible ways. In the first place, Aristotle may never have carried out his expressed intention: he may never have written the fuller explanation of catharsis. In the second place, the reference may be (this was Bernays' inference and is still the prevailing assumption) to the lost second book of the *Poetics*, and we have no way of telling just what Aristotle said there. Or, if there never was a second book of our *Poetics*, as

[61] This is worth emphasizing. The cross-reference is Bernays' only warrant for importing the therapeutic concept into the *Poetics*. But for it, the obvious answer to Bernays would be that his theory is all very well for the *Politics* passage and perhaps for some others, but has nothing to do with the *Poetics*.

MacMahon[62] and Montmollin[63] have argued, he may have expounded the matter in another work περὶ ποιητικῆς.

I abstain from canvassing these hypotheses. To do so would lead far beyond the scope of this book. The fact that they are not and probably never can be anything more than hypotheses should not, I think, weigh against our analysis of the possible meaning of catharsis *in our Poetics.* For my point is precisely that the *Poetics* ought to be interpreted out of itself, if possible, and that the consideration of cross-references elsewhere, and of other possible external evidence, must follow the interpretation of the *Poetics,* not precede it. I will, however, offer a purely personal and perhaps gratuitous hypothesis of my own to account for the apparent discrepancy with the *Politics.* Catharsis, as we have analyzed it, forms part of an extraordinarily tight and subtle nexus of ideas concerning the tragic plot. It stands to reason that such a nexus does not spring into being in a man's mind overnight. It is inherently probable rather than improbable, then, that catharsis in the sense we have suggested was not an original part of Aristotle's thinking about tragedy. And in fact we saw reason to mark the catharsis-clause in the definition of tragedy as a later addition to the text by Aristotle. On the other hand there is good reason to believe that book 8 of the *Politics* is early.[64] It may be, then, that when Aristotle wrote the latter he had in mind a comparatively simple and direct concept of catharsis as a variety of psychic therapy, but that the peculiar, special system of ideas which emerged in time from his study of the tragic plot-structure[65] changed all that and necessitated revisions in his promised explanation of catharsis. If so, the explanation when finally written, or rewritten, would have looked very different from what is implied in the *Politics.* It would have had to attack the problem of catharsis again on a broader front, bringing the structural line of thought into harmony somehow with the medical-therapeutic. Whether Aristotle actually

[62] *Op. cit.* (above, c. 13, n. 65).

[63] Pp. 188-193.

[64] Jaeger, *Aristotle*² 267-292.

[65] I do not mean to imply a "two-strata" theory like Montmollin's. As I see the possible development of Aristotle's thinking about poetry, it does not fall into sharply defined strata separated from each other by a considerable space of time, but may well represent a growth and refocusing of his conceptions within a single, perhaps even a comparatively short, period. Aristotle's pattern of thought in chapters 11-14 is subtle and highly integrated, but none of its premises are such that he could not have had them from the beginning. In other words we seem to have, not successive "strata," but several closely related stages of integration of the same ideas. To attempt to recapture the exact chronological sequence of such a development is hopeless.

wrote such a treatment I do not venture to decide. Perhaps it was too much for him; perhaps it was drafted but never incorporated into any part of the Aristotelian corpus (certainly there is no trace of it in any part that we now possess).

As against these speculations, interesting as they might be if pursued, let us reaffirm that our aim here is to interpret the *Poetics* out of the *Poetics, if that is possible,* and that other tasks and projects must take second place.

There is another defect in our explanation of catharsis: that it turns the latter into a relatively minor operational factor in the poetic economy instead of a major aesthetic (or moral or therapeutic, etc.) concept. But this is not necessarily a very serious fault. As we said earlier, one of the great virtues of the traditional view(s) was its (their) vagueness: a vagueness which made it possible to stretch "catharsis" to cover almost every conceivable variety of literary experience. We have grown used to feeling—again vaguely—that serious literature is hardly respectable unless it performs some "catharsis." "Catharsis" has come, for reasons that are not entirely clear, to be one of the biggest of the "big" ideas in the field of aesthetics and criticism, the Mt. Everest or Kilimanjaro that looms on all literary horizons. But all this may be nothing but a self-propagating mirage. Aristotle does not *tell* us that catharsis is so important, that it is the "biggest" idea about tragedy. If it were, we should expect it to be at least mentioned again by name somewhere in the discussion of tragedy. As it is, pity and fear are mentioned repeatedly, and the tragic pleasure three times; catharsis never appears again, by name, after its sudden appearance in chapter 6.

The last feature of our explanation which may seem to militate against it is that it limits catharsis to complex plots and thus makes it a special concept, whereas the catharsis-clause in the definition of tragedy seems to promise a general one, applicable to all tragedies. To this we must reply that Aristotle does in fact come perilously close to making complex tragedy stand for all tragedy, and that this is especially true so far as the tragic emotions are concerned. Pity and fear were first mentioned in his analysis (9.52a1) precisely in order to introduce the theory of the complex plot, and the standing justification for each of its features was its effectiveness in arousing pity and fear. Aristotle never says in so many words that a simple plot cannot arouse pity and fear, but the implication does not lie far below the surface. Of the possible modes of outcome which he canvassed in chapter 13, those possible to the simple plot were rejected as untragic, and the mode involving *hamartia* (which as we saw is only possible, or only makes sense, in a complex structure, as the necessary foil for recognition) was put forward as the "finest." Similarly in the present chapter, the first two modalities of the *pathos* (no. 1, performed with full knowledge; no. 2, intended with full knowledge, then not performed) are those possible in a simple plot, and they are the poorest.

Actually, if we look back over the *Poetics* from the vantage-point of chapter 14, we see that Aristotle has said very little about the simple plot as such. It is true that chapters 7-9, in so far as they outline the general theory of the aesthetic qualities of the tragic plot, must be applicable to the simple as well as the complex. But these general characteristics serve primarily as a foundation for the superstructure which Aristotle builds in chapters 11-14: the theory of the complex plot. The simple plot is mentioned *as such* only in connection with its worst form, the episodic (9. 51b33-52a1).

Thus everywhere we look we find evidence that for Aristotle complex tragedy is very close to being tragedy *tout court:* as if the simple were another species, not merely an inferior variety of this one.[66] And there are other places in the *Poetics* where we can observe a similar tendency: in the classification of the modes of imitation in chapter 3 (the dramatic mode *is* imitation in the proper or full sense) and in the "history" of poetry in chapters 4 and 5 (the drama *is* poetry, the earlier varieties being essentially attempts to achieve it; the "dramatization of the ludicrous" *is* comedy, other varieties being only "iambic").[67] Aristotle's whole theory is permeated by the conviction that the best or perfect specimen *is* the species in the proper sense. So, from the point of view not merely of perfection of structure but of the emotional "work" of tragedy (since, as we have seen, the structure is for the sake of the "work"), the complex plot is *the* tragic plot, *is* tragedy in the full sense of the word.[68] It follows that in restricting catharsis to the complex plot we are not limiting its significance, by Aristotle's standards. It is a post of honor, like that of peripety and recognition.

But it is not merely a question of limitation to complex plots. A complex play may have a peripety but no *hamartia* and recognition; by the same token it will have no catharsis. The total nexus to which

[66] Cf. the section on episodic plots, where they are characterized in a way that practically assimilates them to the epic. See below on 18. 56a10-15.

[67] See above on 9. 51b11-15.

[68] This is already implicit in the οὐ μόνον . . . ἀλλὰ καί of 9. 52a1-2.

catharsis belongs is defined so tightly by the interlocking of its parts—*pathos, hamartia,* recognition, and catharsis—that it will actually fit only a few tragedies; and in fact that is precisely the state of affairs to which Aristotle calls attention in chapter 13 (53a17-22) and again at the end of the present chapter (54a9-15). It is clear that he was not troubled by any concern for the statistical average. The six heroes mentioned in 13. 53a20-21, as examples of the "few houses" which have provided suitable stories, account between them for about seventy known tragedies (only six of them extant, as it happens);[69] and they do not exhaust the possible list (*loc. cit.,* καὶ ὅσοις ἄλλοις κτλ.). But we cannot tell how many of the seventy plays were complex in Aristotle's sense,[70] though it is reasonable to assume that some of the Sophoclean dramas and most of those by Euripides and later poets were so. Above all, we cannot tell how many fitted the full prescription of *hamartia*—recognition—catharsis.[71] Certainly it is hard to imagine an Orestes-Clytemnestra drama in which the son kills his mother without knowing who she is; yet Astydamas perhaps accomplished a similar feat with Alcmeon.

The sum of the matter is that we cannot tell what proportion of all Greek tragedies exactly fitted Aristotle's prescription for the best plot, but it cannot have been more than a small fraction: perhaps as much as a tenth.[72] Among the extant plays the proportion is spectacular: two (*Oedipus Rex* and *Iphigenia in Tauris*) out of 32. The reasons for this glaring disproportion are not certain either; though it seems fair at least to say that the final choice, so far as it was a choice,[73] of the

[69] Aesch. *Cho., Eum.*; Soph. *O.T., El.*; Eur. *El., I.T.* For details on the rest see the notes on the passage, above *ad loc.*

[70] We can be sure that at least those by Aeschylus were not.

[71] Out of the other complex tragedies mentioned in the *Poetics* we can detect at least two which had a *pathos* involving close kin. One of them, the play cited here (14. 53b34) as the Τραυματίας Ὀδυσσεύς (almost certainly identical with the Ὀδυσσεὺς ἀκανθοπλήξ of Sophocles: see Gudeman 263), is an almost exact parallel to the *Oedipus*: Telegonus kills his father, as an oracle had predicted, and only "recognizes" him afterward. The other, the *Tereus* of Sophocles (16. 54b36), involved *pathê* of the right kind (cutting out of Philomela's tongue; Itys' flesh served up to his father), but no *hamartia.*

[72] Estimating, more or less at random, that half of the 70 plays mentioned above may have done so—probably a liberal guess—and setting this against the 387 known titles of tragedies (see Schmid 1. 2. 87n. 7; the six heroes named by Aristotle do figure prominently in Schmid's list of the commonest titles: *Meleager* 4 times, *Orestes* 5, *Alcmeon* and *Thyestes* 6, *Telephus* 7, *Oedipus* 12).

[73] The seven plays each which we have from Aeschylus and Sophocles are "select." But ten of the extant plays of Euripides come from a complete alphabetical edition, part of which (two rolls) was somehow preserved long enough

tragedies that were destined to survive antiquity was not made on Aristotelian principles. Actually I believe that the fact is a damaging one to Aristotle's credit as a critic, no matter how one looks at it. His principles, which with his characteristic logic he has pushed to a radical conclusion, have led him into a *cul de sac*. They were based too narrowly to begin with, on his exaggerated and one-sided thesis of the overwhelming importance of plot as against all other elements; and their interlocking into the tight nexus we have described had the result of narrowing his scope still more, to two subspecies (our modes nos. 3 and 4) of one variety (the complex plot). It so happened that the knife-edge of his judgment hit square on one masterpiece, the *Oedipus;* but the other play it hit upon, the *Iphigenia,* cannot honestly be called much more than a good melodrama, and meanwhile masterpieces like the *Trojan Women* or the *Bacchae,* to say nothing of the *Oedipus at Colonus* or the *Agamemnon,* remain outside the range of Aristotle's formula. This is not the way one can arrive at an organic comprehension of the best of Greek drama. Tragedy in its greatest days comported things that were not dreamt of in Aristotle's philosophy.

However, our purpose here is to understand the *Poetics,* not to judge it. There is one more thing to be said before we leave the subject of catharsis: that our interpretation of it excludes the possibility of a *comic* catharsis. Comedy has no tragic *pathê,* no *μιαρόν,* to be cleansed; the idea could not possibly be relevant to it.[74]

---

to be conflated with a "select" edition of nine plays; see E. R. Dodds, *Euripides Bacchae,* Oxford, 1944, Introd. xlvii-viii.

[74] For speculations on this subject, and an attempt (with negative results) to find evidence for an Aristotelian doctrine of catharsis in comedy, see Lane Cooper, *An Aristotelian Theory of Comedy,* New York, 1922, 63-90. The source of the idea is of course the *Tractatus Coislinianus,* with its parody of Aristotle's definition of tragedy (on it see Gudeman 145, on 5. 49a31).—The *hamartia* of comedy is painless; see above on 5. 49a31-37.

The Psychology of Tragic Pleasure

ROY MORRELL

Mine is a hackneyed subject, and I should like to say at once that some obvious points which may appear heavily laboured in the first part of this paper, are included not in order to instruct, but to facilitate reference when I come to a psychoanalytical analogy at the end.

I have little room, in my theory, for the jargon of psychological pleasure terms such as Sadism and Masochism. The masochistic element in literature is familiar and it appears distinct from Tragedy. The Romantic mood which finds pleasure in "swooning to death" has, I know, been called tragic, but this is, I believe, a confusion. When Tragedy appears in nineteenth century literature, it seems alien and even shocking to the Romantic sensibility. The argument that the appeal of Tragedy is sadistic is likewise unconvincing: the critic argues—rightly, I think—that literature or drama which openly relishes cruelty repels those of us who are not sadists, yet those of us who are not sadists can find pleasure in Tragedy.

The argument in favour of sadism might, however, be pressed in a different way: it might be said that some "censorship" mechanism enables us to derive sadistic pleasure—those of us who deny that we are sadists—only from something not *too* sadistic, from something not recognizable as sadism. Psychologists do, in fact, extend the term sadism to include not only sexual violence or a relish in inflicting pain inexplicable except through some sexual analogy, but also a more general satisfaction in the discomfiture of others. At one time it seemed to me that tragic pleasure must be explicable in this way. Are not all but the best of men moved to envy the lot of their more energetic or more successful fellows? We may think we are unselfish, or good sportsmen, rejoicing in our friend's success, his windfall, his prize in the sweepstake—he bought only one ticket, lucky fellow, and we had bought ten—we may rejoice in his fat legacy. We cannot blame ourselves, we blame only him, when we quickly detect signs of "uppish-

From *Essays in Criticism,* Vol. VI, 1956, pp. 22-37. Reprinted by permission of the editors.

ness" in him; and we leave him to go his superior way. How quickly and virtuously, on the other hand, do we rally round with demonstrations of friendship and pity, refraining from the least mention of "poetic justice," should he lose his wealth as quickly as he acquired it. Nor is it entirely petty thus to wish for an assurance that Fate is not too unfair, that if she withholds from us her special favours, she does not deal us her worst blows. To see disaster befalling a great and fortunate person dwarfs our own worries and troubles, and makes them more easily bearable. Fate, great personages, disasters befalling them—these are the stuff of tragedy, and that pity should be seen as something related to envy, and therefore undesirable, perhaps indicates that Aristotle was thinking partly along these lines.

Reflection will show us, however, that any such theory is incomplete. It assumes a detachment on the part of the audience; it ignores the fact that most spectators and readers sympathize, or perhaps actually identify themselves with the hero. We may be more sophisticated than the schoolboy who forgets that Jim Hawkins is not himself, but we sympathize with Oedipus, Lear, Othello, Tess and Hugo actively enough to wish to avert the disasters which await them. In short, tragic pleasure does not arise through the gratification of a wish, but in a wish's frustration. This reminder should prevent our toying with psychological pleasure terms, masochism or sadism, dilute them as we may, or with any conception of "poetic justice." Tragedy does not "please" in this sense; it does not please our palate, nor awaken pleasurable anticipation. On the contrary, we resist Tragedy, and try to avert it. The pleasure arises only afterwards, and no small part of the pleasure is the discovery that we have the strength to face a world which is larger than the mere creation of our wishes.

There remain the anthropologists' data of the magical origins of Tragedy. We all know that pain, mutilation, sacrifice, ritual burial, once implied renewal, resurrection, the germination of the seed. But what have such things to do with us today? Having outgrown the magical view of the world, why have we not outgrown Tragedy? It is true that primitive impulses still move us unconsciously. Freud has shown that accidents, breakages and the like, are sometimes instinctive sacrifices, sops to Nemesis. We may not use the word *Hubris,* but we dislike and fear boasting; we touch wood, and hang up mistletoe; and in the same way the tragic experience, in which we suffer vicariously, may still be "good magic" and seem to appease the Fates.

The Fates indeed are merely projections of our anxieties, and if the

Fates have gone, the anxieties remain. And it is in this way, I think, that we usually find the appeal of Tragedy defined today. If art is man's method of imposing a pattern on the disorderly material of life, Tragedy's function is to get under control life's most chaotic and difficult parts. Gilbert Murray said, "In its primitive form, drama was doing beforehand the thing you longed or dreaded to do; doing afterwards the thing that lived in your mind and could not be exorcised."

Modern warfare has shown that man has not outgrown this need for anticipating or exorcising. In Freud's account of war neuroses, he pointed out that the anxious individuals, whose imaginations pictured the horrors of battle in advance, were least liable to shell-shock. He also pointed out that recovery from shock was necessarily accompanied by dreams of the shocking experience. Attempts to cure the patient by diverting his mind always failed; his injured psyche was set on rehearsing and rehearsing the horror in daydreams and in sleep until gradually the experience was brought under control; and cures were accelerated not by removing the patients to the quiet of the country, trying to make them forget, but rather by reminding them of the battlefield, supplementing their imaginings by noises of bombardment and by additional shocks.

All this is well known, but it is interesting because, first, it suggests why surprise is unimportant in Tragedy. Indeed, as Mr. Lucas says, dramatic irony and suspense—with their hints of what is about to happen—far from detracting from the effect of tragedy, only enhance the horror. We can, moreover, see a great tragedy again and again, without diminution of effect: it is, indeed, as if, within our own minds, Tragedy were never a performance, always a rehearsal. Second, Freudian psychology corroborates our previous impression that "Tragic Pleasure" is a phrase which can be used only with reserve, in inverted commas. We are not "pleased" by the destruction of the hero, any more than the soldier is "pleased" either by the shock which penetrates his illusions, or by the dreams by which he seeks to control or exorcise the terror. Pleasure there is indeed, but only afterwards, in the feeling of having gained control, partial or complete, over the chaotic experience.

In the book where Freud develops this theme—that certain human behaviour can be explained only by going, as the title puts it, "Beyond the Pleasure Principle," he analyses examples of play in children, where sometimes, by persistent repetition, the child's psyche obtains control over a painful experience. Freud then compares the psyche to a cell. He sees it as having a highly sensitive interior protected by a hard rind from the cruel shock-laden wind of the real world. Some objective reality may be absorbed into layers of the rind, and defences may be strengthened by marshalling energies from within to resist specific attacks—just as our soldier who was full of "horrible imaginings" before the battle, saved himself from shell-shock. Some adaptation is possible, but the psyche tries to "make do" with the simplest set of illusions which seems as if it might, with luck, work. Except that "work" is hardly the word: the psyche is essentially lazy, seeking to economize effort. Sooner or later, however, an unexpected disaster may break through these too simple defences, and the whole equilibrium of the psyche may be upset until the new experience has been absorbed and brought under control, and a more complex, a less dangerously sensitive, composition established.

There is nothing new in this: it is Gilbert Murray's theory of rehearsing and exorcising, in metaphor. But, as Freud explains, the metaphor of the cell economizing its energy in pursuit of a "pleasure principle" (its little labour-saving ideal home is really the home of the death instincts), but being forced to reorganize itself into more complex life—this metaphor refers these "unpleasure processes," of which the tragic experience is one, to the very principle of life itself. It is thus that the sperm forces the ovum to live, repeating in every individual the process by which organic life began. Whatever disturbances occurred during the cooling of the globe, one imagines life—not real life at first, but merely the potentiality of life—coming into being not once but many times, and fading out again, until some further disturbances intervened, enforcing a readjustment, a complication of the cell, the beginning of a cycle of life, before the simplicity of death could be re-attained.

In this view, then, there are two sets of impulses, one set which can be termed "death instincts," which are innate; and the other set, reacting to disturbing stimulation from the outside, which enable the individual to adapt and to reorganize and to live more complexly—Tragedy exciting the second set. I am simplifying, perhaps; for instance I omit the possibility of innate disturbances which may complicate the life of the psyche by fifth-column activity within. With Freud's name on one's lips one is not likely to forget such impulses as complicated the life of Oedipus, for example. But on the whole I am not misrepresenting Freud, for in this book he does make mention—a single passing mention, but unambiguous—of Tragedy.

By "death instincts" Freud explains that he doesn't mean "suicide instincts." Death is not their immediate, only their ultimate aim; their immediate aim is the preservation of the established life-cycle to death, with the least possible interference or tension. Tragedy's preoccupation with death indicates no alliance with these "death instincts" but rather a desire to rid us of the numbing effect of its terror. But there are obvious reservations to be made here: in many tragedies we are reminded that death is not the worst that can happen to the hero, and I hope to show later that his death has, in addition, a special function to perform.

For the moment the essential function of Tragedy would appear to be the complicating and strengthening of the psyche by means of shocks from outside: not, of course, violent and disorganizing shocks, but mild, preventive, reorganizing ones. The participation in "tragic conflicts" may be a part of such reorganizing; though I am thinking of a toughening less crude than that which some German philosophers have thought desirable. Theoretically it would, I suppose, be possible to present a tragedy so horrible that there resulted a real shock—like shell-shock—from which the patient would have to be cured. In practice, however, we can usually protect ourselves by recalling, if we are forced, that what is hapening on the stage is not "real." There is probably a level of tragedy, involving not too drastic a reorganization of the psyche, at which tragedy is most effective.

But when we come to define this level, and to consider the mechanism by which the tragic experience is conveyed to the audience, it seems to me that we are inevitably defining characteristics in the tragic hero. In Elizabethan tragedy, we are at once aware of the hero's position—Faustus's, Hamlet's, Clermont's, Othello's—a step or so ahead of his age. He develops fine sensibilities at heavy cost; he suffers and fails. The audience follow the hero's aspirations, his explorations in new realms of feeling; they face the possibility that such noble struggles will be thwarted by the insensibility and evil of the men around them, by the weight of the past, by blind chance. Despite the hero's defeat, however, the experience is, for the audience, a reorganization from the old life to the new fuller one; the cell is hindered in its easy acceptance of the old instinctive life cycle, and compelled to live more complexly. I believe great tragedy always has this effect of bringing the consciousness to a threshold between the old and the new, although it may have other methods of doing this than by representing the hero as thus stepping to a threshold or beyond. Nor is the representation of such a hero alone sufficient: the nobility of Clermont is not enough, for instance, to make a great tragedy out of *The Revenge of Bussy D'Ambois.*

None the less, a great hero—one human enough for the audience's sympathy, and remarkable enough to lift their imaginations—is important. It is mainly through the hero's thoughts and feelings that we judge the truth of the world which the dramatist asks us to accept, its "values," its relevance to the possibilities of our own existence. I have already said we feel more than a detached sympathy for the hero; we feel more than "there, but for the grace of God, go I"; we identify ourselves, and go, with him. The extent of the identification varies in different members of the audience, and with different types of Tragedy. Some identification occurs even in Comedy; but the essence of comedy is that identification is partial and temporary and that we are continually dissociating ourselves in laughter. Stephen Haggard and Athene Seyler tell us in *The Craft of Comedy* that actors recognize this, keeping slightly "outside" the parts, self-dramatizing and slightly overcharacterizing, in comedy, but acting realistically and "straight," identifying themselves with their parts and trying to "live" them, empathizing—if I may use this word in a more limited sense than it is normally used in criticism—empathizing in the characters in a serious play. I used the word "realistically" inaccurately as a paraphrase of the actors' word "straight." In fact, too great a degree of realism with its reminders of the particular and commonplace can be distressing to the audience. If the audience too are to empathize in the hero, we should probably agree that a slightly stylized and remote production is more effective; indeed, this matter of "psychological distance" in drama has been explored by philosophers and critics.

My emphasis on the reality of the hero is unfashionable, and went out with Bradley. But although I am willing to defend this emphasis, I realise that the position has its dangers; particularly if adopted by actors. If an actor believes that a play exists for the sake of character, and for his acting of it, the result is frequently disastrous. Nothing repels an audience so much as finding that an actor, with a strong and perhaps highly mannered personality, has "got in" first. I am not arguing that personalities should dominate the play, least of all the personalities of actors. Such domination defeats the whole end of drama, which is not to give scope for actors or actresses (pace M. Cocteau), nor to impress the audience, but to enable the audience to respond and react themselves. And they can only respond naturally and unselfconsciously if the actor has the tact to leave a little of the initiative to them, if he underacts a little, perhaps. And, needless to say, they can only respond if the whole play, the whole action, rings true. Only then can they also be convinced by the hero's part in it. I certainly do not believe that the play should be subordinated to character, none the less I do believe that for the full functioning—the purging—of Tragedy, our credulity, our four-dimensional acceptance, our ability to emphasize in the tragic hero, or bovarize—as Huxley and others have called it—is always relevant. I need hardly distinguish here between bad bovarism and good: if we are tempted to identify ourselves with some hero of less intelligence and capacity for living than ourselves, it is probably to satisfy some dream of affluence or success; in short, to escape. Empathy in a character of a different kind, with a mind and soul larger than our own, requires effort and imagination, and, apart from any ordeal, any adjustment to the harsher realities which may be forced upon us by the tragic development of the plot, the greater awareness into which we are led tallies with the experience we derive from other great art.

Before considering whether this is the whole truth, I should like to recapitulate briefly and add to what I've said about the tragic hero. We have argued that whatever pleasure-principle factors enter, the distinctive appeal of Tragedy can only be explained by going "beyond the pleasure principle"; we suffer an ordeal, face life at its most difficult and complex, but derive pleasure in the new readiness and power we have gained thereby. To enable us to live more complexly and to persuade us that what we are getting is true to life—for it is important that we should not feel that the dramatist is either cheating us or sparing us, treating us as children who cannot be told the truth—we are invited to empathize in a hero of a certain type. We feel more deeply and subtly, act more courageously, more passionately, in him, and all the time with the conviction that it is true to life, a fuller life than our own. We may add that as drama has to work quickly, superficial superiorities, such as those of rank and fortune mentioned by classical critics, may predispose some of us to empathize, though modern class-conscious audiences may prefer other qualities. Whatever else the tragic hero is, however, he should not be dull: some conscientiously proletarian modern writers make a mistake, I think, when they solemnly present with a drab little hero—unless they succeed in making out of him a twentieth-century Everyman. That may be as successful occasionally as the great character who lifts our imaginations, and it may invite our empathy no less.

Edith Sitwell has remarked that Tragedy always opens on a question, "Who?"—Who is the tragic hero? what is his significance? The answer is seldom given as explicitly as in the closing lines of *The Great God Brown*: the Police Captain, you may remember, has given Cybel a few minutes alone with the dying Brown to make him talk; he then comes in and asks, "Well, what's his name?" Cybel answers, "Man," and the Police Officer, his notebook open, asks "How d'yuh spell it?"

The spelling is not difficult: it is either "Everyman," ourselves, whose fate we must endure; or it is "Potential Man," whose powers of living it would be well for the species if we could assimilate.

Nothing of what I have said so far is new, and little, I hope, is controversial. But one point is unexplained: If Tragedy is, as I have described it, a vicarious ordeal, why is the unhappy ending essential? Why cannot the ordeal be provided by a serious and terrifying depiction of the sufferings of the hero, if he recovers from an almost mortal wound to live "happily ever after"? Death, as we know, is not essential. Oedipus lives on for a while; but in his despair, blood streaming from his eyesockets, he is a more terrible symbol of defeat than the hanged Jocasta. Defeat, the end of effective life, the end of hope for the hero—these are essential. His death, in fact, is convenient; but why?

It is true that the death of the hero is occasionally accompanied by the suggestion of a new start. Before the death of Henchard, some of our interest has been transferred to Elizabeth-Jane; Macbeth's death is followed by the coronation of Malcolm; there is even mention of the succession in *Hamlet*; but these are not "happy endings." Between the effect of *Hamlet* and that of *The Winter's Tale* there is a difference of kind not of degree: I know this difference depends not merely on the ending, but differences in the texture of the play throughout; and a key difference, in my view, is that in the Tragicomedy our sympathies are not centred to the same extent on a single person. In this, it seems to me there is a special propriety: that the audience should not be asked to empathize seriously and deeply in a hero who is going, not to die, but to live "happily ever after."

Still, there is this difference in texture and it would be fairer to compare the effect of *Villette* with that of *Jane Eyre,* or the two versions of a Shakespeare tragedy, before and after it had been doctored to "please" Restoration or eighteenth-century audiences. I don't think there can be serious doubt that, despite Aristotle's contrary opinion, the unhappy ending is indispensable for tragic effect, and the ordeal theory is incomplete. Indeed nothing would seem to fit the ordeal theory better than some modern crime fiction. Raymond Chandler does not spare his readers when he describes his hero being taught by some thug to mind his own business, but I have yet to encounter a critic who calls this literature tragic.

The effect of Tragedy is courage; not mere toughness, nor bravado, nor the will to display power, but simply calmness and readiness, the discovery that even in the harshest experiences there is, to quote Richards, "no difficulty"; the difficulty arises from the illusions and subterfuges by which we seek to dodge reality, and which we unconsciously fear are going to betray us.

But how does this change come about? How is it that for a time we are personally participating in the fears and difficulties of the hero, our need to dodge increased; and then that we are, almost suddenly sometimes, freed from these apprehensions, having achieved an impersonal objective attitude?

Freudian psychology helped us with a corroboration before, can it now provide us with an answer? We are again up against the difficulty of providing generalizations which are valid for all types of individuals—I recall a member of the Cambridge English Faculty who claimed that he had never experienced tragic catharsis: clearly my generalizations cannot include him. I put forward no chain of proof, tested at every link, only a kind of analogy which seems to me more plausible at some times than at others.

In pathological "fixations," when the psyche shrinks from developing into maturity, it often turns aside into a fantasy world comparable to the empathizing or bovarizing fantasies which we have been discussing. It is permissible to compare normal with pathological processes, for, as the example of Mme Bovary reminds us, no sharp line divides the two. It is a matter of better or of worse adjustment, and both possibilities are open to all of us.

At all events, with the conception of psychological fixation in mind, we can reframe our question thus, "Does Tragedy provide the individual in the audience with a means of expansion through empathy, through good 'bovarism,' and then, *but only in the destruction of the hero,* free the individual, break his empathy at the point where it is in danger of becoming a fixation, where his fantasies might otherwise usurp the energies required for real life?" If this question is framed correctly, we could say simply that the individual adjusts himself to real life because his fantasy life has died with the hero.

I do not know how general these fixation fantasies are, however, and I should like to establish an analogy between the tragic "empathy-ordeal-disaster" process and some more general fantasy process. But meanwhile one point is worth noting. Freud in dealing with fixations has concentrated mainly on infantile incest fantasies; the tragic function—of enabling one to grow and adjust oneself—might therefore be expressed as breaking free from a fixation, if one had no more to explain than *Oedipus Tyrannus*. But the main point hangs on Freud's reminder that an elaborate fantasy-living is *normal* in children. In their "endless imitation," they enter into fantasies, change them, discard them to meet the demands of real life, return to fantasy play at a moment's notice—they cease being soldiers or Red Indians and rush in to their real dinner, then rush out again to be pirates or shipwrecked mariners—doing safely, easily and normally what no adult can do without serious risk to his sanity. The explanation of this links up with what we said earlier about good and bad empathy: the whole principle of a child's life is growth, expansion; and his normal fantasies are informed inevitably with this expansion; they are, mainly, fantasies of growing up; and he is indeed growing minute by minute; except for the pathological case, the child with the infantile fixation, the child has no past, but only a future which he is constantly realizing. For the adult it is a different matter; every fantasy has the danger of becoming a fixation, a mental cancer growing inward when the normal expansive organic growth has slowed down, a step aside, a turn back to the past—unless, as we have suggested, the fantasy is of a special kind, derived from outside impact, demanding new effort, offering new opportunities of creative, imaginative, expansion.

But we were seeking in the realms of psychology for a more general type of fantasy, for comparison with tragic empathy. Is this not found in the artificially induced fantasy of the "transference," a part of the mechanism by which all psycho-therapeutic analysis was at one time attempted? An account of this mechanism is given in Jung's *Modern Man in Search of a Soul.* Jung describes the failure of Breuer's early therapeutic treatment, which Breuer with deliberate but, as it turned out, most unfortunate reference to Aristotle, called "Catharsis." Breuer's "Catharsis" was simply free confession aided by the probings of the physician, and Jung explains that it "consisted of putting the patient in touch with the hinterland of his mind." It failed because one of two kinds of fixation followed treatment and caused a relapse. In fact, though of course Breuer did not realize it at this stage, it did not purge effectively; the term "Catharsis" had been usurped.

Breuer's treatment seemed to promise success; the patient always improved at first; but then one of two things happened: in some cases, to use Jung's words, "The patient goes away apparently cured—but he is now so fascinated by the hinterland of his own mind, that he continues to practise catharsis to himself at the expense of his adaptation to life. He is bound to the unconscious—to himself." In other cases, as is well known, the patient develops a sense of complete dependence on the physician, and collapses if the connection is severed. Both reactions are in the nature of fantasy-fixations: in the first case, the patient's fantasies are self-contained, they are fantasies about himself; in the second case a fantasy of child-parent dependence—the patient is the child; the physician the parent—is set up, and persists. In short, all Breuer had discovered or rediscovered was the relief and comfort of confession, and the helpless dependence which followed it.

Freud's system of analysis which superseded Breuer's made use of a similar relationship of dependence—the dependence of child-patient on father-confessor-physician—in the preliminary stages, but strove to break this "transference" later. This break was always regarded, of course, as indispensable for a cure; and, when properly successful, it effected something much more in the nature of a real catharsis. The important difference between Freud's analytical "transference" and Breuer's was that Freud's did not merely bring to light a few repressed thoughts and impulses from the "hinterland of the patient's mind," it strove also to bring the patient face to face with some terror, forced him to experience in his fantasy something which had been evaded in the past, something which provided a key to later conduct with its evasions and suppressions. Only if the psycho-analyst is able to lead the patient to a climax of resistance ending in painful temporary collapse, does this treatment end successfully and lead to the eventual readjustment of the patient. This process is different from that of Tragedy mainly in the fact that the patient is led back to a point where a wrong turning had been taken in his past development, where he takes the hurdle he had evaded then, and leaves his old self behind; whereas in tragedy, the individual is led forward. But there are points of comparison too: there is the initial fantasy, there is the postponed and resisted pain, eventually faced either in the death of the hero, or in what may be regarded as the death of the old incomplete self; there is also that oft-discussed, perhaps essential tragic element, "recognition," the "anagnorsis" of Aristotle, which is akin to, perhaps leads to, self-revelation.

I had hoped to explain Tragedy in terms of psycho-analysis and instead find myself expressing the analytical process in terms of tragedy. We can, however, add a few more bricks which seem to fit into the wall of this circular argument. If the effect of tragedy depends, as I believe, upon the end, not merely upon any earlier ordeal; if, not indeed the death of the hero, but the end of what he stands for is essential to release the audience and enable them to adjust themselves to reality, if purgation depends not merely upon the intensity of the transference but indispensably also upon the way it is broken, then we might expect, as a result of empathizing in heroes who do not fail tragically, but instead live "happily ever afterwards," a pathological state of dependence similar to the pathological condition of Breuer's patients. But this is not unlike Mme Bovary's state; and those people who, not making the mistake of Mme Bovary and attempting to live their day dreams, do none the less seek wish-fulfilment dreams in novels and films, are often called, with justice, film or fiction "addicts." Their first need after reading the average novel, or seeing the average film, seems to be to return to the cinema or the fiction library for another one. Whatever exciting or dangerous "ordeals" the addict has experienced vicariously, "purgation" is not one of them, and he attempts no adjustment but remains dependent on his fantasies. He could not continue to empathize in a person who is dead, but he is glad to do so in one who lives happily ever afterwards; and the more he gets from Hollywood or the bestseller-writer, the more dependent he becomes, upon his own fantasies, or upon the dispenser of them. I make the distinction because the tone of certain writers—talking down to the reader, flattering him, comforting him, encouraging his prejudices—has not escaped critical comment. It seems to me not impossible that a reader may get to the point of feeling that the favourite author knows him and his weaknesses and secrets so well that the author is almost in the reader's confidence; and as a sales device, ensuring the complete dependence of the reader upon the physician-confessor-guardian-parent of an author who continually dispenses absolution to the reader for not growing up, it is unrivalled.

Referring to *Hamlet* and *The Winter's Tale* earlier, I suggested that in a Tragicomedy there was a propriety in not inviting so deep and serious an empathy in the hero, as would be proper in Tragedy. The reason is implied in what I have just said: empathy does not break itself, and an author whose theme gives him no opportunity of breaking it, should not—if he intends to deal honestly with his public—invite it very deeply and intensely in the first place. Good Tragicomedy—and perhaps most of us would agree that Tragicomedy is not commonly entirely convincing—but the best Tragicomedy has some of the critical detachment of Comedy; or else it distributes the empathy amongst several characters.

Had I the time I should have liked to mention one or two other points. I think, for instance, that those moments to which Mr. Eliot has called attention, when the hero dramatizes himself and his lonely struggle against the Fates, find a place in my scheme. Such self-dramatization in real life is not amiable; we forgive it, in moments of exceptional stress, in those we know and love, but we take it as weakness. The heroes who do this kind of thing continually from the rise of the curtain on Act I are, as serious tragic heroes, intolerable. In great tragedy we forgive it, as we forgive it in ourselves and in our friends; but the dramatic effect lies in the fact that at such moments, when the audience know the limits of the hero's strength, the nearness of his end, and the hero too knows it, but is desperately hiding the knowledge from himself—at such moments our critical faculty is stirring to waken, and our empathy is, as it were, being worked loose.

I should also have liked to discuss those tragedies which the audience approaches quite detachedly, their critical sense awake throughout. In my view such Tragedies are a different species, and to regard them as the same leads only to confusion in theatrical production and in criticism.

But it is possible here to offer only a brief summary.

Tragedy is man's rehearsal of the harsher realities of life; by it the psyche's cell is forced out of its lethargy, its conservative instinctive life-cycle where it is only delusively secure, and it adapts itself to a more complex readiness for life.

The tragic hero is usually, as Aristotle said, uncommonly great and alive: only if he is great (but we mean by this not merely great in rank) does his downfall impress us with the insignificance of our own petty anxieties and mishaps; only if he is great—better than ourselves—does our attempt to share his experiences increase our own capacity for living. The place of the great hero is sometimes, however, successfully supplied by the figure of "Everyman" or by the representative not of all mankind but of a large group. Exceptionally our empathy may even be elicited by an idea, a "cause," with the success of which the fates of numerous individuals are bound up. This could be said not only of a few modern plays, but also of *Antigone*. Character, or some figure or idea in which the audience can identify themselves exactly as in a great character, is indispensable to tragedy; it must not dominate the action, but it is, despite Aristotle, as indispensable as action. In certain modern plays—*A Streetcar named Desire, Lottie Dundass* and others —the action is adequate, the end is disastrous, but the persons are not tragic characters: their place is not in drama, but in a psychoanalyst's case-book; they are tawdry and second-rate persons with whom no audience can with advantage identify themselves, and their failure, whatever else it may be, is not tragic.

Finally, despite Aristotle, Mr. Lucas and others, the general seriousness of the theme is not enough: the action must end in disaster. More than a bare hint of the "rebirth" or renewal theme is dangerous. A production of *Macbeth,* for instance, which allowed all our sympathy for Macbeth to ebb before the desperate scenes in Acts IV and V, and encouraged us to identify ourselves and our interests in Malcolm, would transform the play into melodrama. But in the tragic end of the hero, and of the hopes we had in him, there is nothing defeatist; for only in his failure is some connection, some "transference" between us and our fantasy life in the play, broken, and our own energies set free.

"Catharsis": An Excision from the Dictionary of Critical Terms

I: D. M. HILL

II: F. W. BATESON

I

Humphry House, the most recent expositor of Aristotle's theory of catharsis, made some good points in his *Aristotle's Poetics* (London, 1956, Lecture VII). In particular I was pleased to see him come out strongly (if briefly) against those commentators who might be called the bowel enthusiasts, who see Aristotle's theory in terms of the only current medical meaning of catharsis. It was good, too, to see him referring at crucial points to D. S. Margoliouth, whose comments on catharsis in the introduction to his *The Poetics of Aristotle* (London, 1911) are in some respects more rewarding than either Butcher's (*Aristotle's Theory of Poetry and Fine Art,* London, third ed., 1902) or Bywater's (*Aristotle on the Art of Poetry,* Oxford, 1909), though these are more frequently cited as authorities. I do not wish, however, to put forward yet another interpretation of the theory, but to raise the question whether, in the light of current usage and of the powerful and pervasive tradition of bowel enthusiasm, we might not to our advantage dispense with the term "cartharsis" altogether.

The enthusiasts can be divided into two groups; those who take the theory to refer to bowel *purgation,* and those who (often implicitly) have in mind the activity in which we find Leopold Bloom engaged in *Ulysses:*

> Asquat the cuckstool he folded out his paper turning its pages over on his bared knees . . . Quietly he read, restraining himself, the first column and, yielding but resisting, began the second. Midway, his last resistance yielding, he allowed his bowels to ease themselves quietly as he read . . .

From *Essays in Criticism,* Vol. VIII, 1958, pp. 113-20. Reprinted by permission of the editors.

Those of the former group, who hold that their interpretation offers a fairly complete analogy of the experience of tragedy, seem to evade the problem of pleasure. Aristotle insisted over and over again that poetry gives pleasure, and he believed that there is a pleasure proper to tragedy. Now a catharsis involving a purgation of the bowel is not in any way a pleasurable experience, at any rate at the time it takes place. Pleasure (if the word can be used at all in this context) only comes afterwards with the introspection which compares one's state of being before the cathartic experience with the state following upon it. Many commentators who have seriously maintained this interpretation have either side-stepped the problem of pleasure and have given prominence to Aristotle's view that pity and fear, the tragic emotions, are forms of pain, or they have in some way confused a medical catharsis with that diurnal activity in which Leopold Bloom was engaged. Commentators of the latter group do not usually, to be sure, baldly state that the experience of tragedy is strictly analogous to simple bowel evacuation, but their insistence on a pleasure element implies it. An example of a commentator with a stake in both senses is Bywater, who at one point in his book acknowledges the *infrequency* of dramatic performances in Greek life (p. 156), but one page earlier maintains that pleasure accompanies catharsis:

> [The tragic excitement] serves as a sort of medicine, producing a *catharsis* to lighten and relieve the soul . . . of the accumulated emotion within it; and as the relief is wanted, there is always a harmless pleasure attending the process of relief.

(There would appear to be a flaw in the argument: it does not follow that because "relief is wanted" the *process* of relief must be pleasurable, but let that pass.) Another commentator taking up a similar position is John Crowe Ransom, who in one and the same paragraph (in "The Cathartic Principle," in *The World's Body*, New York, 1938) talks about the "cathartic pill" and "the pleasure that attends an act of elimination," making no distinction between purgation and ordinary evacuation. One could multiply examples. Indeed, it would be true to say that of the commentators who have relied on a medical interpretation, an overwhelming majority have chosen either bowel purgation, or evacuation, or aspects of both.

It is not hard to see why this should have been so. In the first place the medical uses of the term, originally allowing for qualitative as well as quantitative catharsis, became severely restricted in scope, until now there is virtually only one meaning. Again, the interpretation gained some plausibility from relating pain in physical purgation to pain in tragedy and from the need at certain periods to justify art in terms of morals: a physical purgation provided an apt analogy for religious purification, the purging of sin from the soul. Some plausibility accrued, too, from the ancient identification of deep feeling (especially pity) with the bowel. The biblical phrase "the bowels of compassion" is an instance of this. And it has long been known that the other Aristotelian tragic emotion, fear, could in some circumstances cause an involuntary evacuation of the bowel.

For these reasons, and no doubt many others, Aristotle's theory has been taken to involve the use of a metaphor or analogy relating to the bowel. That the theory does not concern that part of the body, and further, that it does not involve the use of a metaphor or analogy at all, was made clear by Margoliouth. He showed that it was not an attempt to describe a psychological process by means of an analogous physical process, though he might perhaps have stressed more the fact that for Aristotle *any* psychological event (any event of "the soul") had its physiological counterpart, or, more accurately, that any human experience could be described by any of several methods, depending on one's point of view. Aristotle once put the matter thus:

> a physicist would define an affection of soul differently from a dialectician; the latter would define e.g. anger as the appetite for returning pain for pain, or something like that, while the former would define it as a boiling of the blood or warm substance round the heart.
>
> (403a30 ff. Oxford ed. of Works)

And elsewhere he observed that "anything painful or pleasing is generally accompanied by a definite change of temperature in the body." What the dialectician in the *Poetics* called a catharsis of the emotions, the physicist (or his pupil) in the *Problems* defined as a reduction of the "cold" in the black bile. Pity and fear have the same bodily manifestation: both are due to an excess of "cold" in the black bile. They differ only in respect of their "objects": "What we fear for ourselves excites our pity when it happens to others" (1386a27). A reduction of the "cold" means a reduction of the emotions of both pity and fear and constitutes a qualitative catharsis. The principle underlying the catharsis was homeopathic. By applying a small dose of "cold" ("fear chills"), Aristotle thought that excess cold in the black bile would be driven out. This is the principle mentioned by Milton in the preface to *Samson Agonistes*, as many have pointed out, though critics writing after 1924 might also have appreciated that Ida Langdon in *Milton's Theory of Poetry and Fine Art* showed how ambiguous Milton's attitude to Aristotle's theory really was. Although he offered a homeopathic interpretation in the preface, he translated Aristotle's definition on the title page of his poem as

> Tragoedia est imitatio actionis seriae, etc. Per misericordiam et metum perficiens talium affectuum lustrationem.

The meaning of "lustratio" was confined to religious purification. "Purgatio" could be used in that sense too, but it also stood for qualitative and quantitative physical catharsis. To be consistent Milton should have used "purgatio," not "lustratio."

Although Aristotle included the catharsis in his definition of tragedy, it did not by any means constitute the whole of the tragic experience: in fact it was a minor element in it. The "imitation," the peripeteia, the use of metaphor, and other elements listed in the *Poetics,* were the important parts of an intricate and complex and pleasurable whole. Not everyone would have the cathartic experience. Those not susceptible enough to the emotions of pity and fear would not have it, nor (and this is the significant point) would those in whom pity and fear existed in true proportion. Catharsis in tragedy held a position not unlike that of catharsis in music. In fact, *exactly the same* catharsis of pity and fear could be produced in those "specially subject to the feelings of fear and pity" (*Politics,* trans. Sir Ernest Baker, Oxford, 1948, p. 413) by the appropriate *music*. Music specifically designed to effect catharsis gave pleasure to those who had no catharsis:

> We may add that melodies which are specifically designed to purge the emotions are likewise also a source of innocent delight to us all.

If, then, the catharsis of pity and fear was not peculiar to tragedy, the pleasure resulting from it could not of itself provide the "pleasure appropriate to Tragedy." That pleasure of some kind resulted from it is likely from the relevant passage in the *Politics,* where Aristotle, discussing the catharsis in music, talks about "the release of emotion accompanied by pleasure." What, then, did he mean by the "pleasure appropriate to tragedy"? According to House

> the peculiar element, therefore, in the pleasure of Tragedy, as distinct from the pleasures given by other forms of art, is that the pleasure is derived from the imitation of emotions and situations which,

> taken in themselves, or taken as they operate in real life, are forms of pain or causes of pain.

This cannot be the case, for such a description also fits music and epic, both of which are "imitations" and can imitate those things which in real life are forms or causes of pain, and in so doing give pleasure. I do not think that there is an element *peculiar* to pleasure in tragedy. The "pleasure appropriate to Tragedy" is an amalgam of pleasures any one of which is obtainable in other poetic or art forms. That amalgam may or may not include the pleasure of the catharsis, depending on one's emotional balance; but what distinguishes it from the pleasure of other forms of art, what characterises it as the appropriate tragic pleasure, is its *richness*. More pleasures go into the formation of it than into those of other forms, and some of the pleasures exist in it in a more intense form (all those remarks in the comparison between tragedy and epic in the *Poetics* bear witness to the concentration and intensity of the former: epic, for Aristotle, is a kind of dilute tragedy).

Thus the tradition of bowel enthusiasm has caused real harm. In the first place, the enthusiasts have given to catharsis an importance far in excess of its real significance in the tragic scheme. Secondly, their analogy of medical purgation breaks down because it does not provide a pleasure element. Thirdly, their analogies of purgation and of simple bowel evacuation break down in respect of what is removed during the process: (1) what is expelled is expelled completely; and this is not true of the emotions of pity and fear, which the good man possesses in true proportion: (2) what is expelled is noxious and injurious to the body; and there is no true parallel here with the tragic emotions. Fourthly, bowel interpretations bring all the wrong associations: the need for purgatives does not have the same moral force as the need to temper the emotions. Fifthly, there already exists an explanation of catharsis more satisfactory than any which bring in the bowel.

Bearing this in mind, we might ask whether the time has not come when we might profitably dispense with the term "catharsis" altogether. For one thing, the only modern medical meaning is related to the bowel, and any interpretation of Aristotle involving this is dangerously misleading. Aristotle's use of the term has to be identified with a system of human physiology which is now obsolete. If we no longer believe in the system, is not our faith in the theory destroyed? In any event, all expounders of criticism should swear to abjure any form of bowel interpretation. Aristotle, despite a long sojourn in Elysium, has never got over the shock of that precipitate and undignified dash for the jakes.

II

Catharsis is perhaps only one of the excisable terms. Every time I read the *Poetics*—but tell it not in Chicago!—I become more conscious of the central critical vacuum. There are useful marginal tips, of course, much important historical information, and one or two profound generalisations (notably in Chapter IX), but the general critical level at which Aristotle's treatise operates is pretty much that of William Archers' *Play-Making*. It is instructive that his favourite tragedy—the model of the well-made play, was the *Oedipus Rex,* which is as much a melodrama as a tragedy. On the other hand, the greater Greek tragedies, the *Prometheus,* the *Agamemnon,* the *Antigone,* the *Oedipus Coloneus,* the *Hippolytus* and the *Bacchae,* are not even mentioned. And he shows no awareness whatever of such concepts as Hubris, Nemesis, Fate, moderation ("nothing too much"), and "knowledge of suffering," which lie at the very heart of Greek tragedy. Of Aristotle's intelligence there can, of course, be no question. I shall never forget the excitement with which I read the *Poetics* for the first time thirty-seven years ago. But what excited me then was not a new understanding I was acquiring of the nature of tragedy, but the spectacle the *Poetics* provide of the functioning of the analytical process itself. I had found myself inside an exceptionally intelligent intelligence. But even then I realised that most of the *matter* Aristotle analyses is aesthetically irrelevant, the mere superficies of anything that can be called literature. A discussion of tragedy must begin with what differentiates a good tragedy from a bad tragedy: the human values embodied and clarified in it. Aristotle was more interested in plots.

The Nature of the Net; The Spring and the Trigger

T. R. HENN

The Nature of the Net

Know now that God hath overthrown me, and hath compassed me with his net.

Job

. . . if the assassination
Could trammel up the consequence, and catch
With his surcease success. . . .

Macbeth

I. The structure of a play may be considered from three possible points of view. The spectator perceives it in varying degrees of "aesthetic distance," oscillating between some measure of "willing suspension of disbelief" and his knowledge that "from the first act to the last, the stage is only a stage, and the players merely players." His view of the outcome of the action will vary in accordance with his mood, the expectations aroused by the known conventions within which the dramatist is working, the extent to which his awareness of the plot is counterbalanced by the success in emotional communication, and the significant momentum which the fable, if known, may have acquired in his mind. He will be aware of a movement in time and space controlled and terminated by the dramatist; but it seems likely that—particularly in tragedy—the emotional response will produce a further oscillation. He knows that the outcome will obey a predetermined pattern: yet as he watches he becomes aware (as many have testified) that he hopes for a different solution. There is just the possibility that, this time, Desdemona will not be murdered, nor Antony be betrayed. This excited hope carries an intermittent suggestion of free will, the

From *The Harvest of Tragedy,* London, 1956, pp. 35-42, 59-64. Reprinted by permission of Methuen and Co., Ltd.

momentary illusion of a self-generating self-determining action that can perhaps be modified, as in the *Eumenides,* by the intrusion of the irrational.

The dramatist himself is aware of the overriding framework, the compulsions of his form: which, if we are to judge by the accounts of dramatists who have described their own creative activity, modifies and re-shapes itself continually during that process. It may, indeed, become almost a purgatorial experience, as Goethe testified: "I am terrified at the idea of undertaking to write a tragedy, and I am almost convinced that I might destroy myself by that very effort." [1] He is controlling the destiny of his characters, allowing them the sense of momentary escape, and of glimpses of a compulsive pattern which is, in varying degrees and in varying civilizations, of their own making.

If it were possible to perceive the play (in the manner of Pirandello) from the viewpoint of certain of the leading characters, they would become progressively aware of a rigid structure, built up from character and the impact of the Past upon the Present, enclosing a more flexible structure which "gives" momentarily to the demands of *immediate* action. This flexible structure, the illusion of escape which it gives, is the instrument of one kind of dramatic irony, its recoil in obedience to the outer structure one source of the Reversal of the Situa tion. And the protagonists—or the Chorus—will perceive intermittently the nature of the outer compulsive structure, and the fact that this nature is, *from their point of view in the space-time continuum of the play,* beyond explanation save that afforded by momentary intuitions.

In the following pages I have attempted to show, by two images, some qualities of the tragic structure. That of the net is a frequent metaphor in tragedy; as regards its application here I have in mind two forms. The first is the seine, which consists of a long wall of netting, deeper at the middle than at the sides; the wall being extended vertically by a lead-line below, and a cork-line above. The ends are extended by wooden posts, weighted at the foot, and attached by a bridle to hauling-ropes. It is "shot" from the stern of the boat, one hauling-line made fast to a man on shore. Once the net is extended, the boat returns to the shore in a half-circle, the net being dragged both by the boat and by the helper on the shore. The two meet, and the net is drawn slowly, horseshoe-wise, so that its middle, where the purse is

[1] Quoted by Volkelt, *op. cit.,* p. 267 n. See also Erich Heller, *The Disinherited Mind:* and in particular the very illuminating chapter "Goethe and the Avoidance of Tragedy."

formed, comes in last. The fish are enclosed, and as the purse or belly of the net comes nearer, the fish can be seen struggling in the diminishing space. It was this image that Yeats had in mind when he wrote:

> Shakespearean fish swam the sea, far away from land;
> Romantic fish swam in nets coming to the hand;
> What are all those fish that lie gasping on the strand? [2]

There is yet another projection of the thought. Certain kinds of fish—grey mullet, for example, will jump the cork-line as the purse diminishes. A single fish tries; the rest follow. Sometimes straw is floated on the surface of the water to give the illusion of a net above as well as in front; in some parts of the world a raft is placed behind the purse, and on it the leaping fish fall.

The second type is the trammel; a wall of large-meshed heavy netting, forming a wall with lead- and cork-lines, moored across the current. On either side of the main wall hang, loosely, walls of much finer mesh. Fish that move with the current strike the wall, thrust the fine mesh into a bag through the squares formed by the wall of the coarse mesh, and are caught in the purse which they themselves have formed. Both images are applicable to certain kinds of tragedy.

For the seine net, the lead-line of Fate moving onwards disturbs the fish lying on the bottom, or swimming in mid-water: the power applied at either end moves it onwards steadily, yet shapes it intelligently into the horseshoe form. There is no escape above or below; though there may be, for a time, an illusion of freedom, of space to manœuvre, even a sense of companionship with others in misfortune,[3] and a

[2] Reprinted with permission of The Macmillan Company, Macmillan & Co. Ltd, and Bertha Georgie Yeats from *Three Movements* by William Butler Yeats. Copyright 1933 by The Macmillan Company, Renewed 1961 by Bertha Georgie Yeats.

[3] Cousteau in *The Silent World* (pp. 112-13) has a description of a herd of tunny fishes that have been trapped in the inner chamber of a maze of nets because of their habit of swimming, during the spawning-season, with their right eyes towards the shore as if the left were blind. The last stages before the kill in the *corpo* are described thus by the divers among them:

"Life took on a new perspective, when considered from the viewpoint of the creatures imprisoned in the *corpo*. We pondered how it would feel to be trapped with the other animals and have to live their tragedy. Dumas and I were the only ones in the creeping, constricting prison who knew the outcome, and we were destined to escape. Perhaps we were over-sentimental, but we felt ashamed of the knowledge. I had an impulse to take my belt knife and cut a hole for a mass break to freedom.

"The death chamber was reduced to a third of its size. The atmosphere grew excited, frantic. The herd swam restlessly faster, but still in formation. As they passed us, the expression of fright in their eyes was almost human."

strengthening of courage thereby. (Webster's tragedies give some sense of this.) But the progress towards the shore is inexorable; the open space contracts; the meshes stifle the struggles; and with a final motion the fish are flung upon the beach, great and small together.

As to the analogy of the trammel, the workings of destiny are more crude, the current and the instinct to stem it or to follow it, are more compulsive, the self-enmeshing more dramatically the outcome of the struggle to escape.

There is often in tragedy just this sense of the symmetrical tightening of the plot-ropes, the narrowing of the circle in the final stages of the play. Oedipus for long preserves the illusion of freedom, and builds up the continuous irony of the play by his ignorance of the outcome. Macbeth is aware of the narrowing circle, and uses images of a familiar kind to express his own fierce despair:

> . . . I am in blood
> Stepp'd in so far, that, should I wade no more,
> Returning were as tedious as go o'er.[4]

and

> I am tied to a stake; I cannot fly,
> But, bear-like, I must fight the course.[5]

There are, of course, degrees in this illusion of freedom, in the possibility of escape. And the tensions often appear to be distributed among the victims themselves:

> Will you, I pray, demand that demi-devil
> Why he hath thus ensnar'd my soul and body?[6]

II. We can carry some of the images of the net a stage further if we imagine the tragic structure as composed of a series of concentric yielding circles, which gradually diminish in size. For the outer ring we may postulate the First Cause, under whatever name it may be recognized: imperceptible, stable, within the awareness of the spectators and the protagonists; the presence that is felt, for example, throughout the *Iliad,* the object of prayers or imprecations in *King Lear.* Within it there is the ring of Present Action, shifting and changing in its points of pressure, yet linked to a ring immediately outside it, between it and the First Cause, which is the Determining Past. (Perhaps the gods in Homer, themselves symbolizing man's dilemma, lie between the two

[4] III. iv, 136.
[5] v. vii, 1.
[6] *Oth.*, v. ii, 299.

rings; and there also Irony has its first growth.) It is, obviously, in close sympathy with the ring of the First Cause; the connection is a matter for philosophical speculation. Within the third circle, yielding perpetually to their struggles, yet doubly constricted by the two outer circles, the protagonists of the tragedy may be thought to move. Their circle is flexible, giving the illusion of control over the present action and even providing glimpses, through the mesh-wall of the Past, that enable the protagonists to speculate, intuitively or by analogy, on the nature of the First Cause.

The conformation of the circles to the movements and pressure may be seen at their simplest in Greek Drama. The First Cause is not subject to speculation; we do not know why Thyestes was doomed to eat of his children's flesh, or even why the curse should have lighted on the House of Atreus. The Determining Past is stayed and bolted to it; Iphigenia has died at Aulis, and Clytemnestra nurses her wrongs. Within the next ring, Agamemnon is free to refuse to walk on the purple carpet, to commit *hubris;* yet the illusion has only a pathetic value, for Cassandra is prophesying that he must be slain in the Palace. Out of the past the Messenger comes to rob Oedipus of his last hope; and indeed the Messenger is often both the remembrancer of the Past and the architect of the present. In *A Doll's House* the Past is pushed forward intermittently, until the pattern that it is forming becomes clear to the protagonists who might once have altered that past, for Nora Helmer might have left her husband; and this pattern from the past is horribly projected into, and beyond, the Present, even the Present of the final scene. In *Ghosts* the home on Captain Alving's Foundation belongs to the future as much as the champagne and the incestuous kiss belong to the past. Once the final ring has narrowed on the protagonists and crushed them, it expands again and becomes in its turn part of the Determining Past; perhaps to repeat its pattern of nemesis, as in Shakespeare's history plays, upon a fresh shoal of characters round whom the net has again been shot.

III. There are several methods of emphasizing the linkage between past and present. The Greek Chorus has among many functions that of conveying the sense of past momentum, and an artificial helplessness dissociated from the spectators. They are in one sense the guardians of the past, mediating, interpreting it, moralizing upon it, but never developing it into an authoritative pattern that may affect the present. The symbol, confirmed and sanctioned by the past, achieves a growing validity from that fact; and the revelation of its progression is a powerful emotional agent as we view the closing of the net. The pattern may be conveyed, as in Shakespeare's Historical Plays, by a recurrent sense of the nemesis of Kingship, of a repeating intermittent perception of crime and punishment against a patient background which reflects, almost casually, and in minute particulars, the politics of the great. It seems likely that the *sententiae*, and the proverbial lore of Elizabethan drama, served to establish a similar continuity.

A more subtle linkage takes place when the title and framework of a myth is projected into the present, as in Anouilh's *Eurydice*, or O'Neill's *Mourning Becomes Elektra*. The intellectual appeal of "recognition," whether of similarities or of differences in relation to the source-play, is an obvious appeal; yet it is probable that the fable is strongly re-inforced in its re-creation, not only by the scholar's recollection of the earlier pattern, but by the validity attaching to the archetypal qualities of the original formulation. Even more complex patterns are formed by the counterpointing of a Biblical narrative against a classical or modern setting. The "reversed" passage from Ezekiel in O'Casey's *The Silver Tassie* is a case in point, crude but dramatically effective:

> And the hand of the Lord was upon me, and carried me out in the spirit of Lord, and set me down in the midst of a valley.
>
> And I looked, and saw a great multitude that stood upon their feet, an exceeding great army.
>
> And he said unto me, Son of man, can this exceeding great army become a valley of dry bones? . . .
>
> And I answered and said, O Lord God, thou knowest. And he said, prophesy and say unto the wind, come from the four winds a breath and breathe upon these living that they may die . . .
>
> And I prophesied, and the breath came out of them, and the sinews came away from them, and behold a shaking, and their bones fell asunder, bone from his bone, and they died, and the exceeding great army became a valley of dry bones.

IV. In the seine-net image we can communicate the sense of an inexorable external pressure in the progress of tragedy; the progressive constriction of the individual's power of choice; the symmetrical narrowing of the horseshoe; the illusion of liberty in the meshes, or above the cork-line; the final catastrophic hauling of the purse to land. It is applicable to those forms in which there is a strong deterministic aspect.

The image of the trammel is more valid for the self-wrought tragic situation. Fish progress with or against the current,[7] athwart the line of the net. They push forward towards a particular objective. The first obstacle is soft, yielding: they thrust against it, and in so doing push the sagging net through the large heavy meshes of the centre net. Once in the purse which they themselves have formed, the smaller meshes close about them. The further they thrust forward the more secure the trap becomes. They hang in the purse, perhaps to drown in the current, perhaps precariously alive, till the net is hauled and re-set. The responsibility of the presence of the net belongs to the life above the surface of the water. The thrust into the trap is (whatever instinct may drive him forward) the responsibility of the individual fish. So it is, perhaps, in the tragedy born of self-will, or of the sexual instinct, or of the will to power. The victims do not always question what power has set the net across the flood.

It will be seen that in developing this image I have implicitly rejected the proposition that the entire responsibility for tragedy rests upon the protagonists. To Hegel's proposition that "the dramatic character plucks for himself the fruit of his own deeds" I assent, but in a strictly limited sense. The dramatic character, it seems to me, has a limited amount of free-will. For the sake of dramatic consistency he possesses the potency to follow Course A or Course B. He chooses B, either through his *hamartia,* or because of his *hubris,* or both. But, from the spectator's point of view, the action is in a sense predetermined. The plot or net is secured to the Past, and to the principle of evil, that, when once it is loosed, is self-generative. The ending (given the genre) is inevitable, if the mechanics of the net stand the strain of the hauling. If a rent is made deliberately (as perhaps in *Measure for Measure*) or if its shape is changed (as in *The Winter's Tale*) it ceases to function. But to attribute free-will to characters within the given structure as ordered by the dramatist appears to me inconsistent, and to demand presuppositions as to the rationality of character which causes us, too often, to lose sight of the compulsive nature of the pattern, and to lose ourselves in the subtleties of motivation. Yet Fate must not be wholly malignant, and the weakness of *Romeo and Juliet,* as of Hardy's *Weltanschauung,* is that complete malignity makes tragedy without meaning. Man's struggle with himself and with circumstances must have its own virtue; whether in the hope that the net may one day be broken, or in the good that accrues through suffering. The malignant fate may arouse pity and fear; it denies all possibility of

[7] Cf. Cousteau, p. 298, *ante*.

purgation,[8] though it may rid the writer of some "imposthume in his brain." It is here that the net image, which I have used in order to suggest a particular aspect of the tragic response, ceases to be useful. To cry out, with Job, against the compassing of God's net, is human and necessary to convey that agony of apparent entanglement. But the meshes are slashed across in death, and its resolution; and there is sometimes a strange feeling that the victims are returned to reabsorbtion in a new life in the sea.

The Spring and the Trigger

> The spring is wound up tight. It will uncoil of itself. That is what is so convenient in tragedy. The least little turn of the wrist will do the job. Anything will set it going; a glance at a girl who happens to be lifting her arms to her hair as you go by; a feeling when you wake up on a fine morning that you'd like a little respect paid to you today, as if it were as easy to order as a second cup of coffee; one question too many, idly thrown out over a friendly drink—and the tragedy is on.
>
> ANOUILH [9]

> Ce n'est pas par des crimes qu'un peuple se met en situation fausse avec son destin, mais par des fautes. Son armée est forte, son caisse abondante, ses poètes en plein fonctionnement. Mais un jour, on ne sait pourquoi, du fait que ses citoyens coupent méchamment les arbres, que son prince enlève vilainement une femme, que ses enfants adoptent une mauvaise turbulence, il est perdu. Les nations, comme les hommes, meurent d'imperceptibles impolitesses.
>
> GIRAUDOUX [10]

I. We may perceive in both these statements by French dramatists a certain cynicism as to the releasing of the tragic force; yet they express accurately what many critics have felt, and tried to rationalize, in their theory of tragedy. From another point of view, their complaint is an expression of the moral discrepancy felt between the first or second causes of a tragedy and the outcome. If they are indeed right, the *hamartia* is reduced purely to an error of judgement, but an error which

[8] That Hardy obtained a characteristic purgation from his own pessimism is clear. "He is now—this afternoon—writing a poem with great spirit; always a sign of well-being with him. Needless to say it is an intensely dismal poem." (Mrs. Hardy to Sir Sydney Cockerell: quoted J. G. Southworth.)

[9] *Antigone,* p. 34.

[10] *La Guerre de Troie n'aura pas lieu,* p. 188.

possesses an appalling element of the irrational or the capricious both in its inception and its fulfilment. It is therefore necessary to examine the apparent motivations in the tragic action.

It is, I think, true to say that the majority of writers have found the mainspring of tragedy to lie in the Will. Schopenhauer, deriving from Kant and followed by Brunetière, gives us a typical statement of his destructive pessimism:[11]

> It is the Will which constitutes the fundamental reality of the Ego. The Will as a thing in itself constitutes the mind, true and indestructible essence of the will . . . The Will to live is the substance and nucleus of all reality. But it has neither consciousness nor knowledge; it is a blind dynamic urge. The Will is irrational. It acts at random.

This immediately raises the question of the whole moral consciousness in relation to tragedy. If this force is a blind dynamic urge (as we may sometimes feel in the plays of Marlowe or Webster) the tragic feeling will break down unless we can counterweight it with some moral principle. If we split this "urge" into its possible components, we are in a position to consider Nietzsche's account, perhaps the most original and influential analysis of the tragic energy. We must first consider his use of the words *Apollonian* and *Dionysian:*

> The word "Apollonian" stands for that state of rapt repose in the presence of a visionary world, in the presence of a world of *beautiful appearance* designed as a deliverance from *becoming;* the Dionysos, on the other hand, stands for strenuous becoming, grown self-conscious, in the form of the rampant voluptuousness of the creator, who is also perfectly conscious of the violent anger of the destroyer. . . .[12]
>
> The antagonism of these two attitudes, and the *desires* that underlie them. The first would have the vision it conjures up *eternal;* in its light man must be quiescent, apathetic, peaceful, healed, and on friendly terms with himself and all existence; the second strives after creation, after the voluptuousness of wilful creation, i.e. constructing and destroying. Creation felt and explained as an instinct would be merely the unremitting inventive action of a dissatisfied being, overflowing with wealth and living at high tension and high pressure—of a God who would overcome the sorrows of existence by means only of continual changes and transformations,—appearance as a transient and

[11] Any evaluation of Schopenhauer's views would, I think, start with a detailed consideration of his life; and would need to explain his idea of beatitude through negation.

[12] *The Birth of Tragedy,* p. xxv.

momentary deliverance; the world as an apparent sequence of godlike visions and deliverances.[13]

Beneath this curious language we can discern Nietzsche's psychological dualism. Dionysian man is the creator and destroyer, the sinner. He must, in the fashion of Marlowe's Faustus, challenge the gods: he commits sin that good may eventually come. Nietzsche contrasts the Promethean myth with that of the Fall; the first is the heritage of the Aryan, the second of the Semitic.[14] The Promethean action affords a typical illustration of the *pecca fortiter* theme. Fire is of transcendent value to man: but it is given by the gods only as lightning or as the sun, and neither can be under man's control. Therefore Prometheus robbed the gods, and had to suffer; but his sin is active and dignified as compared with the feminine sin of the Fall. Hence "the necessity for crime imposed upon the Titanically-striving individual" and

> this Titanic impulse, to become as it were the Atlas of all individuals, and to carry them on broad shoulders, higher and higher, farther and farther, is what the Promethean and the Dionysian have in common.[15]

And the final end is

> . . . *the mystery doctrine of tragedy:* the fundamental knowledge of the oneness of all existing things, the consideration of individuation as the primal cause of evil, and art as the joyous hope that the spell of individuation may be broken, as the augury of a restored oneness.[16]

But in this world, with its strange blend of superhuman energy with reflective mysticism, pain is perceived as a condition of knowledge. (We should remember that *The Birth of Tragedy* was originally entitled *The Birth of Tragedy out of the Spirit of Music.*)

> The formless and intangible reflection of the primordial pain in music, with its redemption in appearance, thus generates a second mirroring as a concrete symbol or example.[17]

And again:

> Indeed he [the Apollonian Greek] had to recognize . . . that his entire existence, with all its beauty and moderation, rested on a hidden

[13] *Ibid.*, p. xxvi.
[14] *Ibid.*, p. 78.
[15] *Ibid.*, p. 80.
[16] *Ibid.*, p. 83.
[17] *Ibid.*, p. 45.

> substratum of suffering and knowledge, which was again disclosed to him by the Dionysian.[18]

So Nietzsche takes Raphael's *Transfiguration* to illustrate the upper Apollonian world of beauty, with its substratum, the "terrible wisdom" of Silenus. In his desire to give further application to the Prometheus-image, he turns to Oedipus:

> because of his excessive wisdom, which solved the riddle of the Sphinx, Oedipus had to plunge into a bewildering vortex of monstrous crimes: thus did the Delphic god interpret the Grecian past.[19]

Such a position is of course quite untenable; Oedipus' sequence of crimes is not intrinsically connected with his wisdom. It seems that we must look elsewhere for our explanation of the trigger, if not of the spring.

II. As usual, we must return to Aristotle. The Fall takes place: through some error or frailty. The wholly sinless hero appears impossible, unless we set up a counter-puppet by dividing the ethical substance. We are left with the following logical possibilities.

1. We may use Anouilh's image, and assume that there is in the universe this coiled-spring tension, ready at any moment to release its destructive-tragic forces, regardless of the kind or quality of the force that touches the trigger to release the detaining sear. (A development of the image into weapon-detail is, for the moment, useful.) The explosion thus has a completely irresponsible character: and we are compelled to suppose a complete though momentarily static tension as a normal condition of events. We are not, however, given any explanation of how the state of tension has arisen; it is apparently implicit in the nature of the universe. And so we are in a room full of hidden wires connected to booby-traps set by jealously-watching gods, a room in which we must go about our daily business, moving most delicately and invoking the element of luck. But the threat remains. Both explanations, the arbitrary spring and the capricious trigger, seem to me unsatisfactory.

2. Alternatively, we may reverse the hypothesis, and consider Giraudoux's thesis that nations "meurent d'imperceptibles impolitesses." In such a case catastrophe might arise from cumulative inattention to what Chapman called "ceremony." Life is seen as ordered, "pious," disciplined; unceremonious clumsiness may shatter it. One aspect of such a

[18] *Ibid.*, p. 41.
[19] *Ibid.*, p. 40.

state of mind will be the sin of levity, which Tillyard finds at the centre of Eve's sin in *Paradise Lost.* Any lapse from grace will be cumulative, produce a condition in which the cup will suddenly brim over from an apparently trivial addition. A civilization, when it reaches a certain state of deterioration, is ready to be precipitated into tragedy. Something is rotten in Denmark, or in the world of Coriolanus, or in mid-nineteenth-century Norway, or in the Ireland of O'Casey.

This hypothesis is in some ways attractive; but it results inevitably in a drastic reduction of the "seriousness" of tragedy, and blurs the tragic issues. Yet both quotations, Anouilh's and Giraudoux's, have this in common: we *feel* that the tragic action releases a powerful force of sheer evil: that this force has been in a preparatory state of extreme tension: that the initiating action, the trigger, is often unrelated in its seriousness to the force released; and that the pressure upon it may be trivial or capricious. In considering this situation we are touching the problem of evil from another aspect, though we are not concerned with any final evaluation of cause and effect. It is probably best to examine certain tragic openings to see whether any light is thrown on the problem.

Romeo and Juliet affords a simple instance. The tension in the spring is the hatred between the houses of Capulet and Montague; demonstrated at a low level in the opening scene, and on various planes afterwards. The trigger releasing it is Romeo's sudden and seemingly arbitrary infatuation for Juliet. Thereafter the spring expands, as it were, in jerks. In *Macbeth,* as in *Lear,* a series of new political adjustments are taking place. Whether the Witches embody Macbeth's thoughts of ambition, which are suddenly half-confirmed by events, or whether the action of Lear presupposes a cumulative hatred on the part of Goneril and Regan such as Gordon Bottomley imagined, there appears to be enough *potential* disruption in the mere political setting. In Ibsen, and perhaps in Chekhov and Strindberg, we sometimes appear to have two springs, one within the other; a general setting of corruption or ineffectiveness that is not specifically limited to the characters of the play, and a more immediate and personal tension created by the past actions of the characters themselves. It is this inner spring which uncoils, but its action is governed and reinforced by the outer one; and it would appear that the trigger-force is part of a larger decisive pattern rather than an arbitrary or casual action such as Anouilh describes. There is a sense of ripeness, of a saturation point in the cloud of nemesis.

It appears that in general the "trigger" shows a principle in common with that of accident in dramatic structure. Both are legitimate devices, in so far as the apparent arbitrariness of either factor may be considered as tightening or accelerating, or precipitating at a given moment, a train of circumstances which would, without such intervening, have occurred *sooner or later,* but which occur when they do because of the characteristics of the dramatic structure. Within the general circle of causation, the preliminary tension, its capacity for releasing evil or destruction, may be thought to build up, by the mere act of delay, an increasing explosive quality. This impression is given very strongly in the work of Chekhov, whose world of *accidie* and listless romantic despair is shown, by his use of the past in the present, to have accumulated steadily over a long period.

III. It seems that we can best meet the known conditions by the following hypotheses:

1. A general moral Law, on whose component parts we can speculate in detail but whose total operation and pattern is *ex hypothesi* unknowable, orders and controls events.
2. The outcome of that Law, its system of rewards and punishments, *as we understand them,* is also unknown and unknowable.
3. Within its system, and on a lower level than that system, man's will is free to operate on its proper levels, and in obedience to his known ethic.
4. But is therein subject to the Pauline paradox

> "For the good that I would, that I do not: but the evil which I would not, that I do." [20]

5. The *reasons* for the operation of this law may arise from any of the following features, or from any combination of them:
   (*a*) The influence of past evil upon the active present; the quantitative and qualitative connection between the two being unknowable; since the higher system, which operates less unclearly in the past than in the present, is (at best) perceived intermittently: through processes which we can describe in terms of faith, or of mysticism, or of the poetic statement.
   (*b*) the individual will to evil, or to what, in a given sociological context, is perceived as evil.

[20] Rom. vii, 19.

(*c*) the accumulation of past evil set into activity by a breakdown of the ceremonial order of society, and thus generating a favourable condition for a catastrophic cycle.

It will be seen that this position involves the rejection of the Hegelian division of the ethical substance in favour of a relativist doctrine of evil; that is, evil perceived as operative against both a fixed body of ethic, *and* as against a contemporary or local situation which might modify such an ethic.[21]

[21] A number of anthropological examples will occur to the reader.

Tragedy and the "Medium": A Note on Mr Santayana's "Tragic Philosophy"

F. R. LEAVIS

There appeared in *Scrutiny* some years ago (March 1936) an essay by Mr Santayana, *Tragic Philosophy,* in which I have always found valuable stimulus to disagreement. To say "always" is to suggest that I have re-read it a good deal, and I have. In fact, I am indebted to the essay for its use as a stock resort in the discussion of Tragedy with undergraduates reading for the English Tripos. I don't want to suggest that the debt incurred has been purely a matter of opportunities for disagreement. *Tragic Philosophy* exhibits Mr Santayana's characteristic brilliance and wit—that rare wit (not rare in Mr Santayana, of course) which is the focussed sharpness of illuminating intelligence. But it has striking weaknesses (or so I see them), and it is the considerations raised by one of them in particular that I am concerned with here. They are considerations that take me back to a point I made in discussing Johnson's criticism.

Many admirers of Mr Santayana besides myself must have been surprised at the way in which he plays off Macbeth's speech beginning *To-morrow and to-morrow and to-morrow* against the passage attributed by Dante to Piccarda de Donati in which occurs the line

> E'n la sua volontade è nostra pace.

True, earlier in the essay he has said that Shakespeare "like an honest miscellaneous dramatist . . . was putting into the mouths of his different characters the sentiments that, for the moment, were suggested to him by their predicaments." But he unmistakably slips into arguing as if Macbeth's comment on the plight to which the action has brought him may be taken as Shakespeare's, just as Piccarda may be taken as speaking for Dante. Mr Santayana's point, I recognize, is that Shake-

From *The Common Pursuit,* London, 1952, pp. 121-35. Reprinted by permission of Chatto and Windus, Ltd.

speare hasn't a settled and coherent philosophy to set against Dante's—though "possibly if he had been pressed by some troublesome friend to propound a personal philosophy, he might have found in his irritation nothing else to fall back upon than the animal despair of Macbeth. Fortunately we may presume that burgherly comfort and official orthodoxy saved him from being unreasonably pressed." But we are at the same time invited, unambiguously, to take Macbeth's speech as representing such substitute for a philosophy as Shakespeare, in this play, has to offer:

> I questioned at the beginning whether the poetic value of unlike things could be pronounced equal: and if now I compare this whole passage with the passage from *Macbeth* I find that to my sense they are incommensurable. Both are notable passages, if that is all that was meant; but they belong to different poetic worlds, appealing to and developing different sides of the mind. And there is more than disparity between these two worlds; there is contrariety and hostility between them, in as much as each professes to include and to subordinate the other, and in so doing to annul its tragic dignity and moral finality. For the mood of Macbeth, religion and philosophy are insane vapours; for the mood of Dante, Macbeth is possessed by the devil. There is no possible common ground, no common criterion even of taste or beauty.

For the mood of Shakespeare too, we are moved to retort, Macbeth is possessed by the devil: the tragic dignity and moral finality of Shakespeare's world are focussed in Macbeth's cry of "animal despair" only in so far as this refers us, inevitably (one would have thought), to the quite other effect of the total action—the total action in relation to which the speech has its significance. By his plunge into crime, taken in fatal ignorance of his nature—

> If it were done, when 'tis done, then 'twere well
> It were done quickly

—he has confounded "this little state of man" and the impersonal order from which it is inseparable. It is not on his extinction after a tale of sound and fury, signifying nothing, that the play ends, and his valedictory nihilism is the vindication of the moral and spiritual order he has outraged, and which is re-established in the close.

How, one asks, can Mr Santayana have failed to see things so obvious? The answer follows immediately on the sentence of his last quoted;

> We might at best say that both poets succeed in conveying what they wish to convey, and that in that sense their skill is equal: but I

> hardly think this is true in fact, because in Shakespeare the medium is rich and thick and more important than the idea; whereas in Dante the medium is as unvarying and simple as possible, and meant to be transparent. Even in this choice passage, there are stretches of pure scholastic reasoning, not poetical at all to our sensuous and romantic apprehension; yet the studious and rapt poet feels himself carried on those wings of logic into a paradise of truth, where choir answers choir, and everything is beautiful. A clear and transparent medium is admirable, when we love what we have to say; but when what we have to say is nothing previously definite, expressiveness depends on stirring the waters deeply, suggesting a thousand half-thoughts and letting the very unutterableness of our passion become manifest in our disjointed words. The medium then becomes dominant: but can this be called success in expression? It is rather success in making an impression, if the reader is impressed. . . .

The critic who falls so complete a victim to the word "medium" as Mr Santayana here shows himself, doesn't, it is plain, understand the poetic—and the essentially dramatic—use of language that Shakespeare's verse supremely exemplifies. He cannot, then, understand the nature of the organization that goes with that use of language: he cannot appreciate the ways in which the themes and significances of the play are dramatically presented. Take, for instance, this betraying sentence:

> So at this point in *Macbeth,* where Seneca would have unrolled the high maxims of orthodox Stoicism, Shakespeare gives us the humours of his distracted hero; a hero nonplussed, confounded, stultified in his own eyes, a dying gladiator; a blinded lion at bay.

We don't, when we are responding properly, say that "Shakespeare gives us Macbeth's speech": it comes to us, not from the author, but from the play, emerging dramatically from a dramatic context. It offers no parallel to Seneca's "high maxims." And the "philosophy," moral significance, or total upshot, of the play isn't stated but enacted. But for Mr Santayana significance is a matter of "ideas," and "ideas" have to be stated, and so, looking for an epitomizing statement, he excises that speech from the organism to which it belongs and fixes it directly on Shakespeare, and gives us his surprising commentary.

We have only shifted the question a stage further back, of course. How can so subtle an intelligence as Mr Santayana's have let itself be so victimized? The answer, I think, is that he is a philosopher. This is not to suggest that a philosopher can, for his own purposes, safely dispense with the ability to comprehend Shakespearean poetry. On the contrary, Mr Santayana's inappreciation seems to me to go with a naïveté about the nature of conceptual thought that is common among philosophers, to their disadvantage as such. In venturing so far I may be merely exposing myself; but this, I am sure, must be said: to demand that poetry should be a "medium" for "previously definite" ideas is arbitrary, and betrays a radical incomprehension. What Mr Santayana calls "Shakespeare's medium" creates what it conveys; "previously definite" ideas put into a "clear and transparent" medium wouldn't have been definite enough for Shakespeare's purpose. It is in place to quote again here a passage of D. W. Harding on Isaac Rosenberg:

> Usually when we speak of finding words to express a thought we seem to mean that we have the thought rather close to formulation and use it to measure the adequacy of any possible phrasing that occurs to us, treating words as servants of the idea. "Clothing a thought in language," whatever it means psychologically, seems a fair metaphorical description of most speaking and writing. Of Rosenberg's work it would be misleading. He—like many poets in some degree, one supposes—brought language to bear on the incipient thought at an earlier stage of its development. Instead of the emerging idea being racked slightly so as to fit a more familiar approximation of itself, and words found for *that*, Rosenberg let it manipulate words almost from the beginning, often without insisting on the controls of logic and intelligibility.

The control over Shakespeare's words in *Macbeth* (for what Harding describes is the essentially poetic use of language, a use in which Shakespeare is pre-eminent) is a complex dramatic theme vividly and profoundly realized—not thought of, but possessed imaginatively in its concreteness, so that, as it grows in specificity, it in turn possesses the poet's mind and commands expression. To explain how so marvellous a definiteness of conception and presentment can have been missed by Mr Santayana one has to invoke a training in inappropriate linguistic habits—inappropriate, that is, to the reading of Shakespeare: unable to relinquish irrelevant demands, the critic cannot take what is offered; misinformed and blinded by preconceptions, he cannot see what is there.

The case, readers will have noted, has much in common with Johnson's. Mr Santayana too has a way of paradoxically appreciating, while exhibiting his inability to appreciate, like that I have pointed to in Johnson's dealings with Shakespeare:

> But as living poetry, as a mould and stimulus for honest feeling, is Dante for us at all comparable to Shakespeare? Shakespeare, in passages such as this from *Macbeth,* is orchestrated. He trills away into fancy: what was daylight a moment ago, suddenly becomes a candle: we are not thinking or reasoning, we are dreaming. He needs but to say "all our yesterdays," and presently the tedium of childhood, the tedium of labour and illness, the vacancy of friendships lost, rise like ghosts before us, and fill us with a sense of the unreality of all that once seemed most real. When he mentions "a poor player" we think at once of the poet himself, because our minds are biographical and our sympathies novelesque; we feel the misery and the lurid contrasts of a comedian's life; and the existence that just now seemed merely vain now seems also tempestuous and bitter.

Can we say that the author of this cannot understand the Shakespearean use of language, and cannot therefore appreciate the nature and force of the Shakespearean "medium"? What we have here implies, surely, a pretty good analysis of the speech? But Mr Santayana goes on:

> And the rhythms help; the verse struts and bangs, holds our attention suspended, obliges our thoughts to become rhetorical, and brings our declamation round handsomely to a grand finale. We should hardly have found courage in ourselves for so much passion and theatricality; but we bless Shakespeare for enabling us still to indulge in such emotions, and to relieve ourselves of a weight that we hardly knew we were carrying.

These sentences are perhaps not so unequivocal as Johnson's pejorative remarks, but it is nevertheless impossible not to take them as cancelling the appreciation. We relate them to these earlier sentences, and their significant failure to distinguish between irresponsible exuberance and the mature Shakespearean mastery of language:

> Shakespeare was a professional actor, a professional dramatist; his greatness lay there, and in the gift of the gab: in that exuberance and joy in language which everybody had in that age, but he supremely. The Renaissance needed no mastering living religion, no mastering living philosophy. Life was gayer without them.

The implications are plain enough. It would clearly be misleading to say that the critic who can express himself thus can properly appreciate Shakespeare's poetry. He clearly cannot appreciate the organization that has its local life in the verse. He has no inkling of the way in which the mastering living theme commands and controls the words.

It will have been noted that in the former of the two passages just quoted Mr Santayana gives us an account of tragic catharsis. It is peculiarly interesting because in it he associates the cathartic effect with a poetic use (as he understands it) of language. We are bound to question his understanding, and in attempting to provide our own account of a poetic use we find ourselves exploring for a profounder and more satisfactory account of Tragedy—of the tragic—than he implies here, or offers elsewhere in his essay. This at any rate is what, in my experience, gives the essay its peculiar value.

The view of the tragic implied in Mr Santayana's account of catharsis seems a very limited one. Does Shakespearean tragedy, does the tragic in *Macbeth,* amount to no more than this? If so, where can we look for anything profounder? For surely the tragic experience is, or can be, a more important and serious matter than Mr Santayana here suggests?

To postulate a "tragic experience" or "tragic effect" and then seek to define it is to lay oneself open to the suspicion of proposing a solemn and time-honoured academic game. Yet the critical contemplation of the profoundest things in literature does lead to the idea of such an experience, and we can see to it that the attempt at definition shall not be the kind of futility we associate with the Grand Style or the Sublime and the Beautiful. It need hardly be said, for instance, that what we are concerned with will not be found in all tragedies, or in most. And next, it is well to put aside the term "catharsis": its promptings don't seem to be at all helpful, and the exercise of refining upon, or interpreting away, Aristotle's medical metaphor may be left to the unfortunate student who knows that he may be required to "apply" the *Poetics* to Shakespeare, Webster, Racine, Ibsen or Eugene O'Neill in the examination-room. If "calm" may properly be predicated of the tragic experience, it is certainly not "calm of mind, all passion spent" in the natural suggestion of that phrase. According to what seems valid in the current notion of the tragic there is rather something in the nature of an exalting effect. We have contemplated a painful action, involving death and the destruction of the good, admirable and sympathetic, and yet instead of being depressed we enjoy a sense of enhanced vitality.

I take this general account as granted—as recognized for sound as far as it goes. The conditions of something ostensibly answering to it are described by Mr Santayana in his account of the Senecan tragic attitude or philosophy:

> Mr Eliot says that this philosophy is derived from Seneca; and it is certain that in Seneca's tragedies, if not in his treatises, there is a pomp

> of diction, a violence of pose, and a suicidal despair not unlike the tone of this passage. But would Seneca ever have said that life signifies nothing? It signified for him the universal reign of law, of reason, of the will of God. Fate was inhuman, it was cruel, it excited and crushed every finite wish; yet there was something in man that shared that disdain for humanity, and triumphed in that ruthless march of order and necessity. Something superior, not inferior, Seneca would have said; something that not only raised the mind into sympathy with the truth of nature and the decrees of heaven, but that taught the blackest tragedy to sing in verse. The passions in foreseeing their defeat became prophets, in remembering it became poets, and they created the noblest beauties by defying and transcending death.

Mr Santayana seems to imply (he says nothing crude, of course, and he shows considerable suppleness in presenting his case) that Seneca has an advantage over Shakespeare in this tragic philosophy, however the total comparison between the two poets may work out. Without granting this, we may at any rate feel that the formula for the tragic it represents, in Mr Santayana's account of it, deserves pondering. It deserves pondering because, though clearly unsatisfactory, it has (we feel) something of the right form.

It is most clearly unsatisfactory because, in the terms in which it stands, it is equivocal. In spite of the "something superior, not inferior," it reminds us too much of "the bitter beauty of the universe and the frail human pride that confronts it for a moment undismayed." It is, in fact, not clearly enough distinguishable from *A Free Man's Worship:*

> Brief and powerless is Man's life; on him and all his race the slow, sure doom falls pitiless and dark. Blind to good and evil, reckless of destruction, omnipotent matter rolls on its relentless way; for Man, condemned to-day to lose his dearest, to-morrow himself to pass through the gate of darkness, it remains only to cherish, ere yet the blow falls, the lofty thoughts that ennoble his little day; disdaining the coward terrors of the slave of Fate, to worship at the shrine that his own hands have built; undismayed by the empire of chance, to preserve a mind free from the wanton tyranny that rules his outward life; proudly defiant of the irresistible forces that tolerate, for a moment, his knowledge and his condemnation, to sustain alone, a weary but unyielding Atlas, the world that his own ideals have fashioned despite the trampling march of unconscious power.[1]

The tragic experience, however it is to be defined, is certainly not anything that encourages, or permits, an indulgence in the dramatiza-

[1] Bertrand Russell, *Mysticism and Logic,* p. 56.

tion of one's nobly-suffering self. Mr Santayana's Seneca, of course, doesn't propose anything as crude. Nevertheless, as we ponder the "*disdain* for humanity" and the "*defying* . . . death," it strikes us that the Senecan attitude as described is perilously ready to subside into something of a kindred order to the prose of *A Free Man's Worship:* the differences aren't radical enough. We recall Mr Eliot's observations (in *Shakespeare and the Stoicism of Seneca*) on the Senecan influence in Elizabethan drama, and its relation to the trick of rhetorical self-boosting.

And whether Mr Eliot is right or not in associating Othello's self-dramatizing habit with the Senecan influence, he gives us the cue for saying that the attitude represented by Othello's last speech is radically untragic. This is so obvious as to seem, perhaps, not worth saying: Othello, for those who don't join in the traditional sentimentalization of the play, is a very obvious case. The essential point that has to be made is that his valedictory *coup de théâtre* represents a rhetorical inflation, a headily emotional glorification, of an incapacity for tragic experience that marks the ordinary moments of us all.

There is a passage of one of D. H. Lawrence's letters[2] that came into my mind when this point was under discussion:

> I am so sick of people: they preserve an evil, bad, separating spirit under the warm cloak of good words. That is intolerable in them. The Conservative talks about the old and glorious national ideal, the Liberal talks about this great struggle for right in which the nation is engaged, the peaceful women talk about disarmament and international peace. Bertie Russell talks about democratic control and the educating of the artisan, and all this, all this goodness, is just a warm and cosy cloak for a bad spirit. They all want the same thing: a continuing in this state of disintegration wherein each separate little ego is an independent little principality by itself. What does Russell really want? He wants to keep his own established ego, his finite and ready-defined self intact, free from contact and connection. He wants to be ultimately a free agent. That is what they all want, ultimately—that is what is at the back of all international peace-for-ever and democratic control talks: they want an outward system of nullity, which they call peace and goodwill, so that in their own souls they can be independent little gods, referred nowhere and to nothing, little mortal Absolutes, secure from question. That is at the back of all Liberalism, Fabianism and democracy. It stinks. It is the will of the louse. And the Conservative either wants to bully or to be bullied. And the young authoritarian, the young man who turns Roman Catholic in order to put himself under the

[2] *Letters,* p. 247.

> authority of the Church, in order to enjoy the aesthetic quality of obedience, he is such a swine with cringing hind-quarters . . . etc.

The particular justice or injustice of these animadversions needn't be discussed: one wouldn't go to Lawrence for judicial fairness towards persons or parties, and there are necessary political and kindred activities at levels at which the characteristic Laurentian contribution may well appear the reverse of helpful or encouraging. But it is just his part, as he sees it, to insist—with a passionate insistence exasperating to energizers for movements and policies—that there are profounder levels; levels of experience that, though they tend constantly to be ignored, are always, in respect of any concern for life and health, supremely relevant. The most effective insistence would be tragic art. Lawrence, in fact, might fairly (for my present purpose) be said to be pronouncing of the attitudes he stigmatizes that they are incompatible with tragic experience.

At any rate, it is an essential part of the definition of the tragic that it breaks down, or undermines and supersedes, such attitudes. It establishes below them a kind of profound impersonality in which experience matters, not because it is mine—because it is to me it belongs or happens, or because it subserves or issues in purpose or will, but because it is what it is, the "mine" mattering only in so far as the individual sentience is the indispensable focus of experience.

The attainment in literature of this level, and of organization at this level, would seem to involve the poetic use of language, or of processes that amount to that. By the "poetic" use of language I mean that which I described as "dramatic" in discussing Johnson's criticism and the limits to his appreciation of Shakespeare. For Johnson, I said, expression was necessarily statement; critically, he couldn't come to terms with the use of language, not as a medium in which to put "previously definite" ideas, but for exploratory creation. Poetry as creating what it presents, and as presenting something that stands there to speak for itself, or, rather, that isn't a matter of saying, but of being and enacting, he couldn't properly understand. In this he is representative of the eighteenth century, and (the point was made in discussion) it is significant that that century, which went in so much for formal tragedy, should have shown itself so utterly incapable of attaining the tragic. The use of language for the expression of "previously definite" ideas needn't, of course, carry with its social and rational conventions as obviously limiting as the Augustan, but in proposing for the poet as his true business the lucid arangement of ready-minted concepts Mr

Santayana proposes (it seems to me) limitations as essentially disabling for tragedy as the Augustan. It may not be altogether true to say that in such a use of language—in the business of expressing "previously definite" ideas—one is necessarily confined to one's "established ego," one's "ready-defined self." But it does seem as if the "tragic" transcendence of ordinary experience that can be attained by a mind tied to such a use must inevitably tend towards the rhetorical order represented by Mr Santayana's account of Seneca's tragic philosophy (or—shall I say?—by the Senecan attitude as no doubt fairly conveyed by Mr Santayana).

Such an attitude is really an exaltation of the "established ego," and, as we have seen, cannot be securely distinguished from the kind of attitude one strikes. The attainment of the level of experience at which emancipation from the "ready-defined self" is compelled involves an essentially different order of expression; one in which heightening is deepening, exaltation has nothing alcoholic about it, and rhetoric (as in *Othello*—for those who take what Shakespeare offers) is "placed."

It is interesting to see Yeats, in his own way and by his own characteristic approach, making the point in question. He rebels, in his Aesthetically-given youth, against the flatness of the dialogue in post-Ibsenian drama (see *Essays*). Modern naturalistic speech, he feels, precludes beauty and significance. We can never, of course, feel quite safe, reading these protests in Yeatsian prose, against a suggestion of "Rosa Alchemica" and the "trembling of the veil." Nevertheless he makes the necessary points and makes them firmly. You cannot, he notes (see, *e.g.*, p. 339), be passionate in educated modern speech: Ibsen in the attempt to overcome this difficulty invented a conventional rhetoric. Poetry, with attendant non-naturalistic conventions (see the essay on *Certain Noble Plays of Japan*), is necessary in order to provide the distance and the frame without which there can be no intensity of the right kind. And then we come to this (*The Tragic Theatre*): "I saw plainly what should have been plain from the first line I had written, that tragedy must always be a drowning, a breaking of the dykes that separate man from man. . . ." Yeats's intention in this, which is immediately related to his preoccupation with convention and the "medium," has unmistakably the directest relation to what I have been trying to say above.

We might further invoke as obviously relevant Nietzsche's insistence on the Dionysiac. But perhaps after all the Nietzschean witness had better be dispensed with; at the best it introduces a disturbing vibration.

The Nietzschean context is uncongenial to the present purpose, and a glance at it prompts the remark that the tragic calm (if "calm" is the word), while not the product of any laxative catharsis, is not in the least the calm of the tensed and self-approving will.

The sense of heightened life that goes with the tragic experience is conditioned by a transcending of the ego—an escape from all attitudes of self-assertion. "Escape," perhaps, is not altogether a good word, since it might suggest something negative and irresponsible (just as "Dionysiac" carries unacceptable suggestions of the Dark Gods). Actually the experience is constructive or creative, and involves a recognizing positive value as in some way defined and vindicated by death. It is as if we were challenged at the profoundest level with the question, "In what does the significance of life reside?" and found ourselves contemplating, for answer, a view of life, and of the things giving it value, that makes the valued appear unquestionably more important than the valuer, so that significance lies, clearly and inescapably, in the willing adhesion of the individual self to something other than itself. Here, for instance, is D. A. Traversi writing[3] on *Antony and Cleopatra* (with his relative valuation of which, I had better add by the way, I don't agree):

> For death, which had seemed in the Sonnets and early tragedies to be incontrovertible evidence of the subjection of love and human values to Time, now becomes by virtue of Shakespeare's poetic achievement an instrument of release, the necessary condition of an experience which, though dependent upon Time and circumstance, is by virtue of its *value* and intensity incommensurate with them—that is "immortal." The emotions of Antony and Cleopatra are built upon "dungy earth," upon "Nilus' slime," and so upon Time which these elements by their nature imply; but, just as earth and slime are quickened into fire and air, whilst retaining their sensible qualities as constituent parts of the final experience, so Time itself becomes a necessary element in the creation of "immortality."

I quote this for its relevant suggestiveness. It seems to me to compare very interestingly with the following passage from D. W. Harding (whose distinctive strength in criticism—I add, in case I should have appeared to be betraying metaphysical ambitions—goes with a psychologist's approach):

> Death in itself was not his concern, but only death at the moment when life was simplified and intensified; this he felt had a significance which he represents by immortality. For him it was no more than the

[3] *Approach to Shakespeare,* pp. 126-27.

> immortality of the possibilities of life. This immortality and the value he glimpses in the living effort of war in no way mitigate his suffering at the human pain and waste. The value of what was destroyed seemed to him to have been brought into sight only by the destruction, and he had to respond to both facts without allowing either to neutralize the other. It is this which is most impressive in Rosenberg—the complexity of experience which he was strong enough to permit himself and which his technique was fine enough to reveal.[4]

I will not attempt to develop the kind of discussion of Tragedy that the juxtaposition of these passages might seem to promise—or threaten. It suits my purpose rather to note the stress laid by Harding on "complexity" and "technique" (compare Traversi's "poetic achievement"—a phrase that sums up much preceding analysis of Shakespeare's verse), and to note further that he passes on to "impersonality":

> To say that Rosenberg tried to understand all that the war stood for means probably that he tried to expose the whole of himself to it. In one letter he describes as an intention what he obviously achieved: "I will not leave a corner of my consciousness covered up, but saturate myself with the strange and extraordinary new conditions of this life. . . ." This willingness—and ability—to let himself be new-born into the new situation, not subduing his experience to his established personality, is a large part, if not the whole secret of the robustness which characterizes his best work. . . . Here as in all the war poems his suffering and discomfort are unusually *direct;* there is no secondary distress arising from the sense that these things *ought not* to be. He was given up to realizing fully what *was*. He expressed his attitude in *The Unicorn*:
>
> *Lilith:* I think there is more sorrow in the world
> Than man can bear.
>
> *Nubian:* None can exceed their limit, lady:
> You either bear or break.
>
> It was Rosenberg's exposure of his whole personality that gave his work its quality of impersonality.[5]

What Harding says about Rosenberg in these passages has clearly the closest relevance to Tragedy. And it is especially significant, for my theme, that they belong to the essay containing that discussion of the poetic use of language which I have found so useful in defining the limitations, in respect of the tragic, of Johnson and (I suggest) Mr Santayana.

This significance, my main concern in this note, will get a suitable

[4] *Scrutiny,* Vol. III, pp. 362-63 (*The Poetry of Isaac Rosenberg*).
[5] *Ibid.*

parting stress, if we consider I. A. Richards's treatment of "impersonality," which has, on the surface, resemblances to Harding's. Dr Richards deals with "impersonality" and Tragedy together in the same chapter (XXXII) of *The Principles of Literary Criticism*. These pages (245-253) contain some of the most valuably suggestive things in the book, and if, for my convenience, I dwell on the weakness, I have at any rate the justification that they are entailed by Richards's essential Neo-Benthamite ambition, which is irreconcilable with his best insight. (And I am urging that these pages should be read, or re-read.)

The ambition asserts itself characteristically when Richards, having told us that, in the full tragic experience, the "mind does not shy away from anything, it does not protect itself with any illusion, it stands uncomforted, unintimidated, alone and self-reliant," goes on to pronounce toughly (p. 246):

> The joy which is so strangely at the heart of the experience is not an indication that "all's right with the world" or that "somewhere, somehow, there is Justice"; it is an indication that all is right here and now in the nervous system.

For him, of course, Tragedy is the supreme instance of the inclusive organization of impulses; it is "perhaps the most general all-accepting, all-ordering experience known" (p. 247). Experience, for the purposes of the new science, must be reducible to unit impulses, so that evaluation may be quantitative. We are not, then, surprised when we read (p. 248):

> This balanced poise, stable through its power of inclusion, not through the force of its exclusions, is not peculiar to Tragedy. It is a general characteristic of all the most valuable experiences of the arts. It can be given by a carpet or a pot or by a gesture as unmistakably as by the Parthenon, it may come about through an epigram as clearly as through a Sonata.

I must confess myself to have found, with surprise, that I had carried away a wrong impression from this passage—an impression that Richards actually pronounces the tragic experience to be obtainable from a carpet or a pot. But it is easy to see how I came to form it, the argument moving as it does, with so easy and uninhibited a transition. And it is not at all easy to see how Richards can satisfactorily explain the differences between any experience fitly to be called "tragic" and the most inclusively-poised experience a carpet or a pot can be supposed to give. The scientifico-psychological ambition entails his taking his diagrams of poised and organized "impulses" or "appetencies" too seriously: he couldn't go on supposing he took his science seriously if he even began to recognize the remoteness of their relevance to concrete experiences.

This may seem, so late in the day, too obvious a kind of criticism to be worth reiterating; but I want to give it a special point in relation to my main argument. No theory of Tragedy can amount to more than a blackboard diagram, a mere schematic substitute for understanding, unless it is associated with an adequate appreciation of the subtleties of poetic (or creative) language—the subtleties that are supremely illustrated in the poetry of Shakespeare. Such an appreciation, if operative, would have inhibited Dr Richards's reliance on his "impulses" and his "nervous system." This point is not the less worth making because he has always, in his Neo-Benthamite way, been interested in language and the meaning of meaning. He has, since the phase represented by *The Principles of Literary Criticism,* specialized in Semasiology. But no interest in language that is Benthamite in spirit, or controlled by a Neo-Benthamite ambition, can afford to recognize the profoundest aspects of linguistic "communication"—those we find ourselves contemplating when we contemplate in the concrete the nature of tragic impersonality. Such an interest can no more be adequate to them than the Utilitarian calculus—with its water-tight unit self, confined, for all self-transcendence, to external transactions with other selves—could engage on the kind of interest in moral issues taken by George Eliot.

Our Country and Our Culture

LESLIE A. FIEDLER

The end of the American artist's pilgrimage to Europe is the discovery of America. That this discovery is unintended hardly matters; ever since Columbus it has been traditional to discover America by mistake. Even in the days when it was still fashionable to talk about "expatriation," the American writer was rediscovering the Michigan woods in the Pyrenees, or coming upon St. Paul in Antibes. How much more so now when the departing intellectual does not take flight under cover of a barrage of manifestoes, but is sent abroad on a Fulbright grant or is sustained by the G.I. Bill. The new American abroad finds a Europe racked by self-pity and nostalgia (except where sustained by the manufactured enthusiasms of Stalinism), and as alienated from its own traditions as Sauk City; he finds a Europe reading in its ruins *Moby Dick,* a Europe haunted by the idea of America.

The American writer soon learns that for the European intellectual, as for him, there are two Americas. The first is the America of ECA and NATO, a political lesser evil, hated with a kind of helpless fury by those who cannot afford to reject its aid; the second is the America invented by European Romanticism—the last humanistic religion of the West, a faith become strangely confused with a political fact. To the European, the literature of America is inevitably purer, *realer* than America itself. Finding it impossible to reject the reality of death, and difficult to believe in anything else, the European is perpetually astonished at the actual existence of a land where only death is denied and everything else considered possible. Overwhelmed by a conviction of human impotence, he regards with horrified admiration a people who, because they are too naive to understand theory, achieve what he can demonstrate to be theoretically impossible.

From Europe it is easy to understand the religious nature of the American belief in innocence and achievement; to see how even the

From *The Partisan Review,* May-June, 1952, pp. 294-98. Reprinted by permission of the author.

most vulgar products of "mass culture," movies, comic books, sub-literary novels are the scriptures of this post-Christian faith—a faith that has already built up in Western Europe a sizeable underground sect which worships in the catacombs of the movie theaters and bows before the images of its saints on the news-stands. A hundred years after the *Manifesto,* the specter that is haunting Europe is—Gary Cooper! Vulgar, gross, sentimental, impoverished in style—our popular sub-art presents a dream of human possibilities to starved imaginations everywhere. It is a wry joke that what for us are the most embarrassing by-products of a democratic culture, are in countries like Italy the only democracy there is.

It seems to me that it has become absurd to ask whether a democratic society is worthwhile if it entails a vulgarization and leveling of taste. Such a leveling the whole world is bound to endure, with or without political guarantees of freedom; and the serious writer must envision his own work in such a context, realize that his own final meanings will arise out of a dialectical interplay between what he makes and a given world of "mass culture." Even the Stalinists, though they thunder against American jazz and cowboy suits for children, can in the end only kidnap our vulgar mythology for their own purposes. The sense of an immortality here and now, so important to American culture and parodies in Forest Lawn Cemetery, finds its Soviet counterpart in the mummification of Lenin or the touting of Bogomolets; while our faith in progress and achievement finds an *ersatz* in the Five Year Plans and the statistics doctored to assist belief. In its Russian form, what is possible in America has become compulsory, an unofficial rite has been made an orthodoxy. And even in our own country there have been occasional attempts to impose optimism (and eventually, one can only suppose, youth and naiveté) by law.

Yet for us, hope has never become just official, a mere camouflage for actual exploitation, though indeed two generations of writers just before us believed so; and it was their sense of having alone penetrated our hoax of prosperity and happiness that nourished their feelings of alienation. The error of such writers was double (such errors, naturally, do not preclude good writing; being *right* is, thank God, optional for the writer). Not only was the American *mythos* real and effective, the very opposite of the hypocritical and barren materialism it seemed; but also everywhere, down to the last layer of babbitry, there existed beside this belief its complement: an unspoken realization of the guilt and terror involved in the American experience. In his sense of lonely horror, the writer was most one with everyone else.

Precisely the uncompromising optimism of Americans makes every inevitable failure to accomplish what can only be dreamed an unredeemable torment. Among us, nothing is winked at or shrugged away; we are being eternally horrified at dope-addiction or bribery or war, at things accepted in older civilizations as the facts of life, scarcely worth a tired joke. Even tax evasion dismays us! We are forever feeling our own pulses, collecting statistics to demonstrate the plight of the Negro, the prevalence of divorce, the failure of the female organ, the decline of family Bible reading, because we feel, we *know* that a little while ago it was in our power, new men in a new world (and even yet there is hope), to make all perfect. How absurd of our writers to have believed that only they were pained at the failure of love and justice in the United States! What did they think our pulp literature of violence and drunkenness and flight was trying symbolically to declare? Why did they suppose that the most widely read fiction in America asks endlessly, "Whodunnit? Where is the guilt?"

I think we are in the position now to understand that the concept of the "alienated artist" itself was as much a creation of the popular mind as of the artist. It is no accident that Edgar Allan Poe is both the prototype of the American Poet as Despised Dandy, and the inventor of the most popular genres of "mass culture." The image of the drunken, dope-ridden, sexually impotent, poverty-oppressed Poe is as native to the American mind as the image of the worker driving his new Ford into the garage beside the Cape Cod cottage; together they are the American's image of himself. Poe, Crane, Fitzgerald—each generation provides itself with its own lost artist—and their biographies are inevitable best-sellers.

I do not mean to imply that the role of scapegoat is not actually painful for the artist; his exclusion and scourging is the psychodrama of us all, but it is played out in earnest. Poe was in a certain sense a poseur, but he died of his pose; and the end of Fitzgerald was real terror. I want only to insist that the melancholy and rebellious artist has always been a collaborator in American culture—that it is only when he accepts the political or sentimental half-truths of democracy, when he says *yes* too soon, that he betrays his role and his countrymen —and that the popular mind at its deepest level is well aware of this.

Of all peoples of the world, we hunger most deeply for tragedy; and perhaps in America alone the emergence of a tragic literature is still possible. The masterpieces of our nineteenth-century literature have captured the imagination of readers everywhere, precisely because their tragic sense of life renews vicariously the exhausted spirit. In Western Europe, the tragic tension no longer exists; it is too easy to despair and to fall in love with one's despair. Melodrama, *comèdie larmoyante,* learned irony and serious parody—these are the forms proper to the contemporary European mind. In the orbit of Stalinism, on the other hand, despair has been legislated away; justice triumphs and the wicked suffer—there is no evil except in the other. Some lies are the very stuff of literature, but this is not among them; it breeds police forces rather than poetry.

Only where there is a real and advancing prosperity, a constant effort to push beyond all accidental, curable ills, all easy cynicism and premature despair toward the irreducible residuum of human weakness, sloth, self-love, and fear; only where the sense of the inevitability of man's failure does not cancel out the realization of the splendor of his vision, nor the splendor of his vision conceal the reality and beauty of his failure, can tragedy be touched. It is toward this tragic margin that the American artist is impelled by the neglect and love of his public. If he can resist the vulgar temptation to turn a quick profit by making yet one more best-selling parody of hope, and the snobbish temptation to burnish chic versions of elegant despair, the American writer will find that he has, after all, a real function.

Indeed, he is needed in a naked and terrible way, perhaps unprecedented in the history of Western culture—not as an entertainer, or the sustainer of a "tradition," or a recruit to a distinguished guild, but as the recorder of the encounter of the dream of innocence and the fact of guilt, in the only part of the world where the reality of that conflict can still be recognized. If it is a use he is after and not a reward, there is no better place for the artist than America.

Giraudoux' *Tiger at the Gates*: A Review

RICHARD HAYES

The scene is Troy: not the windswept Homeric plains, burning under the vault of night with a thousand campfires, but Priam's holy citadel, which the dogs of war have already begun to foul. Under a hot Asian sun, Andromache and Cassandra await the victorious return of Hector. The fields of Troy are heavy with golden wheat; happiness falls from the sky like a blanket of snow; in her womb, Andromache carries the seed of Hector, yet imperceptibly the light changes—"doom has transfigured everything here with the color of storm." Paris has abducted Helen, and the sibylline Cassandra smells the tiger at the gates. He rouses, opens one eye, stretches and starts to prowl. He pads silently up the steps, and pushes doors open with his snout. Suddenly he is here, in his tawny terror, and at that moment, the splendid Hector arrives triumphantly on the battlements of Troy.

With his entrance, the dramatic energy of "Tiger at the Gates"—which has been ominous and gathering—springs terribly to life. For Hector is the "guardian of the perishable joys," as Mme. Rachel Bespaloff calls him in her essay *On the Iliad*. In the scales of fate, he may weigh only "a young woman and an unborn child . . . hunting, courage, loyalty, love . . . all the leafy thick-set oak trees that grow on the hills . . . the whole race of humble peasants, hard-working craftsmen, thousands of plows and looms, forges and anvils . . . joy of life, belief in life, a response to whatever's natural and good." And the tiger is the enemy of these: the tiger is "the stupidity of men and the wild stupidity of the elements:" the tiger is vanity and self and the destructive impulse. But the tiger is also something more: Destiny—"the relentless logic of each day we live"—and in this terrible embrace of the beast, Hector is crushed. What is tragedy? someone once asked Giraudoux, and he replied: the affirmation of a horrible bond existing

From *The Commonweal*, 25 November 1955, pp. 200-201. Reprinted by permission of the editors.

between man and a greater fate than man's fate. What is the tragic hero? he was questioned further, and answered again: he is a being peculiarly resigned to cohabiting with every shape and every monster of destiny.

Grief and pleasure, passion and relief burn with equal intensity at the center of Giraudoux's variation on a classic theme. The play's texture has the iridescence and shimmer, the hard beauty, of light on shot silk: language cascades and erupts in fountains of liquid sound. (Mr. Christopher Fry's translation has fidelity, power, elegance, steeliness, perfection of cut.) Giraudoux has taken figures from the preliterate, pre-psychological Homeric universe and honeycombed them with sophistication and complexity of motive. Helen is not here the moving finger of remorse drawn across the pages of the *Iliad,* but a creamy blonde vacancy, baleful and inaccessible, yet a hostage of fate, charged with the danger of "one of those rare creatures destiny puts on the earth for its own personal use." Cassandra is a modish sibyl in timeless evening dress; Paris, the seducer son "in a large middleclass family." The chorus of Trojan elders whose reedy voices, in Homer, pipe thinly their praise of Helen's beauty, provides Giraudoux with one of his most resonant motifs. Yet these modifications of myth, so quintessentially Gallic in their irreverent sensibility, occasionally blur the purity of the play's tone. "Intellectual stimulation," M. Georges May has written suggestively in a study of Giraudoux, "is not compatible with the tragic emotion. Giraudoux's delectable and sophisticated humor reduces the tragic tension of the drama. Only irony could tighten it, as Sophocles and Racine exemplified it." And I find everywhere in "Tiger at the Gates" the tragic rhythm, but only once the tragic release: in the long dialogue between Hector and Ulysses, when heightened knowledge moves beyond good and evil, beyond wit and tears and laughter into that chill air where man's fate is determined, and spirit withers at the mercy of punishing circumstance.

Mr. Harold Clurman's production of "Tiger at the Gates" is one of the absolute theatrical occasions of the past decade in New York. By an act of imaginative apprehension such as our theater rarely permits, he has kept the performance in a superb repose, circumscribed yet vibrant with energy, directing our attention to what is always the ultimate center of any Giraudoux play: the mesmerism of the word. I do not imagine Mr. Clurman has done anything finer than this, and I am not forgetting his exquisite dramatic articulation of "The Autumn Garden" and "The Time of the Cuckoo." Mr. Loudon Sainthill's backdrops splendidly suggest the fateful ambience of the myth, as does Mr. Lennox Berkeley's incidental music.

No one of the performances is less than competent, several are triumphs: Miss Leueen MacGrath's crystalline, worldly Cassandra; Diane Cilento's fluting, voluptuous Helen; the tart venom of Catherine Lacey's Hecuba, and John Laurie's frenzied nationalist poet. Mr. Walter Fitzgerald's Ulysses has authority, but the pressure here is a little monotonous, and the surface somehow dull. Mr. Michael Redgrave, as Hector, crowns the evening with an illustration of the passionate dramatic line in action: he gives the play its velocity and weight and momentum. Humanity itself is outraged in his defeat, and when one sees the image of his broken spirit, irresistibly the mind moves forward in time: to Achilles sulking by his black ships; to Hector's plume tumbled in the dust, and Hecuba's screams rending the windy air of Ilium. "The Trojan poet is dead," says Cassandra, brooding as the tiger, Destiny, pushes open the gates of war with his snout. "And now the Grecian poet will have his word."

The Modern Temper and Tragic Drama

LOUIS I. BREDVOLD

Just twenty-five years ago Mr. Joseph Wood Krutch published a volume of essays on *The Modern Temper,* a devastating analysis which has enjoyed enormous prestige and influence among thoughtful people, young and old. It continues even now to find readers who regard it as a sort of classic for our times, and who cannot but admire the courage and candor with which Mr. Krutch has exposed our modern disillusionment. It is still read by college students, who, recognizing the brilliance and the persuasiveness of the writing, defer to it as to an unquestionable authority. The unequal battle between the unprepared college student and *The Modern Temper* has for years been one of the major crises facing undergraduates.

One of the essays, on "The Tragic Fallacy," is particularly troublesome to students of literature. It is a pitiless explanation of why "we read but we do not write tragedies." It admits that "when we turn the pages of a Sophoclean or a Shakespearean tragedy we participate faintly in the experience which created it," but the truth is, we learn, that even when we are most moved by such tragedy "we perceive a Sophocles or a Shakespeare soaring in an air which we can never hope to breathe." The great tragic dramas of the past have faded for us; "we no longer live in the world which they represent, but we can half imagine it, and we can measure the distance which we have moved away." As moderns we would be incapable of even forming by ourselves any conception of "the tragic spirit," and we can think about it only as we find it exemplified in these half-comprehended dramas left us from earlier ages.

The difficulty, says Mr. Krutch, is not a problem of art, but of two worlds, of a mind in the modern world trying to understand a mind from another world. We are separated from Shakespeare and Sophocles by our discovery of "the meanness of human life." A tragedy must have a hero, but "from the universe, as we see it, both the Glory of God

From *The Quarterly Review,* Vol. LXI, No. 18 (May 21, 1955) pp. 207-13. Reprinted by permission of the editors.

and the Glory of Man have departed. Our cosmos may be farcical or it may be pathetic, but it has not the dignity of tragedy and we cannot accept it as such." We have lost the faith that makes possible the tragic vision; we can never recapture that faith because we live in the modern world. For that faith, says Mr. Krutch, was born "out of an instinctive confidence in life which is nearer to the animal's unquestioning allegiance to the scheme of nature than it is to that critical intelligence characteristic of a fully developed humanism." The modern reader of tragic drama is therefore in a dilemma: either he enjoys the drama and gives up his critical intelligence, or he gives up the drama as naive and adolescent.

All this argument is sweeping in its generality. But one may gather from the essay some more specific statements as to how the great tragedy of the past was generated by a view of the world and of man no longer tenable by the modern critical intelligence. First, the moderns have learned that the cosmos is indifferent to them. "They cannot believe that the universe trembles when their love is, like Romeo's, cut off, or when the place where they, small as they are, have gathered up their trivial treasure is, like Othello's sanctuary, defiled." But the man contemporary with Sophocles or Shakespeare, believing that he occupied "the exact centre of the universe which would have no meaning except for him," could naturally assume that "each of his acts reverberates through the universe." Such cosmic importance imparts dignity to the tragic hero. In the second place, "the tragic spirit is in reality the product of a religious faith," whether it be in "God, Nature, or that still vaguer thing called a Moral Order," and because this faith is an "assumption" and not valid for us, we cannot feel that the struggles of the tragic hero are important. It is more modern to conceive of the catastrophe of the tragic hero as not differing essentially from the destruction of bacteria in a test tube. Finally, the modern world has turned from the hero to the common man, as is so evident in our novels as well as in drama. "We can no longer tell tales of the fall of noble men, because we do not believe that noble men exist. The best that we can achieve is pathos, and the most that we can do is to feel sorry for ourselves. Man has put off his royal robes, and it is only in sceptred pomp that tragedy can come sweeping by." We may summarize the argument thus: modern science has destroyed the old illusions regarding the cosmos; consequently, as the older tragedy was written in this obsolete "world," we can no longer be moved by its representation of human life and destiny.

Such observations and sentiments are of course not peculiar to Mr. Krutch. They are the common property of the Modern Mind; we hear them constantly and sometimes utter them ourselves. They seem as indisputable as axioms and circulate among us with as little exercise of the critical intelligence as other clichés. It may be worth while to pause over them and scrutinize them more carefully. It is of course not to the point to reject them just because they are depressing, to accept fiction as truth because it is pleasant. The inquiry should be into the soundness of these generalizations. Are they true to facts? Are they truthful interpretations of tragedy and of human nature? Are they distorted in emphasis?

To illustrate the last point first: Mr. Krutch is certainly safe in saying that we read tragedies now-a-days, but we do not write them. Stated in that way the observation carries the implication that our failure to produce tragedy is a norm by which we may conclude that our reading of older tragedy is fatuous. But it is possible to turn the statement around and say that, although our modern dramatists are not writing any great tragedies, the public nevertheless insists on reading and seeing the great tragedies of the past. Thus the shoe of explanation is put on the other foot. One cannot dismiss lightly the fact that even modern people have some inner necessity for returning to Sophoclean and Shakespearean tragedy, that they find there some deep human satisfaction not given by modern drama. Does this signify that the product of our modern dramatists falls short of what the modern audience craves? If so, the supposedly uniform Modern Mind is only a generalized construct of the critic and fails to take account of the complexities of our contemporary experience.

Mr. Krutch argues ingeniously that we participate only faintly in the experience which the great tragedy of the past evoked when it was written, and that as it gradually fades with time, this tragedy will become "completely meaningless." This argument is not a brilliant example of scientific caution. The comparison it involves is not susceptible of any proof, as we obviously cannot find out the intensity of the emotional reactions of the audience of Shakespeare's day. As for our contemporary experience with these tragedies, a sufficient number of people could easily be produced who can assert with competence that their participation in the greatness of these plays is neither so faint nor so faded as the argument insists. Indeed, Mr. Krutch himself says as much. If we put the old tragedies alongside of a *Ghosts* or a *Weavers,* he says, "we shrink as from the impulse to commit some folly";

the new tragedy will not bear the comparison. Granted. But we would not shrink from the folly of comparison if our experience with Shakespeare were really so faint and superficial.

If the argument about the experience of the modern audience is thus highly dubious, the assumptions regarding the nature of tragic drama are even more so. Mr. Krutch is of course a distinguished critic, and his comments on tragic drama, even in this essay, are often so admirable and illuminating that it would be manifest injustice to say that his own experience of the old drama is either faded or faint. But his doctrinal argument is less felicitous than his appreciations. It is part of his doctrine that our modern enlightened view of the cosmos has made the old tragedy obsolete. We can no longer feel that the tragedies of man are important because we know that the cosmos is indifferent to them. We do not, like Romeo and Othello, believe that the universe will tremble when calamity strikes us. However, if we search the plays we do not find that Othello and Romeo ever express any expectation of such trembling. In fact, Shakespeare was too great a dramatist to need to rely on any cosmic demonstration of sympathy in order to build up the tragic stature and dignity of his heroes. It is likewise futile to search for places in Shakespeare where dignity is imputed to man because he occupies "the exact centre of the universe." Such astronomical ideas are completely irrelevant in the sphere of Shakespearean tragedy, as they are indeed also in our own modern daily life. The archangel Raphael explained to Adam in *Paradise Lost* that his problems in the conduct of life will in no way depend on whether the earth or the sun is the centre of our astronomical system. Raphael's prediction has been justified. We continue obstinately to say that the sun goes down. And when Shakespeare represented on the stage the tragic frustration of a noble romance, or the agony of Othello, victim of Iago's villainy and his own weakness, who threw away a pearl richer than all his tribe, he did not go outside of his story to borrow any cosmic significance. He found all that he needed in human life, even as we also may perchance know it and live it.

All this discussion about the divergent views of the cosmos amounts to an attempt to lay down such a prerequisite for the tragic vision of Shakespeare as no intelligent modern could subscribe to. But it does not inquire first whether the tragic vision does in fact depend on any such a prerequisite. It will be observed that it is a kind of deductive argument evolving out of an assumption, rather than an inductive examination of the tragedy we all agree to call great. We find a similar mode of reasoning in Mr. Krutch's other observations. He says that "the tragic spirit is in reality the product of religious faith," and the word "product" again lays down a prerequisite for tragedy. By "religious faith" we must understand such a faith as was held by a majority, at least, of the theatre audiences of sixteenth-century England, but not to be relied on in addressing audiences of our day. The modern reader must therefore hypothesize in some way this religious faith before he begins a Shakespearean tragedy, for the tragic spirit is derivative from it. This argument, presumably, is not to be taken as a trivial one, implying, let us say, that to appreciate *Macbeth* we must believe in witches, or that *Hamlet* is a sealed book unless we believe in ghosts, and also in Purgatory (the doctrine of which was to Shakespeare's Protestant audience a rank heresy). The issue is surely much more important and reaches to the profound depths of the tragic vision. There can be no doubt that the tragic experience is closely associated with religious feeling, but the sequence of cause and effect seems to be exactly the reverse of the way Mr. Krutch would have it.

Such prologues in Heaven as we find in Goethe's *Faust* and the Book of Job are not standard in tragedy. Like comedy, tragedy deals with human life here on earth, and it can exert no power over us unless we acknowledge it as a truthful representation of human experience. It is an exploration of human destiny which begins *in medias res* and has no theoretical prerequisites. It is not derivative from any doctrines which might conceivably be delivered to the audience by means of a prologue at the opening of the play. The effect of tragedy is not dependent on any insights other than those developed in the course of the action of the play. Even the common belief in the immortality of the soul does not enter into the tragic experience in Shakespeare's plays, any more than in Greek tragedy. Hamlet speaks of it only doubtfully, as he meditates suicide. But when death comes to one of Shakespeare's tragic heroes, destiny has reached, for the purposes of the drama, its completion without anything being said about what may come thereafter.

Those who would penetrate behind the play and formulate the religion of Shakespeare usually succeed only in exposing their own personal convictions. A Roman Catholic scholar once demonstrated to his own satisfaction that Shakespeare was a Catholic; a Protestant scholar that he was a Protestant; an agnostic that he was an agnostic. The great experience of the tragedy they probably all shared in common. Shakespeare eluded all of them, as he eludes all of us, putting between himself and us the action of the play, and that is all he gives us. We must read it and interpret it as we can. We must understand his characters in terms of our common humanity; he has left us no marginal commentary. When Mr. Krutch says that a Shakespearean hero perishes with dignity because "a God leans out from infinity to strike him down," he speaks strangely and apparently in momentary forgetfulness of the plays. Those grand figures perished because they struck themselves down, not without more or less assistance, it is true, from those around them. The moving forces in their destinies were in the human, not a superhuman, sphere and therefore universally understandable as experiences that are possible, alas, to us all.

As has been often observed, there is something strikingly pagan about Shakespeare, precisely because he does not rely on external buttressing for his tragic effects. The idea of divinity is remarkably unimportant dramatically, in no play more strikingly so than in *King Lear,* which many readers think his greatest. This tragedy belongs to legendary Britain, and a Christian God would have been an anachronism; but we need not suppose that Shakespeare was handicapped by chronological difficulties. He produced the effect he wanted, by vague references to "the heavens," oftener "the gods," who are alluded to from time to time as remote existences, too remote, unfortunately, to rescue agonizing mankind from its accumulating woe. They appear to be more wished for than believed in.

> If that the heavens do not their visible spirits
> Send quickly down to tame these vile offences,
> It will come,
> Humanity must perforce prey on itself,
> Like monsters of the deep.

That is all the consolation Albany derives from his faith, as he contemplates the vileness of the daughters of Lear. A revealing turn comes a moment later when he learns that a servant had killed Cornwall, his brother-in-law, just as he was brutally putting out the eyes of Gloucester. Albany can now speak out more certainly, with a touch of triumph:

> This shows you are above,
> You justicers, that these our nether crimes
> So speedily can venge.

No "justicer" leaned out from infinity or sent his visible spirit down to punish Cornwall or protect Gloucester; only a humble but heroic servant meted out punishment and thus vindicated the "justicers"; and

Albany could again believe that some kind of Moral Order was operative in the world of man. Albany needs no messenger from heaven, no divine judgment from Mt. Sinai, to make clear to him that Goneril and Regan are "tigers, not daughters," and that if humanity continues to develop in that direction it "must perforce prey on itself like monsters of the deep." If Cornwall's fate were not evident justice, it could not *show* that there are "justicers" above. Great tragedy, let it be repeated, presents an essentially human story, told in human terms, and providing such insights of its own as our common humanity can share. It can be understood by all the varieties of people who drift in from the streets through the doors of the theatre.

It is also true, however, that the story that unfolds in a great tragedy, rooted though it must be in human nature, presents a view of human destiny that raises issues beyond the power of a stage play to resolve. There are emotional upheavals, insights adumbrating into mystery, awesome revelations, that have the power to shake the complacency, one might think, of even the most hardened materialist, who might well leave the theatre in a momentary mood to say with Hamlet, "for mine own poor part, look you, I'll go pray." For the great theme of tragedy is the problem of evil, from which even the materialist is not immune, the greatest problem mankind has to face, and the inspiration of the greatest literature mankind has so far produced. The tragedian raises metaphysical and religious issues which pass beyond the limits of his art, and on which it is impossible for him as a playwright to commit himself. As has been pointed out, he can not resolve the problem of evil by assuming an existence after death in which rewards and punishments will balance the accounts of justice. Even if scenes of that sort were feasible in the theatre, they would have to be rejected as inharmonious with the tragic experience. No one wants an afterpiece showing Othello and Desdemona united happily in heaven. Tragedy must limit itself to showing heaven and hell as extreme possibilities of our destiny here on earth. The tragic hero is great, not because of any extraterrestrial relationships, but in himself. It is the depths of human nature, not the cosmos, that the dramatist must explore. He must have the creative power to plummet those depths and the dramatic technique to convey his tragic vision to his audience. The essential requirement for reading and writing great tragedy is therefore not a prescribed view of the universe, but a profound, imaginative, and sympathetic insight into human nature.

This, it seems, is where the modern dramatist falls short. He is unable to find in man the dignity and greatness necessary to true tragedy. He is unable, as Mr. Krutch says, to "tell the tales of the fall of noble men, because we do not believe that noble men exist." Against this proposition it must be permissible to expostulate. Are we to receive this universal negative as a scientific finding of the modern sociologist or the modern psychologist? Is this desperate generalization now become an obligatory creed? Is it the truth that "all contemporary minds" feel "that man is relatively trivial"? Our dramatists themselves might possibly have seen not so long ago some commonplace sewing-machine salesman (let us say) descend from the skies over Normandy and with his fellow troopers do heroic battle like the heroes of old. They have greater opportunity, if they can use it, to observe nobility and heroism in other commonplace people less spectacularly employed. It seems a very heavy ideology, indeed, that so dehumanizes a creative artist as to blind him to the very humanity which it is his mission to interpret. Mr. Krutch, like others afflicted with the "modern temper," falls back upon the cosmos as the explanation. "Our cosmos," he says, "may be farcical or it may be pathetic, but it has not the dignity of tragedy and we cannot accept it as such." If the humanity of man can be validly dismissed on such a priori grounds, the modern dramatist has of course only one problem to solve: how to utilize the highly developed technical expertness of the modern theatre to exploit the meanness and triviality of human life into a box-office success.

Because he chooses such limited contacts with human nature the modern dramatist produces a monotony of effect, tense though his play may be with suspense, which contrasts with the rich and variegated patterns of Shakespeare. As a matter of fact, it could be argued plausibly that Shakespeare was master of all the stock in trade of the modern dramatist, but used it in such a way as to justify Dryden's remark that of all ancients and moderns he had the most comprehensive mind. The tragic street battles in *Romeo and Juliet* take their rise in each case in trivial buffoonery by servants; in such a complex pattern even farce may suddenly take on a serious significance. In *Hamlet* Shakespeare created an atmosphere as depressing as can be found in any modern play; Hamlet speaks of Denmark as a prison, or as an "unweeded garden, things rank and gross infest it merely"; a moral miasma has settled over it, more death-dealing and blinding than a smog. And Hamlet is not incapable of some quite "modern" utterances about the farcical aspects of man. He can observe, for instance, that "we fat all creatures else to fat us, and we fat ourselves for maggots." What modern dramatist wouldn't envy Shakespeare that pitiless cynicism! But in *Hamlet* such moods are passing, mere aspects of a complex personality, falling into their proper place in a larger and nobler view of life. And the modern lament about the indifference of the cosmos to the destinies of men is in fact not something new; on that point the older tragedy anticipated the moderns. What Prossor Hall Frye has observed about Greek tragedy is equally applicable to Shakespeare's: "the tragic qualm is perhaps nothing more or less than a sudden and appalling recognition of our desperate plight in a universe apparently indiscriminate of good and evil as of happiness and misery."

It is because he cherishes so dearly a pinched and starved view of human nature that the modern dramatist finds himself incapable of rising above sordid misery and achieving the truly tragic vision. Mr. Krutch himself gives us a good statement of what is lacking in the moderns. We rise from reading the old tragedy, he says, with a feeling of "elation"; more specifically, the old tragedians understood that "it is only in calamity that the human spirit has the opportunity to reveal itself triumphant over the outward universe which fails to conquer it." The statement needs some minor qualification: the triumph of Othello or King Lear was not primarily over "the outward universe." But some sort of triumph there is in great tragedy, and the audience shares in it. For if the tragic vision is to impress us with a sense of profound loss, it must at the same time bring home to us an equally profound sense of the values without which the loss would not be real. As we participate sympathetically in the tragic role of the hero, we clutch more and more firmly certain values which the action of the play reveals to us as infinitely precious to us as human beings. These values appear concretely in the nobility of the characters, especially in the erring hero, and in a Lear, an Othello, an Oedipus they operate as a redemptive power. Matthew Arnold praised Sophocles for seeing life steadily and seeing it whole. This steady vision led Sophocles to a tragical self-knowledge; and, in the words of Werner Jaeger, "to know oneself is for Sophocles to know man's powerlessness; but it is also to know the indestructible and conquering majesty of suffering humanity." Perhaps no Greek drama impresses a modern reader more profoundly and powerfully than Sophocles' treatment of the Oedipus story, in spite of its oracle and sphinx and gods. Oedipus found himself unwittingly guilty of patricide and incest. When he is forced to acknowledge his guilt, he begins his expiation; he blinds himself, wanders many years as an outcast old man, in the deepest misery and agony, his one loyal daughter his only friend and support. But the strength and nobility of his character help him through his long ordeal, and as he ages he grows into a venerable figure. Like Lear, he reaches wisdom through suffering; his nobility is tested by his agony. And therefore even we, moderns as we are, agree that it is right that the gods themselves should at last give Oedipus mysterious release and sepulture. "No mortal eye," says Jaeger, a modern interpreter, "may see the mystery; only he who is consecrated by suffering may take part in it. Hallowed by pain, Oedipus is in some mysterious way brought near to divinity: his agonies have set him apart from other men. Now he rests on the hill of Colonus, in the poet's own dear homeland, in the eternally green grove of the Kind Spirits where the nightingale sings from the branches. No human foot may tread in that place, but from it there goes out a blessing over all the land of Attica."

Is it possible for the modern world to produce great tragic drama? No doubt it is, if dramatists with sufficient ability will give up their a priori inhibitions and see human nature steadily and see it whole. If they can do that, they will find a large and receptive audience awaiting them.